ENCYCLOPEDIA OF
CHESS
WISDOM

ABOUT THE AUTHOR

Eric Schiller, widely considered one of the world's foremost chess analysts, writers, and teachers, is internationally recognized for his definitive works on openings. He is the author of 87 chess books including Cardoza Publishing's definitive series on openings, *World Champion Openings*, *Standard Chess Openings*, and *Unorthodox Chess Openings* — an exhaustive opening library of more than 1700 pages. He's also the author of *Encyclopedia of Chess Wisdom, Gambit Opening Repertoire for White, Gambit Opening Repertoire for Black, Complete Defense to King Pawn Openings, Complete Defense to Queen Pawn Openings*, and multiple other chess titles for Cardoza Publishing. (For listings of all chess titles published by Cardoza Publishing, go online to www.cardozapub.com.)

Eric Schiller is a National and Life Master, an International Arbiter of F.I.D.E., and the official trainer for many of America's top young players. He has recently been reappointed as official coach of America's best players under 18 to represent the United States at the Chess World Championships. He has also presided over world championship matches dating back to 1983, runs prestigious international tournaments, and has been interviewed dozens of times in major media throughout the world. His games have been featured in leading chess journals and newspapers including the venerable New York Times. Schiller has helped design some of the most popular chess software being used today. Eric Schiller's web site is www.chessworks.com.

Eric, who has trained many of the brightest chess prodigies and students of all levels, adds four decades of the experiences at the chessboard to bring readers the whole world of chess.

Eric is the senior editor of the free online chess magazine, www.chesscity.com

---

NEW CARDOZA PUBLISHING BOOKS BY ERIC SCHILLER

STANDARD CHESS OPENINGS - The new standard on opening chess play, references every important opening and variation played - more than 3,000 opening strategies! The standard reference book necessary for competitive play. *A must have!!!* 768 pgs, $24.95.

UNORTHODOX CHESS OPENINGS - The comprehensive guide to contains more than 1,200 weird, contentious, controversial, unconventional, arrogant and outright strange opening strategies. Great against unprepared opponents. *Great Fun!* 576 pgs, $24.95.

WORLD CHAMPION OPENINGS - Covers the essential opening theory and moves of every major chess opening and variation as played by *all* the world champions. Learn the insights, concepts and secrets as used by the greatest players of all time. 384 pages, $21.95

COMPLETE DEFENSE TO QUEEN PAWN OPENINGS - This aggressive counterattacking repertoire covers Black opening systems against virtually all chess opening except for 1.e4 (including flank games), based on the powerful Tarrasch Defense. 288 pages, $16.95.

COMPLETE DEFENSE TO KING PAWN OPENINGS - Learn a complete defensive system against 1.e4 based on the mighty Caro-Kann, a favorite weapon of many great players. All White's options are shown with plans for Black to combat them all. 288 pages, $16.95.

WHIZ KIDS TEACH CHESS *Eric Schiller and the Whiz Kids* - Today's greatest young stars, from 10 to 17 years of age–tells of their successes, failures, world travels, and love of the game. At the heart of this book is a chess primer with large diagrams, clear explanations, and winning ideas. Lots of photos, 160 large format pages, $14.95.

ENCYCLOPEDIA OF CHESS WISDOM, *The Essential Concepts and Strategies of Smart Chess Play* by Eric Schiller The most important concepts, strategies, tactics, wisdom, and thinking that every chessplayer must know, plus the gold nuggets of knowledge behind every attack and defense, all in one volume. 432 pages, $19.95.

Get online now to learn more about upcoming titles! www.cardozapub.com

---

ENCYCLOPEDIA OF
CHESS
WISDOM

THE GOLD NUGGETS OF CHESS KNOWLEDGE

Opening, Middlegame, Endgame,
Strategies, Tactics, Psychology, and More...

The Essential
Concepts &
Thinking
that Every Chess
Player Must
Know

Eric Schiller

CARDOZA PUBLISHING

CARDOZA PUBLISHING
Authoritative and Readable Books for Chess Players
Chess is Our Game

Thanks to Jordy Mont-Reynaud for helping with the proofreading

PRINT HISTORY

First Edition	November 1998
Second Edition	February 2000
Third Edition	February 2003

Library of Congress Catalog Card No: 2002109178
ISBN: 1-58042-088-5

CARDOZA PUBLISHING
P.O. Box 1500 Cooper Station, New York, NY 10276
Phone (800)577-WINS

TABLE OF CONTENTS

THE MIDDLEGAME

THE MIDDLEGAME 125

STRATEGY 215

TACTICS, SACRIFICES, AND COMBINATIONS 257

ANALYSIS — 337

TRAINING — 350

PSYCHOLOGY — 360

A NOTE FROM ERIC...

The reader will find a great deal of wisdom in this book. This knowledge was not created in my own mind, of course, but comes from the many teachers, friends and opponents I have encountered in over three dozen years of active chessplaying and 15 years of writing on chess. It is not possible to trace the source of each idea. I've quoted authors who have stated a particular concept whenever I feel that they put it better than I ever could, or because the quote is well known. For the most part, however, the influences lie submerged, their journey into my chess philosophy irrecoverable.

Therefore I'd like to mention some of the strongest influences on my game, so that you'll have some idea where all this chess wisdom comes from. My father taught me the game when I was four and half years old, and I had no formal instruction other than his advice, experience, and a wealth of chess literature that I discovered a few years later. America did not have any chess training at the time, and I doubt I could have located such resources if they did exist. At the Manhattan Chess Club and Marshall Chess Club in New York City I was able to receive valuable advice from such venerable chess writers as Al Horowitz, Hans Kmoch, and Edward Lasker. Grandmaster William Lombardy was very helpful to me and other young players at the Manhattan, and when I migrated downtown to the Marshall, many different masters provided instructive competition, including the late Leslie Braun.

In the 1980s, I entered the international ranks and also earned the title of International Arbiter at the encouragement of Ray Keene, whose classic study of Aron Nimzowitsch was one of my favorite books. Ray also got my writing career going, at first with articles for various chess journals and then in full length books for the British publisher B.T. Batsford. I lived in England then, as a housemate of such strong players as Keene, Jon Tisdall, and Murray Chandler. I made frequent visits to Bob Wade, who gave me free run of his fantastic chess library. I also learned a lot of chess at the King's Head Pub, where most of these players, and other stars such as Jon Speelman, were regular visitors. In fact, the analysis of one of the most fascinating adjourned positions of my career took place there. We'll see that game in the section on stalemate.

When it comes to endgame play, the greatest teacher or all has recently passed away. I am not referring to a human teacher, but to the practice of adjourning games overnight. Adjournments have all but disappeared, as we'll learn in the "rules" chapter. I learned some invaluable lessons in endgame play while working out my own adjourned endgames or helping others. The best lessons, though, were the analysis sessions conducted with strong players. Grandmaster Vlastimil Jansa and I spent most of one of the Gausdal Internationals examining each other's many adjourned games. As captain of several American teams at international competitions, I sometimes stayed up all night working out difficult endgames with other team members. At Graz, in 1981, we had to work on the marathon contest between John Fedorowicz and Johnny van der Wiel for several days!

As the 80s progressed, I learned more about organizing chess tournaments and was on the staff of several World Championship events, usually as chief of the press center. There the best chess journalists from all over the world, including Oswaldo Leonxto Garcia, David Goodman, Jon "Ace Reporter" Tisdall and famous veterans Leonard Barden, Harry Golombek and Miguel Najdorf, held court. Many of the tales in this book were brought to the world through their reporting.

I started writing on chess during the 1980's and had the fortune of teaming up with strong players who led me to a deeper understanding of the game. Grandmasters Leonid Shamkovich, Ray Keene, Garry Kasparov, Joel Benjamin, and Lev Alburt became colleagues and friends. Many promising young players helped out on some of these projects.

When I help with the training of many of our young stars, I try to go beyond the pure chess teaching to the psychological and social aspects of the game. The education of a chessplayer must include familiarity with the great players and greatest tournaments. These topics are covered in the latter chapters of the book.

I owe a deep debt of gratitude to all of those mentioned above, and countless others who have given me the opportunity to learn some of the secrets of the Royal Game.

This third edition is dedicated to the memory of my friend and frequent co-author, Grandmaster Eduard Gufeld, who passed away in 2002. He had a great and infectious love for the game, and was a great promoter of the artistic side of the intellectual battle.

INTRODUCTION

Chess is a sea in which a gnat may drink and an elephant may bathe. —**Proverb (India)**

The most important concepts, strategies, tactics, wisdom, and thinking that every chessplayer must know, plus the gold nuggets of knowledge behind every attack and defense, are collected together in this book with the goal of bringing you greater pleasure and increased success at the chessboard.

From opening, middlegame, and endgame strategy, to psychological warfare, strategy, preparation, and tournament tactics, and bonus sections on rules and etiquette, the *Encyclopedia of Chess Wisdom* forms the blueprint of knowledge, power play and advantage at the chess board. Step-by-step, you will be taken through the thinking behind each essential concept, and through examples, discussions, and diagrams, shown how you can use this wisdom to fully impact a game to your advantage.

The *Encyclopedia of Chess Wisdom* is a compendium of important chess concepts as passed down from generations of teachers, players, and scholars. This book is unique, however, in presenting important counterexamples to most of these crucial concepts. Each bit of wisdom contains at least a grain of truth, and this

Every science borrows from all the rest, and we cannot attain any single one without the encyclopedia.

–Glanvill

> *All of the important aspects of the game are contained here, from the opening to the endgame, from the psychology of the game to the rules of behavior...*

book will help you pick out the useful ideas while avoiding mistaken interpretations.

Chess fans have received tips from the best players in the form of instructional books which have been available for centuries. Much of this wisdom is valuable and you'll find quotations from many great chess players and teachers throughout the book. The passage of time, however, has forced us to re-evaluate some of these statements. In the discussion of each crucial concept I will point out whenever the old formula may no longer apply. Important corrections based on modern thinking can be found throughout the book.

All of the important aspects of the game are contained here, from the opening to the endgame, from the psychology of the game to the rules of behavior. Although it is impossible to cover any of these in great depth, you will get a good introduction to the key concepts, and will be shown examples from practical play to emphasize each point. A bibliography of recommended books is included so that each topic can be explored in greater depth.

The material is presented with many diagrams and discussion in prose. I've tried to explain everything as clearly as possible, but that doesn't mean that the book is just for beginners. Those starting out on their chess journey will find all of the classic knowledge enlightening, but more advanced players will benefit both from the repetition of important fundamentals they have overlooked, and more importantly, will be ready to absorb the many counterexamples that are provided. Even accomplished masters will find new material here, more weapons to add to their practical arsenal.

This is an encyclopedia in the old sense, an attempt to bring together advice on a wide range of chess subjects. Since entire books are devoted to many of the individual topics presented here, it is not possible to go into any great depth on any single subjects. I have had to confine myself to a single example for each theme. Because progress in chess is largely a matter of pattern recognition you can only expect to understand each of these ideas conceptually. To reinforce each of the con-

> *This is an encyclopedia in the old sense...*

cepts you'll need to consult more detailed works, or simply play enough games and study enough games so that they become second nature to you.

Browse this encyclopedia for general knowledge, or turn to specific sections on aspects of the game which interest you. Some of the material will no doubt be familiar to all but beginners, but you'll find much of the traditional wisdom called into question here. To enable beginners to master the game, important concepts are often oversimplified and contradictory situations are conveniently ignored.

Many different chess themes are often seen in a single game, even in one position! Use the index at the back of the book for additional examples of key concepts. The more positions you learn, the easier it will be for you to recognize the opportunities in your own games.

A GUIDED TOUR

It makes sense to start at the beginning of the game, in the **opening** phase. We'll cover a lot of ground in this critical area. We'll begin with the concept of development, bringing your pieces into battle. The vast subject of opening theory will be introduced with specific discussion of standard, gambit and unorthodox openings. You'll learn how openings get their names, and examine a collection of opening traps. Then we will look at each individual piece and how it is best used in the opening phase of the game.

> *It makes sense to start at the beginning...*

When most of the forces have been brought into play, we enter the **middlegame**. The art of attack and defense is our primary interest here. The concept of the initiative and exploitation of weaknesses also play a significant role. Once again, we will consider the role of each piece and in a discussion of the tricky transition between the middlegame and the endgame.

The **endgame** is one of the most complex battle grounds in the game of chess. In addition to our usual treatment of the individual properties of each piece, we will present tips on a range of important issues such as the opposition, making material, zugzwang, and profitable exchanges. You'll find a dozen important endgame positions which are required knowledge for successful endgame play.

We move onto elements of chess **strategy** including piece coordination, control of the center, space, and the essentials of pawn structure. Tactical operations are presented in the next chapter. We look at **tactics, sacrifices, and combinations**. A collection of checkmating and stalemating patterns completes the chapter.

Advice in the art of chess **analysis** is the next topic. We'll discover that assigning numeric values to each of the chess pieces is a task much more difficult than appears a first sight. The mental gymnastics of chess analysis and calculation are investigated, leading to some practical tips on analyzing in time pressure.

Chess **training** is the subject of many books. Many conflicting views have been presented but there is a consensus on many of the best ways of studying chess games. You'll learn how to study classical games, opening strategy, middle game technique, tactics, endgame strategy, and more. Chess is **psychological** warfare too. A lot of chess games are won because one player adopted the correct psychological attitude. You'll learn how to question authority, manage the clock, and take advantage of your intuition. Many other practical situations provide instructive lessons in the handling of critical positions.

The later sections of the book contain wisdom of a different nature. Some aspects of chess **etiquette** and even the **rules** of the game are not widely known. A bewildering variety of new time controls have been introduced, for example. We'll take a look at many different ranking systems and explained some differences between the local and international rules. You'll find some **recommended reading** to help you continue you're journey into chess at the end of the book.

THE OPENING

Every great journey begins with a single step.

When you sit down to play a game of chess, you had better be in full command of your opening strategies! From amateur levels to the World Championship matches, opening preparation is playing a greater and greater role in contemporary chess.

Nevertheless, you can usually get through the opening if you follow some of the general advice passed down through the ages. We'll start by considering the most important topic of all—developing your pieces. Then we will look at the tricky question of move order. Based on this foundation, we can learn how to build an opening repertoire. Specific opening strategies are the subject of many books. Some present an overview of many different openings, while others examine a variation or subvariation in detail. In fact, entire books are devoted to analysis of openings which start only after each side has made a dozen moves or so, and some of these books run into hundreds of pages!

The naming of openings is a complex and controversial area, and you'll see why tempers flare when arguments arise. Political and cultural biases, even "political correctness," has muddied the waters considerably. On a more objective level, openings can be divided into many categories. There are even elaborate code systems used to characterize them. We'll visit all of these topics.

Turning to more concrete matters, we will then look at some opening traps. These are usually based on hidden tactics and are seen many times in tournament play. Each of your pieces can pull off amazing things in the opening. Traps are not always necessary though, and we'll consider the proper role of each piece in the early stages of the game.

As we will do throughout the book, we'll take a critical look at some of the conventional advice, and try to make sure that the other side of the coin is examined as well.

DEVELOPMENT

Your initial task in the opening is to get your army mobilized. You can't expect to launch an effective attack with just one piece, or a couple of pawns, or just scatter your pieces around the board and hope something turns up. It takes a coordinated and powerful fighting force. Putting your pieces in their proper positions early in the game is known as **development**.

Development involves three separate factors which are seen not just in the opening. The great Siegbert Tarrasch described the entire game of chess as a combination of force, space, and time. From the starting position, you want to maximize the amount of force at your disposal. You also want to control as much of the board as possible, so that the enemy has fewer useful posts for his own pieces. Finally, you want to achieve these goals sooner than your opponent, and therefore control the tempo of the game.

The best developing move is one in which you move a piece so that it attacks an undefended enemy piece, or a piece of greater value, and yet is not itself attacked. In the starting position, you have no such moves.

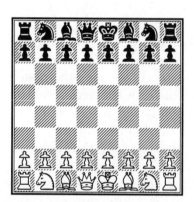

There are 20 legal moves. Each pawn can move either one or two squares forward, and each knight has a choice of two squares. No matter what you do, you can't get any of them into position to attack an enemy piece, even a lowly pawn. You need to develop pieces with longer range, such as bishops, rooks, or the queen. One move, 1.e4, opens a pathway for both a bishop and a queen. This also controls important central territory. That is why it is considered a strong move. On the other hand, this pawn is a little vulnerable, and can be attacked immediately by 1...d5 or 1...Nf6. Usually, the attacks come later. In any case the potential weakness of the e-pawn leads some players to prefer 1.d4, instead, or a flank opening with 1.c4 or 1.Nf3.

There are many generalizations concerning how the opening phase of the game should be carried out. Many are presented in this section. Most openings used by professionals conform to these principles, and unorthodox openings violate at least two of them. Yet there are also many popular openings which break the laws from time to time, and we'll meet a few of them along the way.

Beginners would do well to adopt a simple, three step plan of development. This formula is simplistic and of course cannot be followed slavishly, but as a general guide it is excellent advice.

1. First, get a pawn to the fourth rank in the center on one of your first two moves.

2. Then castle your king to safety.

3. Finally, move your pieces off the back rank so that your rooks are connected, that is, have no pieces blocking the line between them.

OCCUPY THE CENTER WITH PAWNS

Each player should try to place at least one pawn on the fourth rank of the d-file or e-file during the first two moves. The **"ideal pawn center"** is achieved when you get both pawns to the center.

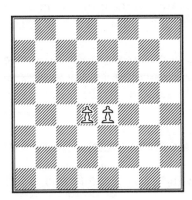

This is the goal that White, who has the privilege of moving first, wants to achieve as soon as possible. In the old days, occupation of the center with pawns was considered almost obligatory. That's why they call it the ideal pawn center. As we shall see modern thinking does not consider an ideal pawns center to be obligatory but still holds that it is a pretty good thing.

Most of Black's opening strategies are designed to prevent the erection of the ideal pawn center. Against 1.d4, Black can play 1...d5, 1...Nf6, or 1...f5, and the e-pawn cannot be brought to e4 except as a dubious sort of gambit. If White starts out with 1.e4, Black has many good choices, including direct central pawn play with 1...e5, 1...c5, or 1...d5. There is also a delayed central plan with 2...d5, supported by 1...c6 or 1...e6. Black can even attack the e-pawn with 1...Nf6.

Classical theoreticians were certain that it was necessary to prevent White from establishing the ideal pawn center. In the 1920s, however, the Hypermodern Revolution overthrew this dogma, and such openings as the King's Indian Defense became respectable. The Four Pawns Attack, one of the variations of the almost omnipresent King's Indian, starts out **1.d4 Nf6; 2.c4 g6; 3.Nc3 Bg7; 4.e4 0-0; 5.f4 d6.**

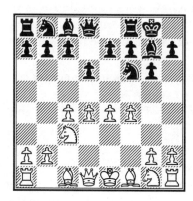

White has made four pawn moves, but completely dominates the center. The center is subject to fierce counterattacks from the flank by ...c5, and if the White d-pawn advances to d5, then it can be hit again by ...e6. The current verdict on this line is that it is too ambitious for White.

The old ideal of a broad line of pawns in the center of the board turns out to be flawed, in that it can easily fall apart if not sufficiently supported by pieces. Let's look at a game which illustrates the dangers of the broad pawn center. Watch White's center disintegrate.

CHRISTIANSEN - KASPAROV
Moscow (Interzonal), 1982
1.d4 Nf6; 2.c4 g6; 3.Nc3 Bg7; 4.e4 d6; 5.f4 0-0; 6.Nf3 c5.

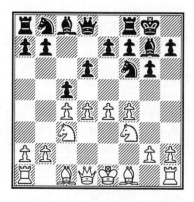

The first blow against the central formation. If White's d-pawn remains in place, it will be captured and then the dark squares in the center are weak.

7.d5 e6.

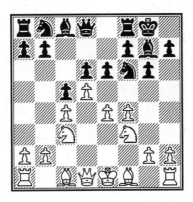

A new front is opened, at d5. **8.dxe6.** 8.Be2 exd5 is more common. White can then capture with the e-pawn, which opens the e-file and breaks up the center. Recapturing with the c-pawn maintains the pawn center, but the pawn at e4 is a target. There is another option, the exciting advance of the e-pawn to e5. 9.e5!? dxe5; 10.fxe5 Ne4 leaves the White center vulnerable.

8...fxe6.

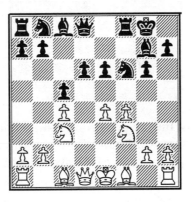

Black's pawns look weak, but they are hard to attack, and will soon take up solid positions. **9.Bd3.** The bishop would be better off at e2, since Black is going to take control of d4 and e5. **9...Nc6; 10.0–0 Nd4!; 11.Ng5?!** Too ambitious. Capturing at d4 would have allowed Black to build a strong center, similar to what we will see later at move 17. Retreating the knight from c3 to e2 was relatively best. **11...e5!**

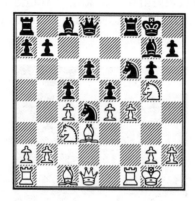

Black's center is stronger than White's, despite the backward pawn at d6. **12.f5 h6; 13.Nh3** White can try to play sacrificially, but after 13.fxg6 hxg5; 14.Bxg5 Kasparov points out that Black gets a good game with 14...Be6; 15.Nd5 Bxd5; 16.exd5 e4!; 17.Bxe4 Qe7; 18.Bd3 Rae8; Or 13.Nf3 gxf5; 14.exf5 Nxf5; 15.Nxe5 dxe5; 16.Bxf5 Qd4+! **13...gxf5; 14.exf5 b5!**

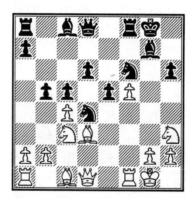

Another assault against White's once proud pawn center. Working from the flank is typical hypermodern strategy. **15.Be3?** White could have maintained the balance with 15.Nxb5! Nxb5; 16.cxb5 d5. **15...bxc4; 16.Bxc4+ Kh8;** Kasparov will not advance the d-pawn to d5 yet, because then the center is vulnerable. **17.Bxd4 cxd4; 18.Nd5 Ba6!; 19.Nxf6 Bxc4.**

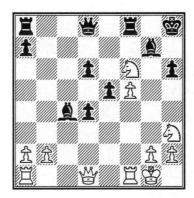

Once White owned the center, but now it belongs to Black. The central pawns, combined with the bishop pair, provide a decisive advantage, but Christiansen sacrifices the exchange to introduce some tactics. Kasparov avoids all the pitfalls and shoves the pawns down White's throat.

20.Nh5 Bxf1; 21.Qg4 Qd7; 22.Rxf1 d3! 23.Qf3 d2; 24.g4 Rac8; 25.Qd3 Qa4; 26.Nf2 Qd4!; 27.Qxd4 exd4.

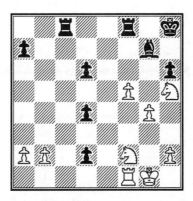

Black's pawns are tripled, but the endgame is winning.

28.Nf4 Rfe8; 29.Ne6 Rc1; 30.Nd1 Bf6!; 31.Kf2 Bg5; 32.Ke2 Rc5!; 33.Kd3 Re5; 34.Nxg5 hxg5; 35.Rf2 Re4; 36.h3? Re3+!; 37.Kxd4 R8e4+; 38.Kd5 Re2; 39.Rf3 Re1; 40.f6 Rf4. White resigned.

The Classical Lines, with a more conservative central pawn formation, are more popular. The next diagram shows a typical position.

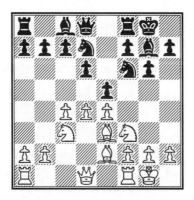

The King's Indian is so popular that it is impossible to believe that the ideal pawn center by itself is guaranteed to confer an advantage in the opening, but if properly supported, it can be the spawning ground for middlegame attacks. In the Saemisch Variation of the King's Indian Defense, White supports the center with a pawn, and uses pieces and the advance of the h-pawn to attack the enemy king.

In the following game, White shows how control of the center can be exploited.

PORTISCH - PINTER
1975 Hungarian Championship
1.d4 Nf6; 2.c4 g6; 3.Nc3 Bg7; 4.e4 d6; 5.f3 0-0; 6.Be3 Nc6; 7.Nge2 Rb8; 8.Qd2 Re8; 9.h4.

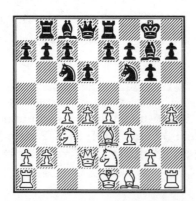

White has a full pawn center and is ready to castle queenside. The kingside attack does not need the bishop at f1, because White has queen, rook, and bishop aimed at the kingside and a knight can play a significant role. Black tries to get some counterplay on the queenside. He would like to open lines on the queenside, anticipating castling.
9...a6; 10.h5 b5; 11.hxg6 fxg6; 12.Bh6 Bh8; 13.Bg5.

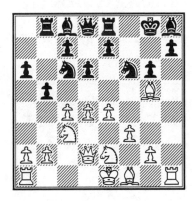

White places the bishop at g5, where it attack the enemy knight which is an important defender of h7. The stopover at h6 on move 12 was designed to push the enemy bishop to an inferior square. Because White controls the center, Black can't bring the knight from c6 to aid in the defense.

13...Rf8; 14.0-0-0 Na5; 15.Nf4 c6; 16.g4 b4; 17.Nb1 Bxg4. Desperation. Black gives up a piece for two pawns, but the knight at f6 must sooner or later leave the board, leaving h7 crippled.

18.fxg4 Nxe4; 19.Qh2 Nxg5; 20.Ne6! The knight at g5 must not move because of the weakness of h7. **20...b3; 21.Nxg5!** Black resigned.

This game made it all look easy, and indeed the Saemisch Variation rarely manages such quick kills. The King's Indian is considered fully playable for Black, nevertheless, the dangers of allowing your opponent to enjoy an unmolested pawn center must not be underestimated.

RIM PAWNS SHOULD STAY CLOSE TO HOME

The a-pawn and the h-pawn are important defenders. Until you castle, it is generally wise to keep them on the second or third ranks. Advancing to the fourth rank to attack the enemy king should be delayed until after development is complete. The advance of the h-pawn weakens g3, and if the f-pawn has departed from f2, that weakness can prove fatal. So we see another tradeoff. You can't win without advancing some pawns, but each advance comes at a price.

In the next game, White embarks on an adventure up the h-file before removing his king from the center. Rapidly occupying attacking positions for minor pieces, the thought of king safety is far from his mind. It shouldn't have been.

TURNER - VOLOSHIN
Lilie, 1997
1.d4 Nf6; 2.Nc3 d5; 3.Bg5 Nbd7; 4.e3 g6; 5.Nf3 Bg7; 6.Ne5 c6; 7.f4 0-0; 8.Bd3 Ne8; 9.h4? Nxe5; 10.fxe5.

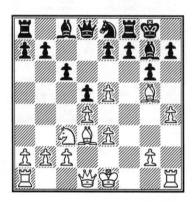

White's center, open f-file, greater space, and kingside attack look impressive. In reality, Black stands better after blasting the center with a pawn break.

10...f6!; 11.Bf4. 11.exf6; exf6; 12.Bf4 f5 will be very good for Black, when the knight gets from e8 to e4. **11...fxe5; 12.dxe5 Qc7.** Both e-pawns are weak, defended only by a nervous bishop at f4 which is attacked by Black's rook. White's minor pieces are no more effective than their Black counterparts.

13.h5 g5! This technique is often effective against a premature h-pawn advance. The h-file remains closed, making it hard to attack. In this case, the poor overworked bishop collapses, and the game falls apart. **14.Bxg5.** 14.Bg3 Bxe5; 15.Bxe5 Qxe5; 16.Qe2 Qg3+ wins with a bishop or rook pin.

14...Qxe5; 15.h6 Qg3+. White resigned. It is only fitting that the final move exploited the weakness created by the premature advance of the h-pawn.

THE G-PAWN DOES NOT ADVANCE PAST THE THIRD RANK

Theoreticians have poured scorn on the double advance of the g-pawn early in the game. This hasn't stopped true fans from pushing the g-pawn to the fourth rank during the very first moves of the game. At the professional level, such behavior is usually greeted with brutal punishment, but among amateurs the survival rate is greater.

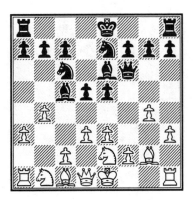

In this position after eight moves in Kranzl vs. Dorn, 1993, White has most of the kingside under control. However, the h4 square remains weak after the advance of the g-pawn, and the g3 square, despite being covered by the knight at pawn, is still a little shaky because the h-pawn has moved. Black attacked the rook at a1, then retreated the bishop to work on the dark squares.

8...e4; 9.d4 Bb6; 10.Bb2 Ng6. The knight leaps to h4. **11.Bf1 Nh4.** Black threatens mate at f3!

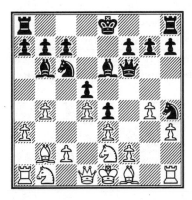

12.Nd2. This is forced, but the White king is now unable to castle to safety. Black can simply develop and work on the queenside, preparing to open lines so that the queenside will never be a refuge for the enemy king. The f3-square can be exploited at any time, but there is no rush.

12...a5; 13.b5 Ne7; 14.Nf4 0-0; 15.c4 c6; 16.Qb3 Bc7. White is ready to castle, but never gets time. The immediate threat is the capture at f4. **17.Ng2 Nf3+!** Well timed! **18.Nxf3 Qxf3.**

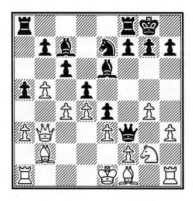

Castling is still out of the question. After a pair of pawn moves White tries to trade queens, but neglects the mating net.

19.c5 a4; 20.Qd1? Ba5+! White resigned.

THE F-PAWN STAYS HOME

The square in front of the king's bishop is the most vulnerable point in the defensive armor. The pawn that resides there both protects the king from attack and, more importantly, protects both the g6 and e6 squares. Therefore it should not advance without good cause.

In Wedervang vs. Jorgensen, Holbak, 1983, a critical position was reached after eight moves. The White kingside is under assault. Black plans ...h5 followed by ...h4. White panics, and tries to chase away the enemy queen.

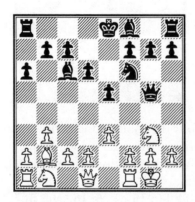

9.f4? White should have realized that this pawn might be needed at f3 to guard the g4-square. There is a tactical miscalculation as well. Black seems forced to capture at f4, otherwise the e-pawn is lost. The weakness created by the advance of the f-pawn makes it possible to ignore the threats at e5.

9...Qh4!; 10.fxe5 Ng4.

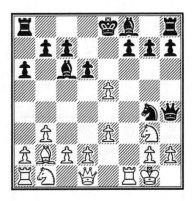

White cannot defend the h-pawn, and it cannot advance without losing the knight. After 11.h3 Qxg3, White cannot capture at g4 because of mate at g2. **11.Rf2 Qxh2+; 12.Kf1 Nxf2; 13.e4 Nxd1.** White resigned.

DO NOT ADVANCE PAWNS BEYOND THE FIFTH RANK

It is inadvisable to advance a pawn beyond the fifth rank unless it makes at least one, and preferably two or more captures along the way. This is based on the concept of preserving time, since otherwise a White pawn takes four moves to reach the sixth rank without achieving any tangible results.

DON'T MOVE A PIECE TWICE IN THE OPENING

Almost every beginner has heard this maxim, which is rarely followed. Actually, it is perfectly acceptable to move a piece twice in the opening if one of the moves is a capture. Even the Mexican Defense, sometimes known as the Black Knights Tango, dances on the boards of professional players. For examine, the following position is seen after 1.d4 Nf6; 2.c4 Nc6; 3.d5 Ne5; 4.e4 e6.

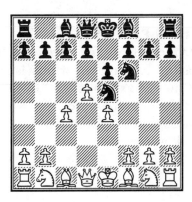

Black has moved nothing but knights and a single pawn, and with 5.f4, another knight move is forced. Yet in this position White almost never advances the f-pawn, as the large pawn center is vulnerable.

A better piece of advice is: Don't move a piece twice in the opening unless you are forced to do so, or if there is no other way to maintain an initiative. Consider the popularity of the knight leap in the Karpov Variation of the Caro-Kann Defense, which runs 1.e4 c6; 2.d4 d5; 3.Nc3 dxe4; 4.Nxe4 Nd7; 5.Bc4 Ngf6; 6.Ng5.

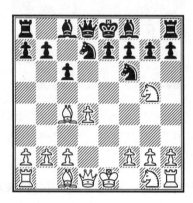

The knight will eventually be driven back by ...h6, with further loss of time, but it accomplishes the important task of forcing Black to place a pawn at e6, locking in the bishop at c8. In addition, it avoids an exchange for the enemy knight, which would reduce White's attacking force. The advance of the knight to g5 is considered the only way for White to play for the advantage in this variation.

Edward Lasker points out a more specific form of this rule. It is not a good idea to exchange a knight that has moved twice for a knight that has moved only once. The same holds true for bishops. If you are going to move a piece around the board in the opening, make sure that each step has a purpose that will last even if the wandering piece is exchanged for a newly developed one. Otherwise, the exercise will have been a pointless waste of time.

MOVE PIECES RATHER THAN PAWNS

Many books advise you to move only one or two pawns in the opening, concentrating on piece development instead. A common formula is that the ideal opening should involve two pawn moves (e4 and d4 as White) and two minor piece moves (Nf3 and Bc4, Bb5, or Nc3) in the first four or five moves.

There is a grain of truth here, but in fact many standard openings involve lots of pawn moves. Consider the following:

Semi-Slav Defense: Noteboom Variation

1.d4 d5; 2.c4 e6; 3.Nc3 c6; 4.Nf3 dxc4; 5.a4 Bb4; 6.e3 b5; 7.Bd2 a5; 8.axb5 Bxc3; 9.Bxc3 cxb5; 10.b3.

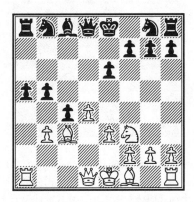

This is a very popular opening. Even though White has played ten moves, and Black nine, White has only two developed pieces, and Black's forces are all on their home squares. In 19 moves, 13 pawn moves have been made! The current verdict is that the Noteboom is playable for both sides. This is an extreme example, but it does demonstrate that the conventional wisdom about development has major exceptions.

It is better to concentrate on the role of pawns in the opening, not the number of pawn moves. Pawns should advance in the following circumstances:

- To engage in battle for central territory
- To support a fellow pawn in the center
- To allow bishops to get into the game
- To capture enemy forces
- To undermine the enemy pawn center

DEVELOP KNIGHTS BEFORE BISHOPS

This is an old oversimplification which really doesn't apply anymore. It is better to think in terms of the king's knight alone, as White. Openings involving Nc3 before Nf3 are not as popular as they once were, especially in the King Pawn Games. In many Queen Pawn Games, the relative entries of the knights are often unimportant, and transpositions are frequent.

The idea behind the old wisdom is that knights tend to be developed in close proximity to the center. Knights at c3 and f3, for example, control d4, e4, d5, and e5. It is harder for bishops to achieve this. You could fianchetto both bishops, but they are likely to be blocked by knights. In the diagram below, these two strategies are compared.

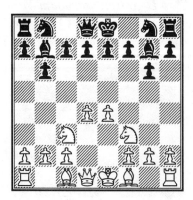

White can continue development easily enough, but if Black brings the knights to their natural posts, then the bishops will be blocked. In addition, the knights can reach their desired posts without the need to make pawn moves. The bishops require twice as long to get into position.

Now that the ideal pawn center is not considered any guarantee of an advantage, openings with an early bishop deployment have become more respectable, none more so than the Trompowsky Attack **1.d4 Nf6; 2.Bg5.**

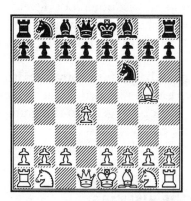

This move has no direct role in the construction of the ideal pawn center, but that is not the goal of this opening. The bishop can sometimes capture at f6, but often the knight jumps to e4 to avoid capture. The knight may be driven back later. This is a very complicated opening and is currently under examination on the chessboards of the top players in the world.

A more extreme case is the failure to develop either knight early in the game. The opening of Euwe vs. Maroczy, Amsterdam 1921, shows the danger of delaying knight development. The Black king is trapped in the center, unable to castle.

1.e4 e5; 2.f4 Bc5; 3.Nf3 d6; 4.c3 Bg4; 5.fxe5 dxe5; 6.Qa4+ Bd7; 7.Qc2 Qe7; 8.d4 exd4; 9.cxd4 Bb4+; 10.Nc3 Bc6; 11.Bd3.

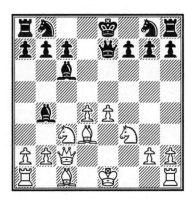

Black's king seems safe enough, but the unavailability of castling should be cause for some concern. It is hard for the knights to be developed because White owns the center, and the bishop at c6 is artificially placed. In spite of all this, Maroczy feels compelled to go after the pawn at e4.

11...Bxc3+?; 12.bxc3 Bxe4. A temporary sacrifice, thanks to the pin on the e-file. **13.Bxe4 f5; 14.0-0! fxe4; 15.Qb3!** White threatens to capture at b7. **15...c5; 16.Ba3 Nf6.**

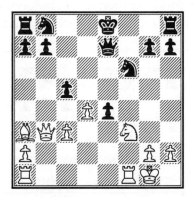

Finally, a knight is developed at move 16. But there are still impediments to castling. The knight at f3 therefore remains taboo, as White would bring a rook to e1 and win the enemy queen. Euwe won quickly.

17.Bxc5 Qf7; 18.c4 b6; 19.Ng5 Qd7.

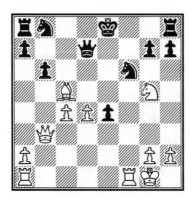

The knight at b8 still hasn't moved, and the one at f6 is about to be removed.

20.Rxf6!! gxf6; 21.Nxe4 Qe6; 22.Re1 bxc5; 23.Nxf6+ Kf7; 24.Qb7+. Black resigned. While it is not necessary to develop knights before bishops, one mustn't neglect the development of knights altogether!

BISHOPS STAY NEAR THE CENTER

A bishop should not move to b5 or g5 unless there is an enemy piece to attack or a check to give. It can become too exposed there. Indeed, even in the venerable Spanish Game, the bishop gets chased. Observe: **1.e4 e5; 2.Nf3 Nc6; 3.Bb5 a6; 4.Ba4 b5; 5.Bb3.**

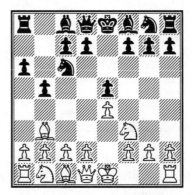

The bishop has made three consecutive moves, but arrives at a safe and useful post. Black has gained space on the queenside, but the pawn structure is vulnerable to an eventual advance of White's a-pawn to a4. Such compromises lead to a balanced game with chances for both sides.

HER MAJESTY STAYS IN THE SAFETY ZONE

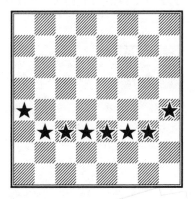

The safety zone is bordered by the ⌐   ⌐e dots in the diagram. The squares with the dots are definitely risk   be easily attacked, but the queen often uses these squares for a speci⌐   look at those later when we discuss the queen in detail.

Generally, queens belong behind pawn⌐   involved in a direct attack. This indicates that you won't find queens t⌐   rd early in the game.

CASTLE KINGSIDE AS SOON AS YOU ⌐

There is no doubt that Napier is correct i⌐   ot to castle just because you can. Nevertheless in most circumstances   do so as soon as possible, especially for beginners. The king in th⌐   in great danger but is usually safe in a castled position. Since castlin⌐   normal developments there are very few circumstances under which it   a mistake.

In the game Stein vs. Gufeld, from a tournam⌐   ⌐67, the game started quietly enough.

*C*astle when you will, or if you must,
    but not when you can.

–Napier

STEIN - GUFELD
Tbilisi, 1967

1.d4 Nf6; 2.c4 g6; 3.Nc3 Bg7; 4.e4 d6; 5.Nf3 0-0; 6.Be2 e5; 7.Be3 Qe7; 8.0-0? This is in fact a blunder which leads to an advantage for Black. 8.d5 is the correct move.

8...Nxe4!; 9.Nxe4 exd4; 10.Nxd4 Qxe4. Black has an extra pawn, but even more significant is the weakness of the a1-h8 diagonal.

Except in rare circumstances where castling needs to be delayed in order to see what the opponent is up to, you should get your king to safety as soon as possible. All authorities agree with this. The king is safer in the castled position because the files leading to the king are more likely to remain closed. Central files often open up early in the game. The vulnerability of the f7-square is lessened because a rook will protect the pawn, which can also be defended by a bishop or queen at e8.

Illustrating the protected f7

Chess isn't so simple, of course. If kingside castling were such a priority, then White would always move 1.e4, 2.Nf3, 3.Bc4 (or 3.Bb5) and 4.0-0. In fact, that is not especially common now.

Instead, White usually aims to castle in the first eight moves or so. There are some major exceptions in common openings of the modern era, and let's take a look at some of these to see why castling is sometimes delayed until even later in the game.

Sveshnikov Sicilian
1.e4 c5; 2.Nf3 Nc6; 3.d4 cxd4; 4.Nxd4 Nf6; 5.Nc3 e5; 6.Ndb5 d6; 7.Bg5 a6; 8.Na3 b5; 9.Nd5 Be7; 10.Bxf6 Bxf6; 11.c3 0-0; 12.Nc2.

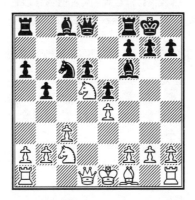

White is in no hurry to castle in this position. The king is not in any danger, and a pawnstorm on the kingside remains a serious option. A game between Tiviakov and Yakovich from the 1997 Russian Championship continued **12...Rb8; 13.h4 Be7; 14.Nce3 Be6; 15.g3 Qd7; 16.Qf3 Bd8; 17.h5 h6; 18.Nf5 Bxf5; 19.Qxf5 Qxf5; 20.exf5 Ne7; 21.Nxe7+ Bxe7; 22.Bg2 Rfc8.**

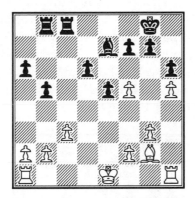

Now it is finally time to castle. Although the king often belongs in the center during the endgame, it is safer in the corner. The game was eventually drawn.

King's Indian: Saemisch Variation

The Saemisch Variation of the King's Indian Defense also allows White the luxury of late castling. In the 1997 Linares super-tournament, Garry Kasparov defended the Black side twice against this line, and White took plenty of time before castling. Kasparov managed only one draw from these two games, so late castling certainly wasn't punished!

IVANCHUK - KASPAROV
Linaret, 1997

1.d4 Nf6; 2.c4 g6; 3.Nc3 Bg7; 4.e4 d6; 5.f3 0-0; 6.Bg5 a6; 7.Qd2.

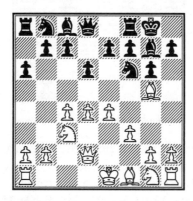

White seems clearly headed for early queenside castling. The way is clear. Black's 6th move, however, discourages that plan, since the queenside can be ripped open by ...b5. Black has several plans. An immediate consideration is whether or not to challenge the center with ...c5. That's what Kasparov chose against Ivanchuk. **7...c5.** A different plan allows White to plant a pawn at d5 before Black can advance the c-pawn.

Facing Dreyev, Kasparov chose 7...Nbd7; 8.d5 Ne5; 9.Rd1 c6; 10.dxc6 bxc6; 11.b3 Qa5, leading to a sharp game. 12.Na4 Qc7; 13.Ne2 Nh5; 14.Nec3 f5; 15.exf5 gxf5; 16.f4 Ng4; 17.Be2 h6; 18.Bh4 d5; 19.Bxg4 fxg4.

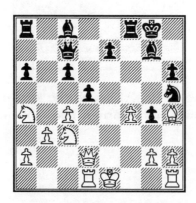

White's king is now exposed in the center, so Dreyev castled with 20.0-0. After 20...d4; 21.Ne2 c5; 22.Nb2 a5; 23.Rde1 Bf5; 24.Nd3 a4; 25.Ne5 axb3; 26.axb3 Bf6; 27.Bxf6 exf6; 28.Nd3 Ra3; 29.Nec1 Ng7; 30.Re2 h5; 31.Rfe1 Rf7 the game was eventually drawn.

Returning to the Ivanchuk game, play continued **8.d5 b5; 9.cxb5 Nbd7; 10.a4 Qa5; 11.Nge2 Nb6; 12.Nc1.**

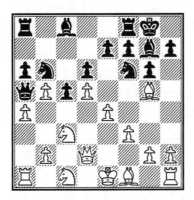

This is a typical maneuver in the Saemisch. White has a hard time castling, since c1 and f1 are still occupied. The advance of the f-pawn to f3 also creates possibilities for Black on the a7-g1 diagonal should White choose to castle kingside. **12...axb5; 13.Bxb5 Ba6; 14.N1a2 Bxb5; 15.axb5 Nh5; 16.Rb1 Bd4; 17.Bh6 Rfe8; 18.b3 e6; 19.dxe6 Rxe6; 20.Be3 Bxe3; 21.Qxe3 d5; 22.b4 Qa3; 23.bxc5 Nc4; 24.Qd4 Nf4.**

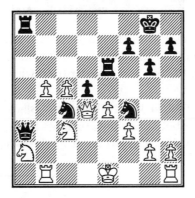

Perhaps Black reasoned that White cannot castle here, because of a tactical trick. It doesn't work. **25.0-0 Qxa2; 26.Rf2! Qa3; 27.Nxd5.** White has three pawns for the piece, and the queenside passed pawns are a serious threat. Not only that, but the knight at f4 is under attack. Kasparov exchanges queens, but the endgame is hopeless. **27...Qd3; 28.Qxd3 Nxd3; 29.Rc2 Na3; 30.Ra2 Nxc5; 31.Rba1.** The pawn armada is stopped, but it costs Black a piece. **31...f5; 32.Nc7 Re5; 33.Nxa8 Nxb5; 34.exf5 gxf5; 35.Nb6 Nc3; 36.Rc2 Ne2+ and** Black resigned.

In examining almost 60,000 games played in 1997, less than one percent saw castling after move 25. One of the rarest sights in all chess is castling after move 40. Krabbé's *Chess Curiosities* lists only seven examples up to 1985. I found only one in 1997. Here is an example of delayed queenside castling. The game below is truly amazing. Black manages to delay castling until move 43, and castling proves to be the winning move! You can hardly blame White for failing to take the move into account, because castling had been impossible for a long time.

POPOVYCH - IVANOV
New York, 1983
1.e4 c5; 2.Nf3 d6; 3.d4 cxd4; 4.Nxd4 Nf6; 5.Nc3 Nc6; 6.Bg5 Qb6; 7.Nb3 e6; 8.Bd3 Be7; 9.0–0 a6; 10.Qe2 h6; 11.Bh4 Ne5.

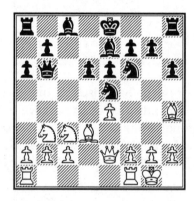

Black often delays castling in the Richter-Rauzer variation of the Sicilian Defense. The Black king is well protected at home. Castling kingside has the drawback that White can later capture at f6, forcing a recapture with the pawn in some circumstances.

12.Kh1 Ng6; 13.Bg3 h5; 14.f4 h4; 15.Bf2 Qc7. Black is not ready to develop the bishop and castle queenside, because the future of the bishop has not yet been determined. It can crawl to c6 via d7, or go to b7 after the advance of the b-pawn. **16.Be3 b5; 17.a4 b4; 18.Nd1 Bb7; 19.Nf2.**

From this point Black can castle in either direction.

19...h3. 19...0–0; 20.Rad1 looks better for White, who will have a free hand on the kingside. 19...0-0-0 is not playable because of 20.Bxa6. **20.Nxh3 Nxe4.** Black must equalize the material. **21.Kg1 d5.** 21...0-0; 22.Rad1 is also good for White here. Queenside castling continues to fail to the capture of the a-pawn.

22.Nd4 Bd6. Black gangs up on the f-pawn. **23.Rac1 Rh4.** The plan of kingside castling is put to rest, though manual castling with Kf8-g8 remains an option. **24.c4; bxc3.** Black could have tried capturing at f4.

25.Bxe4! dxe4; 26.Rxc3 Qd7.

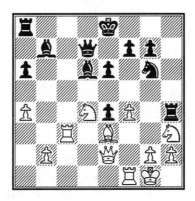

The queen is forced to abandon the c-file, and now castling is not legal.

27.f5 Ne5; 28.fxe6 fxe6; 29.Ng5 Bd5; 30.h3 White eliminates the threat of ...Ng4. **30...Bb4; 31.Rc2 Be7; 32.Qf2!** The f-file is open for business. The king cannot escape the center. **32...Rh6; 33.Qg3 Rf6.**

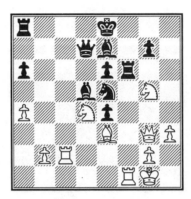

34.Bf4. 34.Rxf6 gxf6; 35.Qh4! Black would then be in serious trouble, for example 35...fxg5; 36.Qh8+ Kf7; 37.Qxe5 Qxa4; 38.Rf2+ Ke8; 39.Nxe6 Bxe6; 40.Qxe6 and Black will soon capitulate.

34...Nd3; 35.Rc7 The invasion of the seventh rank is usually fatal. **35...Qxa4; 36.Ngxe6 Bxe6; 37.Nxe6 Rxe6; 38.Qxg7 Nxf4; 39.Qg8+ Bf8; 40.Rxf4 Qd4+; 41.Kh1 Qd1+; 42.Kh2 Qd6.**

After a fast and furious race to time control, Black holds an extra piece but the king is under assault. White should have played 43.g3 here, after which there are excellent winning chances, but instead forgot about castling.

43.Rcf7?? 0–0–0! The Black king is safe at last. White doesn't even have a check. The pin on the rook at f4 is decisive. **44.g3 Bh6;** White resigned. The queen and rook at f4 are both under attack.

KEEP UP WITH YOUR OPPONENT

There are two ways of looking at development during the opening. You can take an absolute view, being concerned only with your own position. This is in some ways very useful, as it keeps you from getting sidetrack by your opponent's play. At the same time it is important to look at development from another perspective, the relative development of each side. When you are still in the opening, and it is your opponent's turn to play, spend some time calculating which side is ahead in development, and take that differential into account as you develop your plans.

If you have a lead of three or more tempi, then you can start looking for attacks and combinations right away. Even a move or two may provide the foundation for a decisive assault. A game between Tartakower and Mieses, from the great international tournament at Baden Baden, 1925, saw Black utterly neglect development in the early stage of the game.

1.d4 f5; 2.e4 fxe4; 3.Nc3 Nf6; 4.g4 d5; 5.g5 Ng8; 6.f3 exf3; 7.Qxf3! e6; 8.Bd3 g6; 9.Nge2 Qe7; 10.Bf4 c6; 11.Be5 Bg7; 12.Qg3.

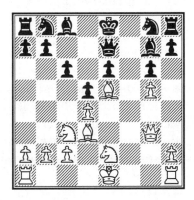

White has developed all four minor pieces and the queen. Black has just a queen and bishop in the game. Black is already in a hopeless situation. The knight at b8 is under attack, and must move to a useless position at the edge of the board.

12...Na6. Black cannot play 12...Nd7? because of 13.Bd6 Qd8; 14.Rf1 Ne7; 15.Bc7 and the Black queen is trapped. After **13.0-0 Bd7; 14.Bd6 Qd8; 15.Qf4** Black resigned, with no defense to the threats of 16.Qf7#, and 16.Qf8+ Bxf8; 17.Rf8#.

HANG ON TO YOUR PIECES

You need superior firepower to win most battles, so sacrificing material in the opening should only be used when there is clear compensation. Giving up material early in the game is known as gambit play, and we will examine gambit chess openings in a separate chapter.

Gambiteers will argue that there is considerable compensation for the sacrificed material. Usually open lines, rapid development, control of the center and limited enemy counterplay can be found in the best opening gambits. Still, as they say, "A pawn is a pawn." A pawn in the hand is worth the risk, in many cases. With extra material, you can exchange pieces to win in the endgame, a topic presented later in the book. Of course, you'll have to survive the middlegame first. Lessons on defense are located in the strategy chapter.

OPENING REPERTOIRE

An opening repertoire is a collection of openings that a player uses more or less regularly. Every experienced chessplayer has an opening repertoire, whether it is just a few moves deep or extensively analyzed out to move thirty. Some players prefer a narrow repertoire, while others like to explore a wide range of strategies.

Developing an opening repertoire is a task which should not be taken lightly. Decisions made in a few moments can influence your game for years. There are many ways to build your opening set. You can examine the games of strong players and emulate them. To see how the very best players handle the opening phase of the game you might consult *World Champion Openings*. You can also consult many books which are devoted to opening repertoires. To browse the many different opening possibilities, check out *Standard Chess Openings, Gambit Chess Openings* and *Unorthodox Chess Openings* and other fine chess books from Cardoza Publishing.

There is some general advice on opening repertoires, but much of it is very bad. Many teachers simply pass on their own opening preferences to their students, regardless of whether the openings are suitable for less advanced players. The openings you choose early in your career should be respectable and in common use among strong players, not necessarily modern stars but visible at some point in the hands of top professionals.

We'll get into specific recommendations in the training chapter, but at the outset I'd like to expose one of the myths that continue to appear in books which are supposed to help you become a better player. You often read that it is important to choose openings which fit your "style." Unless you are an accomplished master, the term "style" is irrelevant. You don't have a style, you have a set of weaknesses. Using only openings which attempt to avoid those weaknesses will leave them festering like a disease, with no cure in sight.

That said, it is certainly true that most players who enjoy a sharp attacking game prefer to open 1.e4, though, as the great David Bronstein says, that can be "somewhat dangerous because tactical complications can arise almost immediately." He recommends 1.d4 or 1.Nf3. Most top players have played at least two of these three moves. None, as far as I know, have more than a transient belief that one is better than the other.

MOVE ORDER

When we choose to play a certain opening, it is because we want to achieve a certain type of position, ideally a specific position we have studied at home. Some of these positions can be reached by many different move orders. These are known as transpositional openings. Suppose we want to reach the starting position of the Classical Variation of the Tarrasch Defense, as Black.

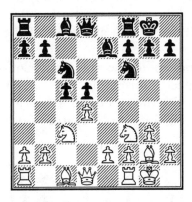

Since the Tarrasch Defense is classified as belonging to the Queen's Gambit Declined, the natural start to the game is **1.d4.**

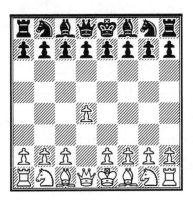

In almost all opening books you will find the move order of the Classical Tarrasch given as 1.d4 d5; 2.c4 e6; 3.Nc3 c5; 4.cxd5 exd5; 5.Nf3 Nc6; 6.g3 Nf6; 7.Bg2 Be7; 8.0-0 0-0. There are, however, many other paths. For example:

A. 1.c4 e6; 2.Nc3 (2.d4 d5; 3.Nc3 c5 arrives at the same position.) 2...d5; 3.d4 c5 rejoins the main line at White's fourth move.

B. 1.Nf3 d5; 2.g3 c5; 3.Bg2 Nc6; 4.d4 e6; 5.0-0 Nf6; 6.c4 Be7; 7.cxd5 exd5; 8.Nc3 0-0.

C. 1.g3 d5; 2.Nf3 c5; 3.Bg2 Nc6; 4.d4 e6. 5.0-0 Nf6; 6.c4 Be7; 7.cxd5 exd5; 8.Nc3 0-0.

D. 1.b3 d5; 2.Nf3, c5; 3.Bb2 Nc6; 4.g3 Nf6; 5.Bg2 e6; 6.0–0 Be7; 7.c4 0–0; 8.cxd5 exd5; 9.d4 is the Larsen Variation of the Classical Tarrasch.

E. 1.e4 c6; 2.d4 d5; 3.exd5 cxd5; 4.c4 Nf6; 5.Nc3 g6; 6.Nf3 Bg7; 7.Be2 0–0; 8.0–0 Nc6 is a reverse Tarrasch.

The move order used in the books is just the conventional one, but has no other special status. As Black, we are most likely to reach the position we want after 1.c4, because after 1.d4 d5; 2.Nf3 White can choose many different plans, many of which do not involve the advance of the c-pawn to c4, which is crucial to our position. After 1.c4 e6, however, Black will play 2...d5, and most of the time, White will oblige by playing d4 early in the game.

You can't force your opponent to play your choice of opening. Even the openings which involve setting up a specific formation, such as a Stonewall, can be thwarted by radical means. Some players like the Stonewall Attack for its aggressive kingside play, and aim to set up the following formation regardless of Black's moves (so we'll show the Black side in the starting position).

If we look carefully at the position, we can see that there are only two logical candidates for our first move in the game. Since we need to pile up piece on the d-file and f-file, the d-pawn and f-pawn must quickly advance to the fourth rank. So 1.d4 and 1.f4 are our candidates. The problem with **1.f4** is that it allows the sharp From Gambit with **1...e5!?**

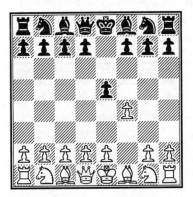

This can be a truly dangerous gambit. Fortunately, we can decline it if we wish, and even transpose to the King's Gambit (1.e5 e5; 2.f4) with **2.e4.**

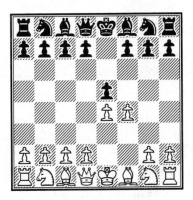

This is quite different from the Stonewall Attack, however, so let's try the alternative move order **1.d4.**

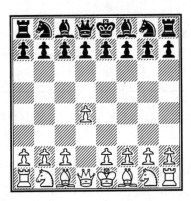

The gambit approach with 1...e5? is bad, as we will see later in the book.

Black can try 1...c5, which is a form of the Benoni Defense. That does not prevent White from playing a Stonewall formation, so we needn't worry about that.

The Dutch Defense with 1...f5 is another matter.

Nothing stops us from advancing 2.f4, but it is now a rather silly and pointless move. Instead of trying to play a Stonewall at all costs, White is better off learning a separate approach to use against the Dutch, and there are many available. Choosing a move order is as important as your decision on which openings to include in your repertoire!

OPENING THEORY

Opening theory is the collective wisdom and experience of the chess community. When we say that theory considers an opening good, or bad, we mean that the prevailing opinion in the latest published work comes to this conclusion. Opening theory is always subject to revision, and changes can take place either over many years, or as a result of a single new idea.

There are some players, Hungarian Grandmaster and former World Championship candidate Lajos Portisch among them, who have no interest in spending time and energy working on the subtleties of their opening strategies. They view the opening as an overture. Their only concern is to emerge from the opening with a playable game. This is not such a bad attitude. In our day the opening phase of the game has been over emphasized so much that many players study nothing but opening theory. In fact their studying time would be much better spent working on endgames and middle game theory.

> *Your only task in the opening is to reach a playable middlegame*
>
> *–Portisch*

If you compare the results of games where one side had in opening advantage with those where the opening ended in rocky quality or even an advantage for the other side, you'll find that there is very little correlation with the actual results of the game. Chess games are lost through mistakes. It doesn't really matter which stage of the game sees these mistakes. If you emerge from the opening with an equal game or even a slight disadvantage there is usually no risk of losing unless you make a serious error. So the question naturally arises, why spend so much time trying to achieve the small advantage in the opening when you can play chess with slightly less aspiration in the initial stage of the game and nevertheless arrive at a position from which it is entirely possible to win the game?

At the very highest levels of chess a small opening advantage may be significant. In amateur play it rarely is.

FASHION RULES!

At any given time, chessplayers and theoreticians will proclaim certain openings to be playable and discard many others. At the end of the 19th century, the *British Chess Magazine Guide to the Openings* discussed the important openings of the day. This book contained only a few openings, not considering any others worthy of serious analysis. Let us see how the century old opinions hold up today. All quotes are from this venerable book, except as noted.

Italian Game (Giuoco Piano)

1.e4 e5; 2.Nf3 Nc6; 3.Bc4 Bc5.

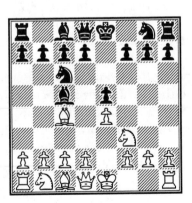

The opening which everybody knows–so far. Though rarely played in professional tournaments of matches, it is still deservedly popular with amateurs.

Until quite recently it was certainly true that almost anyone familiar with the game had at least a passing acquaintance with the Italian Game. These days, however, many players do not adopt the King Pawn Game (1.e4 e5) as part of their student repertoire, choosing the popular Sicilian Defense instead when playing Black. As White, the Italian Game is still popular with amateur players. There are fewer followers among professionals, and in those cases where White does use the opening, it is usually not for its excitement, but for its solid positional foundation.

Evans Gambit

1.e4 e5; 2.Nf3 Nc6; 3.Bc4 Bc5; 4.b4.

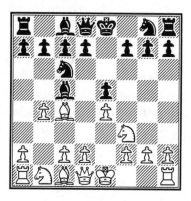

Since 1834 it has been analyzed down hundreds of variations. In his able examination of the Gambit in Chess Openings A. & M., Mr. Freeborough uses up no less than 120 columns of analysis, plus nearly 300 additional notes.

Having fallen into obscurity, the Evans has made a few appearances in top level competition in the 1990s and the trickle-down effect has made it once again a popular opening in amateur games. Several important new books have also helped to popularize it. It is interesting that the resurgence of interest in this old opening was brought about by the top stars of our own time, especially 1993 World Championship challenger Nigel Short.

Max Lange Attack

1.e4 e5; 2.Nf3 Nc6; 3.Bc4 Bc5; 4.0-0 Nf6; 5.d4.

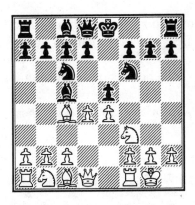

Excepting the Evans Gambit, this is the most lively offshoot of the Giuoco Piano. Like the Evans, the Max Lange Attack is a true gambit, involving the early sacrifice of a pawn for the sake of rapid development.

This particular form of the Max Lange Attack is a rare sight now since the pawn at d4 can be captured by the bishop. Used mostly by lower rated players, it nevertheless continues to score very well for White. The Max Lange is more frequently reached through the Two Knights Defense, and is now classified as a branch of that opening. Indeed, the Two Knights, with 3...Nf6, is considered the primary response to 3...Bc5.

Two Knights Defense

1.e4 e5; 2.Nf3 Nc6; 3.Bc4 Nf6.

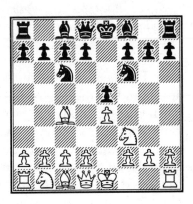

To players desirous of avoiding the dangers of an Evans or a Max Lange Attack, or the dullness of a possible Giuoco Pianissimo, this defense may be recommended as perfectly satisfactory.

This logic rings false now. The Two Knights contains some of the sharpest positions in the King Pawn Games, and Black usually adopts it when looking for a fight. There is no reason to fear either of White's sharpest plans, 4.Ng5 or 4.d4, provided that one is familiar with the treacherous paths of opening theory.

Spanish Game (Ruy Lopez)

1.e4 e5; 2.Nf3 Nc6; 3.Bb5.

The object of playing the bishop to b5 was evidently to still threaten the Black e-pawn by an attack on the defending knight–a simple though, as was soon proved, barren idea, the appreciation of which caused the practical abandonment of the opening. In the last thirty or forty years, however, the "Ruy" has become extremely popular the move of the bishop is no longer played with a view to an immediate and direct attack, but as helping on White's development while leading to a tiresome and cramped game for Black, in which early attempts at retaliation are almost invariably disastrous.

Although fairly low down in the hierarchy, the author clearly notices the rising status of the Spanish Game at the end of the 19th century. It soon became the most important of all of the King Pawn Games, and is still by far the most respected opening plan involving 1.e4 e5. All of the great 20th century masters have some experience with it, and World Champions from Steinitz to Kasparov have contributed greatly to the theory. In most opening manuals, the Spanish Game occupies as much space as all the other King Pawn Games combined. In fact, 1998 saw renewed interest in the Spanish, which has been a frequent quest in recent tournaments. This trend continues today.

Scotch Game

1.e4 e5; 2.Nf3 Nc6; 3.d4.

The proffered pawn must be taken, or Black soon gets a very bad game. ... It is, moreover, better for Black not to play 3...Nxd4, but 3...exd4, when if White replies 4.Bc4 we have the Scotch Gambit, and if 4.Nxd4, the Scotch Opening, the latter form being the most frequently adopted now-a-days. In either case, the result should be a free and interesting game, affording great scope for brilliant combination both in attack and defense.

The Scotch Game has been a bench warmer for a long time. After a brief renaissance in the early 1990s, motivated in large part by Kasparov's patronage in the 1990 title match against Karpov, it is now almost dormant. The Scotch Gambit, on the other hand, is firmly entrenched in the amateur repertoire, though it has fewer followers among professionals. The general view is that the complications have all been worked out, and that White cannot secure an advantage in any part of Scottish territory. While most lines lead to sterile positions, there is renewed interest in Steinitz's old defense 4.Nxd4 Qh4!?

Russian Game (Petroff Defense)

1.e4 e5; 2.Nf3 Nf6.

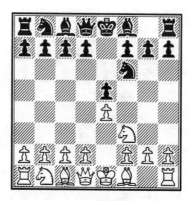

To the numerous players who dislike the Ruy Lopez, the Petroff may be recommended as on the whole the most satisfactory method of avoiding that troublesome attack, though, as the analysis now stands, Black has to be content with getting a slightly inferior game.

Still chugging along, for the same old reason. White's advantage in the Russian Game tends to be microscopic. This tiny advantage can easily disappear after just one imprecise move by White. Many good defensive players, such as Artur Yusupov, are quite comfortable defending the Black side. It is not often used when a win is required by Black, because the tendency for the game to end in a draw is pronounced.

Center Game

1.e4 e5; 2.d4.

Strictly speaking, this opening is usually not a gambit, there being no sacrifice of material but merely an exchange of pawns. When, however, it is played as a gambit, White secures full compensation by his rapid development.

None but the most eccentric players use the Center Game in serious competition now. The Center Gambits are considered dubious, though the Göring Gambit (2...exd4 3.Nf3 Nc6; 4.c3) has a following in amateur games. The ancient Danish Gambit (2...exd4 3.c3) has been rehabilitated. The main line in authoritative opening manuals of the 1970s was judged to be better for Black, but now the evaluations are less clear. The main problem with both gambits is that Black can strike back in the center with ...d5 immediately, declining the gambit and securing an equal game.

Vienna Game

1.e4 e5; 2.Nc3.

At present, in one or another of its numerous varieties, it rivals in general popularity the Ruy Lopez itself. The distinctive feature of this opening is its being a deferred attack, where the queen knight is brought out before the King's Gambit move (f4) is played, thus augmenting the force of the latter move.

The old Bishop Ruy Lopez has nothing to fear from his Austrian cousin. The Vienna Game, at least as a prelude to the King's Gambit formation, is not a significant contender in the popularity contest of the openings. A modern approach, developed by Mieses and others, is to adopt a kingside fianchetto, placing the knight at e2 rather than f3, so that the scope of the bishop is not impaired.

Allgaier Gambit

1.e4 e5; 2.f4 exf4; 3.Nf3 g5; 4.h4 g4; 5.Ng5.

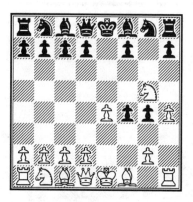

Mr. Gunsberg, when conducting the so-called Chess Automaton, was rightly partial to this opening. It is never dull, and dullness would have been the one unpardonable sin for "Mephisto" to commit. ... What Mr. Gunsberg has to say about it amounts to this: I find that I win more games the more I play this opening. Though perhaps not quite sound, I have tried it with success even in match play.

This opening has fallen off the map. In a database of recent games, it was seen only once, in a minor amateur encounter. All authorities consider this opening to be refuted. What has changed since Gunsberg's time?

The answer to the question lies in the greater familiarity with opening theory among modern players, even amateurs. The Allgaier might work against uninformed opposition, but now anyone who accepts the King's Gambit and follows up with 3...g5 is thoroughly prepared to meet it.

King's Gambit Declined

1.e4 e5; 2.f4.

There are two good declining moves at Black's disposal, and two which are inferior. The two good replies are 2...Bc5 and 2...d5.

The range of inferior replies has been extended considerably, but both 2...Bc5 and 2...d5 are the preferred moves when Black is in no mood to accept the King's Gambit. There is nothing wrong with taking the pawn, however, and many reliable defensive strategies have been established.

French Defense

1.e4 e6.

> *A comparison of games recorded at different periods shows us, however, that whereas in Jaenisch's time Black scored 56 per cent ... the proportion has now altered to White scoring 66 percent, and Black only 34.*
>
> *But in spite of this, strangely enough, the opening has not diminished in popularity, a fact that must be ascribed to the nervous desire to limit White's choice of attacks, and above all to avoid that old man of the sea, the Ruy Lopez.* –B.C.M. Guide to the Openings

The French is one of the most favored openings of our time, but not for the reasons which led players to it in the last century. The defense which once cooperatively abandoned the center has been transformed into a fighting opening. Nevertheless, the limited scope of the bishop at c8 still discourages many players from adopting it. World Champions Botvinnik and Petrosian patronized it, and though no modern champions use it, many top contenders do.

Where are the two most popular openings of our time—the Sicilian Defense and the King's Indian Defense? They are not even mentioned! The Sicilian had been played from time to time in the 19th century, but the Indian Games (1.d4 Nf6) had not yet been explored seriously.

THE ONLY CONSTANT IS THAT THINGS CHANGE

Although many openings have been studied to depths of dozens of moves, important innovations frequently cause chess theoreticians and tournament players alike to re-evaluate even the most popular opening strategies. Sometimes, a new idea around move 30 can force a player to abandon an entire variation which begins at, say, move 9. Sharp openings involve treacherous tactical situations where danger can arise from unexpected sources. Years may be needed to uncover the hidden resource.

At the top levels of professional chess, a new move may seem to be only a slight twist on an old idea. Yet the difference can be an enormous one, as we see in this example from the best in the business.

GELFAND - KASPAROV
Novgorod, 1997
1.d4 Nf6; 2.c4 e6; 3.Nf3 b6; 4.a3 c5; 5.d5 Ba6; 6.Qc2 exd5; 7.cxd5 g6; 8.Nc3 Bg7; 9.g3 0-0; 10.Bg2 d6; 11.0-0 Re8; 12.Re1 Nbd7.

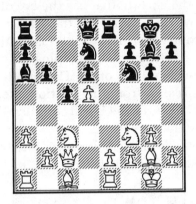

This position is very sharp, and has been seen frequently in the past three decades. In the *Encyclopedia of Chess Openings*, a considerable amount of analysis is devoted to the position. The main line there follows a 1987 game between Yusupov and Timman, which will be mentioned below.

13.h3. 13.e4 has been tried in this position, in anticipation of the problems White faces after 14.e4 in our game. Accelerating the plan is even worse. 13...Ng4; 14.Bg5 Qc7; 15.Bf4 Nde5; 16.Rad1 b5; 17.h3 Nxf3+; 18.Bxf3 Ne5; 19.Be2 c4 gave Black typical Benoni counterplay in Popov-Kastanieda, St. Petersburg 1998.

13...b5! The immediate occupation of the e5-square was considered best, until this game. 13...Ne5; 14.Nxe5 Rxe5; 15.e4 Re8; 16.Be3 Nd7; 17.f4 c4; 18.e5 was the official line, considered slightly better for White on the basis of 18...dxe5; 19.d6 Rc8; 20.f5 with strong pressure in Yusupov-Timman, Tilburg 1986.

14.e4. The alternative, 14.Bf4, must be examined, as the present game may wipe out 14.e4.

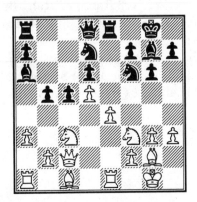

Black had previously tried bringing the queen to b6 and the rook to c8, a logical plan, but one which turns out to be awkward for Black in a number of games. Kasparov came up with a new plan, using the queen on the light squares instead. This plan is not at all obvious. 14.Bf4 is presently being countered by 14...Nb6!? It is now this line, rather than the advance of the e-pawn, that has the eye of the theoreticians.

14...Qc8! This is the move that overturned the verdict of the theoreticians. As you can see, it does not seem to make as much sense as putting the queen on the more active square, b6. Kasparov has other plans, keeping it open for use by the knight at d7. Then, the diagonal from c8 to h3 is open. That subtle point, which plays a major role in the game, is not easily seen from the position after White's fourteenth move. 14...Rc8; 15.Be3 Qc7; 16.Bf1 Qb7; 17.Bf4 is still considered better for White, as in Van Wely-Kamsky, Amsterdam 1996.

15.Bf4 b4; 16.Na4 b3. Black's initiative is strong, and the potential of the bishop at g7 is felt at b2. **17.Qxb3 Nxe4; 18.Qc2 Ndf6.**

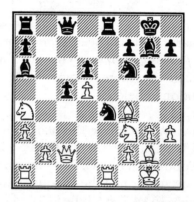

Kasparov's plan has succeeded in building a strong position. His opponent, feeling the pressure, launches a desperate kingside attack, but this just leads to a further weakening of the position which proves fatal.

19.g4? 19.Nd2 Nxd2; 20.Qxd2 Qd7 is given by Kasparov's second, Dokhoyan. **19...Qd7; 20.g5 Nh5; 21.Bh2 f5; 22.Nc3 Rab8; 23.Rab1 Bxc3; 24.bxc3 Rxb1; 25.Rxb1 Bc4; 26.Nd2 Nxd2; 27.Qxd2 f4; 28.Re1 Re5; 29.Re4.** Exchanging rooks would have provided a bit more defense.

29...Rxe4; 30.Bxe4 Qxh3. The White pawns just drop off the board. **31.Bg2 Qg4; 32.Qe1 Ng7; 33.f3 Qxg5; 34.Qb1 Nf5; 35.Qb8+ Kg7; 36.Qxa7+ Kh6; 37.Qf7 Bf1; 38.Kxf1 Ne3+; 39.Ke1 Qh4+; 40.Ke2 Qxh2; 41.Kd3 Nf5.** White resigned.

STANDARD CHESS OPENINGS

Standard chess openings are the ones that you are most likely to encounter in tournament chess. One way to recognize a standard chess opening is going to a chess bookstall or catalog. If a great many books have been written about the opening and its variations, then it is almost certainly a standard opening.

Standard openings display a fine sense of balance, with any violations of opening principles justified by concrete positional factors. If a player gambits a pawn, there is usually a substantial lead in development, control of the center, and an initiative as compensation. When Black accepts a constricted position, then it is usually one without any glaring weaknesses that can easily be exploited by White.

These openings are discussed in detail in *Standard Chess Openings*, but here is a list of some of the most important standard openings. Considering the problem of transpositions, it is not simple to decide how to slice up the opening pie. The *Encyclopedia of Chess Openings* uses 500 different codes to classify the openings. The system is not without flaws, but since it is in such widespread use, we'll adopt it in our search for the most popular openings of 1997. Consulting the 1.5 million game Caxton Chess Database, I found over 60,000 games from that year, and here is how the popularity breaks down. (For more recent survey results see www.chesscity.com.)

You may be surprised to see some unfamiliar names here, but we'll soon see that is due to the nature of this particular system of classification. Many diagrams will probably not be familiar to you unless you are an advanced player.

The first number in the parenthesis indicates the number of games found with the opening in the Caxton Chess Database; the letter and number combination following indicates the ECO code.

THE MODERN APPROACH

Sicilian Defense: Alapin-Sveshnikov Variations
1.e4 c5; 2.c3 (1592, B22)

Modern Defense
1.e4 g6 (970, B07)

Scandinavian Defense
1.e4 d5 (937, B01)

Rat Defense
1.e4 d6 (761, B06)

Queen Pawn Game
1.d4 d5; 2.Nf3; Nf6 with 3.Bf4,
3.g3, or other 2nd moves
(720, D02)

Sicilian Defense: Lasker-Pelikan Variation
1.e4 c5; 2.Nf3 Nc6; 3.d4 cxd4; 4.Nxd4
(644, B33)

Unorthodox Openings. Anything except 1.d4, 1.e4, 1.c4, 1.Nf3, 1.f4, 1.b3 (578, A00)

Sample Unorthodox Opening
1.g3

French Defense: Advance Variation
1.e4 e6; 2.d4 d5; 3.e5 (571, C02)

Sicilian Defense: Closed Variation
1.e4 c5; 2.Nc3 (567, B23)

Caro-Kann Defense: Advance Variation
1.e4 c6; 2.d4 d5; 3.e5 (522, B12)

Trompowsky Attack
1.d4 Nf6; 2.Bg5 (522, A45)

King's Indian Attack
1.Nf3 Nf6; 2.g3 d5; 3.Bg2 (500, A07)

This is an interesting list, and certainly not what we would expect to find. The nature of the ECO classification system lends prominence to certain openings. Some major openings span dozens of the 500 available codes. The King's Indian Defense occupies the entire range of E60 though E99, a total of 40 codes. No wonder none of the individual codes reaches the top dozen. Let's consider the reason for the popularity of the openings listed above.

The Sicilian Defense leads almost inevitably to sharp tactical positions. Players who don't like a brawl as White therefore turn to the quiet Alapin-Sveshnikov Variation, to keep the atmosphere of the game civil.

The Scandinavian Defense and Trompowsky Attack are two openings which have genuinely soared in popularity, and each benefits from being squeezed into a single code. The enormous popularity of the Scandinavian Defense was influenced by the 1995 PCA World Championship where it was used by challenger Viswanathan Anand. British Grandmaster Julian Hodgson and 1997 United States Champion Joel Benjamin have brought the Trompowsky into fashion among top players.

Similarly, the Advance variations in both the French and Caro-Kann Defenses have been gaining more followers, though in the French it is still primarily a weapon used by amateur players.

The Lasker-Pelikan Variation is indeed popular, though unlike the "major" Sicilians, it has one code instead of ten. It is by no means the most popular approach to the Sicilian, but has some friends in high places, Vladimir Kramnik among them.

The Modern Defense and Rat Defense cover a lot of ground, with highly transpositional variations leading to the Pirc, Pterodactyl, Sicilian, and King's Indian Defenses. Squeezed into a couple of codes, it receives undue prominence here. The Queen Pawn Game is covered in several codes, but a variety of approaches fall under the rubric D02. Transpositions to other openings, such as the Catalan, can also be launched here. The category of unorthodox openings is even broader, with most of White's legal first moves included there. This has always been one of the major shortcomings of the ECO system.

The King's Indian Attack and Closed Variation of the Sicilian are primarily used by amateur players seeking to avoid the complexities of main line openings. In the case of the Sicilian, the code B23 includes the Grand Prix Attack, 1.e4 c5; 2.Nc3 and 3.f4, which enjoyed a brief moment in the limelight during the 1980s, but is almost never seen in top competition now.

There are other systems of classification by codes, but they tend to suffer from the same shortcomings when it comes to using them for statistical comparisons. A rival system from *New in Chess* has a more hierarchical and flexible structure, but transpositions are still a problem. Throughout this book, the conventions of the Caxton Named Opening Database are used. You can download this file from Chess City Magazine (www.chesscity.com).

THE TRADITIONAL APPROACH

If we abandon the ECO system in favor of more traditional opening designation, a quite different picture emerges. Here are the top ten openings, together with the number of games in the 1997 database. You should find these diagrams more familiar.

Sicilian Defense
1.e4 c5 (9834)

King's Indian Defense
1.d4 Nf6; 2.c4 g6; 3.Nc3 Bg7 (5687)

Queen's Gambit Declined
1.d4 d5; 2.c4 e6 (4871)

Spanish Game
1.e4 e5; 2.Nf3 Nc6; 3.Bb5 (4333)

King Pawn Game
1.e4 e5 (3953)

Gruenfeld Defense
1.d4 Nf6; 2.c4 g6; 3.Nc3 d53 (923)

English Opening
1.c4 (3275)

Queen Pawn Game
1.d4 d5 (3099)

Italian Game
1.e4 e5; 2.Nf3 Nc6; 3.Bc4 (2478)

Nimzo-Indian Defense
1.d4 Nf6; 2.c4 e6; 3.Nc3 Bb4 (1837)

This list is much more rational. Sometimes the old ways are better. The Sicilian Defenses, all starting 1.e4 c5, dominate the scene, seen in about one out of every six games played. That shows how wonderfully diverse and entertaining our game is. The

King's Indian here includes some lines from the Modern Benoni, though not the Benko Gambit.

Is it any surprise that the Sicilian and King's Indian, the foundation of the repertoires of both Gary Kasparov and Bobby Fischer, hold center stage? The traditional Queen's Gambit Declined and Spanish Games are close behind. The Queen Pawn game includes the Trompowsky Attack and the Torre Attack, among other popular amateur openings. The Nimzo-Indian includes much of the popular Panov Attack which is shared with the Caro Kann Defense. Two move orders reach the same position: 1.e4 c6; 2.d4 d5; 3.exd5 cxd5; 4.c4 Nf6; 5.Nc3 e6; 6.Nf3 Bb4 or 1.d4 Nf6; 2.c4 e6; 3.Nc3 Bb4; 4.e3 c5; 5.Nf3 cxd4; 6.exd4 d5. The Caro-Kann (1.e4 c6) was in any case a close runner-up.

The traditional approach runs into problems with transpositions. An ideal system would indicate all paths leading up to the key position, as well as all branches emerging from it. Such a system has not yet been proposed in anything but concept.

GAMBIT CHESS OPENINGS

A gambit is the offer of some material, usually a pawn, in the opening phase of the game, in return for which some concrete advantage is gained. Gambits have always been popular. The Queen's Gambit is one of the most common strategies in the Queen Pawn Openings. In modern times, gambits are more frequently seen there than in the King Pawn openings, but a century ago the situation was reversed.

Tarrasch intended the comment below to be humorous, though he himself was not known for gambit play. Yet there is a grain of truth here. The gambit openings provide a path to quick victory against hapless opponents, yet against a strong player, the material investment may never pay off.

Q: What is the object of playing a gambit opening?

A: To acquire a reputation of being a dashing player at the cost of losing the game.

–Tarrasch

Gambits are usually characterized as sound or unsound. In a sound gambit, the person offering the material ("gambiteer") receives adequate positional compensation, usually involving a lead in development, vulnerability of the enemy king, or a powerful initiative. Here are some examples of gambits, presented in descending order of respectability. We start with gambits which are part of

the standard opening repertoire and continue on to those which are clearly unorthodox openings. Then we will compare the values of each, taking into account the three
forms of compensation we just discussed.

Queen's Gambit

1.d4 d5; 2.c4.

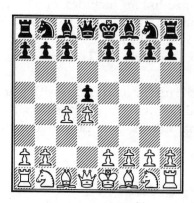

If Black captures at c4, White will eventually control the center, and will also re-
gain the pawn, which cannot be defended, for example:
2...dxc4; 3.Nf3 b5?

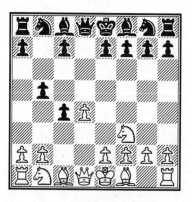

White can undermine Black's pawn chain with **4.a4.** Now Black must defend with
4...c6 since defending with the a-pawn allows White to capture on b5 and the pawn at
a6 would be pinned to the rook at a8. Now White can obtain an advantage with **5.axb5**
cxb5; 6.b3, but also good is **5.e3**, for example **5...c6 Bd7; 6.Ne5 e6; 7.axb5 cxb5;
8.Qf3.**

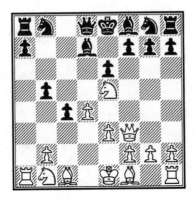

This led to immediate resignation in Blackburne-Fleissig, Vienna, 1873. Black gets mated at f7 or loses the rook at a8.

King's Gambit

The King's Gambit is not quite as strong as the Queen's Gambit, because Black can capture the pawn and hold onto it, though there is a positional price to pay. In fact, it is not so common to see this approach in top level games, as Black usually prefers to return the pawn for an equal position. Still, let's see what happens if Black does keep the profits.

2...exf4; 3.Nf3 g5. The pawn at f4 is defended. Sometimes White ignores this and sets up an attack with 4.Bc4, but a more direct confrontation begins with the immediate **4.h4.** This is the standard recommendation for White.

This was a popular line back in the 17th century.

4...g4. Black makes another pawn move, leaving his pieces undeveloped, but he attacks the Nf3 which must move.

5.Ne5. This is the Kieseritzky Gambit, the main continuation for White. Black has tried no less than eight methods of defense, but in this book only two will be discussed.

5...d6.

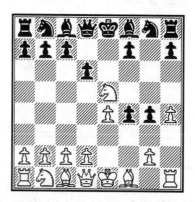

The Kolisch Defense is a fairly simple concept. Black takes the initiative to buy time for development.

6.Nxg4 Be7; 7.d4. Some modern books prefer 7.d3 Bxh4+; 8.Nf2 Qg5; 9.Qd2 but 9...Bg3; 10.Nc3 Nf6; 11.Ne2 Qe5! is an improvement on 11...Bxf2+; 12.Kxf2 Ng4+; 13.Kg1 Ne3; 14.Nxf4 Nxf1; 15.Kxf1. Now after 12.Nxg3 fxg3 and Black is better, Winants-Almasi, Wijk aan Zee 1995. **7...Bxh4+; 8.Nf2.**

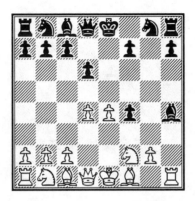

8...Qg5! It is important to avoid being too greedy. Black must not be tempted by 8...Bxf2+; 9.Kxf2 Nf6 since after 10.Nc3 Qe7; 11.Bxf4 Nxe4+; 12.Nxe4 Qxe4; 13.Bb5+ Kf8; 14.Bh6+ White wins: 14...Kg8; 15.Rh5 Bf5; 16.Qd2 Bg6; 17.Re1 Qg4; 18.Re8# Morphy-Lyttelton, Birmingham 1858.

9.Nc3 Nf6; 10.Qf3.

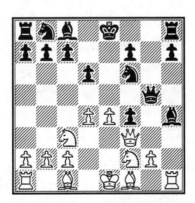

Black has an extra pawn, but the pawns on the f-file are weak. The critical factor is the pin on the knight at f2, which keeps the initiative in Black's hands.

10...Ng4!; 11.Nd1Nc6; 12.c3 Nxf2; 13.Nxf2 Bg3.

14.Kd1 Be6; 15.Nh3. 15 d5? Ne5! is good for Black.
15...Qg7; 16.Be2!

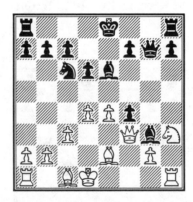

This position has been the subject of much discussion, from the great Paul Keres to modern King's Gambit scholars. For our purposes, the important point is that Black has held on to the pawn long enough to secure significant positional advantages. The king will find shelter on the queenside. White's seemingly strong center is in fact vulnerable at e4.

The latest theory runs **16...0–0–0; 17 Nxf4; Bxf4; 18 Bxf4 d5; 19 e5; Bf5; 20.Kc1** as given in the 1995 book by Maser and Raingruber, but Black can play 20...Rhg8 with a firm grip on g4. 21.Bh6 can be countered with 21...Qg6, followed by ...Bg4. The king does not seem well-placed at c1, and it will be hard to activate the rook at a1.

Although White does not emerge from the opening with a disadvantage, the King's Gambit is unlikely to secure a meaningful advantage and is therefore not seen frequently in professional games.

Schara Gambit

The Schara Gambit is a gambit for Black. It is an offshoot of the Tarrasch Defense, starting **1.d4 d5; 2.c4 e6; 3.Nc3 c5,** where **4.cxd5** is met by **4...cxd4!?**

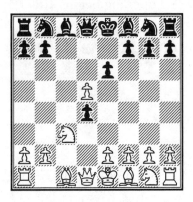

Gambits for Black are riskier, because in addition to the material deficit, there is usually a deficit in development, a result of White's privilege of moving first. When Black offers a pawn, it is often a long term investment. This is best illustrated in the main line.

5.Qa4+ Bd7; 6.Qxd4 exd5; 7.Qxd5 Nc6; 8.Qd1 Nf6; 9.e3 Bc5; 10.Nf3 Qe7.

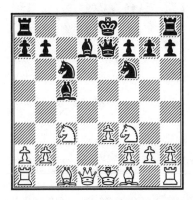

Black remains a pawn down, but is ready to castle in either direction. White needs two moves to complete castling, and it is hard to bring the bishop at c1 into the game. Current theory holds that Black has enough compensation for the pawn, but there is certainly risk for Black, especially if queenside castling is intended. As far as aggresive Black gambits are concerned, this is about as good as it gets. The most repeated gambit for Black is the Benko Gambit (1.d4 Nf6; 2.c4 c5; 3.d5 b5!?), but that is quite atypical, aiming for long-term positional pressure on the queenside rather than an attack on the enemy king.

Blackmar-Diemer Gambit

The Blackmar-Diemer Gambit is a popular opening among amateur players, but has no following at all among professionals. White gives up a pawn for some open lines and attacking chances. The opening begins **1.d4 d5; 2.e4 dxe4.**

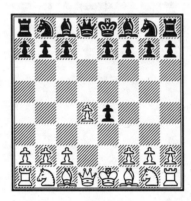

White now develops with tempo, playing **3.Nc3.** Black can now opt out of the gambit by transposing to the French Defense with 3...e6 or Caro-Kann with 3...c6, or can accept the offer with **3...Nf6; 4.f3 exf3; 5.Nxf3.**

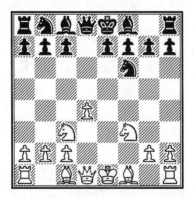

White has an open e-file and f-file to work with, but not much else. Black can erect a solid defense with 5...g6, followed by a fianchetto and kingside castling. 5...e6 is also good. Despite the fanatic devotion of some gambiteers, the Blackmar-Diemer Gambit has never been respectable. The missing pawn is rarely regained, and with good defense White should go down to defeat. It succeeds from time to time in amateur play because of weak defensive skills, not any inherent value.

Cochrane Gambit

When White sacrifices a pawn, the investment is modest. But when a whole piece is sacrificed, there is great risk. Nevertheless, there are some established piece gambits which are playable among amateurs. The Cochrane Gambit dates back to the 19th century, and has found new life in the 1990s. The opening starts off as a quiet Russian Game with **1.e4 e5; 2.Nf3 Nf6; 3.Nxe5 d6** but instead of retreating the knight, Black sacrifices it at f7 with **4.Nxf7.**

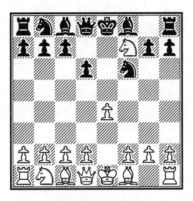

Black must capture, of course. **4...Kxf7.** White now takes control of the center and develops quickly, hoping to build a strong attack.

5.d4 g6; 6.Bd3 Bg7; 7.0-0 Re8; 8.e5 dxe5; 9.dxe5 Nd5; 10.f4 Kg8; 11.Qe1 Nc6; 12.Nc3.

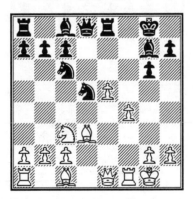

Black now systematically exchanges pieces, easing the defense.

12...Nxc3; 13.bxc3 Bf5; 14.Qe2 Qd7; 15.Rb1 Bxd3; 16.cxd3 Nxe5!; 17.fxe5 Rxe5.

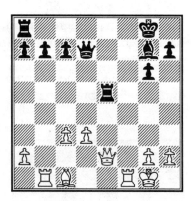

Black has returned the material for a clearly superior endgame, which he went on to win in Luukkonen vs. Lauk, Finland Team Championship Moscow, 1997. Of course not all games work out this well for Black, and the current evaluation of the Cochrane Gambit is that it is dubious, but still unclear.

Latvian Gambit

Moving down the scale of acceptability, we have a gambit for Black which is considered by most authorities to be unsound. The Latvian Gambit is, however, very popular among amateurs, who hope to catch opponents by surprise. The Latvian is hard to refute at the board. The opening begins **1.e4 e5; 2.Nf3 f5.**

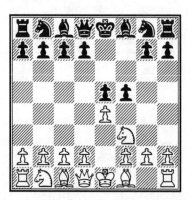

This is a sort of King's Gambit reversed. Black is down a tempo, but the presence of the knight at f3 is not always a good idea early in a King's Gambit. If White now captures at f5, Black can advance the e-pawn and force the knight to move. For this reason a capture at e5 is preferred.

3.Nxe5 Qf6. The early deployment of the queen is typical of the Latvian. **4.d4 d6.**

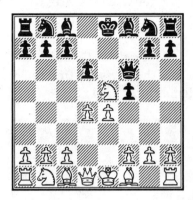

Here White almost always plays 5.Nc4. The complications usually work out in White's favor, but this is not the place to discuss them. Unsound openings often have quiet alternatives that guarantee White at least an equal game. When confronted by an unfamiliar opening, such a cautious path is often best. In the position of the diagram White has another move, **5.Nd3** which is generally overlooked or dismissed with the recommendation **5...fxe4; 6.Nf4.**

Kosten's book, *The Latvian Gambit*, counters this with 6...Qf7 followed by ...d5 and ...Bd6. After 7.Nc3, however, White controls d5. For this reason a recent game saw a different approach for Black. **6...c6** and White grabbed control of d5.

7.d5 Qe5. The queen needed to be repositioned, but it is not clear that this is the best square. **8.Na3 Nf6; 9.Nc4 Qf5; 10.g3.** The idea is to place the bishop not at g2, though that is a fine square, but at h3, where it can wreak havoc on the c8-h3 diagonal. **10...g5.** Necessary, to blunt the force of Bh3.

11.Bh3 g4; 12.Ne3! Qd7; 13.Nh5! Qf7; 14.Nxf6+ Qxf6; 15.Bxg4 and a game between two players who have participated in the US Championship ended brutally. Ivanov vs. Karklins, Chicago 1995 lasted just another dozen moves.

15...Nd7; 16.f3 exf3; 17.Bh5+ Kd8; 18.0-0 Ne5; 19.Bxf3 Nxf3+; 20.Rxf3 Qg6;

21.dxc6 bxc6; 22.Qd4 Bg7; 23.Qh4+ Ke8; 24.Bd2 Rf8; 25.Rxf8+ Bxf8; 26.Re1 Kd7; 27.Nd5. Black resigned.

Englund Gambit

Descending even deeper into the abyss, we find the disreputable Englund Gambit, which offers a pawn immediately after **1.d4 e5.**

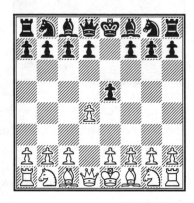

White captures the pawn, and Black spends a lot of time trying to get it back. **2.dxe5 Nc6; 3.Nf3 Qe7.**

Gambits And Their Compensating Factors

The following table shows the compensation provided in each of these gambits. Below we will look into other important factors in the evaluation of gambits. In each case, we'll take a typical position after ten moves. In an attempt to remain objective, I have selected the main lines from popular opening manuals as a sample.

| | | Vulnerable | |
	Development	Enemy King	Initiative
Queen's Gambit	Good	No	Yes
King's Gambit	Good	Yes	Yes
Schara Gambit	Good	Somewhat	Yes
Blackmar-Diemer Gambit	Good	Somewhat	Yes
Cochrane Gambit	Nothing special	Yes	Yes
Latvian Gambit	Nothing special	No	A little
Englund Gambit	Nothing special	No	A little

GAMBITS AND THEIR COMPENSATING FACTORS

Let's look at each of these gambits and see what compensation can be found.

Queen's Gambit

1.d4 d5; 2.c4 dxc4; 3.Nf3 Nf6; 4.e3 e6; 5.Bxc4 c5; 6.0-0 a6; 7.a4 Nc6; 8.Qe2 cxd4; 9.Rd1 Be7; 10.exd4 0-0.

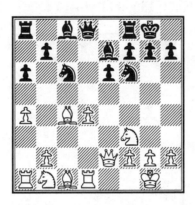

White has regained the pawn, which is just about inevitable in most lines of the Queen's Gambit Accepted. Therefore the question of compensation does not arise. White has a nice isolated d-pawn position, since the pawn is well supported. Black can be content as well, seeing the standard blockading maneuver ...Nd5 in the near future. Computers evaluation the position as dead even, and I'd be comfortable on either side of the board.

King's Gambit

1.e4 e5; 2.f4 exf4; 3.Nf3 g5; 4.h4 g4; 5.Ne5 Nf6; 6.Bc4 d5. Black returns the pawn to blunt the power of the enemy bishop.

7.exd5 Bd6. The White pawn at d5 is just in the way, and helps Black to defend! **8.d4 0-0; 9.Bxf4 Nh5; 10.g3 f6.**

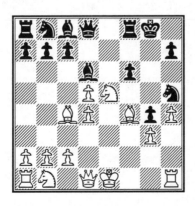

White offered the initial gambit, but it is Black who holds the extra pawn. Both sides need three moves to complete development. Since the knight at e5 is under attack, Black has the initiative. White's king is certainly vulnerable. Because the position is highly tactical, let's follow the action a bit further. Most of these moves are considered forced.

11.Nxg4 Qe8+; 12.Kd2 Nxf4; 13.gxf4 Bxf4+; 14.Kc3 b5; 15.Qf3 h5; 16.Qxf4 hxg4.

Black still has the initiative, attacking the bishop at c4. White has an extra pawn, and the threat of a discovered check is meaningful. Both kings are a bit airy. Surprisingly, after all this time, neither side has completed development. This is not an easy position to evaluate. It was reached in a correspondence game between Grasso and Pampa, published in 1995. Computers consider the position almost two pawns better for White. Nevertheless, human analysts consider the situation unclear.

To learn more about gambits, check out *Gambit Chess Openings*. That book includes over 900 gambits! If you are interested in good lines against popular gambits in the Open and Closed games, you might want to look at *Survive and Beat Annoying Chess Openings,* which I co-wrote with John Watson, or our older *Big Book of Busts* which includes a wide range of openings.

Schara Gambit

1.d4 d5; 2.c4 e6; 3.Nc3 c5; 4.cxd5 cxd4; 5.Qa4+ Bd7; 6.Qxd4 exd5; 7.Qxd5 Nc6; 8.Nf3 Nf6; 9.Qd1 Bc5; 10.e3 Qe7.

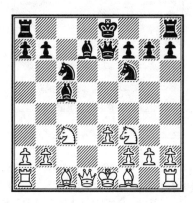

Black remains a pawn down, but is way ahead in development, and needs only to castle to complete the task. White is four moves away from castling. The initiative is within reach, using threats such as queenside castling with potential discovered attacks against the White queen, advancing the kingside pawns, or weakening the kingside defense by exchanging the knight at c6 for the one at f3 by bringing it to e5. The White king will not easily find shelter. All in all there is robust compensation, though computers are not impressed, awarding a half-pawn advantage to White.

Blackmar-Diemer Gambit

In this case the recommended line in the *Encyclopedia of Chess Openings* is rather pathetic and typical of its treatment of unorthodox openings. We'll follow the main line as given by Gary Lane, a leading authority on the opening.

1.d4 d5; 2.e4 dxe4; 3.Nc3 e5; 4.Be3 exd4; 5.Bxd4. 5.Qxd4 Qxd4; 6.Bxd4 Nc6; 7.Bb5 Bd7; 8.0-0-0 0-0-0 is all that is in ECO, and it is known to be better for Black.

5...Nc6; 6.Bb5 Bd7; 7.Nge2 Qh4. This position is evaluated by Lane as equal. The following moves seem natural. **8.Qd2 0-0-0; 9.0-0-0 a6; 10.g3 Qh5.**

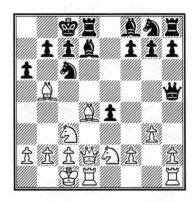

Black has an extra pawn and holds the initiative thanks to the attack on the bishop at b5. White is fully developed, and Black requires two more moves to get the minor pieces on the kingside into the game. Neither king is particularly vulnerable. We conclude that Black does not have enough compensation here. The calculating machines claim an advantage of more than a pawn.

Cochrane Gambit
1.e4 e5; 2.Nf3 Nf6; 3.Nxe5 d6; 4.Nxf7 Kxf7; 5.d4 c5; 6.dxc5 Bg4; 7.Be2 Be6; 8.0-0 Nc6; 9.f4 Kg8; 10.Nc3 dxc5.

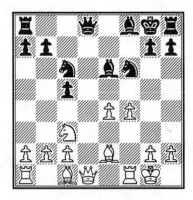

White's material deficit is not great, holding two pawns for the sacrificed knight. Black has a safe king, but will have difficulty developing the rook from h8. The open d-file can be used for exchanges, and d4 is firmly under control. The evaluation of the experts is that White has just about enough to justify the investment, but had better capitalize on it before too many pieces leave the board. From the machine's point of view, Black is a pawn ahead.

Latvian Gambit

1.e4 e5; 2.Nf3 f5; 3.Nxe5 Qf6; 4.Nc4 fxe4; 5.Nc3 Qg6; 6.d3 Bb4; 7.Bd2 Bxc3; 8.Bxc3 Nf6; 9.Bxf6 gxf6; 10.dxe4 Qxe4+.

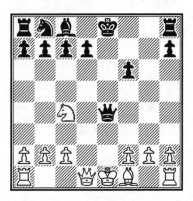

Material is equal, but both man and machine recognize White's advantage here. Nothing is to be gained by exchanging queens, but after the simple retreat of the knight, as in a 1971 correspondence game between Strautins and Castelli, White will complete development quickly and take advantage of Black's vulnerable king and shattered pawn structure.

Englund Gambit

We have already been introduced to the Englund Gambit, whose reputation remains terrible despite recent attempts at rehabilitation. Yet we are presented with a misleading picture by ECO here. That esteemed authority relegates the opening to a footnote, even though it has a near fanatical following among some amateur players. We look at their recommended line, and mention some counterpoints from Stefan Bücker, a specialist in the opening.

1.d4 e5; 2.dxe5 Nc6; 3.Nf3 Qe7; 4.Qd5 f6; 5.exf6 Nxf6; 6.Qb3 d5; 7.Nc3 d4; 8.Nb5 Bg4; 9.Nbxd4 Nxd4; 10.Nxd4 0-0-0; 11.c3.

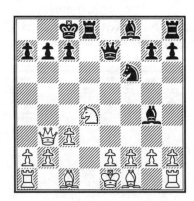

Looking at this position, there is every reason for skepticism regarding compensation for the two pawns. Sure, Black has a lead in development, but the awkward position of the bishop at f8 means that two more moves are required to claim full development. White needs four moves to get castled. This is not such a problem because the king is safe at e1. Neither side can lay claim to the initiative. Putting it all together, the computer evaluation of a pawn and a half advantage for White seems reasonable. This analysis completely ignores work in the 1980s by Bücker, who demonstrated the superiority of **7...Bd7!** His main line continues **8.Qxb7 Rb8; 9.Qxc7 Qc5; 10.Qf4 d4.**

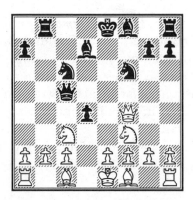

In Bücker's version, the lead in development is retained, but the material deficit is even greater, at three pawns. The last move maintains the initiative, as the knight must now flee c3. Neither king is especially vulnerable, however. Computers give White an advantage of almost two pawns, but Bücker relies on 11.Nd1 being countered by 11...Bd6 12.Qg5 Nb4, not considering the exchange of queens with 13.Qxc5 Bxc5; 14.Bf4! The spectacular 14...Nxc2+; 15.Kd2 Bb4+; 16.Kxc2 Bf5+ does not succeed, because of 17.e4 dxe3+; 18.Bd3 and Black's attack is repulsed.

GAMBIT SUMMARY

We have spent a great deal of time on the topic of evaluating gambits, because amateurs are often tempted by the enthusiasm of gambiteers and lack objective methods for evaluating them. In general, there are serious drawbacks to many gambits, making them unsuitable for use by professionals. At lesser heights, the openings may bring success and are often fun to play. You must, however, keep in mind the nature of compensation provided by each gambit. Conservative players will want to see a lot of compensation before investing a pawn, while risk takers will not mind if the official tally comes up short.

It is time to reverse the coin, and consider how a peace-loving chessplayer can avoid the tactical pitfalls of gambit play by declining gambits.

DECLINING A GAMBIT

The safest method of dealing with most gambits is to simply refuse the gift and continue with development. Not all gambits allow this approach. We'll take another look at our seven typical gambits and see how safely they can be declined.

The Queen's Gambit is usually declined with **1.d4 d5; 2.c4 e6.**

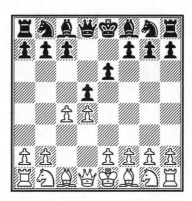

Black supports the pawn at d5 and does not allow White to construct the ideal pawn center, since 3.e4 is met by 3...dxe4. This is the Diemer-Duhm Gambit and it is not considered very good, as the pawn at c4 does little to help White, and deprives the bishop of access to c4 or b5.

The King's Gambit can be declined in many ways. One popular method is the Falkbeer Countergambit, **1.e4 e5; 2.f4 d5!?**

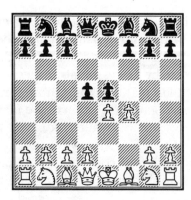

The idea is that after 3.exd5, Black can advance 3...e4 and cramp White's position. It is even possible to offer a real gambit with 3...c6. Transposing to the King's Gambit Accepted lines with 3...exf4 is also good.

The Schara Gambit can be declined by wimpy plans such as **1.d4 d5; 2.c4 e6; 3.Nc3 c5; 4.cxd4 cxd4; 5.Qxd4 Nc6; 6.Qd1 exd5; 7.Nf3.**

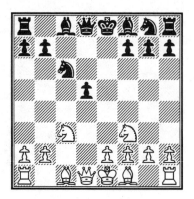

This transposes to a normal Tarrasch Defense after 7...Nf6, but 7...d4 is also possible. I'd much rather be Black in the latter case.

The Blackmar-Diemer Gambit is easiest to decline, but White does get to build the ideal pawn center. After **1.d4 d5; 2.e4,** Black can choose between the Caro-Kann Defense with 2...c6 or the French Defense with 2...e6. Of course, those are only viable options if you already play those openings, since they are major openings which require a great deal of study. An often recommended alternative is to take the pawn but to let White recapture it, striking in the center instead after **2...dxe4; 3.Nc3 e5!?**

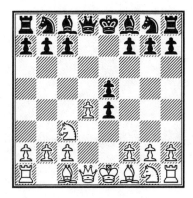

White can capture at e5, but only at the cost of entering an endgame which is not likely to appeal to the sort of gambiteers who play the Blackmar-Diemer.

The Cochrane Gambit simply can't be declined. The impudent knight at f7 cannot be ignored. Nor is there any easy way to return the material right away. By waiting until the right moment, as we saw above, Black can eliminate the central pawns at the cost of a knight, restoring material balance with a more peaceful game.

Declining the Latvian Gambit is inadvisable, but after accepting, one can choose a quiet line such as **1.e4 e5; 2.Nf3 f5; 3.exf5 e4; 5.Ng1 Nf6; 6.d3.**

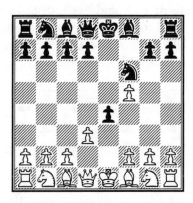

This is a sort of King's Gambit in reverse, with an overextended pawn at e4. I prefer White's position, though other theoreticians evaluate it as about equal.

There is really no point in declining the Englund Gambit. White can turn the tables and offer a gambit with 2.e4, leading to the Göring or Danish Gambits, or can choose a solid approach with 2.c3, a sort of reversed Caro-Kann, which can mutate into an Exchange Variation of the Queen's Gambit Declined after 2...exd4 3.cxd4 d5.

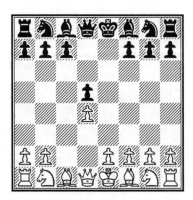

It is hard to believe that someone who plays the Englund Gambit would be content in the stodgy and dusty lines of the Queen's Gambit. This is an example of psychological warfare in the opening, a subject we will return to in the Psychology chapter.

UNSOUND GAMBITS

Many gambits are considered unsound. If the opponent plays the approved moves the gambiteer should go down in flames. That's fine in theory, but in practice there is still danger at the door. Even if a gambit is unsound, it can be venomous. Often a single inaccurate move in defense can lead to disaster. In the Englund Gambit, about which we have had nothing good to say so far, there is a famous trap.

1.d4 e5; 2.dxe5 Nc6; 3.Nf3 Qe7; 4.Bf4 Qb4+; 5.Bd2 Qxb2; 6.Bc3? White must develop the knight to c3 instead. 6...Bb4!; 7.Qd2 Bxc3; 8.Qxc3.

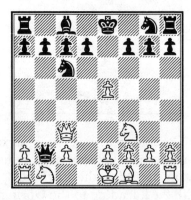

Things seem to be under control, but there is the small problem of 8...Qc1 checkmate! I played the Englund Gambit in school, and won with this trap many times. It is not a good opening however, and it didn't take a college education to encourage me to give it up. I gave up all of my unsound gambits, but found a new temptation—unorthodox openings.

UNORTHODOX CHESS OPENINGS

Unorthodox chess strategies involve apparent violations of opening principles such as those seen throughout this section of our book. Sometimes the term "Irregular Opening" is seen, but no one seems to agree on which openings are standard and which are irregular, and the judgments certainly change over time. Consider these examples:

In the book of the first German Chess Congresses (1879 and 1881), the moves 1.e3 and 1.Nf3 were classified as irregular.

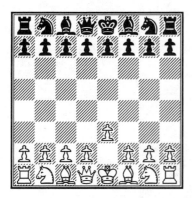 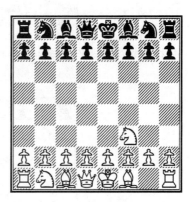

The former is usually just transpositional, leading to more familiar openings once White is forced to declare some sort of plan. The latter is now considered a standard opening, whether it later transposes to another opening or not. In the 1883 event we find 1.c3 appearing, and that certainly remains in the irregular category.

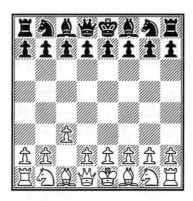

The other debut, 1.g3, is considered slightly inferior to plans with a preliminary 1.Nf3, because it allows Black to play 1...e5.

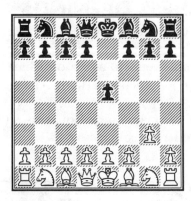

On the other hand, the Wade Defense 1.Nf3 d6; 2.g3 e5 can lead to the same stake in the center.

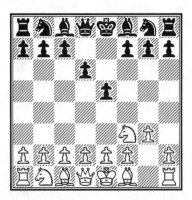

That's why 1.g3 is often considered a normal flank opening, joining 1.c4, 1.Nf3, and sometimes 1.d3.

By the turn of the century, more experiments had taken place. At the Kaiser jubilee tournament of Vienna, 1898, many were relegated to the cabinet of irregularities including 1.d4 c5, the Benoni, which was later refined by adding a preliminary ...Nf6.

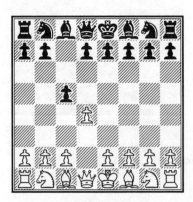

The Modern Benoni, 1.d4 Nf6; 2.c4 c5 is considered a standard chess opening now, though it was considered suspect for many decades.

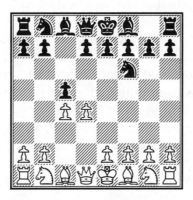

David Baird's favorite 1.d4 d6 was not appreciated at the time. It has become a standard transpositional device.

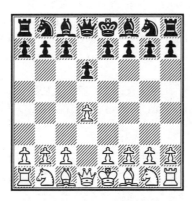

Assuming Black does not want to place the pawn at d5, this is one of the least committal options available.

The entire Indian complex, 1.d4 Nf6, was in fact considered irregular.

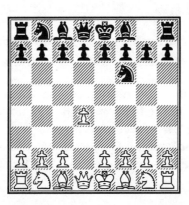

This is the starting position for many of today's most popular openings, including the King's Indian, Queen's Indian, Gruenfeld Defense and Nimzo-indian.

Bird's 1.f4 also remained in the odd bins, despite its frequent appearance in games by Bird and Caro (of Caro-Kann fame).

As the views on acceptable openings liberalized in the 20th century, any opening which was seen in the hands of competent players was a candidate for consideration. The term "irregular" was confined to openings which seemed too radical. The exponential growth of the chess community continued for some time, and any opening that seemed to have a logical basis was excluded.

Eventually two camps developed. The vast majority of players were content to apply one of the thousands of acceptable opening strategies. A few iconoclasts continued to indulge in bizarre and heretical experiments. Sometimes these resulted in innovations which found their way to the chessboards of Grandmasters. The World Champions, however, were unimpressed.

Then one day there was an opening shot heard around the world. It came from the town of Skara, where the 1980 European Team Championship was taking place. Tony Miles, the first Grandmaster from England, had the Black pieces against World Champion Anatoly Karpov. On the very first move, he boldly adopted the St. George Defense, developed by Michael Basman, a leading theoretician of unorthodox opening play. And to everyone's amazement, he won the game! Here it is.

KARPOV - MILES
European Team Championship, 1980

1.e4 a6!?

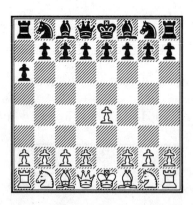

This must have been quite a psychological blow. Facing a World Champion, Miles chooses a move which had never been seen in a game between two Grandmasters. Karpov referred to it as the "Incorrect Opening."

2.d4 b5; 3.Nf3 Bb7; 4.Bd3 Nf6; 5.Qe2 e6; 6.a4 c5; 7.dxc5 Bxc5; 8.Nbd2. Karpov reacts with quiet development. 8.axb5 axb5; 9.Rxa8 Bxa8; 10.Bxb5 Nxe4 would have been welcomed by Black.

8...b4; 9.e5 Nd5; 10.Ne4 Be7. Black's pawn structure looks awkward, and one has to wonder about the long term safety of the Black king on the kingside.

11.0-0 Nc6; 12.Bd2 Qc7; 13.c4 bxc3; 14.Nxc3 Nxc3; 15.Bxc3 Nb4; 16.Bxb4 Bxb4; 17.Rac1 Qb6; 18.Be4 0-0.

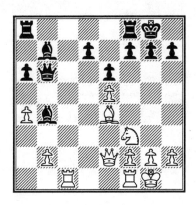

19.Ng5. An interesting position. Many commentators suggest a classic sacrifice at h7 instead, but it was dismissed by Karpov. He shows 19.Bxh7+ Kxh7; 20.Ng5+ Kg6; 21.Qg4 f5; 22.Qg3 Qd4 is given by Karpov, claiming that Black can defend. I can't agree. 23.Nxe6+! Qg4; 24.Nxf8+ Rxf8; 25.Qxg4+ fxg4; 26.Rc4 a5; 27.Rxg4+ and White has rook and three pawns for the bishop pair, definitely much better for the rooks. For example: 27...Kf7; 28.Rf4+ Ke7; 29.Rxf8 Kxf8; 30.Rd1 Bc6; 31.b3 and White's winning plan is to bring the king to a2 to defend the b-pawn, and then use the rook to support the advance of the pawns on the kingside.

19...h6; 20.Bh7+ Kh8; 21.Bb1 Be7; 22.Ne4 Rac8; 23.Qd3?! Karpov claimed that this was his only serious error in the game, and that 23. Rcd1 would have maintained an advantage.

23...Rxc1; 24.Rxc1 Qxb2; 25.Re1 Qxe5; 26.Qxd7. The endgame is hopeless, and Karpov eventually went down to defeat. **26...Bb4; 27.Re3 Qd5; 28.Qxd5 Bxd5; 29.Nc3 Rc8; 30.Ne2 g5; 31.h4 Kg7; 32.hxg5 hxg5; 33.Bd3 a5; 34.Rg3 Kf6; 35.Rg4 Bd6; 36.Kf1 Be5; 37.Ke1 Rh8; 38.f4 gxf4; 39.Nxf4 Bc6; 40.Ne2 Rh1+; 41.Kd2 Rh2; 42.g3 Bf3; 43.Rg8 Rg2; 44.Ke1 Bxe2; 45.Bxe2 Rxg3; 46.Ra8 Bc7.** White resigned.

The result was gleefully heralded by unorthodox "deviants" everywhere, but this is a rare case. Most of the time, unorthodox openings do not stand up to the test of time.

Of course some opinions do not change. The Grob Attack, **1.g4**, is described by Henry Bird (for whom the opening 1.f4 is named):

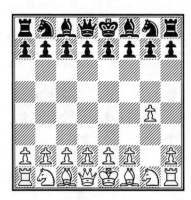

This opening we have adopted for a change on one or two occasions, with our friend Mr. Boden. It gives a slightly inferior game to the first player, and has, we fear, little beyond novelty to recommend it.

Contemporary thinking is that the opening is simply bad, though there are a number of amateur players and a few professionals that use it. These unusual but sometimes fascinating openings are catalogued in *Unorthodox Chess Openings.* In an earlier book, *Unorthodox Openings,* they were divided into four categories: The Good, The Bad, The Ugly, and The Twilight Zone.

Just because an opening is unorthodox does not mean that it is bad. If the opening is a *good* one, it can be used regularly. An *ugly* opening might work against an inferior opponent. Using *bad* openings should cause you grief at the chessboard. The inhabitants of the Twilight Zone are considered suspect, but there is no conclusive evidence that they are unplayable.

Evaluating unorthodox openings is as difficult for the amateur as evaluating gambits. The enthusiasm of the "deviants" can sometimes overwhelm good judgment. On the other hand, once in a while they are right, and it just takes time for the rest of the world, and the old fuddy-duddy theoreticians, to catch up.

We will take a set of four openings involving an early double advance of the g-pawn, that horror of horrors we met in the chapter on development.

GOOD

We don't have to look far to find an example of a good opening with an early g4. One of the most popular weapons against the Caro-Kann Defense is the Van der Wiel Attack in the Advance Variation.

1.e4 c6; 2.d4 d5; 3.e5 Bf5; 4.Nc3 e6; 5.g4.

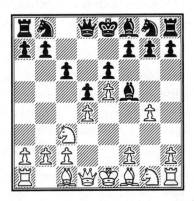

The advance of the g-pawn is justified on several grounds. It's primary advantage is that it threatens to bring its colleagues up the h-file or f-file to trap the enemy bishop. The closed pawn structure helps to shelter the White king. Black will gain some counterplay in the center with ...c5 and ...Nc6, and the game remains sharp and unbalanced.

BAD

Much of the time the early advance of the g-pawn is a bad idea. It presents White with a clear target, and the neighboring squares become weak. The Macho Grob variation of the Borg Defense, **1.e4 g5; 2.d4 h6**, is a good example.

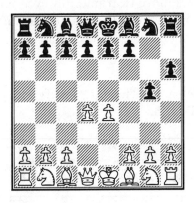

A game between Grandmaster Granda Zuniga and Candidate Master Chaplin, at the 1997 National Open saw White relentlessly hammer away at the weaknesses on the kingside.

3.Nc3 d6; 4.Bc4 Nf6; 5.Nf3 c6; 6.e5 Nd5; 7.0-0 Nxc3; 8.bxc3 d5; 9.Bd3 Bg4; 10.h3 Bxf3; 11.Qxf3 e6; 12.Rb1 b5; 13.Qh5 a6; 14.f4! The Grandmaster cracks open the case. **14...gxf4; 15.Rxf4 Ra7; 16.Rf6.** Now the h-pawn falls, and the game quickly falls apart.

16...Qc8 ;17.Bxh6 Bxh6; 18.Rxh6 Rxh6; 19.Qxh6 Nd7; 20.Rf1 Nf8; 21.Qh8 Re7; 22.Qg8 Qc7; 23.h4 c5; 24.h5 cxd4; 25.h6 Qxe5; 26.h7 Qe3+; 27.Rf2 Qc1+; 28.Bf1. Black resigned.

UGLY

The vast majority of openings with an early g4 are just plain ugly. They do not lead to a losing position, but leave the player with long-lasting problems caused by the weaknesses of the kingside. Joel Benjamin and I classified the Polish Spike, **1.b4 Nf6; 2.Bb2 g6; 3.g4** as ugly.

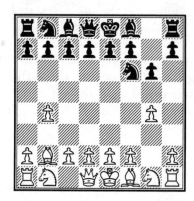

White's primitive threat of g5 is countered by **3...Bg7**, when 4.g5 Nh5 is not at all bad for Black. If White shows more restraint, however, and plays **4.h3**, then the position holds a little more promise. Nevertheless, the advanced pawns are exposed and weak. Black also has an advantage in development.

TWILIGHT ZONE

A number of early g-pawn are difficult to classify with confidence. Several of these are in the Dutch Defense, 1.d4 f5.

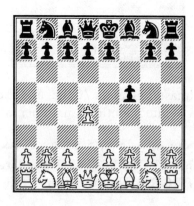

The f-pawn is an inviting target, and the advance of the g-pawn to the fourth rank has been played immediately, or after a preparatory move such as 2.h3.

In the end, it doesn't really matter what theoreticians say about unorthodox openings. Few amateur players are prepared to meet them, so you should rely on the general principles of development and piece placement whenever they spring up. There is no need to keep these radical ideas out of your repertoire, but it is dangerous to rely on them as your primary weapons. A well prepared opponent can embarrass you if your opening fails to meet standards of playability.

Tartakower's words still ring true. If the worst possible result of a correctly played opening is an inferior, but not necessarily losing position, then you can probably get away with using it. You will be giving your opponent an advantage, if they can find it. Even then, the advantage must be exploited, and this is not easy to do. It is easy to overplay a position, and then lose as a result.

> *If an Opening is Dubious, it is Playable.*
>
> — Tartakower

There is a special pain that comes with losing to a dubious opening. You sometimes feel as though victory should be yours by right when the opponent deviates from accepted forms of opening play. This is faulty logic. A dubious opening provides the opponent with an opportunity to gain easy equality as Black, or a significant advantage as White. Taking advantage of these opportunities may mean departing from familiar territory, or accepting a position with more tactics than are comfortable.

Sometimes it is better to take a more modest approach. During the game, concentrate on the position, and forget about the fact that there may be a known solution to your problem buried in some book. You probably don't even know the name of the strange formation staring at you from the board.

NAMES OF CHESS OPENINGS

To those who like tidy, well organized systems, the naming of chess openings is a distasteful subject. Not only is there no coherent system involved, ugly political issues have led to many openings having multiple names.

Following are some of the ways in which standard openings are named, with examples.

Nationalities: Spanish Game, Russian Game, Scandinavian Defense, Italian Game
Cities: Vienna Game, London System
Famous Players: Ruy Lopez, Petrov Defense, Polugayevsky Variation, Nimzowitsch Variation
Player Duets: Richter-Rauzer Attack, Panov-Botvinnik Attack
Animals: Hedgehog Formation, Orangutan, Pterodactyl, Rat, Lizard
Characteristics of the Position: Two Knights Variation, Giuoco Piano (Quiet Game), Center Counter Game, Stonewall Attack.
Unusual: Fried Liver Attack, Noah's Ark Trap, Nescafe Frappe Attack

---

Now comes the fun part. There are actually fewer different openings in that list than you might think! The Spanish Game is also known as the Ruy Lopez, as are Petrov (or Petroff) Defense and Russian Game. The Center Counter Game and the Scandinavian Defense are one and the same. The English Attack and English Defense are not. The Fried Liver Attack, Giuoco Piano and one of the many Two Knights variations are all part of the Italian Game. The Hedgehog Formation belongs to the Sicilian Defense, and the quite unrelated English Opening as well.

To add to the confusion, there is a lot of variation in the second term. Hedgehog Variation and Hedgehog Formation are usually the same thing. Spanish Opening and Spanish Game are identical. Nimzowitsch Variation and Nimzowitsch Defense are quite different. Aron Nimzowitsch was a productive fellow and most major openings have a Nimzowitsch Variation somewhere.

There are code systems with notations such as E17 (ECO) or SI47.25 (NIC), but these are not generally used in conversation and commentary.

TRAPS

Traps have brought ruin to many a chessplayer. There is hardly anyone who has not fallen victim to one. An opening trap is an opening variation which contains a tactical trick. If you fall into the trap, you lose enough material to cost you the game. There are thousands of opening traps, many of which involve tempting, but poisoned, offerings. Here is a recent crop, from 1997.

Many traps take advantage of a queen check at h5 leading to the capture of an enemy piece on the fifth rank. This theme is not easy to see. In the example following, the diagram position holds great danger. To sense it, however, you need to see the queen at d1 capturing the bishop at c5, and that is not at all obvious. It requires cooperation by Black to make it happen. The opening is the Nimzo-Larsen Attack.

MARTINKOVA - SVOBODA
Klatovy, 1997
1.b3 e5; 2.Bb2 Nc6; 3.e3 Bc5; 4.Bxe5.

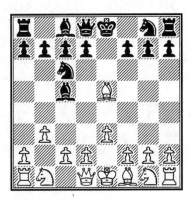

4...f6?? 4...Nxe5; 5.d4 Bd6; 6.dxe5 Bxe5 is no worse for Black.
5.Bxc7 Qxc7; 6.Qh5+. Black resigned.

REWITZ - NICOLAISEN
Aarhus, 1997

In this game a master teaches a candidate master that there are hidden reefs even in the earliest stages of the game. This is a very unusual case where the loser is the one who has chosen an unorthodox opening strategy but is not prepared for a simple and logical plan by White. The opening is Franco-Sicilian Defense.

1.e4 e6; 2.d4 c5; 3.d5 Nf6; 4.Nc3 exd5; 5.e5 d4?? Black must play 5...d5 or 5...Qe7 followed by d4.

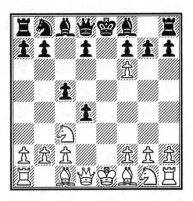

6.exf6. Resignation is not necessarily forced, but Black was devastated that he missed 6...dxc3? 7.Qe2+.

At the end of our discussion of gambits we mentioned gambits against the Dutch Defense, using an early advance of the g-pawn. Here a master delivers a powerful lesson to his amateur opponent.

JOHANSSON - HERNBACK
Swedish Open Championship, 1997

The openings are Dutch Defense and Mongredien Defense. **1.d4 f5; 2.h3 Nf6; 3.g4 fxg4; 4.hxg4 Nxg4; 5.Qd3 Nf6??** Black must play 5...g6 instead, when 6.Rxh7 fails to Rxh7 7.Qxgb+ Rf7; 8.Qxg4, White has only a pawn for the exchange.

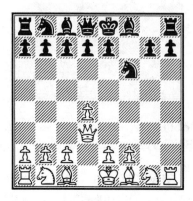

6.Rxh7. There is no defense to mate at g6 that saves the rook. Black resigned.

ZWEEDIJK - SAALHEIM
Vlissingen, 1997

Sometimes even a mate in one escapes our notice. There is a feeling that a mere minor piece can't cause a fatal accident to happen to the enemy king, but that is exactly what happens in this game. The opening is the St. George defense.

1.e4 b6; 2.d4 g6; 3.Bc4 Bb7; 4.Nc3 f5; 5.exf5 Bxg2; 6.fxg6

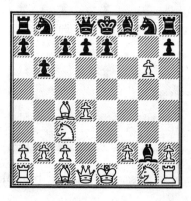

There is no rush to take the rook, which isn't going anywhere. After 6...e6, there is no catastrophe facing Black. In this game, Black calmly took the rook with **6...Bxh1** only to run into **7.Bf7 checkmate!**

The move order is important even in the most flexible formation. In this game Black carelessly plays an "obvious" move and gets hammered by a powerful sacrifice.

GOH WEI MING - SIHOMBING
World Cities Championship, 1997
1.e4 d6; 2.d4 Nd7; 3.Nf3 a6; 4.Bc4 b5??

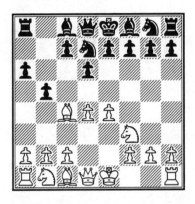

The bishop is attacked, but doesn't have to retreat! Black should have defended the critical f7-square with 4...e6.

5.Bxf7+ Kxf7; 6.Ng5+ Kg6. The king cannot retreat to e8 because then the queen would be suffocated after 7.Nd6. **7.Ne6 Qe8.** The queen escapes. The king does not. **8.Qg4+ Kf7; 9.Qf5+ Ngf6; 10.Ng5+.** Black resigned, faced with mate in two.

The best way to avoid traps is to develop your pieces to useful squares where they will not be in any immediate danger. Positioning your pieces properly is one of the fundamental skills in the opening. In the following chapters, we will take this task apart piece by piece.

Sometimes you will find yourself the victim of a trap. In this case you are often faced with a difficult task. Escape is sometimes possible, as you will see in my game against Baudo Mercere in the Saving Lost Positions section.

OPENING ROLE OF EACH PIECE

OPENING ROLE OF THE PAWNS

Beginners, cognizant of the fact that a pawn can promote to a more valuable piece by reaching the eighth rank, often hurl their pawns forward early in the game. Intermediate players wait until the enemy has castled, and then launch a pawnstorm on the flank that contains the enemy king. Masters, however, usually hesitate to advance pawns recklessly. Pawns cannot move backwards, unlike their fellow pieces. Once advanced, they cannot retreat. Therefore each pawn move must be considered carefully.

White tries to place pawns at e4 and d4, where they occupy and control important central territory. Black wants to either prevent White from doing this, or prepare to counterattack against the center with either pawns or pieces.

IDEAL PAWN CENTER

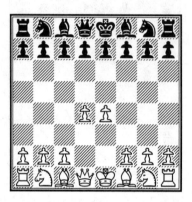

White's traditional goal in the opening has always been establishing control of the center of the board by planting pawns at both e4 and d4. That's why the central formation is known as the "ideal pawn center," though it is only strong if well supported by other pieces. From these squares, White also fights for control of c5, d5, e5, and f5. If White can achieve, and (importantly!) maintain this ideal pawn center Black will have great difficulty deploying forces effectively.

Therefore Black usually takes measures either to prevent White from building the ideal pawn center or to try to smash it once it is there. The former approach is known as the classical style. The latter is the hypermodern style. The modern style is a combination of both strategies.

Classical openings include the Open Games with 1.e4 e5 and Closed Games with 1.d4 d5.

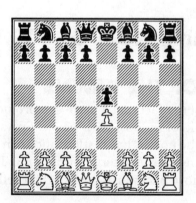

OPEN GAME

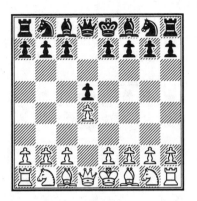

CLOSED GAME

In each case White is prevented from establishing the ideal pawn center because the companion pawn would be subject to capture.

The Hypermodern Revolution of the 1920s brought an awareness that it is sometimes acceptable to allow White to occupy the center as long as that center can later be attacked. The best known examples of hypermodern openings are the King's Indian Defense and Modern Defense, where Black uses a fianchetto to undermine the center.

King's Indian Defense
1.d4 Nf6; 2.c4 g6; 3.Nc3 Bg7; 4.e4

Modern Defense
1.e4 g6; 2.d4 Bg7

White can also adopt a hypermodern strategy, allowing Black to enjoy the ideal pawn center. This is rare, however, as usually White plays either Nf3 or c4 to restrain Black's options during the first two moves.

The ideal pawn center is a valuable asset if it is strong. It controls important territory which can be used to transfer your pieces around the board. If you allow your opponent to build one, you must take measures to weaken it. Let's look at some ways of dealing with the problem as Black.

CLASSICAL PREVENTIONS

Black can thwart both of White's plans by playing symmetrically. This was the preferred plan until the end of the 19th century. 1.e4 e5 leads to the Open Games. These include the Spanish and Italian games, as well as a variety of gambits.

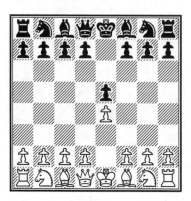

1.d4 d5 brings about a Closed Game. The Queen's Gambit and the Slav Defense are the best known closed games.

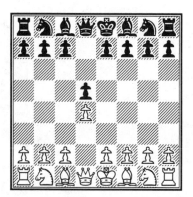

In each case, the counterplay against White's center is usually reinforced by the presence of a knight at f6 to put more pressure on the e4-square. White can rarely maintain the center for long, even if it can be achieved briefly.

It may be said that the classical prescription is the best way to fight for the center, but there is a drawback to the approach. Positions can often become sterile, with Black suffering from an excess of symmetry and feeling the disadvantage of moving second. This has led more impatient players away from the old strategy.

ROMANTIC INTERVENTIONS

In the Romantic era, Black would allow White to build the ideal pawn center, but would quickly strike back. For example, in the Caro-Kann Defense, White achieves the goal after **1.e4 c6; 2.d4**, but Black plays **2...d5** and White cannot maintain control of e4.

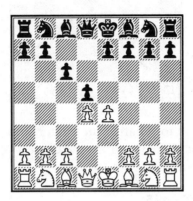

Usually White plays **3.Nc3** and then Black captures at e4. So White's ideal pawn center cannot be sustained.

In the Queen Pawn Game, **1.d4**, Black still played **1...d5** and White continued with **2.c4.**

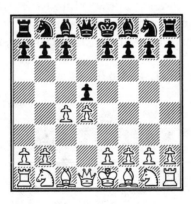

Now instead of timid defense with 2...c6 or 2...e6, some Romantic players experimented with 2...e5, the Albin Countergambit, or accepted the gambit with 2...dxc4, inviting White to play 3.e4.

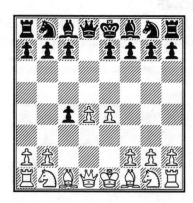

Black found a lot of ways to go after the center immediately, with 3...e5!?, 3...c5 and even 3...Nc6. The major shift away from the Closed Games did not come until the hypermodern revolution took place.

HYPERMODERN INVENTIONS

The Hypermodern School was more like a 1920's version of a 1960s American college campus, with revolution breaking out all over the place. Wild and unorthodox parties were not unheard of, and young turks such as Aron Nimzowitsch and Richard Reti were not only questioning authority, they were ridiculing it.

Not only did the Hypermoderns allow White to set up an ideal pawn center with pawns at e4 and d4, they were willing to allow a pawn at c4, too. The King's Indian Defense, not even a footnote in turn of the century texts, is perhaps the best example of the new approach.

1.d4 Nf6; 2.c4 g6; 3.Nc3 Bg7; 4.e4 0-0.

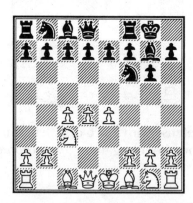

White's pawn dominate the center, and at first it seemed that the path to the advantage lay in 4.e5, chasing the knight, or 4.f4, expanding the pawn center even more. When those proved unsuccessful, White turned to more conservative play with simple development. In each case, however, the pawn center can become the target of a counterattack.

A classic example of a counterattack is seen in Letelier vs. Fischer, from the 1960 Olympiad at Leipzig.

LETELIER - FISCHER
1.d4 Nf6; 2.c4 g6; 3.Nc3 Bg7; 4.e4 0-0; 5.e5 Ne8; 6.f4 d6; 7.Be3.

White seems to have everything under control. Fischer blows up the center with a blow from the flank. **7...c5!** This rips apart the pawn chain. Black sacrifices a pawn for an active position.

Leipzig, 1960
8.dxc5 Nc6; 9.cxd6 exd6; 10.Ne4 Bf5; 11.Ng3 Be6; 12.Nf3 Qc7.

Black could also have achieved a good position by capturing at e5, but the center must eventually fall.

13.Qb1 dxe5; 14.f5 e4; 15.fxe6 exf3; 16.gxf3 f5; 17.f4 Nf6; 18.Be2 Rfe8; 19.Kf2 Rxe6.

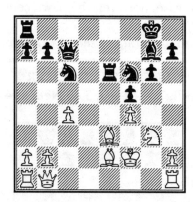

How the picture has changed! There is nothing left of the center but the fraying edges at c4 and f4. Fischer used the open e-file to good effect.

20.Re1 Rae8; 21.Bf3 Rxe3; 22.Rxe3 Rxe3; 23.Kxe3 Qxf4+. White resigned. There is no way to save the game.

As a practical matter, your decision on how to handle your pawns is a matter of taste. Whether or not you choose to station pawns in the middle of the board, it must always be the center of your attention. Overextended pawns are a definite liability in the endgame unless they have adequate support, as we will see later in the section on transition to the endgame.

Pawns dominate the board numerically, but it is the pieces which give chess its fascinating possibilities. We now turn to an examination of the roles of each piece, in ascending order.

OPENING ROLE OF THE KNIGHTS

As a general rule, White knights belong at c3 and f3, Black knights at c6 and f6. The knight more frequently reaches the kingside post than the queenside post, because c3 (c6) is often used by a pawn, supporting the ideal pawn center. We usually see this formation in a major variation of respectable openings, and rarely in disreputable openings. There are plenty of examples, and few counterexamples. In the Tarrasch Defense, all four knights reach the destination. In the Trompowsky Attack, we see a counterexample.

Tarrasch Defense
1.d4 d5; 2.c4 e6; 3.Nc3 c5; 4.cxd5 exd5; 5.Nf3 Nc6; 6.g3 Nf6; 7.Bg2 Be7; 8.0-0 0-0.

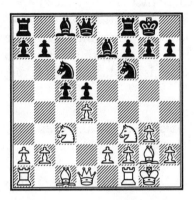

In the Classical Tarrasch, all four knights take up their normal positions, where they can influence play in the center.

Trompowsky Attack
1.d4 Nf6; 2.Bg5 Ne4. Black's knight often leaps to e4 in response to the attack by the bishop. One popular line runs **3.Bf4 c5; 4.f3 Qa5+; 5.c3.**

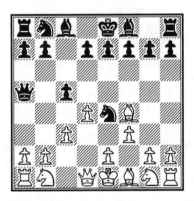

White will not be able to use either c3 or f3 for a knight. Black's knights may eventually find their way to c6 and f6.

OPENING ROLE OF THE BISHOPS

There are several schools of thought concerning best placement of the bishops, and much depends on the central pawn formation. In each case, bishops are stationed on at least one open diagonal, and often simultaneously defend key squares while attacking at long range.

There are four well established approaches. Classical players liked to send the bishops to the fifth rank on the knight's file. Romantic players kept them a little closer to home, but in a position where they could strike at enemy weaknesses. Some players liked to mix the two, in combination with an exchange of e-pawns. The Hypermodern revolution brought the fianchetto formation into vogue. Adventurous spirits sometimes adopt an edge approach, allowing the bishops to work from the side of the board. Each of these approaches is valid, and each is discussed below.

CLASSICAL: B5/G5

Petrosian loved to place a bishop at g5, and even wrote a lecture about why it held such a fascination for him. The strategy is seen in extreme form in a variation of the Four Knights Game.

1.e4 e5; 2.Nf3 Nc6; 3.Nc3 Nf6; 4.d4 Bb4; 5.Bg5 d6; 6.Bb5 0-0; 7.0-0 Bg4.

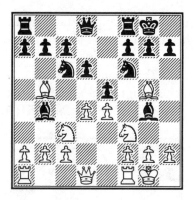

Usually we do not find all four bishops employed in this way, but a bishop in this extended position does place strong pressure on a knight, which is often pinned to a royal piece.

The drawback to the extended bishop strategy is that the bishop is exposed, and can be driven back by an advance of a rook pawn. In the Nimzo-Indian (1.d4 Nf6; 2.c4 e6; 3.Nc3 Bb4) and French Winawer (1.e4 e6; 2.d4 d5; 3.Nc3 Bb4) the bishop must often be exchanged for a knight at c3, and this can provide a long term asset to White.

ROMANTIC: C4/E3

This formation is commonly seen in the Sicilian Defense, where it is especially fashionable against the Dragon Variation. From c4, one bishop strikes directly at the weak square f7, and the other can form a battery with the queen, as in the Yugoslav Attack.

Sicilian Dragon: Yugoslav Attack
1.e4 c5; 2.Nf3 Nd6; 3.d4 cxd4; 4.Nxd4 Nf6; 5.Nc3 g6; 6.Be3 Bg7; 7.f3 Nc6; 8.Qd2 0-0; 9.Bc4.

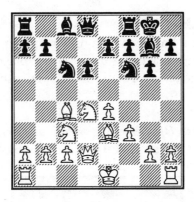

When Black adopts a fianchetto formation, the f7-square is an inviting target for a bishop at c4. Black doesn't want to play ...e6, which will create holes on the dark squares. White's attack on the kingside is fierce, but it is well known that Black is not without counter-chances on the queenside. The bishop at c5 is undefended. Black can play ...Ne5, forcing the bishop back to b3. Then, with a little support on the c-file, Black can plant the knight at c4 to interfere with the bishop's line of sight.

EXCHANGE: D3/G5

Placing one bishop at d3 and another at g5 is a strategy that fits will with the exchange of central pawns in the opening. This is the normal deployment in the Exchange Variations of the Queen's Gambit Declined.

Queen's Gambit Declined: Exchange Variation
1.d4 d5; 2.c4 e6; 3.Nc3 Nf6; 4.cxd5 exd5; 5.Bg5 c6; 6.Qc2 Be7; 7.e3 0-0; 8.Bd3.

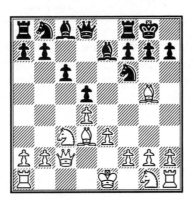

The bishop at g5 can sweep the knight at f6 from the board, leaving the pawn at h7 insufficiently defended. Black usually plays **8...Nbd7**, eliminating that threat but locking in the bishop at c8. White's bishops work very well together in this variation.

HYPERMODERN: FIANCHETTO

The fianchetto formation has become a fully respectable, though it was once considered strange and inferior. It is acceptable for either player to fianchetto one or both bishops, and quadruple fianchetto formations are seen, especially in the English Opening.

English Opening: Symmetrical Variation
1.Nf3 Nf6; 2.g3 g6; 3.b3 Bg7; 4.Bb2 0-0; 5.Bg2 c5; 6.c4 Nc6; 7.0-0 b6; 8.Nc3 Bb7.

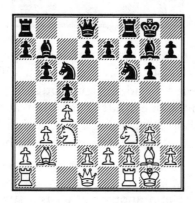

The total symmetry of this picture may immediately be broken by the advance of White's d-pawn to d4, or may persist for a while after more modest moves. The bishops hide behind the knights for the moment, but have access to greater scope once the knights move. This is an extreme case, of course, usually we see only one or two fianchettoes in an opening.

EDGY: A3/A6/H6/H3

Bishops rarely work effectively from the rim, but there are a few cases where a bishop on the rook file can be useful. This strategy is most frequently seen in the Queen's Indian Defense.

Queen's Indian Defense: Nimzowitsch Variation
1.d4 Nf6; 2.c4 e6; 3.Nf3 b6; 4.g3 Ba6.

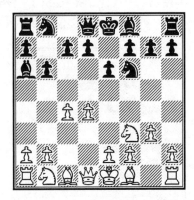

Since White has signaled an intention to fianchetto on the kingside, the pawn at c4 is a target. Black's move attacks this pawn, and can later add more pressure with ...d5. Still, a6 is hardly a good post for the bishop and in the long run it often retreats to b7.

OPENING ROLE OF THE ROOKS

Rooks generally belong on open files, but in the opening, the files generally remained closed or are only partially open. Therefore you have to consider placing your rooks on files which will be opened later. Another strategy, perhaps more appropriate in the opening, is to place rooks behind pawns that you plan to advance early in the game. Using such big guns for mere support may seem like overkill, but later in the game the pawns can advance, and open up more space.

Against the Paulsen Variation of the Sicilian Defense, White often lines up the rooks on the e-file and f-file, preparing the crucial advance of the f-pawn.

Sicilian Defense: Paulsen Variation

1.e4 c5; 2.Nf3 e6; 3.d4 cxd4; 4.Nxd4 a6; 5.Nc3 Qc7; 6.Bd3 Nc6; 7.Nb3 Nf6; 8.0-0 b5; 9.f4 d6; 10.Qf3 Bb7; 11.Bd2 Be7; 12.Rae1 Rc8; 13.Qh3 g6; 14.Nd1 0-0.

We follow the game Moe vs. Hansen, Espergarde, 1977.

White plans a kingside pawn storm. The knight will come to f2 and threaten to work from g4.

15.g4 Nd7; 16.g5 Rfe8; 17.Nf2. Black can no longer allow f5 to be used by White, so felt compelled to play **18...f5 18.exf5 exf5** but after **19.Bc3** obtained a clear advantage. **19...Bf8 20.a4 Qb6** followed, and a sacrifice finished things off.

21.Bxf5 gxf5; 22.g6 h6; 23.Qxf5 Nde5; 24.fxe5. Black Resigned. The rooks took no direct part in the attack, but there presence gave the necessary boost to the kingside operation.

OPENING ROLE OF THE QUEEN

We saw earlier that the queen generally remains within the safety zone.

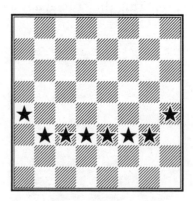

The dots represent squares where the queen is exposed. In this section we look at the cases where a White queen occupies one of those squares early in the game.

Queen at a4: Catalan Opening

In many varieties of the Catalan and Queen's Gambit, a4 is used to give check and recover a pawn at c4. We can see this technique used frequently. Although the queen winds up at c4, where it is a bit exposed, Black has already paid a price by abandoning the center.

1.d4 Nf6; 2.c4 e6; 3.g3 d5; 4.Nf3 Be7; 5.Bg2 0-0; 6.0-0 dxc4; 7.Qa4.

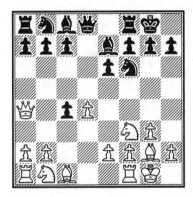

Black cannot hold onto the pawn, so play usually continues **7...a6; 8.Qxc4 b5; 9.Qc2.** White has retreated the queen back into the safety zone. Chances are considered roughly equal.

Sometimes the queen recovers a pawn at d4 instead.

Queen at a4: Schara Gambit

1.d4 d5; 2.c4 e6; 3.Nc3 c5; 4.cxd5 cxd4; 5.Qa4+.

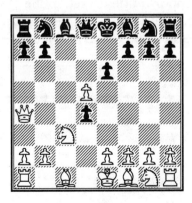

After **6...Bd7; 6.Qxd4** White has regained the pawn.

The queen is often stationed at b3. There are three different motivations. The first is when it supports a pawn at c4, leading to situations similar to the lines where the queen goes to a4, eventually capturing a pawn at c4. The second is when it forms a battery with a bishop at c4, to put pressure on f7. The third is to offer an exchange of queens when an enemy queen sits at b6.

Queen at b3: Gruenfeld Defense: Russian Variations

In the Gruenfeld Defense there is a group of variations which begin with an early queen sortie by White. The reward is a complete control of the center, including an ideal pawn structure.

1.d4 Nf6; 2.c4 g6; 3.Nc3 d5; 4.Nf3 Bg7; 5.Qb3 dxc4; 6.Qxc4.

Black has many plans here, but in each case White can safely play 7.e4 and dominate the center.

Queen at b3: Evans Gambit

In the Evans Gambit, as in many gambits in the Open Games where White plays an early c3, there are early opportunities to set up the Qb3/Bc4 battery.

For example, Fischer vs. Fine, New York 1963, started out **1.e4 e5; 2.Nf3 Nc6; 3.Bc4 Bc5; 4.b4!? Bxb4; 5.c3 Ba5; 6.d4 exd4; 7.0-0 dxc3?! 8.Qb3.**

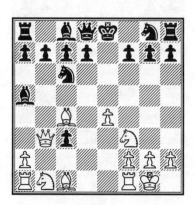

The game didn't last long.

8...Qe7; 9.Nxc3 Nf6?; 10.Nd5! Nxd5; 11.exd5 Ne5; 12.Nxe5 Qxe5; 13.Bb2 Qg5; 14.h4! Qxh4; 15.Bxg7 Rg8; 16.Rfe1+ Kd8; 17.Qg3! Black resigned.

Queen at b3: Slav Defense

1.d4 d5; 2.c4 c6; 3.Nf3 Nf6; 4.e3 Bf5; 5.Nc3 e6; 6.Nh4 Bg4; 7.Qb3 Qb6. The Slav starts out as a closed game, and the queen is relatively safe at b3.

This creates great tension in the position. Both sides are reluctant to capture the enemy queen, opening the a-file and bringing another pawn closer to the center. Yet each side must constantly consider the effects of such an exchange. The queens may stare at each other for dozens of moves before any action is taken.

Queen at c3: Queen's Indian Defense

The queen can land at c3 as a result of a recapture, when Black uses a minor piece to capture a knight there. This is seen in the main line of the Queen's Indian Defense.

1.d4 Nf6; 2.c4 e6; 3.Nf3 b6; 4.g3 Bb7; 5.Bg2 Be7; 6.0-0 0-0; 7.Nc3 Ne4; 8.Qc2 Nxc3; 9.Qxc3.

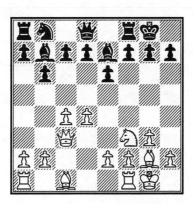

The capture with the queen keeps the pawn structure intact. White can move the knight from f3 to exchange light squared bishops, and has easy development. Achieving the ideal pawn center will be impossible after 9...f5, and Black can be satisfied.

Queen at d3: Gurgenidze Defense

The main risk in bringing a queen to d3 is that it can be harassed by a knight at b4 or bishop at f5. When this is not the case, the queen can function well there. Closed positions such as the Gurgenidze System, often allow this setup.

1.e4 c6; 2.Nc3 g6; 3.Nf3 Bg7; 4.d4 d5; 5.e5 Bf5; 6.Bd3 Bxd3; 7.Qxd3.

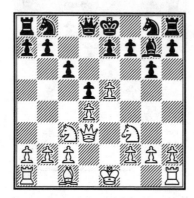

White's queen is quite safe here, and the development of the remaining pieces can take place quickly.

Queen at e3: Center Game

The queen cannot serve well from e3. It blocks the e-file, often interferes with the development of the bishop from c1, and is vulnerable to attack. This position is characteristic of the Center Game, an opening which has rarely been seen in serious play, at least during the twentieth century.

1.e4 e5; 2.d4 exd4; 3.Qxd4 Nc6; 4.Qe3 Nf6.

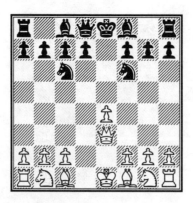

Black's knights are in position to go after the White queen, and Black can also try to maneuver the bishop to b6 via a check at b4 and retreat to a5, adding further insult to her majesty.

Queen at f3: Muzio Gambit

The queen comes to f3 in many openings as a result of a Black capture at f3. Usually Black gives up a bishop for a knight there, so the slight exposure of the queen is acceptable. The queen can aim directly at f7, the weakest point in the enemy camp. The most spectacular example of this is the Muzio Gambit, one of the King's Gambits.

1.e4 e5; 2.f4 exf4; 3.Nf3 g5; 4.Bc4 g4; 5.0-0 gxf3.

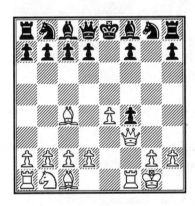

White has sacrificed a knight for a potent attack on f7. To stop this assault, Black plays **6...Qf6** and White invests another pawn with **7.e5 Qxe5; 8.d3**, bringing the dark squared bishop into the game. Wild complications ensue, and the mysteries of the positions remain unresolved after a century of work.

Queen at g3: Center Game

If a White queen sits at g3, it has usually arrived there late in the opening, creating a direct threat against a Black king castled on the kingside. It is most often seen in the Center Game, and Black has little to fear. Consider the following typical example, from a game between Weglarz and Ciruk in the 1997 Polish Team Championship.

1.e4 e5; 2.d4 exd4; 3.Qxd4 Nc6; 4.Qe3 Nf6; 5.Nc3 Bb4; 6.Bd2 0-0; 7.0-0-0 Re8; 8.Qg3.

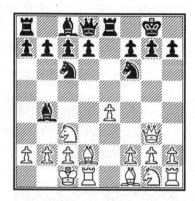

It looks as though White has something going, but Black could have demolished White's hopes with **8...Rxe4!; 9.Nxe4 Nxe4; 10.Qf4 Bxd2+; 11.Rxd2 Nxd2; 12.Qxd2** and White has nothing to show for the pawn.

Queen at h4: English Opening

The h4-square is a useful attacking post, and the queen is relatively safe there. It is hard to attack her with a knight, and if Black deploys a bishop, then White can usually counter with Bg5. Garry Kasparov uses this technique in one line of the English Opening.

    1.Nf3 Nf6; 2.c4 g6; 3.Nc3 d5; 4.cxd5 Nxd5; 5.Qa4+ Bd7; 6.Qh4.

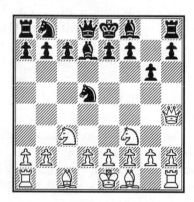

OPENING ROLE OF THE KING

As has been mentioned many times already, it is the obligation of the king to head for safety by castling early in the game. The center is only safe when there are plenty of guards and few entrances. An open e-file is a sure sign to get out of the center! Just in case you need reminding, here are checkmates, from two moves to six! All examples have actually been played!

Fools Mate (Two Moves)
1.g4 e5; 2.f3?? Qh4#

Suicide (Three Moves)
1.e4 e5; 2.Qh5 Ke7?? 3.Qxe5

The suicide mate has a twin:
1.e4 d5; 2.exd5 Qxd5;
3.Ke2?? Qxe4#

Delayed Suicide (Four Moves)
1.e4 e5; 2.f4 Bc5; 3.fxe5 Qh4+;
4.Ke2 Qxe4#

Lone Bishop Mate (Five Moves)
1.f4 e5; 2.fxe5 d6; 3.exd6 Bxd6;
4.Nf3 Nc6; 5.h3 Bg3#

Smothered Mate (Six Moves)
1.e4 c6; 2.Nc3 d5; 3.Nf3 dxe4;
4.Nxe4 Nd7; 5.Qe2 Ngf6; 6.Nd6#

Never forget that when you open up a line to your king, it acts as an invitation to enemy pieces. They may quickly invade your house and cause you much pain. Do not allow it!

The opening requires quite a bit of study at the professional level, but can be a real distraction to amateurs who just want to play chess without a lot of specific opening preparation. Beginners can follow the advice I give to my students, a simple 3 step plan:

1. Put a pawn in the center
2. Castle
3. Let your rooks see each other along the first rank

If you accomplish those three goals without losing any material, you will likely have a good enough position heading into the middlegame.

TRANSITION

The transition from the opening is a murky one. It is hard to define any clear boundary, and traditional definitions, whether based on number of moves or number of pieces developed, are pretty useless. Some openings have been analyzed out almost to move 40! As a practical matter, the opening is over when you no longer remember the next move you have to play, and simple development is no longer an option.

At this point there are two things you absolutely must do. First, you need to figure our what your opponent is up to. The enemy plan may require some short term or long term action on your part. Then, you must create your own plan.

Let's take a step forward and what we do next.

THE MIDDLEGAME

Before the Endgame, the Gods played the Middlegame.

Once the forces have been developed, the middlegame begins. Here strategy and tactics predominate. These are crucial subjects we will deal with later. There are other important topics, however. An attack can be carried out in many ways, and an appropriate defense must be found against each assault. In order to achieve strategic flexibility and maximum combinative power you need to place your pawns and pieces on optimal squares. You must avoid creating weaknesses which can be exploited by the opponent. These matters will be discussed in the present chapter.

ATTACK

A successful attack is the most satisfying achievement in a chess game. There is a special pleasure that comes from breaking down enemy defenses and cornering the enemy king. In the 19th century, players strove to attack at all costs. Early in the game all available force would be brought to bear on the enemy position. Winning the game involved either successfully carrying out the direct attack, or using the attack to force the opponent to make concessions, after which a win could be achieved by positional and technical means.

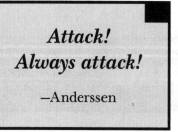

*Attack!
Always attack!*

—Anderssen

Of the quote in the box: Nonsense! Utter nonsense! As Steinitz would later demonstrate, you simply can't expect to attack successfully unless you have the positional basis to do so. Premature attacks are doomed to failure. Even the mighty Mikhail Tal sometimes couldn't resist the temptation to attack before conditions were ripe.

TAL - SMYSLOV
Soviet Championship Qualifier 1977
1.e4 e5; 2.Nf3 Nc6; 3.Bb5 a6; 4.Ba4 Nf6; 5.0-0 Nxe4; 6.d4 b5; 7.Bb3 Be7; 8.Nxe5 Nxe5; 9.dxe5 Bb7; 10.Qg4. The opening is the Spanish Game.

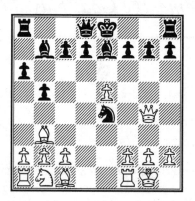

White's attack is premature. There are two bishops and a queen which can take part. Black does not seem to have many defensive resources, but in order to attack White will need to weaken the kingside by advancing the f-pawn. The attack looks promising, but lacks sufficient preparation. Notice that the White queenside is completely undeveloped.

10...0-0. Black simply castles, knowing that there is nothing to fear, because the knight at e4 can assist with the defense if needed, but is also in position to attack f2. **11.f3 Ng5!** The immediate attack would also have been premature! 11...Bc5+; 12.Kh1 Nf2+; 13.Rxf2 Bxf2; 14.Bg5 would have given White a strong attack, with no counterplay for Black. This would surely be worth the exchange.

12.f4!? Although criticized by some commentators, this move is the only consistent way to continue the attack. 12.Nc3 was recommended, but 12...Kh8; 13.f4 f5! 14.exf6 Bc5+; 15.Kh1 Qxf6 is clearly better for Black. **12...Ne4; 13.f5 Kh8.** 13...Bc5+!; 14.Kh1 Kh8; 15.Nc3 Nf2+; 16.Rxf2 Bxf2 was an even stronger plan. **14.Rf3 Bc5+.**

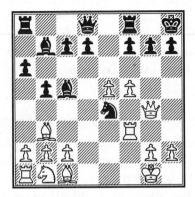

The counterattack begins. Notice that White has no real threats on the kingside.

15.Kf1. 15.Be3 Qe7; 16.f6 is refuted by 16...Bxe3+; 17.Rxe3 Nxf6!; **15...d6; 16.f6 g6!** This shuts down White's attack. The only route to the Black king lies on the h-file, but Black's attack is faster.

17.Qh4 dxe5; 18.Ke2 Qd4!; Black threatens to check at c3 with the knight, winning the White queen. **19.Rh3 Qf2+; 20.Qxf2 Nxf2; 21.Rh4 Ne4; 22.Bh6 Nxf6; 23.Bxf8 Rxf8.** Black went on to win without much difficulty.

> *If the defender is forced to abandon the center,*
> *then the attacks almost play themselves.*
>
> —Tarrasch

One of the hardest concepts for a beginner to grasp is the importance of the center of the board. While a player may go to great lengths to avoid losing material and keep the king safe, control of the center is rarely a priority. This is partially a result of the influence of the hypermodern school of chess.

In the 1920s, some revolutionary thinkers, led by Richard Reti and Aron Nimzowitsch, pointed out that classical chess pundits had placed too much emphasis on the occupation of the center by pawns. A casual reading of their work has led many players to believe that they did not to think that control of the center plays in important role in the game of chess. Nothing could be further from the truth.

These great chess players were well aware that when the opponent is allowed to control the center, a great many attacking possibilities will arise. There pointed was simply that control of the center is not achieved merely by occupying up with pawns and if those pawns are not properly supported then that the center is in fact weak and is subject to counter attack.

There are many types of attacking formation. Choosing the right one requires taking into consideration the defense setup. Attack and defense are inextricably intertwined. We'll adopt the attackers point of view for the moment, and investigate effective attacking formations. More examples will be presented in the chapter on Defense, in the section Pawns Protect the king. Then we'll look at some more general recommendations.

PAWNSTORM AGAINST FIANCHETTO FORMATION

The pawnstorm is an effective method of attack against a fianchetto formation. Because the enemy kingside has been weakened by the advance of the g-pawn, White's pawns do not have as far to go before they reach a position where they can destroy the protective barrier. This theme is seen to good effect in the Dragon Variation of the Sicilian Defense, where pawnstorms rage on both flanks.

YUFEROV - GRODZOV
Lvov, 1966

1.e4 c5; 2.Nc3 Nc6; 3.Nge2 g6; 4.d4 cxd4; 5.Nxd4 Bg7; 6.Be3 Nf6; 7.Bc4 0-0; 8.Bb3 d6; 9.f3 Bd7; 10.Qd2 Qb8; 11.h4 Rc8; 12.0-0-0 b5. The opening is Sicilian Defense.

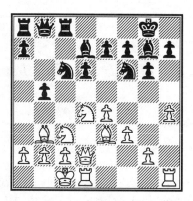

White has not handled the opening particularly well. The queenside formation is a bit artificial. Black should have advanced the a pawn to attack the knight at b3. White now carries out the standard kings side attack and cracks open the h-file.

13.h5 Na5; 14.hxg6 Nxb3+; 15.Nxb3 hxg6; 16.Bh6 Bh8.

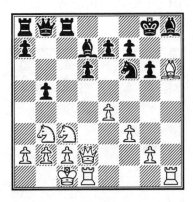

Perhaps Black did not appreciate the danger here. The bishop at h6 is in the way of White's attack. However, it can easily be moved.. **17.Bf8!! Rxf8; 18.Rxh8+ Kxh8; 19.Qh6+ Kg8; 20.Nd5!** Black resigned, since there is no way now to stop mate on the h-file, once the rook is transferred there.

CENTRAL ATTACK AGAINST UNCASTLED KING

The central attack against an uncastled king is not as common in modern chess as it was in the past century. This is simply a result of the fact that even beginners understand the need to castle and usually remove their king from the center as soon as possible. It is easy to understand that if central files are open, an attack can easily be carried out. Many players, however, tried to rationalize leaving the king in the center when there seems to be enough defensive force available to protect it. Often the target of White's operation is the vulnerable square at f7 which we will examine below. Let's start with the case where the Black king is forced to remain in the center and a successful attack is carried out even though the e-file and f-file are unavailable.

BONCH OSMOLOVSKY - BARANOV
Moscow, 1954
1.e4 e5; 2.Nf3 Nf6; 3.d4 exd4; 4.e5 Ne4; 5.Qxd4 d5; 6.exd6 Nxd6; 7.Bd3 Qe7+; 8.Be3 Nf5?! The opening is Russian Game.

Black should be attending to development, so that the king can escape the center. The knight performed a useful defensive function, keeping the d-file closed. See how this move gives White the opportunity to win brilliantly.

9.Bxf5 Bxf5; 10.Nc3 Qb4?! More adventurism. Did Black really think that White would consent to an exchange of queens? **11.Qe5+ Be6; 12.0-0-0.**

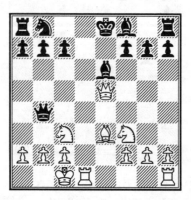

12...Nc6; 13.Qxc7 Rc8; 14.Qf4 Qa5; 15.Qg5 Qa6; 16.Rhe1. White plans Nd5, since the bishop must stand guard on the e-file. **16...Nb4; 17.Nd4 Rxc3.**

Now for one of those moments every chessplayer lives for! **18.Qd8+!! Kxd8; 19.Nxe6+ Ke7.** Even worse is 19...Ke8; 20.Nxg7+ Bxg7; 21.Bg5+ Be5; 22.Rd8#. **20.Bg5+ f6; 21.Nd8+** Black resigned, faced with nothing but futile thrashing for a couple of moves.

ATTACK ON F7 AGAINST UNCASTLED KING

The most accessible point of attack in an uncastled position is at f7. Beginners often fall victim the to the attack on that square because they fail to notice what should be fairly obvious threats. More interesting is the case where a defender relies solely on a few pieces to guard the key squares. It is often thought that you need only have enough defensive force to counter immediate attacks. Underestimating the weakness of the key square usually leads to disaster as in this case.

The following position was reached after 27 moves in Boleslavsky vs. Steiner, Saltsjobaden Interzonal, 1948.

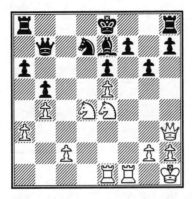

Black's king is still stuck in the center. The e-file is completely blocked, and of no use at all, and the d-file is defended by the knight. The bishop at e7 controls both f6 and d6.

27.Rxf7!! Qd5; 28.Rxe7+ Kxe7; 29.Qh4+ Kf7; 30.Nd6+ Kg7; 31.Qe7+ Kh6; 32.Re3. Black resigned.

SACRIFICE AT F6 AGAINST CASTLED KING

Once the king has castled, the vulnerability of f7 is usually reduced but there are new objects for attack. While the square is only defended once in the initial position, after castling, the pawn enjoys the support not only of the king and a rook, but usually is protected by a knight at f6. In the next chapter, you will see these in more detail.

Our present concern lies one square closer on the f-file. The knight at f6 not only defends the pawn to his rear but also protects the weakling at h7. The removal of this knight is therefore one of the most important goals of White's attack. There are of course slow ways of chasing the knight away including the advance of the g-pawn but sacrificial means are also often employed.

This idea is illustrated nicely in the game Parma vs. Capelan, Solingen 1968, which we pick up after 16 moves.

White plays the thematic sacrifice and cripples Black's defenses.
17.Rxf6! gxf6; 18.Nd5 Rd8. 18...Kg7; 19.Qg3+ Kh8; 20.Qh4 wins. **19.Nxf6+ Kf8; 20.Rc1 Be6; 21.h4!** White is not losing time with this move because now there is no threat of a back rank mate, and the Black queen must now move.

21...Qd3; 22.Qh6+ Ke7; 23.Qg5 Kd6; 24.Nc5. White's control of the c-file has paid off. **24...Qb5; 25.Nxe6 fxe6; 26.Qd2+.** Black resigned. The game would not have lasted much longer. 26...Ke7; 27.Rc7+ Kxf6; 28.Qg5#.

CAPABLANCA'S RULE

Capablanca's rule is quite simple. You need to attack with more force than the defender can use in defense. For the most part chess is not a game of super heroes. A single piece can only be asked to do so much. It is true that there are some occasions when the one piece can strike and destroy an enemy target, but for the most part pieces must work together. In Forgacs vs. Tartakower, from the great St. Petersburg tournament of 1909, White's pieces do not seem to be in attacking position. Black has just advanced the b-pawn to b4 at move 16.

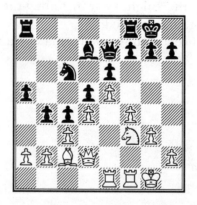

Except for the bishop at c2, none of White's pieces directly attacks the kingside.

The chain of pawns, however, does not allow Black's pieces to get into defensive formation. White quickly opens up lines to increase the attacking force.

17.f5! exf5; 18.g4! The sacrifice of two pawns leads to an overpowering position. **18...fxg4; 19.Ng5! g6; 20.Rf6 Kg7; 21.Ref1 Be8; 22.Qf4 Nd8.**

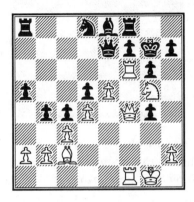

Now all of White's pieces are in attacking position. Black is doing the best he can to cope with the assault, but the f-pawn is still insecure, because it is pinned. A final pawn sacrifice puts the game to rest.

23.e6! Ra6; 24.Qe5 Kh6; 25.R1f5 fxe6; 26.Nf7+ Qxf7; 27.Rh5+ Kg7; 28.Rxg6# In the following position from a game between Alexander and Szabo at Hilversum, in 1947, White is attacking with two knights, one rook, and the queen. Black doesn't have very much in the way of defense. His bishop, queen and rook are in the neighborhood of the king but they have very little influence on the edge files. We join the game after move 20.

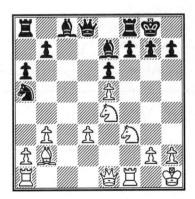

White sacrifices a piece, appreciating that the remaining pieces provide enough ammunition to carry on the fight against the enemy king. **21.Nf6+!! gxf6.** 21...Bxf6 loses to 22.exf6 g6; 23.Qe3; 21...Kh8 only postpones disaster for a while. 22.Qh4 Qxd3; 23.Ng5 h6; 24.Rf3! Qg6; 25.Rg3 is most unpleasant for Black. **22.Qg3+ Kh8; 23.exf6 Bxf6; 24.Ne5.**

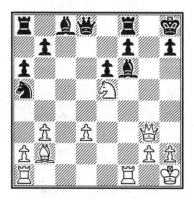

With the e-pawn out of the way, the bishop now participates in the attack from b2. Notice that Black's rook, knight and bishop on the queenside cannot possible aid in the defense. The only White piece which has no role in the attack is the rook at a1, but even it can be activated quickly enough.

> *An attacking complement of four pieces will generally be sufficient to force the mate, allowing one of them to be sacrificed along the way.*
>
> — Freeborough and Ranken

24...Bxe5. 24...Nc6 is too slow. 25.Nxc6! Bxb2; 26.Nxd8 Bxa1; 27.Nxf7+ is a simple win. 24...Bg7 falls to 25.Rxf7 Rg8; 26.Ng6+ hxg6; 27.Qh3+ Qh4; 28.Qxh4#.

25.Bxe5+ f6; 26.Rxf6. Black resigned, since the sky is falling after 26...Rxf6; 27.Rf1.

When you attack with four pieces you have more than enough power to destroy the enemy King. If the king is protected by a solid barrier of pawns and some supporting pieces, your best plan is to give up one of your pieces or smash the pawn barrier. Your remaining three pieces will always be at least as powerful as a queen so you needn't worry about having sufficient material to complete your assignment.

World Champion Mikhail Botvinnik appreciated this concept, as he demonstrated against Chekhover at Moscow 1935. After 18 moves, the following position was reached.

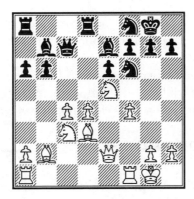

Since Black has three defenders on the queenside, Botvinnik brought the knight into the game from c3. **19.Nd1 Ra7; 20.Nf2 Qb8; 21.Nh3 h6; 22.Ng5 hxg5; 23.fxg5 N8d7**.

Unfortunately, he gave his opponent some chances to survive after **24.Nxf7 Kxf7; 25.g6+**, which has been the subject of a great deal of analysis. With the simple 24.Nxd7, however, he could have achieved a winning position.

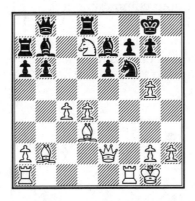

No matter how Black recaptures, the position cannot be held. 24...Rxd7 25.gxf6 Bxf6; Material is equal, but White can sacrifice and win. 26.Rxf6! gxf6; 27.Qg4+ Kf8; 28.Ba3+ Black loses by force. 28...Rd6; 29.Qg3 Ke7; 30.c5 bxc5; 31.dxc5! Rd8; 32.c6+ Rd6; 33.Rb1! What a collection of pins! Or 24...Nxd7; 25.Rxf7!! Bd6; 26.Qxe6 Bxh2+; 27.Kh1 Bxg2+; 28.Kxg2 Qg3+; 29.Kh1 and Black has nothing better than 29...Qd6; 30.d5! Qxe6; 31.dxe6 Be5; 32.Bxe5 Nxe5; 33.Rxa7 Nxd3 but now 34.Rd7 wins. Of course it is all to easy to find such moves after the game, but during the game this would have been difficult to spot.

SIMPLIFY TO WIN

The easiest way to win a game is to achieve a winning endgame. Mating attacks must always be carried out with precision, but extra material is useful even if you don't make the most of every move.

When you have a material advantage, try to hold on to it. You may think that you can afford to return the material for good attacking chances, but such things are intangible. Only give it back if you see a very clear result to your attack.

BRING THE OTHER ROOK INTO THE ATTACK!

If I had to single out just one piece of advice from this entire book, it would be this: bring the distant rook into the attack! So often an attack fails because there just isn't enough firepower. A rook sits idly at a1 while the other pieces attempt to go after the enemy king without its help.

In the games of masters and Grandmasters, a quiet move which centralizes a rook in the early middlegame often passes without comment, but is the key to a successful attack.

Future World Champion Wilhelm Steinitz showed his appreciation of the centralized rook in this position from his game against De Vere at Paris, 1867.

> *A piece in the hand is worth a mate in the bush.*
>
> —Loyd

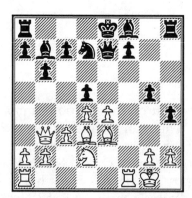

White's position holds great promise, but the pin on the pawn at e4 prevents White from capturing at d5. Steinitz calmly played **15.Rae1!** Black castled with **15...0-0-0**, to break the unfortunate potential pin of queen to the king, but on **16.exd5** he felt compelled to resign since there is nothing to do about the threat of 17.d6 and 18.Rxf7.

Former World Champion Max Euwe and future champion Bobby Fischer met over the board at the New York tournament of 1957, and the young man was taught the lesson of the centralized rook.

16.Rae1! Euwe anticipated that the infiltration at h7 is going to happen sooner or later, so he places a rook on the e-file to keep the enemy king from fleeing to the queenside.

16...Nb4; 17.Qh7+ Kf8; 18.a3! Nxc2. Now the d5-square lacks sufficient support. **19.Ncxd5 Rxd5; 20.Nxd5.** Fischer resigned, since Euwe was ready to play Qh8 mate. Advancing the g-pawn would only offer temporary respite after the bishop on f6 is captured by the knight.

Check out the example later on in the section on the vulnerability of g7, and see just how important this centralizing rook move is!

ATTACK WHERE YOU HAVE THE PAWN MAJORITY

It is often remarked that the most appropriate targets for an attack are on the side of the board where you have a majority of pawns. In most openings, a pair of pawns will be exchanged in the center, leaving an unbalanced position at the start of the middlegame. Consider the following position from Brunker vs. Pihajlic, Buenos Aires Olympiad, 1978. We join the game at move 23, with Black to move.

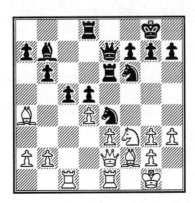

White's position is certainly a mess. You would think that the weaknesses at e3 and g3 would be the target of Black operations. Instead, it is the simple pawn majority on the queenside that delivers the decisive blow, very quickly.

23...c4!; 24.Bc2 b5!; 25.a3 a5! The advance of the pawns is the inevitable. **26.Kh2 Ba6.** A slight pause, while the bishop gets into position. **27.Rb1 b4!; 28.Bg1?** 28.axb4 axb4; 29.Ra1 was probably the best defense, but White's position is still terrible. **28...bxa3.** Black cooperatively demonstrates the theme of weakening the control of c3, but there was a simple mate, which he missed. 28...Ng4+!!; 29.hxg4 Rh6+; 30.Nh4 Qxh4+; 31.gxh4 Rxh4# **29.bxa3 Nc3;** White resigned.

In modern chess, however, attacks with fewer pawns on the attacking side are more common. After all, the lack of a pawn means that you have access to an open file. In most cases, pawns on the attacking side just get in the way of your pieces, and you must find clever ways of removing them.

The most striking counterexample to this rule can be found in the Sicilian Defenses. All of the most important variations in that opening rely on queenside pawn attacks.

Sicilian Defense: Najdorf Variation

The traditional main line of the Najdorf runs:

1.e4 c5; 2.Nf3 d6; 3.d4 cxd4; 4.Nxd4 Nf6; 5.Nc3 a6; 6.Bg5 e6; 7.f4 Be7; 8.Qf3 Qc7; 9.0-0-0 Nbd7; 10.g4 b5; 11.Bxf6 Nxf6; 12.g5 Nd7.

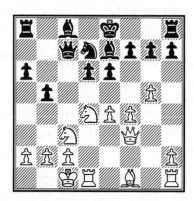

Black will advance the queenside pawns and attack on the c-file. White's attack crucially relies on being able to get rid of at least one of the kingside pawns to open up files for the rooks.

Another opening which frequently sees a minority attack is the Queen's Gambit Declined. That is an attack against a pawn structure, not the king, so we will discuss it in the section on pawn structure.

INITIATIVE

The initiative is one of the hardest chess concepts to define. For many players, it is a matter of subjective feeling, rather than anything which can be calculated and evaluated. You hold the initiative when your opponent must react to your threat or plan. While the enemy is in reactive mode, your plans determine the flow of the game. An attacker must always have the initiative.

It is often said that one or more positional features of the game guarantees one side or another an initiative. This is best viewed as a dynamic situation, not a static one. If you control the center, for example, your pieces have more freedom of movement, which creates more opportunities for the initiative. Nevertheless, a dramatic move can often shift the initiative from one side to another.

ZAMIKHOVSKY - NYEZHMETDINOV
Kharkov, 1956

1.d4 Nf6; 2.c4 g6; 3.Nc3 Bg7; 4.e4 d6; 5.f3 0-0; 6.Be3 Nbd7; 7.Qd2 c5; 8.Nge2 a6; 9.0-0-0 Qa5; 10.dxc5 dxc5; 11.Kb1 b5; 12.Nd5. The opening is King's Indian Defense.

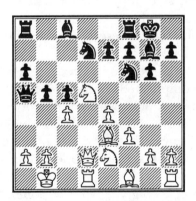

White has malicious intent on the kingside. This move is a form of the knight leap trap, because if Black captures the queen then White wins a pawn by capturing at e7 with check before recapturing the queen. Therefore the retreat of the queen to d8 would seem to be indicated. Nyezhmetdinov chooses to seize the initiative instead, even at the cost of material.

12...Nxd5!!; 13.Qxa5 Nxe3; 14.Rc1 Nxc4. Black has a powerful bishop, an attacking knight, and an extra pawn for the queen. More important, however, is the attack on the queen, which maintains the initiative.

15.Rxc4!? Probably best. By returning an exchange White smashes the pawn structure and blunts the initiative. **15...bxc4; 16.Nc3 Rb8!** Black sets up some threats. The White queen cannot move because then the knight at c3 falls, because the b-pawn is pinned. White's last move, and next move, are necessary to get development going.

17.Bxc4 Ne5! The attack on the bishop at c4 regains the initiative. **18.Be2 Be6**. The bishop moves into position to attack via c4. **19.Rd1.**

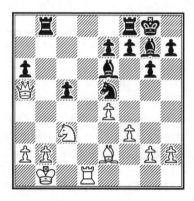

19...Bc4. This move keeps the initiative, but results in a draw. Commentators have suggested that there was a more effective plan, but I am not sure it holds up under scrutiny. 19...Nc6 is the suggested improvement. The idea is that ...Nb4 will be very strong. The capture at c5 was dismissed as suicidal, but is it? 20.Qxc5 Nb4; 21.e5 cuts off the bishop. Again the initiative is preserved with an attack on the queen. 21...Rfc8; 22.Qe3 Bf5+; 23.Ne4 Bxe5; 24.b3 Nc2; 25.Qc1.

Here Black could repeat the position with 25...Nd4; 26.Qe3 Nc2 etc., or maybe even try for more with the complicated 25...Bd6!? Best of all, Black can simplify into a winning endgame with 25...Be6, after which White does not seem to have anything better than 26.Qxc2 Rxc2; 27.Kxc2 Bxh2; 28.Bxa6 where Black plays 28...Ra8 with a clearly superior position. In any case, after the bishop move the game concluded.

20.Rd2 Nc6; 21.Qa3 Be6; 22.Qxc5 Nb4; 23.a3 Rfc8; 24.Qxc8+ Rxc8; 25.axb4 and a draw was agreed.

To maintain the initiative, keep giving your opponent something to worry about. A series of threats is most effective, but sometimes a mere declaration of war is sufficient. When you castle on the opposite side of the board from your opponent, you are stating that battles will rage on both flanks. When you launch your attack, your opponent must take into account the situation many moves later.

The best illustration of this can be found in the Dragon Variation of the Sicilian Defense, particularly in the Yugoslav Attack. In this wild opening both kings are under assault. Black will almost always sacrifice an exchange at c3 to open up the enemy king. This has become commonplace but before the Second World War it was still a relatively fresh idea. The game between Weaver Adams and Rauch at the 1938 American Chess Congress was remarkable in many respects. We join it after White has just tried to get the king to safety with 24.Kb1. The typical sac works quite effectively here.

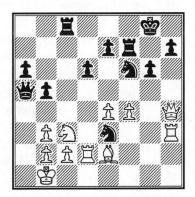

24...Rxc3!; 25.bxc3 Qxc3; 26.Rd3. 26.Rxe3 Qxe3; 27.Qe1 Nxe4; 28.Rd3 Qxf4;
29.Rf3 Nd2+ would have been a quicker death.

26...Qxc2+; 27.Ka1 Qc1+; 28.Ka2 Nc2. Every Black move contains a venomous
threat. In this case, ...Qa1 will now be checkmate, so White must advance the pawn.
29.b4.

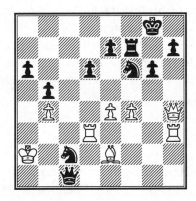

Black eventually won, but missed 29...Qa1+; 30.Kb3 Qb1+; 31.Kc3 Nxe4#!

In the middlegame, an initiative can be blunted in several ways. We'll discuss some
of those in passing in the next chapter, where we deal with defense. Before moving on,
however, it is worth mentioning a common misunderstanding among amateur players. It is often thought that an initiative can be reduced by exchanging pieces. This is
not true. An attack can be diminished in this way, but not the initiative.

> *Remember that after the exchange it is still your move*
>
> — Locock

The ancient wisdom from Locock remains true today. If you have the initiative, exchanging a pair of pieces does not diminish it. After your opponent recaptures, it is still your turn to move. You are still the one controlling the flow of the game. As long as you can present new problems for your opponent, the initiative remains in your hands.

Now we will turn the board around, and look at the middlegame from a defensive viewpoint. After all, if one player has the initiative, the other must necessarily be on defense.

DEFENSE

The first task of the defense is to realize that defense is necessary. When on the attack, it is sometimes difficult to shift gears into defensive mode. It is, after all, more fun to attack. Often you may be conducting an excellent attack only to be destroyed by a devastating and unexpected counterattack. We will turn to the topic of developing a sense of danger in the psychology chapter.

In this chapter we will discuss the five different types of defense, the role of the pawns in defending the castled king, how to salvage a hopeless position, and the use of exchanges to ease the defense. Finally, we will consider what is known as prophylaxis, which takes preventative measures to prevent the opponent from achieving his strategic goals.

TYPES OF DEFENSE

The great chess scholar Hans Kmoch, from whom I learned quite a bit as a young player at the Manhattan Chess Club, divided defensive plans into five categories: passive, active, automatic, philosophical, and aggressive. Circumstances dictate which ones are most appropriate. Sometimes you just have to cover up and fend off enemy blows. Perhaps there are some enemy weaknesses that you can pounce on, or your pieces may be summoned to take up positions to ward off future attacks. When things are really looking bad, psychological or other desperate measures may be required.

Passive Defense

Passive defense is directed toward countering immediate enemy threats. The opponent attacks one of your pieces, you defend it by bringing another piece to support it.

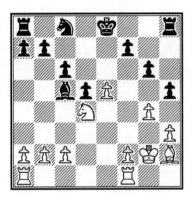

In Matulovic vs. Karaklaic, Yugoslavia 1967, Black just attacked the knight at d4 with the bishop at c5. Using passive defense, White advanced the c-pawn to c3.

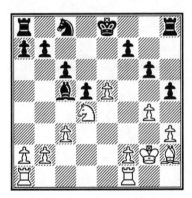

This proved to be the wrong choice. A more active defense, retreating the knight to b3 while attacking the bishop, would have been wiser. Black soon exchanged the bishop for the knight, obtaining a superior good knight vs. bad bishop endgame.

Passive methods lose the initiative, as many scholars have noted. A passive defense must be reserved as a plan of last resort, when nothing else leads to a playable game.

Active Defense

Active defense uses counter-threats and counterattacks to prevent the enemy from competing a mission. Here is a position similar to the previous example, at least as far as the immediate threat is concerned.

In the game Unzicker vs. Larsen from the 2nd Piatigorsky Cup in 1966, White uses the same move, but this time it is active defense, because it attacks the enemy queen.

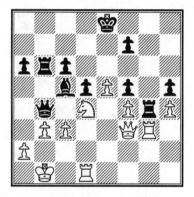

Black was unable to make any significant progress and the game was soon drawn.

Automatic Defense

Automatic defense employs a strategy of mobilizing forces as quickly as possible. It is seen to great effect in the games of Tarrasch and Capablanca. This type of defense should, indeed, be "automatic." Your best chances of defending a weak position is to bring your pieces into positions where they can either defend critical squares or launch counterattacks. Our example is the fifth game from the 1910 World Championship, where David Janowski, the challenger, had Black. We join the game after 12 moves.

    13.Ncb5! The knight not only defends its partner at d4, it can also create threats at a7.

    13...Nf5; 14.Rc1. Ignoring the threat at e3, Lasker continues to mobilize. **14...Nxe3; 15.fxe3 Qxe3+; 16.Be2 Be7.** 16...Bb3 is not as clever as it looks. 17.Nxa7+ Kc7; 18.Ndb5+ Kb6. If the king retreats, then the queen captures the rook followed by Rc8#. 19.Rxc6+ bxc6; 20.Qxd8+ and White wins. **17.Rc3.** White intends to castle. This will not only bring the king to safety, but also allows the rook to undertake active operations on the f-file.

    17...Bh4+; 18.g3 Qe4; 19.0-0 Bf6.

Lasker now uses the rook to eliminate the powerful bishop at f6.

    20.Rxf6! gxf6; 21.Bf3 Qe5. The rest is simple. **22.Nxa7+ Kc7; 23.Naxc6 bxc6; 24.Rxc6+ Kb8; 25.Rb6+ Kc8; 26.Qc1+ Kd7; 27.Nxe6 fxe6; 28.Rb7+ Ke8; 29.Bc6+.** Black resigned.

Philosophical Defense

Philosophical defense tries to lure the opponent into a false sense of security. If the superior side's concentration slips even for a moment, especially in a complicated situation, then immediate escapes are possible. When you have a bad game, you can try to turn the position into a war zone. Create as many tactical traps as you can while still maintaining enough defense to ward off immediate defeat.

This strategy sounds fairly simple but in fact it is double-edged. When you create more tactical opportunities for yourself, you are usually providing the opponent with an equal number of chances. It is like two boxers abandoning finesse and entering a brawl. A lucky punch can end the contest quickly.

Our example is taken from a game between Billy Colias, a young master who died prematurely in 1993, and Ed Friedman, another Chicagoan with a strong passion for attack. It was played in 1985, at the University of Chicago.

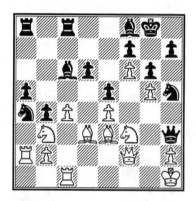

White has just played 24.Ra2 in preparation for a doubling of rooks on the a-file. Black recognized that the situation was bad, and threw caution to the winds with an ambitious sacrifice.

24...Nxb2!?; 25.Rxb2 a4; 26.Nbd2 a3; 27.Ra2 d5!? Philosophical defense unbalances the position at all costs! **28.Bf1 Qe6.** Black offers another piece! **29.cxd5 Bxd5; 30.Rxc8?** 30.exd5 was better, because the exchange of rooks brings another attacker to c8, but White has lost the defender. 30...Qxd5; 31.Nc4 and White is comfortably ahead. The young master was overconfident, and, assuming that two extra pieces would be more valuable than three pawns, followed the dictum "simplify to win," which we discuss elsewhere in the book.

30...Rxc8; 31.exd5 Qxd5; 32.Bc4?! This would have been more effective with the rook at c1, as mentioned in the previous note. **32...Rxc4!; 33.Nxc4 Qxc4; 34.Rc2 Qe6.**

The two passed pawns on the queenside are almost equivalent to a rook. In the endgame section, we show that these pawns, if they both reach the 6th rank, are even stronger than a rook!

35.Bc5 b3; 36.Bxf8 bxc2; 37.Bxa3. White has given up the rook, but has a bishop for two pawns, and the pawns do not appear to be strong. Ah, but they are! **37...Qd5!; 38.Kg1?** White naturally wants to break the pin, especially since he was in deep time trouble. 38.Qe3 Nf4; 39.h3! was best. I am sure Friedman would have tried 36...h6 here, with an unclear position. If White doesn't preserve some pawns, it will be hard to win the endgame.

38...Qd1+; 39.Qf1 e4!; 40.Ne5 e3; 41.Nf3 e2; 42.Qe1. White covers all the promotion squares, but in the end it costs him a piece. **42...Qd3?!** Good enough, but there was a simpler win. 42...Nf4 followed by ...Nd3 would have finished White off immediately. **43.Qb4 Qe3+; 44.Kg2 Nf4+; 45.Kg3 e1Q+; 46.Qxe1 Ne2+; 47.Kg2 Qxa3.** White resigned. A thrilling contest to the end!

Aggressive Defense

Aggressive defense abandons all attempts at stopping the enemy attack, instead launching an attack with maximum speed and force. Often material will be sacrificed, as in the following example, from a game Zinn vs. Matulovic, Maribor 1967.

1.e4 c5; 2.Nf3 e6; 3.d4 cxd4; 4.Nxd4 Nc6; 5.Nc3 Qc7; 6.Be3 a6; 7.Bd3 Nf6; 8.0-0 Bb4; 9.f4 Bc5.

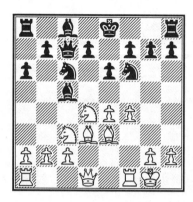

The White knight is attacked. It could be passively defended by Nce2 and c3, but White chose instead the aggressive continuation. Because White's position was not bad, this was not a desperate philosophical defense but is rather an active defense justified by a good position with a lead in development and control of the center.

10.Nf5! The kingside attack proved effective. **10...Qb6; 11.Nxg7+ Kf8; 12.Bxc5+ Qxc5+; 13.Kh1 Kxg7** did leave White down a piece, but the Black forces are useless on the home rank, and development is far in the future. In fact, it is not until move thirty that either rook or the bishop leave the back rank, and that move loses a rook.

14.e5 Nd5; 15.Ne4 Qe7; 16.Qh5 f5; 17.Nd6 Rf8; 18.g4 Kh8; 19.gxf5 exf5; 20.c4 Nc7; 21.Bxf5 Ne6; 22.Rf3 Ncd4; 23.Bxh7 Nxf3; 24.Be4+ Kg7; 25.Qxf3 Nxf4; 26.Rg1+ Kh8; 27.Qg4 a5; 28.Bf5 b5; 29.Qxf4 Qh7; 30.Qe4 Rxf5; 31.Qxa8 Rf8; 32.cxb5. Black could resign here, as White's passed pawns on both flanks are unstoppable.

32...a4; 33.Nxc8 Qc2; 34.Qg2 Qxg2+; 35.Rxg2 Rxc8; 36.Rd2 Rc1+; 37.Kg2 Rc5; 38.b6 Rb5; 39.Rd6 Rxb2+; 40.Kg3 Kg8; 41.h4 Kf8; 42.h5. Black resigned.

PAWNS PROTECT THE KING

> *I know at Chesse a Pawn before the King is ever much played upon.*
>
> — Bacon (1604)

Pawns which lie in front of the king form a protective barrier. That's why such pawns often become the target of enemy invasions. When Black castles kingside, sacrifices at f7, g7, and h7 are very common. In this chapter we will examine typical exploitation of each of these vulnerable squares.

Vulnerability of f7

The king can be drawn into a vulnerable position in the center by means of a sacrifice at f7, so Black must always be on guard against this threat. In a game between Acs and Sukharisingh at the December 1996 edition of the monthly Grandmaster Internationals in Budapest, we see Black's monarch executed by swarming White forces. We pick up the game after the first two dozen moves.

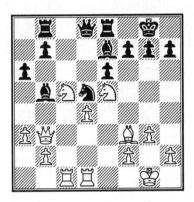

White boldly sacrificed both knights to bring the king to the center of the board. **25.Nxf7 Kxf7; 26.Nxe6 Kxe6; 27.Re1+**.

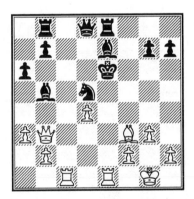

The king cannot retreat to the d-file without losing the knight at d5, with check.

27...Kf6; 28.Bxd5 Bd6. Black might have tried 28...g6. **29.Qf3+ Kg5; 30.Bf7!?** White further restricts the area around the Black king.

30...Rxe1+; 31.Rxe1 g6; 32.h4+ Kh6; 33.h5 Bd7? Black should have tried 33...Qg5, though White is better after capturing at g6. 33...Bc6 34.d5 Bd7 is a bit better than the game, since White cannot use d5 for the queen. Still, 35.Kg2 Kg7; 36.Be6 keeps the pressure on. If Black captures, then a check from c3 is possible.

34.hxg6 hxg6; 35.Qd5 Bc6; 36.Qe6 Kg7; 37.Qxg6+ Kf8. Black resigned.

Well Defended f7

We join the game Banas vs. Kouatly, Trnava 1986, after 19 moves. White sees that all the pieces are ready to attack except the rook at h1. He invests a rook to weaken the enemy king position and bring the other rook into the fight with a check. Black's defense is more than adequate, however. It is true that the rook at a8 and bishop at c8 are once again prisoners. There is a hidden resource, however. The pawn at d7 guards e6, creating the defensive possibility of ...Re6. This reduces the effect of a bishop check at c4. Black has enough material to give some back. It is important that the queen and knight are in the neighborhood, if not in the most useful positions.

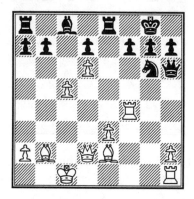

20.Rxf7? Kxf7; 21.Bc4+ Re6!; 22.Rf1+ Ke8. The king is now safe. **23.Bxe6 dxe6.**

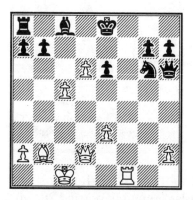

The f7-square is still vulnerable, but White is attacking only with queen and rook, and Black can survive with the help of the bishop at c8, which is now free to move. **24.Qf2 Kd8; 25.Bd4 e5; 26.Qf7 Bd7; 27.Qg8+ Be8; 28.d7 Kxd7.**

The Black position is ugly, but the attack on the bishop at e5 slows White's momentum. The extra knight and pawn are too much, and after a few checks White gives up.

29.Qd5+ Kc8; 30.Qe6+ Bd7; 31.Qg8+ Kc7; 32.Qd5 Rd8. White resigned.

Vulnerability of g7

A queen and dark squared bishop are a potent weapon against the castled king. The bishop can be sacrificed at g7, leaving Black extremely vulnerable on the dark squares. We see it at work after just 17 moves in Spassky vs. Korensky, Sochi 1973.

18.Bxg7 Kxg7; 19.Qf6+ Kf8; 20.Rhf1. The attack is raging, and Black cannot erect a suitable defense.

20...Rc7; 21.Nxd5 exd5; 22.e6 Qxa2; 23.e7+ Kg8; 24.Qxf7+ Kh8; 25.e8Q+ Rxe8; 26.Qxe8+ Kg7; 27.Qe5+ Kg8; 28.Qg5+. Black resigned.

Well Defended g7

To defend against an attack based on g7, you should try to keep your pieces in positions where they can get back to the kingside. Rooks on the back rank are not of much help. In Tseshkovsky vs. Rajkovic, Yugoslavia 1994, Black correctly judged that the control of e5 would present the necessary path. We pick up the game after 18 moves.

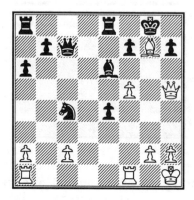

19.Bxg7 Kxg7; 20.Qg5+ Kf8; 21.Qh6+ Ke7. If the White rook were at d1 instead of a1, then 22.f6+ would finish matters. This shows that the sacrifice was not properly prepared.

22.fxe6. 22.Rad1 loses to 22...Bd7!; 23.Qg5+ f6; 24.Qg7+ Kd8; 25.Qxf6+ Kc8. **22...Qe5!;** This is the resource White missed, probably counting on 22...fxe6?; 23.Rf7+! Kxf7; 24.Qxh7+ where White wins. **23.Rxf7+ Kd6; 24.Rb1.** There is nothing better.

24...Rxe6; 25.Qh3 Re7; 26.Rf5 Qe6; 27.g4 e3. White resigned.

Vulnerability of h7

At the edge of the board, the poor h7-pawn never gets much support. At first it has a mighty rook as a guardian, but after castling, the rook is far away at f8, while the king at g8 must worry about his own safety and can't provide much defense to the pawn. The king is more concerned with the h7-square than the loyal soldier that occupies it. In Sakharov vs. Cherepkov, Soviet Union 1969, White's pieces seem far away from the Black king, and the rook has just been brought to d6 at move 34 to provide additional defense along the rank. What could possibly go wrong?

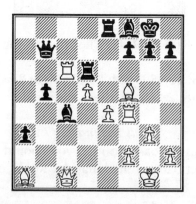

35.Bxh7+!! Kxh7; 36.Rxd6 Bxd6; 37.Rh4+. Black resigned, because of 37...Kg8 38.Rh8+!! Kxh8; 39.Qh6+! Kg8; 40.Qxg7#. This is only one of many mating patterns. You'll find more in the chapter on mating positions.

Well Defended h7

In this position after move 19 of Cooper vs. Gufeld, Hastings Challengers 1992, White attempts, to capitalize on the fact that Black seems to have only a rook available for direct defense, and the rook is not able to cope with the invading flank pawns. The investment of a piece is logical, though no clear win can be calculated. Black has a very important resource, however. The rook can come to a6 and then defend along the open rank.

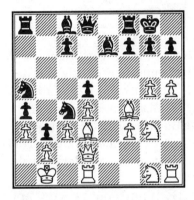

The sacrifice was followed up by a vigorous pawn advance.

20.Bxh7+!? Kxh7; 21.g6+ Kg8! Black cannot get greedy and allow the king to be lured to open ground, as then White's counterplay on the h-file can be deadly. **22.Qh2 Bg5.** Black stares down one of the attackers.

23.h6 gxh6; 24.g7 Re8!

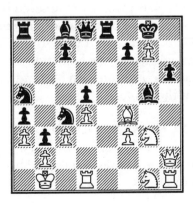

This quiet move leaves the enemy pawn alone. It does no harm, and helps protect the king by keeping more dangerous pieces off of g7.

25.N1e2 Ra6! Lateral defense. Black now has the situation under control. **26.Rdg1 Qf6; 27.Ne4!? dxe4; 28.Bxg5 Qxf3; 29.Bxh6.**

The White bishop is in the way, but given one move White will remove it from the h-file and threaten Qh8#. Black must act quickly and decisively.

29...Nxa3+!; 30.Ka1. The knight cannot be captured. 30.bxa3 loses instantly to 30...Qd3+ 31.Ka1 Qc2. **30...Qd3!** Black threatens a deadly smothered mate with ....Qb1+ and ...Nc2#. **31.Nf4 Nc2+!** If Black sacrifices the queen, then White can now return the favor, since the queen covers c2 from h2. **32.Kb1 Na3+; 33.Ka1 Nc2+; 34.Kb1 a3!** After a repetition to ease the time pressure, Black finishes the job by marching the a-pawn down the board.

35.Nxd3 a2+; 36.Kc1 a1Q+. White could resign, but probably this was played in severe time pressure so the game stumbles past the time control.

37.Kd2 Nc4+; 38.Ke2 exd3+; 39.Kf3 Bb7+; 40.Kg3 Rg6+; 41.Bg5 Re3+; 42.Kg4 Rxg5+; 43.Kf4 Re4+. White resigned.

COUNTERATTACK IN THE CENTER

The notion that a flank attack is properly countered by action in the center is not new. Countless games have demonstrated the wisdom behind this simple idea. Whenever you are attacked on a flank, you should turn to the center for countermeasures, since if they are available they will usually turn the tide in your favor. In the next game, we see the flank advance lead to a position with a stranded pawn, rooted to its square, while White enjoys a party in the center.

SUETIN - BONDAREVSKY
Soviet Championship, 1963

1.e4 e5; 2.Nf3 Nc6; 3.Bb5 a6; 4.Ba4 d6; 5.0-0 g5? This is a premature attack. Later we will see the central counterattack used against a flank operation which has a bit more support.

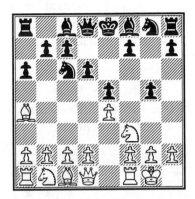

The opening is Spanish Game. Seeing the White king nestled on the kingside, Black launches a pawn storm. White properly reacts by operating the center.

6.d4! g4. Black is committed. **7.Bxc6+ bxc6; 8.Ne1 exd4; 9.Qxd4.** The centralized queen is powerful, and can reach other useful squares.

9...Qf6; 10.Qa4 Ne7; 11.Nc3 Bd7; 12.Qa5 Kd8; 13.Nd3 Bg7.

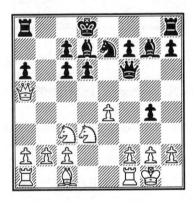

As Suetin himself pointed out, White has been making a lot of queen and knight moves, while leaving the queenside undeveloped. This violation of opening principles is justified, even though Black is almost fully developed and ready for the middlegame. Black's attack is not far advanced, but White must still keep the initiative. The counter-attack, launched in the center at move six, continues.

14.e5! Qf5. Black cannot even think of capturing the pawn and opening up the d-file. **15.Re1 d5; 16.Ne2 Ng6; 17.Ng3 Qe6; 18.Bg5+ Kc8; 19.Nc5 Qe8.** Black's forces have been driven back, and White controls the play in the center and on the queenside. He now eliminates the enemy bishop at g7 and then wins the a-pawn, obtaining a decisive advantage.

20.Nh5! Rg8; 21.Nxg7 Rxg7; 22.Nxa6 Ra7; 23.Be3 Rxa6; 24.Qxa6+ Kd8; 25.Bg5+ Ne7; 26.Bf6 Rg6; 27.a4 Bc8; 28.Qd3 Kd7; 29.a5 Bb7; 30.b4 Ng8; 31.c4 Qe6; 32.Qd4 Ke8; 33.b5 cxb5; 34.cxb5 Ne7; 35.Qc5 Qd7; 36.Rac1. Black resigned.

Attacks are not always premature, but a central counterattack against a flank operation is generally the correct prescription anyway. The next game is one of the most famous examples of the central counterattack.

ALEKHINE-BOOK
Margate, 1938

1.d4 d5; 2.c4 dxc4; 3.Nf3 Nf6; 4.e3 e6; 5.Bxc4 c5; 6.0-0 Nc6; 7.Qe2 a6; 8.Nc3 b5; 9.Bb3 b4. Opening is Queen's Gambit Accepted.

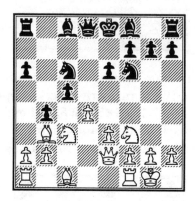

Black's flank operation is understandable. If the knight moves, then White loses control of d5. Alekhine reacts by seizing the opportunity to operate in the center.

10.d5! Na5. 10...exd5; 11.Nxd5 Nxd5; 12.Rd1 followed by e3-e4 gives a clear advantage to White.

11.Ba4+ Bd7; 12.dxe6 fxe6; 13.Rd1. Black still has the threat at c3, and may as well execute the capture, because at least then the knight cannot help in the attack. **13...bxc3.** Or 13...Be7; 14.Bxd7+ Nxd7; 15.Ne5 Ra7; 16.Qh5+ g6; 17.Nxg6 hxg6; 18.Qxh8+ Bf8; 19.Qg8! The invading queen inflicts a lot of damage in a solo performance.

14.Rxd7!! Nxd7; 15.Ne5 Ra7; 16.bxc3 Ke7. A strange looking move, but the alternatives are not pleasant. This game is analyzed in greater detail in *World Champion Combinations*, but I'll add one line against the move most recommended by computer programs. After 16...Qh4; 17.f4 c4; 18.g3 White has just one pawn for the rook, but Black must give back at least an exchange at d7, and White need not hurry to take it. The Black king is trapped in the center.

17.e4! Nf6; 18.Bg5. The deadly Qh5+ is in the air. **18...Qc7; 19.Bf4 Qb6; 20.Rd1.** The complete domination of the center, and the total lack of counterplay from Black, gives White adequate compensation for the rook even though there is only one pawn in hand. **20...g6.** All roads lead to disaster. 20...Nb7; 21.Nc4; 20...Ra8; 21.Bg5 Rd8; 22.Nd7 Qc7; 23.e5 or 20...Rg8; 21.Bg5 h6; 22.Qh5 g6; 23.Nxg6+ Rxg6; 24.Qxg6 hxg5; 25.e5! Nd5; 26.Qe8#.

21.Bg5 Bg7; 22.Nd7! Rxd7; 23.Rxd7+ Kf8; 24.Bxf6 Bxf6; 25.e5 and Black resigned. The conclusion might have gone 25...Qb1+; 26.Rd1 Qf5; 27.exf6 Qxf6; 28.Qxa6 Qxc3; 29.Qxe6 h5; 30.Qc8+ Kg7; 31.Qc7+ Kh6; 32.Qf4+ Kh7; 33.Rd7+.

In these games White's position was by no means hopeless when the counterattack was launched. We turn next to those dire, but all too frequent situations where we find ourselves in a hopeless mess, but must find some way to survive.

SAVING LOST POSITIONS

When your back is to the wall it is easy to give up hope, but there are many miracles to be found. Some are swindles, tactical traps that you spring on overconfident and careless opponents. Others involve the sort of resolve and ingenuity that only the human spirit can bring to the game. Machines cannot make use of psychological factors. They give no credit to a variation just because it would be described by a human as complicated. We saw in the game Colias vs. Friedman that complications can lead easily lead the superior side astray.

In the book *Saving Lost Positions*, Grandmaster Leonid Shamkovich and I presented many cases of resourceful play, leading a player out of the depths to the safety of a draw, or sometimes a win! My very favorite example (not counting those where I was the lucky survivor!) was played by Garry Kasparov at the 1982 tournament in Bugojno, Yugoslavia, against Jan Timman, a future World Championship challenger. Both players would rather forget this game out of embarrassment, but I won't let them, because it is simply too instructive! I witnessed this fascinating struggle.

TIMMAN - KASPAROV
Bugojno, 1982
1.d4 Nf6; 2.c4 g6; 3.Nc3 Bg7; 4.e4 d6; 5.f3 0-0; 6.Be3 Nc6; 7.Nge2 a6; 8.Qd2 Rb8; 9.h4 b5; 10.h5 e5; 11.d5 Na5; 12.Ng3 bxc4; 13.0-0-0 Nd7; 14.hxg6 fxg6; 15.Nb1 Rb5?

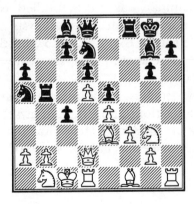

The opening is King's Indian Defense. Kasparov just missed the following tactics, which cost him the rook at b5. He was counting on meeting 16.Na3 with 16...Nc5, but Timman has a stronger move.

16.b4 cxb3. If the knight retreats then the a-pawn comes to a4 and traps the rook. **17.Bxb5 c5; 18.dxc6 axb5; 19.Qd5+.** 19.cxd7 Nc4; 20.dxc8Q Qxc8; 21.axb3? Nxd2+; 22.Kxd2! would have given White a rook and two knights for queen and pawn, in a position where the king could easily be kept safe from harm. **19...Rf7.** 19...Kh8 would have run into a familiar checkmating pattern. 20.Rxh7+ Kxh7; 21.Rh1+ Bh6; 22.Bxh6.

20.axb3 Nf8; 21.Qxd6 Qe8. White should now take care to secure the king, but instead tries to find some way to win the game via direct attack. After all, he is up the exchange and two pawns, though one is being returned immediately. **22.Qd8** 22.Kb2! Nxc6; 23.Ne2 was a stronger plan. **22...Qxc6+; 23.Kb2 Qa8!**

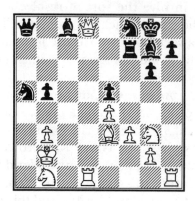

An amazing and unexpected development! Black defends the bishop at c8 and gets ready to attack on the a-file.

24.Rc1 Nc4+!; 25.bxc4 Rd7!; 26.Qe8 bxc4; 27.Nc3 Qc6!; Black is perhaps better now. There is the tremendous threat of ...Rd2+. **28.Kc2 Rd2+.** Here, to everyone's shock and amazement, the players agreed to a draw! Kasparov was just happy to have survived the debacle, and Timman was still befuddled as to how things could have gone so wrong from a winning position. Most analysts consider the position after 29.Kxd2 Qxe8; 30.Nd5 Be6; 31.Rxc4 Bxd5; 32.exd5 Qb5; 33.Rc5 Qb2+; 34.Rc2 Qb4+; 35.Ke2 Qb5+; 36.Kf2 Qxd5! to be about equal, since the queen and pawn should be able to cope with the two rooks.

If you want to see my own greatest Houdini act (or one of them, for I am far too often called upon to salvage positions and extricate myself from a real mess), see the Stalemate Chapter and look at the King's Head Stalemate, which was played in the same year. And if you'd like to see me fall for some of these tricks, take a look at *Development of a Chess Master,* which has many examples of instructive errors I have made.

> *The true sweetness of chess, if it can be sweet, is to see a victory snatched, by some happy impertinence, out of the shadow of apparently irrevocable disaster.*
>
> — H.G. Wells (1898)

If you have a bad position, don't be too miserable. Seek the magic tactic which can save your position! If you manage to swindle your opponent, you can take great pleasure in it. But please, don't rub it in after the game. For if a miracle save brings you great pleasure, the effect on the opponent is almost always the opposite. On conclusion of the game, conduct the post-mortem amicably and try to understand your opponent's foul mood. Among adult players, an offer of a beverage is often considered appropriate.

Fortunately, you won't always find yourself in a hopeless position. Most of the time a small error will simply lead you into an uncomfortable position. The next section will give some tips on how to cope with that unpleasant situation.

EXCHANGE PIECES TO EASE THE DEFENSE

When you are under attack, a lot of enemy guns can be firing at your position. It only makes sense that you should try to reduce the number of attackers, and if you have to exchange a piece of the same value, that is an acceptable price to pay.

White seems to have a strong attack going in Jansa vs. Ilic, Nis 1983. With his 28th move, White advances the pawn to e5, attacking Black's knight. This sacrifices a pawn, but White has strong pressure on the kingside and in the center. White will inevitably get the pawn back, as the pawns at e6 and b6 are weak. Black reacts correctly by exchanging pieces, reducing White's attacking force.

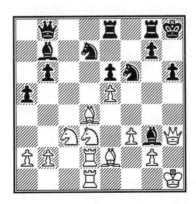

28...Bxe5; 29.Nxe5 Nxe5; 30.Re1 Rd8; 31.Bb5 Nf7; 32.Qxe6. Black now uses a tactical operation to remove a pair of rooks and minor pieces from the board.

32...Rge8; 33.Bxe8 Rxe8; 34.Qxf7 Rxe1+.

Although the White queen and bishop are still in attacking formation, Black has the initiative and is on the attack. **35.Bg1 Qf4.** White is given time to attack, but nothing can be accomplished.

36.Rd8+ Kh7; 37.Rd4 Qxd4. White resigned.

While it is recommended that you exchange pieces as part of a defensive strategy, note that this only applies when you are at least equal in material. If you are behind in material, exchanges led to endgames where the material advantage has a great deal of influence on the outcome. A shrewd attacker will be content to pick off one of your pawns, and then start trading pieces until a winning endgame is reached.

PROPHYLAXIS

Aron Nimzowitsch, the great Hypermodern player, used the term prophylaxis to refer to taking preventative measures in anticipation of an enemy move. It was not his original idea, and in fact dates back to Philidor in the 18th century. Prophylactic moves are very hard for beginners to understand. They are not made in response to a direct threat. Instead, they lay the groundwork for future defense. This concept is illustrated in a game known as the Mysterious Rook Move game between Kupchick and Capablanca at Lake Hopatong, 1926. We pick it up after White's 20th move.

20...Rh6. This move is intended to prevent White from arranging a kingside break-through with h3 and g4. That is the only purpose of this move, and it is entirely defensive in nature. He tries to infiltrate the kingside, but his efforts are futile. The Black defense will hold, and it is only a matter of time before the assault is turned back.

21.Be1 g6; 22.Bh4 Kf7! More prophylaxis. The f8 rook can be used on the g- or h-file. **23.Qe1 a6.** The counterplay begins. White's kingside attack has fizzled. Black is ready to win on the opposite flank.

24.Ba4 b5; 25.Bd1 Bc6; 26.Rh3 a5; 27.Bg5 Rhh8; 28.Qh4 b4; 29.Qe1 Rb8; 30.Rhf3 a4; 31.R3f2 a3. Black is destroying the base of the pawn chain, as recommended in the pawn structure section.

32.b3 cxb3; 33.Bxb3 Bb5; 34.Rg1 Qxc3; 35.Qxc3 bxc3; 36.Rc2 Rhc8; 37.Bh4 Bd3; 38.Rcc1 Rxb3; 39.axb3 a2. White resigned, not wanting to suffer the likes of 40.Ra1 Bb1; 41.Be1 c2; 42.Bd2 Ba3; 43.Bc1 Bxc1; 44.Rxc1 Rc3; 45.Kg1 Rd3; 46.Kf2 Rd1 wins. A most amusing final position!

OVERPROTECTION

A special form of prophylaxis is overprotection. This is another concept that was refined by Nimzowitsch. It was the cornerstone of his defensive philosophy. The idea is that if you control an important square, you should reinforce that square. We'll take one of Nimzowitsch's favorite examples, his game against Rubinstein from the Carlsbad tournament of 1911. Black has just played 19...Ne7, retreating from f5.

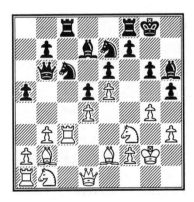

Black has a comfortable game, because the pawn at d4 is an inviting target. If it falls, White's game will quickly collapse. Nimzowitsch applies the principle of over-protection to guard the weakling. **20.Na3!** White has delayed the development of the knight until a strategy is prepared. The knight will be stationed at c2, to overprotect the pawn at d4. **20...Nb4; 21.Nc2 Rxc3; 22.Bxc3 Nxc2; 23.Qxc2.** The knight is no longer at c2 to protect the d-pawn, but Nimzowitsch has a powerful substitute available. **23...Rc8; 24.Qb2!** The pawn will be overprotected by the mighty queen. It is the only significant weakness in White's position, and there is nothing Black can do to overpower it.

24...Bb5; 25.Bxb5 Qxb5; 26.Bd2! Another guard "shows his teeth," as Nimzowitch puts it. **26...Bf8.** An exchange would leave Black with an inferior position as a kingside attack is possible. **27.Rc1 hxg4; 28.hxg4 Rc6; 29.Qa3!** The queen switches from defense to offense, even though she is exposed to attack. **29...Rxc1!** Nimzowitsch had hoped for a chance to part with the lady. 29...Nf5; 30.Rxc6 Bxa3; 31.Rc8+ Kg7; 32.gxf5 with a strong attack, since the bishop will get to f6 via g5.

30.Qxc1. White has the advantage now, though it is just an open file, really, and Black had no difficulty holding the game. **30...Nc6; 31.Bh6 Be7; 32.Bg5 Qe2; 33.Bxe7 Nxe7; 34.Qf4 Qe4.** The queens were exchanged, and the position was eventually drawn.

That covers some broad defensive guidelines. Before we move on to the next topic, there is one important, and often overlooked, piece of advice which you should certainly take to heart.

> ***W****hen protecting a piece, always ask whether it might be captured anyway.*
>
> — Tarrasch

Tarrasch provides the following illustration:

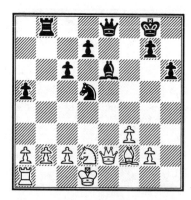

White can defend the b-pawn with **1.Nc4** or **1.Rb1**, but in either case Black can capture it anyway, as after **1...Rxb2!** Any capture at b2 allows the devastating infiltration of the knight at c3, with check, picking off the queen.

We have finished our survey the art of defense. There is of course much more to know, but these guidelines should help you avoid the consequences of inferior or passive positions. Many other defensive ideas are mentioned in other sections of the book. Our next topic is the role of each piece in the middlegame.

MIDDLEGAME ROLE OF EACH PIECE

MIDDLEGAME ROLE OF THE PAWNS

In the middlegame, pawns are generally used to open lines or to harass enemy pieces. They advance purposefully, and some, such as the king's guard, remain home in defensive positions. At all times, preservation of a healthy pawn structure is a consideration, since otherwise the endgames will be nasty, brutish and short.

The advance of a pawn in the center can open up a valuable diagonal or rank. Recall Forgacs vs. Tartakower, examined in the section on Capablanca's Rule. There the advance of a pawn led to a complete destruction of Black's position. Pawns that are in the way of your pieces are expendable, the usual goal being to open up lines. Sometimes, the idea is simply to liberate a square, for use by another piece.

A pawn can easily be sacrificed in the middlegame, and this sets up tactical possibilities on the square that was just vacated. In the next example, a little pawn causes a lot of trouble when supported by a loyal knight. We join Vaganian vs. Short, Skelleftea 1989 after White's 38th move, with time control just over the horizon.

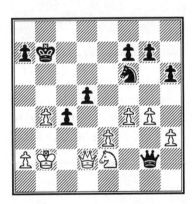

Black has no pieces in attacking position, but after **38...c3+!!** White loses quickly. The game ended in White's resignation after **39.Qxc3 Qxe2+**. If 39.Kxc3, the knight fork 39...Ne4+ wins, while on 39.Nxc3 the queen falls. Three captures, no solutions!

Pawns should only march forward when their advanced positions can be supported long enough for the foot soldiers to accomplish their missions. In a military operation, soldiers invading a beach are supported by gunfire from neighboring positions. Your pawns deserve the same protection. The more pieces the pawns have watching their backs, the better. We'll see many more middlegame strategies for pawns in the section on pawn structure in the Strategy chapter.

MIDDLEGAME ROLE OF THE KNIGHTS

Knight need to attack from short range. They are best stationed in the middle of the board, where they can quickly reach any critical area. A knight at d4, for example, can get to b5, c6, e6, or f5 to help an attack, or retreat to b3, c2, e2, or f3 to assist with the defense. Placing a knight in the center is often unavailable in the opening, as knights in the center are vulnerable to attack. In the middlegame, however, they are more likely to be safe in the center.

Move Knights Forward

– Tranmer

The following position was reached in Ciocaltea vs. Pribyl, Bucharest 1975, after White's 26th move, bringing the queen to e2.

Black loses his nerve here and panics. The rook should have passively moved to d7. White would still have a stronger game, but no immediate win is in sight.

26...g5?; 27.fxg5 f4; 28.Qh5! The bishop at e3 can be sacrificed. **28...Kg8.** This is necessary, to protect the rook. **29.g6! hxg6; 30.Bxg6 Rg7; 31.Rg1!**

White sets a trap. If Black captures the bishop then Bf7 is checkmate.

31...Nxg6; 32.Rxg6 Qa6; 33.Rxg7+. Black resigned. The knight will capture the pawn at e6, with check and mate to follow. Another example of a tremendous knight at d4 is seen in the Bad Bishop section below.

MIDDLEGAME ROLE OF THE BISHOPS

The bishop is usually used in attack during the middlegame. The bishops, if not impeded by their own pawns, easily find open diagonals toward the enemy king. In these cases we have a "good" bishop. In the section on the endgame we will see a related concept of good vs. bad bishop.

GOOD BISHOP

When a bishop can be stationed on a long and unimpeded diagonal, the bishop can be very strong. In Larsen vs. Bednarsky, from the 1967 Havana tournament, the powerful bishop was worth sacrificing a rook for. Here is the situation after 24 moves, with Black just having advanced the f-pawn to f5.

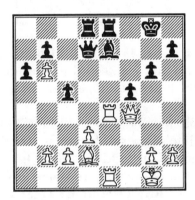

25.Bc3! White offers a whole rook just to get to the key diagonal! **25...fxe4; 26.Qe5 Bf8.** 26...Bd6 loses to 27.Qh8+ Kf7; 28.Qxh7+ Ke6; 29.Rxe4+ Kd5; 30.Qxd7 Rxd7; 31.Rxe8 **27.Qh8+ Kf7; 28.Rf1+ Qf5.** Black has no choice but to give up the queen, but that does not stop the attack. **29.Rxf5+ gxf5; 30.Qf6+ Kg8; 31.Qg5+ Kf7; 32.Qxf5+.** White gobbles up five pawns in a non-stop feast. **32...Kg8; 33.Qg5+ Kf7; 34.Qf6+ Kg8; 35.Qh8+ Kf7; 36.Qxh7+ Ke6; 37.Qxe4+ Kd6; 38.Qxb7 Rd7; 39.Qxa6 Ke6; 40.b7+ Bd6; 41.Qc4+** Black resigned. There was no point in delaying the inevitable until the adjournment session.

> *Bishops may be moved backwards*
>
> – Tranmer

BAD BISHOP

In the middlegame, a bad bishop is one with no scope. A bishop with no more than a couple of legal moves is not able to contribute much to either attack or defense. In Quinteros vs. Panno, Argentinean Championship 1969, Black has misplayed the opening and has a terrible bishop. The knight at d4 dominates the board, arriving on that key squares on White last move.

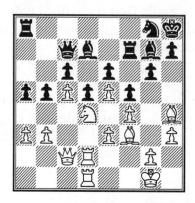

27...Bf8; 28.g4 Qa7; 29.Rc1 b4; 30.a4 Be7; 31.Bxe7 Nxe7; 32.g5. White has exchanged dark squared bishops and can afford to shut down the dark squares. The threat is simply to advance the h-pawn to h5, and infiltrate via the h-file. Black found a clever defense.

32...h5!; 33.gxh6 Rh7. Black will recapture at h6 with the rook. There will be no rapid decisive attack, but White's superior bishop is effective in the long run.

34.Rh2 Qc7; 35.h4 Rxh6; 36.Qg2 Qd8; 37.Kf2 Qg8; 38.Rg1 Qf7; 39.Qh1 Rg8; 40.Rg5 Rg7. It was only a matter of time before White broke through on the kingside. **41.Qf1 Bc8; 42.Qh1 Rgh7; 43.Rh3 Qf8; 44.h5 Qe8; 45.Rh4 Qf8; 46.Qg1 gxh5; 47.Rgxh5 Ba6; 48.Rxh6 Rxh6; 49.Rh5 Rxh5; 50.Bxh5 Qh6; 51.Qg5.**

The cunning bishop often retreats, to take up a new position and carry out an attack. It is easy to misinterpret a bishop retreat as a passive move. For a bishop, every square except the four corners of the board is a pivot square which can be used as a launching pad for a new operation.

We see this idea in action in the game Kasparov vs. Gavrikov, from Frunze 1981.

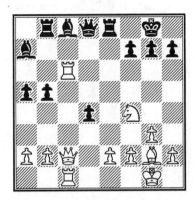

The bishop will travel to d5, then back to f3, where it will pivot first to h5, and then, in sacrifice, to g6. The g6-square is the key to the entire operation.

21.Bd5 Bb6; 22.Qb3 Re7; 23.Bf3 Re5; 24.Bh5! g6; 25.Bxg6!! This final act by the bishop rips apart the enemy position and leads to a forced win. **25...hxg6; 26.Rxg6+ Kf8; 27.Rh6 Ke7; 28.Rcc6 Rf5; 29.Qf3 Bc7; 30.Qe4+ Re5; 31.Ng6+!!** Another piece gives up its life at this critical square. **31...fxg6; 32.Rh7+ Kf8; 33.Qxg6** Black resigned.

THE BISHOP PAIR

A pair of bishops is generally considered better than a bishop and a knight, both in the middlegame and in the endgame. This difference is more obvious in the endgame, as we shall see later. In the middlegame, our current concern, a pair of bishops can work well together, because between them they can cover squares of both colors, while individually they are confined to squares of the same color.

We turn to one very famous game to demonstrate both the principle and its contradiction. This magnificent battle took place at the great tournament in Hastings, 1895, and featured Lasker against Chigorin, one of the top players at the time. It is presented in full, for the drama of bishops against knights is introduced in the very first moves, though it does not end until deep into a long endgame. The notes to this game concentrate only on this aspect of the struggle. The game is rich in other treasures that you can discover by studying it carefully.

LASKER - CHIGORIN
Hastings, 1895

1.d4 d5; 2.Nf3 Bg4; 3.c4 Bxf3; 4.gxf3 Nc6. By transposition we have the Chigorin Defense, a branch of the Queen's Gambit Declined usually reached via 1.d4 d5; 2.c4 Nc6; 3.Nf3 Bg4; 4.Nc3 Bxf3; 5.gxf3. The use of knights against bishops is characteristic of the opening, which was one of Chigorin's favorites.

5.Nc3 e6; 6.e3 Bb4; 7.cxd5 Qxd5; 8.Bd2 Bxc3; 9.bxc3.

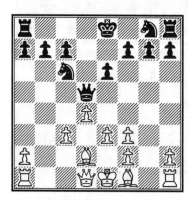

Steinitz described the situation this way: "Chigorin's practical genius is almost privileged to defy theoretical modern principles, but I must consistently dissent. Black's game is inferior; White's two bishops and his compact center will more than neutralize the drawback of the doubled f-pawns. The open files for the rooks ought also to outweigh the isolation of the two rook pawns, which are practically inaccessible to Black's attack.

This game was similar to a game Steinitz himself had played against Chigorin in their 1891/92 match.

9...Nge7; 10.Rg1. Tempting, but advancing in the center would have been a stronger plan. 10.e4 Qh5; 11.Rb1 would have been more logical. Chigorin, who was fond of such maneuvers, would likely have responded 11...Rb8. **10...Qh5; 11.Qb3.** The absence of a bishop at c8 makes itself felt.

11...Nd8; 12.Qb5+. Note that the pawn at g7 is taboo, because Black can bring a knight to g6, trapping the rook. 12.Rg3 Qxh2; 13.e4 Qh4; 14.c4 would have been worth a pawn, according to Steinitz.

12...Qxb5; 13.Bxb5+. The exchange of queens is not bad, but we are now in an endgame, and there are so many pawns make it hard to exploit the long range power of the bishops.

13...c6; 14.Bd3 Ng6.

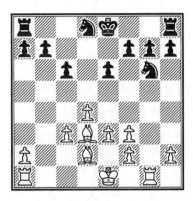

15.f4? This turns the dark squared bishop into a bad bishop. For some reason, Lasker simply refuses to create the ideal pawn structure by advancing the e-pawn. 15.e4 e5; 16.d5 would surely be a bit better for White.

15...0–0; 16.Ke2 Rc8. According to Levenfish, White has a significant advantage, not only because of the bishop pair, but also thanks to the strong pawn center. However, Lasker does not find the correct plan. He concentrates on the kingside, where the knight at g6 is sufficient to defend against the threats, aided by a timely ...f5. Instead, he could have secured a strong position by repositioning his bad bishop to a more useful diagonal.

17.Rg3 17.Bc1 c5; 18.Ba3 b6; 19.f5 exf5; 20.Bxf5 Rc7; 21.Rad1 when the central pawns threaten to advance. This is the right way to play the position for White. Both bishops are stronger than the horses. **17...c5; 18.Rag1** White should be doing something about the doubled pawns by advancing to f5.

18...c4; 19.Bc2 f5!

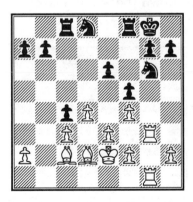

This strong move shuts down the bishop pair. Although Black's pawns look weak, it is actually the weakness of White's pawn structure that is made permanent.

20.Bc1 Rf7; 21.Ba3 Rc6; 22.Bc5 Ra6; 23.a4 Nc6; Chigorin repositions the knights to more effective squares. **24.Rb1 Rd7; 25.Rgg1 Nge7; 26.Rb2 Nd5; 27.Kd2 Ra5?** A waste of time, but in the closed position it does not lead to anything terrible. Some commentators recommend 27...Nf6 intending to bring the other knight to d5, but it is too slow. 28.f3 Ne7; 29.Rb4 wins a pawn.

28.Rgb1 b6; 29.Ba3 g6; 30.Rb5 Ra6! Black admits the earlier error. Pride should never stand in the way of a correct move! **31.Bc1 Nd8; 32.Ra1 Nf7; 33.Rbb1.**

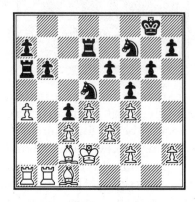

33...Nd6? This is an error, because it gives White a chance to break in the center. Black had a strong move. 33...g5!; 34.fxg5 Nxg5; 35.Bb2 Ne4+; 36.Bxe4 fxe4 would have been a good endgame for Black, despite the weak pawns. The knight is on a great square, and the bishop has no useful function. Steinitz points out that Black will continue by bringing the rook to g7 with a winning attack.

34.f3 Nf7; 35.Ra3 g5. Too late. **36.Ke2!** 36.fxg5 Nxg5; 37.Ke2 Rg7 would have placed the White kingside in danger. **36...gxf4; 37.e4 Nf6; 38.Bxf4 Nh5; 39.Be3 f4!** The pawns at f4 and c4 shut down the White bishops, at least temporarily. **40.Bf2 Ra5!;** Black overprotects the e5-square. **41.Rg1+ Kf8.**

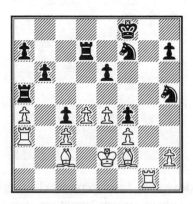

Chigorin had anticipated this position.

42.Raa1. 42.e5 b5; 43.Bxh7 allows 43...Nxe5!! 44.Rg8+ Kf7; 45.dxe5 b4! 46.cxb4 Rxe5+; 47.Kf1 Nf6!; **42...e5.** The game quiets down for a bit as the players search for plans.

43.Rab1 Ng7; 44.Rb4 Rc7; 45.Bb1 Ne6; 46.Rd1 Ned8; 47.Rd2 Nc6; 48.Rb5. White finally gets some action going. **48...Rxa4; 49.dxe5 Nfxe5; 50.Bh4 Rg7; 51.Kf2 Rg6; 52.Rdd5.**

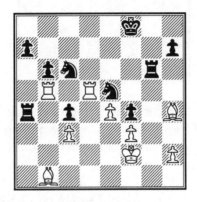

The bishops are pathetic, while the knights dominate the enemy rooks. **52...Ra1.** 52...Rh6 would have been more effective, as Steinitz pointed out, even though Koblentz, a master trainer, claimed that the move Chigorin played was best. 53.Bg5 Rxh2+; 54.Kf1 Ra1; 55.Bxf4 Rxb1+! 56.Rxb1 Rh1+; 57.Kf2 Rxb1; 58.Bxe5 Nxe5; 59.Rxe5 Rc1 and Black should win the endgame.

53.Bd8 Nd3+; 54.Bxd3 cxd3; 55.Rxd3? White has a resource in 55.Bc7! Ra2+; 56.Kf1 Rgg2; 57.Rxd3 Rxh2; 58.Kg1. Steinitz claims that it is not clear that Black can win. 58...Rag2+; 59.Kf1 Rc2; 60.Kg1 doesn't get anywhere. **55...Rag1.** The threat of mate at g2 brings victory. **56.Rf5+ Ke8; 57.Bg5 R6xg5.** White Resigned.

MIDDLEGAME ROLE OF THE ROOKS

Rooks belong on open files. If there is only one open file, rooks should be doubled on that file. That's most of what you need to know about the use of rooks in the middlegame. Even when a file seems to be inaccessible, there are ways of cracking it open, as Hennings demonstrated against Hamann at the 1967 tournament in Harrachov.

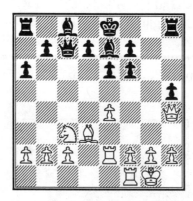

White has just played Re2, clearly intending to double rooks. To what end, since the e-file seems shuttered forever. Black properly anticipates an eventual Nd5 and opening of the file, and slides the king off the dangerous line. However, this does not deter White from carrying out his plan.

14...Kd8; 15.Nd5!! exd5; 16.exd5 d6; 17.Rfe1 Bg4; 18.f3. White does not mind the slight weakening of his king's position. **18...Qc5+; 19.Kh1 Bxf3.** This is an attempt to get some counterplay on the diagonal after 20.gxf3 Qxd5, but White keeps the focus on the open file.

20.Rxe7! Bxd5; 21.Qxf6 Rg8; 22.Be4! This blocking move is available because of White's control of the file. **22...Kc8; 23.Qf5+ Be6; 24.Bxb7+ Kd8; 25.Qxc5 dxc5; 26.R7xe6! fxe6.** Black resigned before White had time to capture at a8.

There are however a few more tips that are less obvious. Rooks can also make use of ranks, using a device known as a **rook lift**. We examine a game Potocnik vs. Lampic, from the 1994 Ljubljana Open.

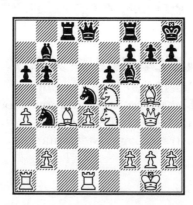

White brings the took to the h-file not from d1, but from a1. The rook lift brings it to a3, then h3. On the h-file, it delivers the final blow in an overpowering attack. The rook at d1 remains to stand guard over the pawn at d4, which anchors the center. This plan is also another example of Capablanca's rule. White has a lot of force massed on the kingside, but not enough to win as things stand.

18.Ra3 Rc7. 18...Be7 threatens to fork the bishop and knight by advancing the pawn to f6. 19.Rh3 is still strong. 19...f6; 20.Bh6! g5; 21.Qh5 and Black can resign. 19...Bxg5; 20.Nxg5 Kg8; 21.Nxe6! White wins a lot of material. 21...fxe6; 22.Qxe6+ Kh8; 23.Ng6#.

19.Rh3 Bxg5; 20.Nxg5 Nf6. 20...h6 21.b3 leaves Black at a loss for a good move. The overprotection of f7 by the queen leads to a loss of material. 21...Qf6; 22.Ngxf7+ Rfxf7; 23.Rf3! **21.Bxe6 Nxg4.** Accepting the queen sacrifice leads to mate, but there was no surviving the position in any case. 21...Bd5; 22.Qh4 h6; 23.Ngxf7+ Rfxf7; 24.Nxf7+ Rxf7; 25.Bxf7 Bxf7 was relatively best, but the rooks and pawns are much better than the three minor pieces.

22.Ng6+ Kg8; 23.Rxh7. Black resigned. Rooks can also be sacrificed to undermine the enemy king position or center. We'll see examples of those in the chapter on sacrifices.

MIDDLEGAME ROLE OF THE QUEEN

Should the queen take up a position in the middle of the board? Opinions differ greatly. Tisdall, for example, holds that the queen belongs in the middle of the board whenever that is feasible. Traditional scholars warn against placing the queen in the center because then it is vulnerable to attack from enemy forces. The classic conflict between piece activity and exposure is seen in this dynamic. Mikhail Tal shows us the danger of the queen in the center in his game as Black against Gradus from the 1953 Latvian Championship.

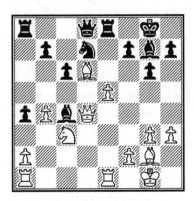

White has just brought the queen to d4 to protect the pawn at e5. The bishop at c4 is now attack. There are three pieces attacking it, and three defending it. It looks like a strong move. But the queen at d4 is vulnerable to two threats. Black can capture the queen if the knight and bishop get out of the way. In addition, if Black has a knight at e5 instead of the White pawn, there is the threat of a discovered attack on the queen with ...Nf3+.

18...Nxe5!; 19.Rxe5. 19.Bxe5 Qxd4; 20.Bxd4 Bxd4; 21.Rxe8+ Rxe8; 22.Rc1 Bxc3; 23.Rxc3 Re1+; 24.Kh2 Bxa2 is an easy win for Black. **19...Rxe5; 20.Bxe5 Qxd4; 21.Bxd4 Bxd4.** White resigned.

Kosten, on the other hand, insists that the queen should be placed behind pawns, to keep her safe. Perhaps the wisest policy is to bring the queen as close to the center as you can provided she has a healthy escort of pawns in front of her.

MIDDLEGAME ROLE OF THE KING

King safety must never be neglected in the middlegame. Most of the successful attacks we have seen in this book, and indeed in most games, are due to an insecure king position. Capablanca's rule forces us to keep a sufficient number of defenders around whenever there are enemy pieces in the neighborhood.

On the other hand, and it seems that in the Royal Game there is always another hand, a bold king may sometimes be a decisive asset. Consider the following fascinating duel between Karpov and Alexander Zaitsev (Not Igor, his future trainer) at the 1970 tournament in Kuibyshev. On the 15th move, White offered up a knight at f7, and Black responded with a check, moving the bishop from an attacked position at d6 to an attacking position at g3.

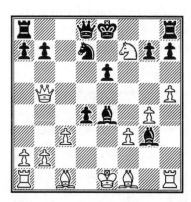

16.Ke2. Every great journey begins with a single step. **16...d3+; 17.Ke3 Qf6; 18.Kxe4.** Fortune favors the brave! The king is actually fairly safe in this exposed position, because Black's pieces are not in position to attack.

18...Qxf7; 19.Rh3 a6; 20.Qg5 h6? This leads to defeat, and was the result of tactical misappraisal of the variation 20...e5! 21.Rxg3 Nc5+; 22.Ke3 0-0; 23.Rh3 Rad8; 24.Bd2 Ne4! If White captures the knight, then Black will quickly deliver checkmate. This is a long way down the road, and many strong players would miss it. Instead, Karpov is given a chance to recover. The King quickly retreats to a safe haven.

21.Qe3 e5; 22.Kxd3 Bf4; 23.Qg1 0-0-0; 24.Kc2 Bxc1; 25.Rxc1 Qxa2; 26.Rh2 Rhf8; 27.Rd2 Qa4+; 28.Kb1.

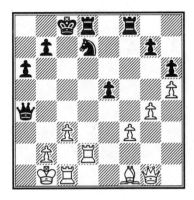

The game has quieted down, with the king safe at home after a long and perilous journey. Karpov used his considerable technique to squeeze out a win at move 71.

WEAKNESSES

An attack is more likely to be successful if the target is weak. In chess, weaknesses take many forms. There are structural weaknesses, involving holes in the pawn chain. We examined these in the section on Pawn Structure. We find positional weaknesses, where our pieces lack coordination or have limited mobility. A third type of weakness is the lack of sufficient defensive force, and this is a cause of much ruin. These latter two types are the subject of the present chapter.

PROVOKING WEAKNESSES

A strong opponent will not voluntarily weaken the position, so you need to find ways to provoke weaknesses. In the opening, the most vulnerable point in the enemy position is at f7(f2). How can we weaken that square? If Black has already advanced the d-pawn, we can use a pawn sacrifice at e6 under some circumstances. This lures the pawn from f7 to e6, exposing the Black king. The same idea can be seen in the middlegame. Any piece can be used for this purpose. In Kindermann vs Robatsch, from Trnava 1987, we see one of the finest examples of this sacrifice.

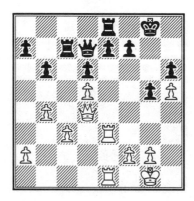

This is a fantastic example of the sacrifice at e6. It is very deep, so deep that none of the computer programs I fed it to could solve it in any reasonable amount of time. We humans can calculate it more easily, because Black's position is so static that there are few reasonable candidate moves.

26.Re6!! fxe6; 27.Qe4 e5. 27...exd5; 28.Qg6+ Kh8; 29.Qxh6+ Kg8; 30.Re6. 27...Kh8; 28.Qg6 exd5; 29.Qxh6+ is the same as the capture at d5 on move 27. **28.Qg6+.** The moves are now forced.

28...Kh8; 29.Qxh6+ Kg8; 30.Qxg5+ Kh7; 31.Qg6+ Kh8; 32.Qh6+ Kg8; 33.Re3 Qg4; 33...e6 34.Rg3+ Qg7; 35.Rxg7+ Rxg7; 36.dxe6 Rge7; 37.Qg6+ Kh8; 38.h6 leaves Black in complete agony, with no useful moves. White will simply advance the g-pawn.

34.Rg3 Qxg3; 35.fxg3 Rf8; 36.Qg6+ Kh8; 37.g4 Rc4; 38.g5 Rcf4; 39.Qh6+ Kg8; 40.g6. Black resigned.

MAKE SURE YOUR PIECES ARE MOBILE

An advantage in space also restricts the movement of enemy forces. The side with less mobility cannot maneuver pieces into useful positions. This makes it easy for White to build and exploit positional advantages. In a correspondence game between Bailey and Johnson, Black obtained a miserable position where the pieces could barely breathe.

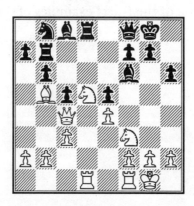

In this position Black has no useful moves. White can inflict serious damage at f6 by capturing the knight at d7 and then taking the bishop.

18...Nb8. There isn't much choice. 18...Qd6; 19.Rd3 gives Black problems on the d-file, for example 19...Be7; 20.Rfd1 Bf8; 21.Nh4 Kh8; 22.Nf5 Qe6; 23.Nde7! Qxc4; 24.Bxc4 g6; 25.Nd6 Bxe7; 26.Nxb7 Bxb7; 27.Rxd7 Rxd7; 28.Rxd7. **19.Nxf6+ gxf6; 20.Rxd8 Qxd8; 21.Qe2!** This quiet move is effective because Black still has no useful mores. White will reclaim the d-file and work on the weak squares on the kingside.

21...Bd7; 22.Rd1 Qe7; 23.Nh4. Black must cope with the unpleasant fact that the bishop at d7 is the crucial defender, but it can be removed at a moment's notice and there is no way to preserve it.

23...Kh7; 24.Qh5 Rc7. 24...Bxb5 lets White win brilliantly with 25.Nf5 Qf8; 26.Rd8!! A rook lift ends the game quickly anyway. **25.Rd3 c4; 26.Nf5 Qf8; 27.Rh3.** Black resigned.

EXPOSED PIECES

Most pieces have the greatest mobility when they are near the center of the board. On the other hand, pieces that are in center of the board are subject to attack. British theoretician Michael Basman places great emphasis on the need to keep your pieces from becoming too exposed to enemy attacks. An exposed piece may be a piece of lesser value, such as pawn or a mighty queen. Pawns are only exposed if they are unprotected, but the queen is considered exposed whenever she is in a position which might be attacked by enemy forces no matter how much support she has. Other pieces are exposed to a greater or lesser extent depending on what sort of pieces might be attacking them.

We saw an example of an exposed queen in the section on the queen above. Let's now see how the exposure of a rook can allow the opponent opportunities to gain time and seize the initiative. Our example is the end of a game between Ciocaltea and Minic, from Varna 1969.

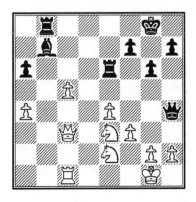

White has two pawns for the exchange. The pawn at c6 is marching forward toward the promotion square. Black is in trouble and should be defending against the threat by moving a rook to c8.

37...Qe7? This cuts off the retreat of the rook, which is exposed and has no room to maneuver. **38.Nd4 Re5.** 38...Rf6; 39.Ng4 is almost humorous, but Black wouldn't find it funny.

39.c6 Bc8; 40.Nd5! Qd6; 41.c7 Rb7; 42.Qc6!

Black cannot afford to exchange queens.

42...Qa3. 42...Qxc6; 43.Nxc6 Re8; 44.Nf6+ shows that even on the back rank Black's rook cannot escape! **43.Qc3 Qa2.** 43...Qxc3; 44.Rxc3 leaves Black powerless against the threat of Nc6.

44.Nc6 Rb2; 45.Qxe5. Black resigned. After one check at g2 there would be no further defense.

The king is the piece which must be protected at all costs, so leaving it exposed is very dangerous. The slow moving king is pretty easy to hunt down. When the king can be flushed out of the castled position, chances of survival are slim. Once in a while, however, his majesty manages to seemingly defy the laws of chess and reach a safe haven.

This position was reached in Spassky vs. Miles, Bugojno 1978. The White king is naked, and the next move allows it to be attacked.

26.Nc5 Bxc3. 26...Rd1+; 27.Ke2 drives the rook back because of the threat of Rc8. This threat effectively prohibits the rook from playing a major attacking role. **27.Ne4 Bd4; 28.c3 Bb6; 29.Ke2!** This bold king move gives Black a lot to worry about in any endgame, because it is closer to the action. If the queens and rooks are removed, White wins easily. The king is actually safer at e2 than on f1, because there are no checks on the f-file.

29...Qd7; 30.Qxd7 Rxd7. The rook and minor piece endgame is inferior, but not hopeless yet. **31.c4 Rd4; 32.Ng5 h6??** A blunder, but Black was in great difficulty anyway. **33.Rc8+** Black resigned, since when the king moves, the knight forks at e6.

Keep Forces On Both Sides Of the Board When Kings Are Castled on the Same Side

One of the things I noticed early on in the career of Gary Kasparov is the tendency for his opponents to let their pieces be bundled up on a side of the board far away from the King.

> *Human life very much resembles a game at Chess: for, as in the latter, while a gamester is too attentive to secure himself very strongly on one side of the board, he is apt to leave an unguarded opening on the other so doth it often happen in life.*
>
> — Fielding

This was brought to my attention in brutal fashion in Graz, Austria, where I was captain of the 1981 United States team at the World Youth Team Championship.

The task of facing rising star Gary Kasparov fell to John Fedorowicz, who was not yet a Grandmaster. With increasing concern I saw John's pieces assemble on the left side of the board. Devastation soon followed.

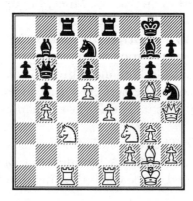

Fedorowicz had just played 25...Qb6, which meant that the queen and bishop at b7 could no longer take part in the defense. White can afford to invest material in the attack, and Kasparov does.

26.exf5! Rxe1+; 27.Rxe1 Bxc3; 28.Re7! Rc4. 28...Nhf6; 29.Qh6 forces mate. 28...Nf8; 29.Be3 Qd8; 30.Rxb7 illustrates the problems Black was facing. Time pressure was mounting here. **29.Qh3 Bc8?;** 29...Nf8; 30.Be3 is decisive, according to Kasparov, but it isn't that simple. After 30...Qd8; 31.Rxb7 Rxb4; 32.Ng5 Rb1+; 33.Bf1 Qc8; 34.Ra7 Qxf5; 35.Qxf5 gxf5; 36.Rxa6 White is only a little better.

30.fxg6 Ndf6; 31.Bxf6 Nxf6; 32.gxh7+ Kf8; 33.h8Q+ Kxe7; 34.Qg7+. Black resigned.

TRANSITION

Most important aspects of the transition period between the middlegame and the endgame lie in the latter area. It is important to anticipate the types of endgames which can arise after various sets of pieces leave the board through exchanges. The better your understanding of endgames, the easier the transition is. For amateur players, this is one of the most difficult periods of a chess game. It takes years to acquire the endgame skills which can provide navigation through this treacherous territory. Precise endgame knowledge is necessary, but there are a few guidelines that can help.

Your first concern must be the pawns. A healthy pawn structure is the key to long life in the endgame. If your pawn structure is sick you soon will be too. You can see the consequences of a weak pawn structure in the Strategy chapter later in the book. Here, we will explore the other common trap, the overestimation of the value of an extra pawn. Knowing which endgames win for the side with one extra pawn is essential to successful endgame play. The key to successful transition is knowing when to exchange pieces. Certain advantages will lead to victory simply removing pieces from the board in a systematic fashion. Our final topic therefore will be how to simplify to win.

MATERIAL ALONE IS NOT ENOUGH!

You will want to exchange pieces and head for an endgame if you have a material advantage, but remember that some pawns are useless, as we saw above in the chapter on pawns. Even the advantage of a whole piece may not be enough in many cases.

White's position is not good. Black has a healthy extra pawn and when the bishop retreats from c4 Black will defend the pawn at d6 by retreating the bishop to d8. White tries a bold sacrifice, even though he is already down a pawn.

43.Nxb6 dxc4; 44.Nxc4 a4; 45.b6 Nd7; 46.b7! White uses the threat of promotion to free the b6-square. 46...Nb8; **47.Nb6 Kg8; 48.Nxa4.** White has two connected passed pawns for the piece, one at b7. That is sufficient compensation.

48...Be8; 49.Nb6 Kf7; 50.Nc8 Bc6. White is able to simplify the position, but the powerful pawn at b7 falls. **51.Nxe7.** 51.Ng6 does not save the game. The bishop cannot stay in place, so some dark squares will be weakened.

That is not enough to save the position. 51...Bg5! will sooner or later get the bishops off the board and create a pawn juggernaut. 52.Nd6+ Kg7; 53.Bf4! Ng4; 54.Bxg5 hxg5; 55.Ne7 Bd7; 56.Kb4 f4; 57.Kc5 (57.Kc3 f3; 58.Kd2 f2; 59.Ke2 Ba4; 60.Ng6 Bc2 and the bishop comes to d3.) 57...f3 58.Ne4 (58.Nc4 f2; 59.Nd2 Ne3; 60.d5 transposes to the main line.) 58...f2 59.Nd2 Ne3; 60.d5 exd5; 61.Nxd5 Nxd5; 62.Kxd5 Bc6+; 63.Kd6 Bxb7; 64.Kc7 White wins back the piece, but the king is too far from the kingside to help stop the pawns. 64...Bf3!; 65.Kxb8 Bxh5; 66.Kc7 g4; 67.Nf1 Kg6; 68.Kd6 Kf5; 69.Ng3+ Kf4!; A nice touch. White is now allowed the luxury of being a piece up, but is hopelessly lost. 70.Nxh5+ Kf3; 71.e6 f1Q White can eventually get the pawn to the promotion square, but the queens will be immediately exchanged and the Black g-pawn promotes. 72.e7 Qd3+; 73.Ke6 Qc4+; 74.Kf6 Qc6+; 75.Kf7 Qd5+; 76.Kf8 Qxh5; 77.e8Q Qxe8+; 78.Kxe8 g3 and Black wins.

51...Kxe7.

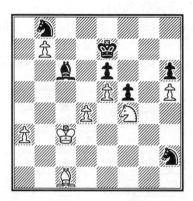

White must now lose the b-pawn, but gets the h-pawn in return. Black still has an extra piece.

52.Ng6+ Kf7; 53.Bxh6 Bxb7; 54.Bf8 Nd7; 55.Bc5 Ng4; 56.Bb4 Ne3; 57.Kd2 Nd5; 58.Ke2 Nxb4; 59.axb4. White has two pawns for the bishop. The pawns are weak, however. Black has a passed pawn too.

59...Nb6; 60.b5 Bd5; 61.Nf4 Bc4+; 62.Kf2 Bxb5; 63.h6 Bd7. More promising was 63...Bc4; 64.Kg3 Nd5; 65.Nxe6 Kg6; 66.Ng7 Bd3; 67.Ne6 Kxh6; 68.Nf4 Be4; 69.Nxd5 Bxd5; 70.Kf4 Kg6.

64.Kg3.

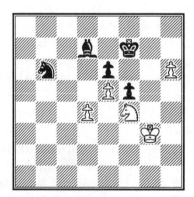

64...Nd5? 64...Kg8! was correct, preventing White's pawn from reaching h7. Black relied too heavily on the material advantage. 65.Kh4 Kh7; 66.Kg5 Nd5; 67.Ng6 f4; 68.Nf8+ Kg8; 69.Nxd7 is refuted by 69...f3! The pawn cannot be stopped. Still, 69.h7+ Kh8; 70.Kg4 Ba4; 71.Ng6+ Kxh7; 72.Nxf4 Nxf4; 73.Kxf4 Bc6 is a simple win for Black. **65.h7!** This move takes indirect control of g6, allowing White's knight to escape.

65...Kg7; 66.Ng6! Kxh7. Black gets the pawn, but White wins back the piece with a check at f8. **67.Nf8+ Kh6; 68.Nxd7 Kg5; 69.Nf8 f4+; 70.Kf3 Kf5; 71.Kf2**.

The game was agreed drawn here, as neither side can make progress.

SIMPLIFY TO WIN!

We have seen that an advantage in the endgame can be material, positional, or both. When we have an advantage, we want to increase the significance of the advantage by exchanging pieces. With fewer pieces on the board, the opponent has fewer resources to use to counteract our advantage. A strong player understands when the advantage is large enough so that it should lead to victory. This is not usually a matter of calculations. A master understands many endgame principles, which will appear in the next section, and can draw a general conclusions by studying the relationship of remaining pieces to the pawns structure.

We see a small advantage tuned into a quick endgame win in Popovic vs. Bellin, from the 1980 edition of the traditional Hastings tournament. White seizes the opportunity to exchange pieces to enter a winning endgame.

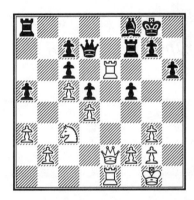

23.Re8! Rxe8; 24.Qxe8 Qxe8; 25.Rxe8 Re7. Black is a bit too cooperative. 25...f4 is still a struggle, if an unpleasant one. **26.Rxe7 Bxe7; 27.f4!** White has insured that the bishop will not be activated. The a-pawn is utterly defenseless, though either the king or the knight will need to undertake a long journey to win it.

27...Bf6; 28.Ne2 Kf7; 29.Kf2 Kg6; 30.Ke3. The d-pawn is now safe. **30...Kh5; 31.a4!** The a-pawn becomes a fixed target. **31...g5; 32.b4!** Black resigned. There is no way to stop White from getting a pawn to a8. For example 32...axb4 33.a5 gxf4+ 34.gxf4 b3 35.a6 b2 36.Nc3 Bh4 37.a7 Be1 38.a8Q Bxc3 39.Qe8+ and checkmate follows.

On the other hand, don't rush to exchange pieces indiscriminately. As we saw in the Philosophical Defense section, this can lead to danger.

THE ENDGAME

To be capable of conducting an endgame to the distant goal with clarity, firmness, and complete familiarity with all its tricks and traps is the sign of the first-class Master.
—*Mieses*

There is no accepted definition of when the endgame begins. In general, it is safe to describe the position has an endgame if neither side has more than four pieces not counting the pawns or the king. The endgame is one of the most studied aspects of chess. Thousands and thousands of pages have been written on the subject. For the purposes of this book, I'm just going to concentrate on some very general, broad principles. There is so much more you need to know. Some advice on acquiring necessary endgame skill is in the training section on studying the endgame.

Our survey will include the possibility for attack in the endgame, the role of each piece, and a selection of positions. We will pay particular attention to the bishop and knight, as minor piece endgames are very sophisticated. Amazing drawing possibilities seem to lurk in every corner. The importance of king position is discussed in the section on the opposition. The need to keep sufficient material on the board to force checkmate is illustrated.

Endgames with kings, pawns, and knights, often are decided by setting zugzwang, forcing your opponent to make a losing move (when passing, if allowed by the rules, would save the game). Knowing when to trade pieces is also essential to good endgame play. We'll see how that tactic can bring victory swiftly and easily. Finally, you'll see some positions which must be mastered by all aspiring chessplayers.

ATTACK IN THE ENDGAME

Direct attacks against the king rarely succeed in the endgame. Capablanca's Rule indicates that the opponent should have sufficient defense unless the pieces are scattered to the corners of the board. If four pieces are needed for successful attack, then the every single piece must be attacking effectively. This can happen only in rare cases when the defense is inadequate.

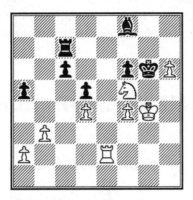

In Mukhutdinov vs. Karatorossian, at the 1995 French festival Cappelle la Grande, White had to find a clever win, because the advantage of an extra pawn is only temporary.

52.Re8! Bxh6. 52...Rf7; 53.Ra8 gives White a decisive advantage on the queenside. 53...Bb4; 54.Rg8+ Kh7; 55.Rc8 wins the c-pawn.

53.Re7 Rc8?? Suicide! 53...Rxe7; 54.Nxe7+ Kf7; 55.Nxc6 Ke6 was the best Black could hope for, though after 56.Nxa5 f5+; 57.Kf3 there isn't much point in continuing. **54.Nh4#.**

> *The endgame is the North Star by which a course may be set in both the opening and middlegame.*
>
> — Collins

There are many different types of endgames. There are endgames without any pawns, and there are many endgames with nothing but pawns. We will briefly survey a sample of endgame positions, but the theory of the endgame occupies many hundreds of pages in specialized books. In fact there is an entire book devoted to the subject of king, rook, and pawn vs. king and rook!

It takes a lifetime to study the endgame, so consider material in this chapter some first steps for the beginner, and some practical tips for the more advanced player. Later on in the book, you'll get advice on how to study the endgame. One thing is for sure, the more time you spend in your endgame study, the better your results will be in competition.

If you are familiar 🔄 with basic endgame theory the *then* you can adjust your opening and middlegame strategies to provide you with the greatest possible opportunities in that crucial stage of the gain. By avoiding weaknesses in your opening pawn structure, you reduce the chance that the opponent will simply exchange pieces in the middle game and leave you with a miserable endgame. In the middlegame, you must not only occupy your thoughts with visions of smashing through unchecked to the enemy king. You must all ways consider the types of endgames might arise if pieces leave the board.

When you see that you can achieve a favorable and perhaps winning endgame by exchanging pieces there is no need to seek out brilliant combinations and swashbuckling attacks.

ENDGAME ROLE OF EACH PIECE

ENDGAME ROLE OF THE PAWNS

The pawns, mere foot soldiers in the opening and middlegame, take on special significance in the endgame, where they can advance up the board and transform themselves into queens, rooks, bishops, or knights.

An extra pawn in the endgame is often all that is needed to deliver victory. One of

> *The theory of the endgame proper is concerned to a large extent with the conversion of an advantage of one pawn into a win.*
>
> — Fine

the most difficult questions in all of chess, however, is whether or not an advantage of a single pawn is sufficient to win. A chess game only has three possible results — win, loss, or draw. You get no credit at all for achieving a drawn game or having extra material. So when is one pawn enough?

That is a question that lies at the heart of endgame theory. It can be answered only by careful and lengthy study. We'll look at an example of pawn promotion, where the extra pawn leads to victory. Then you'll see that in many cases, an extra pawn is utterly useless.

TRY TO PROMOTE YOUR PAWNS!

Amateurs who like to play gambits should keep in mind Mason's words. Each time you give up a pawn you have one less potential Queen. Pawns must be preserved so that they live long enough to be transformed into another, more powerful piece. Think of them as crawling caterpillars who will become flying butterflies.

> *E*very pawn is a
> potential Queen.
>
> — Mason

Remember, too, that you don't have to take a new queen. Sometimes a lesser piece can be more useful. Consider the following position, from a game between two consultants against Capablanca in 1899.

White won by promoting to a knight with **1.e8=N!** On any other promotion, even though it would be discovered check, Black could capture the queen at d8 with the rook from a8. With a new knight at e8, we have a discovered double check, and even though both enemy pieces are under attack, there is only time to capture one of them, so Black can't touch either one, but must move the king out of check. Then the queen captures the rook at a8 and the win is simple, so Black resigned instead.

> *"The Eighth Square at last!"* she cried. *"Oh how glad I am to get here. And what is this on my head?"*
>
> — Carroll (Through the Looking Glass)

A ROOK PAWN CAN BE USELESS!

Remember that a pawn on the rook file often leads to drawn endgames. There is not enough room to maneuver, and the enemy king can find itself in a stalemate position. The best known draws are those with king and pawn against king, and even an extra bishop draws if it is of the wrong color.

The Black king just hangs around in the corner and there is no way for White to flush him out. You would think that every experienced player realizes this, but that is not the case.

ENDGAME ROLE OF THE KNIGHTS

Knights are the tacticians of the endgame. At short range they create threats, especially against pawns. Because of their ability to leap, they can infiltrate closed positions better then their more powerful companions.

Knight and pawn endings are among the most difficult to calculate because of the possibility of myriad tactical threats. In addition, sometimes repositioning a knight requires a long maneuvering strategy. Both of these factors can be seen in the following endgame where I played Black, against Wunnink at the 1997 Groningen tournament. White has just played **42.Nd3.** The notes presented below are taken from my *Complete Defense to the Queen Pawn Game*, where the full game is analyzed.

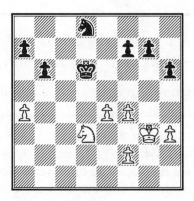

White had counted on the last move to keep the Black king out. The endgame strategy is not simple. If the Black king tries to infiltrate the queenside prematurely, White will be able to advance the central pawns, or somehow break down the defensive pawn barrier. In a book devoted to an opening repertoire, there is no space for a detailed analysis of the endgame, but strategically there are several stages. First, Black makes a passed pawn on the queenside. Next, the pawn is advanced to tie down the White knight. Third, the kingside pawn formation is clarified. Finally, the Black knight embarks on a remarkable journey to take up a defensive post, after which Black can safely win the White knight.

42...Ne6; 43.Kf3 b5. This is the most direct way of creating the passed pawn.

44.axb5 Nd4+; 45.Ke3 Nxb5. Stage one accomplished. **46.f5.** I didn't think this move was as good as retreating the knight so that the Black pawn cannot advance so quickly. 46.Nb2 g6; 47.f3 is correct. Note that the Black a-pawn cannot go to a5 because of Nc4+. Such tactics are always under foot.

46...a5!; 47.f4 a4; 48.Kd2 a3; 49.Nc1.

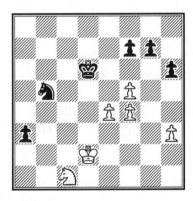

Stage two achieved, the pawn is advanced and the White knight must be very careful not to allow it to reach a2. Black cannot maneuver a knight to b4 to assist.

49...Kc5. The king must play an active role, threatening to advance toward the White pawns. **50.Kd3 Nd6; 51.Na2 h5.** This pawn wants to advance to h4, so that it will eventually be closer to the promotion square after Black maneuvers the knight to capture the pawn at h3.

52.h4 f6; 53.Nc1. White just moves the knight back and forth. Black must somehow try to entice White to advance the pawn from e4 to e5, where it will be weaker. Then the knight will need to move to e7 to make sure the pawns cannot advance, even with the help of the White king. Under those circumstances, Black will be able to use the king effectively on the queenside.

53...Nc4; 54.Na2 Nb2+; 55.Kc3 Nd1+; 56.Kd3 Nf2+; 57.Ke3 Ng4+. This is a useful post for the knight. Black threatens to play ...Kc4, so White's king must stay somewhere near the center.

58.Kd3 Nh2; 59.Ke3 Kc4; 60.e5.

This move is forced, but another goal has been achieved. Any other plan by White is too slow, as the Black king is ready to take out the enemy knight.

60...Ng4+; 61.Ke4 Nh6! The knight heads to e7, the ideal defensive post. **62.Nc1 Ng8; 63.Na2 Ne7.** White is now lost. There are no White threats on the kingside, so the Black knight can be hunted down.

64.Nc1 Kc3; 65.Na2+ Kb2; 66.Nb4 a2; 67.Nxa2 Kxa2; 68.Kd4 Kb3. 68...Nxf5+; 69.Kd5 Nxh4; 70.exf6 gxf6; 71.Ke6 Ng2 would have been a more efficient end to the game.

69.Kc5 Nxf5; 70.exf6 gxf6; 71.Kd5 Nxh4; 72.Ke6 Ng2. White resigned, because the king cannot catch the h-pawn. 73.f5 Ne3; 74.Kxf6 h4; 75.Kg5 Nxf5; 76.Kg4 Kc2 is a simple win.

If the endgames themselves are complicated, one underlying feature is simple enough. In many circumstances you need two extra pawns to win, since exchanges can reduce a one pawn advantage to nothing by sacrificing the knight for the last enemy pawn. The easiest knight endgames to win are those with pawns on both sides of the board.

These are favorable because your opponent must devote either the knight or the king to prevent you from creating a passed pawn on the side of the board where you have more pawns. Let's look at a celebrated endgame between Kholmov and Moiseyev, played in the Russian city of Uzhgorod in 1972. We join it after Black's 42nd move. The analysis below incorporates suggestions of both Kholmov and endgame specialist Edmar Mednis, whose endgame books are recommended in the bibliography.

White has a potential passed pawn on the kingside. Black's strong knight at c5 attacks b3, keeping the White knight from taking part in the offensive maneuvers. The plan for White is to deflect the Black king to the kingside, sacrificing the extra pawn if necessary, and using the White king to attack and devour the Black queenside pawns. White wants to create a passed pawn on the h-file, which is further from the queenside than the g-file.

43.h5! Ke6. 43...Ne6 is a better defense. From e6, the knight helps to control g5. 44.Nf3+ Kf6; (44...Kd5; 45.g5 hxg5; 46.h6 Nf8; 47.Nxg5 is a simple win.) 45.Kd3 Nc7; (45...Ng5; 46.Nd2 Nh3; 47.Kc4 Nf2; 48.Kb5 Nxg4; 49.Kxb6 Ke6; 50.Kxa5 Nf6; 51.Kb6 Nxh5; 52.a5 Nf4; 53.a6 Nd5+; 54.Kb7 Kd7; 55.a7 Nc7; 56.b4 h5; 57.b5 h4; 58.b6 wins.) 46.Kc4 Ke6; 47.g5 hxg5; 48.Nxg5+ Kf6; 49.Ne4+ Kg7; 50.Nc3 Kh6; 51.Nd5 Ne6; 52.Nxb6 Kxh5; 53.Nd7 Kg5; 54.Nc5 Nc7; 55.Nb7 Kf5; 56.Nxa5 and the pawn will advance without difficulty. So even with best play, Black was already lost.

44.Kd4 Nd7; 45.Nc4 Nf6. 45...Nc5; 46.Nxa5! Nxa4; 47.bxa4 bxa5; 48.Kc5 and White wins. 48...Ke5; 49.Kb5 Kf4; 50.Kxa5 Kxg4; 51.Kb6 Kxh5; 52.a5 Kg4; 53.a6 h5; 54.a7 h4; 55.a8Q h3; 56.Qh1 etc. **46.Ne3 Kf7; 47.Kc4 Nd7; 48.Nf5! Ne5+; 49.Kb5 Nxg4; 50.Kxb6 Ke6.** White sacrifices the knight, as the three pawns can win without any help.

51.Nxh6! Nxh6; 52.Kxa5 Kd7; 53.Kb6 Kc8; 54.Ka7 Black resigned. The b-pawn marches up the board, while the knight must remain on the kingside to guard against the advance of the h-pawn.

ENDGAME ROLE OF THE BISHOPS

Bishops are long range operators in the endgame. With short range pieces on the board and fewer pawns in the way they can often cover half the board — all those squares which are of the same color. This creates a dilemma, however. Pawns may be placed on the same color squares as that of the bishop so that they may be defended. Or should you place them on the opposite color, so the bishop has greater mobility?

The answer in most cases is to place the pawns on the opposite color from your own bishop, but of course you must take into account an enemy bishop. If you have a bishop that operates on the white squares, and your opponent has a bishop that operates on the dark squares, the dark squared pawns of your opponent will be vulnerable to attack. If, on the other hand, the bishops are of the same color, then you want your opponent to place pawns on squares that can be attacked by your bishop.

Therefore, if you have a dark square bishop, and so does your opponent, you want pawns to be on lights squares where they cannot be attacked, and you want your opponent's pawns to be on dark squares because then you can attack. The role of the Kings, except in exceptional circumstances, should be balanced. Let's look at a classic case.

This position comes from Pillsbury vs. Billecard, played at the German Chess Congress of 1900.

All of White's pawns are on dark squares, except one. Black's pawns occupy the light squares. You might think that the White king should try to come to g5, but that wasn't really the threat. Instead, White plans to swing the bishop to the h3-c8 diagonal.

47.g5! The immediate attempt to storm the position would fail: 47.Kg5 Kxe5; 48.Bxg6 Bxg6; 49.Kxg6 c5! It is Black who wins the king and pawn endgame. Remember, in a minor piece endgame every pawn ending must be considered.

47...Be8; 48.Bf1. Black now miscalculated the king and pawn endgame and made things easy. **48...Bd7?** A suicidal miscalculation. White would at least have to find a good move to win against 48...Bf7; 49.Bh3+ Ke7; 50.Ke3 Be8; (50...Ke8; 51.Kd4 Kd8; 52.Kc5 Kc7; 53.e6 Bg8; 54.Bg4 also let's the White king get to the key d6-square.) 51.Kd4 Kd8; 52.Kc5 Kc7; 53.e6! Black cannot keep the enemy king from getting to d6.

49.Bh3+ Ke7; 50.Bxd7 Kxd7; 51.Ke3! Ke6; 52.Kd4 Kf5; 53.Kc5 Black resigned. White wins the race easily. 53...Kxe5; 54.Kxc6 Kf5; 55.Kxb5 Kxg5; 56.Kc6 Kf5; 57.b5 g5; 58.b6 g4; 59.b7 g3; 60.b8Q.

BISHOPS OF OPPOSITE COLOR

In endgames with few pawns, bishops of opposite color usually draw. When the pawn count dwindles, the last remaining pawn can be picked off by the bishop, even if the bishop is lost. Here is a typical example.

White can make no progress. If the pawn advances, the Black bishop captures it and White cannot win. If the pawn stays put, Black can just shuffle the bishop on the h2-b8 diagonal forever.

White has more chances with two or three pawns, but unless some of them are connected, a win can still be difficult. Averbakh tells us that if we can put our bishop in a position to keep both enemy pawns from advancing, while our king keeps the enemy monarch from infiltrating, we draw. Here is a study of his, from 1950, which proves the point.

If we have to defend this position as Black, our task would seem to be grim. White has two extra pawns, and a more centralized king. We have our bishop in perfect position, blockading one pawn and, with the help of the king at g5, preventing White from advancing to f4. White cannot make progress on the kingside, so must turn to the queenside.

1.Kd5 Kf6! The bishop at c7 keeps the pawn from advancing to f4, so the king is free to roam. The retreat to f6 is designed to keep the enemy king from getting to e6, and later, d7.

2.Kc5 Ke7; 3.Kb5 Kd8! The king now overprotects c7, so the c-pawn cannot advance. The f-pawn is also immobile. If **4.Ka6 Bf4; 5.Kb7**, then Black keeps the dark squares under control with **5...Bc7.** The position is therefore a draw.

BISHOPS VS. KNIGHTS

In general bishops are better than nights in the endgame because bishops can operate from a safe distance while knights must approach their targets in order to succeed. The complexities of these endgames fill many books, but the superiority of the bishop must not be underestimated. We examine the game Wade vs. Barcza, from the 1952 Interzonal, starting after 53 moves.

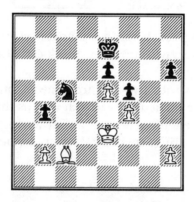

The White bishop is in an ideal configuration with the enemy knight, and vice versa. Each piece restricts the scope of the enemy piece as much as possible. White's pawns are on dark squares, but against a knight, as opposed to an enemy bishop, this is a liability. The pawns are easily attacked. White has the move, and the initiative. Black's pawn at b4 is weak, and can be won by the White king. This leaves the king too far from the f-pawn. Therefore the capture at b4 must be perfectly timed.

The game continued **54.Kd4 Nd7; 55.Bd1.** The bishop takes up a post at b3, to keep pressure on the pawn at e6. This tethers the Black king to a defensive position.

55...Nb6; 56.Bb3 Kd7; 57.Kc5 Nc8. The b-pawn will fall, but then the knight will get to e7 and g6, winning the f-pawn. **58.Ba4+.** 58.Kxb4 Ne7; 59.Kc5 Ng6; 60.Bc4 Nxf4; 61.b4 Ng6! White continues to suffer from the weakness of the kingside pawns. 62.Kd4 Nh4; 63.Be2 Kc6 keeps the bishop at e2 on guard against a fork at f3, and no progress can be made.

58...Kc7; 59.Bb3. 59.Kxb4 Ne7; 60.Bb3 Kd7 and the knight gets to g6 and wins the f-pawn. **59...Kd7.**

60.h4! A bold but necessary more. If the White pawn is allowed to get to h5, then Black will not be able to use the g6 square to maneuver, and no threat can be created against the f-pawn. The Black b-pawn can then safely be captured. Black cannot allow this, and therefore sacrifices the h-pawn to slow White down.

60...h5; 61.Ba4+ Kc7; 62.Bd1 Ne7; 63.Bxh5 Nd5. Black does get the f-pawn, but White has a dangerous outside passed pawn. The queenside pawns are irrelevant, for the moment.

64.Bf3 Nxf4; 65.h5 Kd7; 66.h6 Ke7. Black must try to stop the h-pawn with the king if possible. The knight cannot do the job, as we will see. **67.h7 Ng6; 68.Bh5 Nh8.** The only way to stop the pawn, but now the knight is permanently trapped in the corner unless Black can force the bishop to abandon the post at h5.

69.Kxb4 Kf8; 70.Kc5 Kg7; 71.b4 Kh6. A last, desperate attempt to get the bishop to move, but the bishop is of no further use to White, who simply promotes the b-pawn. **72.b5.** Black resigned. The knight cannot get over to the queenside in time.

Nevertheless, it is important to have a healthy bishop. A knight, even if not particularly well posted, is often superior to weak bishop. The following endgame, from Delaney vs. Akesson at Groningen 1980, is very instructive.

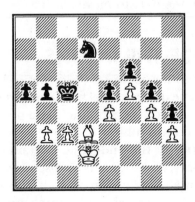

Black has a potential outside passed pawn on the a-file, and you might think that the winning plan lies on the queenside. It does, in a way, but the real advantage is on the kingside. The pawn at e4 is weak. If it falls, the whole game goes. Therefore the king must get to d4. Black achieves this by eliminating all the queenside pawns, the supposed source of his obvious advantage.

Play continued **37...Nb6; 38.Kc2 b4!** White cannot capture this pawn, as it would give access to d4 after Black recaptures with the a-pawn.

39.Kd2 a4! White is forced to capture the Black pawns before they break through the barrier and promote. **40.cxb4+ Kxb4; 41.bxa4 Nxa4.**

This position has even material, and the bishop can protect e4, h3, or both as needed. How then can the position be lost? In fact, Black wins using the same threat as throughout the endgame, the infiltration of the king at d4.

42.Ke3 Kc3; 43.Be2. 43.Bf1 Nb2 leads to the same thing. **43...Nb2; 44.Ba6 Nc4+!** As in so many endgames, the king and pawn endgames are the key. **45.Kf3.** 45.Bxc4 Kxc4; 46.Ke2 Kd4; 47.Kf3 Kd3 is a well known thematic win. **45...Kd4.** White resigned, faced with the threat of ...Nd2+. If the king retreats, then the knight goes to d6 and wins the pawn. The exchange at c4 leads to a lost king and pawn endgame. 46.Bxc4 Kxc4; 47.Ke3 Kc3 wins as in the note to move 45.

ENDGAME ROLE OF THE ROOKS

Rooks belong on the seventh rank or on open files or behind passed pawns in the endgame. Only in the endgame do rooks feel truly comfortable on their home squares! It is not easy to give general advice on handling these powerful weapons. Thousands of pages have been written on the subject of rook endings, but every scholar agrees that rooks must remain active in the endgame. Certain endgames must be part of every chess player's vocabulary, and they will be discussed below as part of the dozen positions you should be thoroughly familiar with. In this section, we look at the key concept of rook activity. We also examine situations, not uncommon at all, when a rook must do battle against one or two mere pawns. They are more complicated than they seem!

Choosing a single representative example is particularly difficult, because well played rook endings are among the most cultured pearls in chess. Analysis of a single endgame can run dozens of pages, and then, even if written by a World Champion, may need to be revised by scholars to correct errors. So instead of a detailed autopsy in a complicated chess murder mystery, let's consider the broader theme of the active rook.

We turn to one of the most analyzed endgames of all time, to demonstrate the difficulty of rook endgames not only at the board, but even under the microscope in the chess laboratory. The game was played at the 1956 Alekhine Memorial in Moscow. World Champion Mikhail Botvinnik handled the White side, while Miguel Najdorf, who remained an active player his entire life, into his 90s, defended the black side. The position is the dreaded R+4 vs. R+3 endgame, and it is presented with a condensed analysis from Botvinnik, Euwe, Aronin, Kopayev, and Lilienthal. I have checked it with a powerful computer program, and added a few notes of my own. Make sure you pay attention to the role of the horizontal check in this endgame!

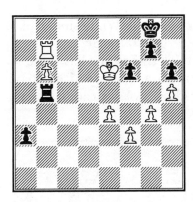

White anticipates the trade of queenside pawns and gets ready for the four vs. three endgame. **58.f4!** The king is now in a position to defend all the kingside pawns.

58...a2; 59.Ra7 Rxb6+; 60.Kf5 Rb7. Necessary, for if 60...Rb2 then 61.Kg6 Kf8; 62.Ra8+ Ke7; 63.Kxg7 Rg2; 64.Ra7+ Ke6; 65.g5! White wins.

61.Rxa2 Kf7; 62.Ra5 Rc7; 63.Rd5 Ra7; 64.e5 fxe5; 65.fxe5 Ke7; 66.e6 Ra4. This provides more resistance than 66...Ra6; 67.Rd7+ Kf8; 68.Kg6 Rxe6+; 69.Kh7. **67.g5.**

67...hxg5? A serious strategic error. White has no intention of capturing it, but will use it as a shield for the king. The defense of the second rank was called for. **68.Rd7+ Kf8; 69.Rf7+ Kg8; 70.Kg6 g4; 71.h6!** Pure tactics. White gets the g-pawn out of the way so that f6 can be used. **71...gxh6.** 71...Ra8; 72.hxg7 g3; 73.e7 Ra6+; 74.Rf6 is another White win.

72.e7 Ra8; 73.Rf6. Black resigned. White simply plays the rook to d6 and then to d8. 73...g3 74.Rd6 Re8; 75.Rd8 g2; 76.Rxe8#.

67...Ra7! is the strongest defense. White has three sensible moves here. They are the check at d7, the capture at h6, and Re5, which defends the e-pawn so the king can get to g6. It turns out that trading rooks or capturing at h6 only draw, but putting the rook at e5 is very strong.

Let's examine each. We can dismiss 68.Rd7+? Rxd7; 69.exd7 Kxd7; 70.Kg6 because 70...hxg5 71.Kxg7 g4; 72.h6 g3; 73.h7 g2; 74.h8Q g1Q+ draws.

So, let's turn to the capture at h6. 68.gxh6 gxh6; 69.Rb5 Rc7. 70.Rb6 prepares the way for the king to get to g6, but it is not quite enough to win. It is a long way to the draw. Computers get completely lost in such positions, because the horizon, where the draw appears, is too far away. 70...Rc5+; 71.Kg6 Re5; 72.Kxh6 Kf6!!

The White king cannot move, and the play takes us toward a well-known position. (72...Rxe6+?? would have been a decisive blunder. 73.Rxe6+ Kxe6; 74.Kg7 and the pawn promotes.) 73.Ra6 Rf5!; (73...Rxe6?? loses as before.) 74.Ra1, giving up the e-pawn, is the only available attempt to make progress. 74...Kxe6; 75.Kg6 Rf6+; 76.Kg7 Rf7+; 77.Kg8 Rb7. This is a useful position to remember, because it shows how to defend against a rook pawn. 78.Rf1 White cuts off the enemy king from the promotion file. It is a standard technique in winning endgames. 78...Rb5.

The pawn is attacked and must advance. 79.h6 (79.Rh1? Kf6; 80.h6 Rb8+; 81.Kh7 Rb7+ forces the draw.) 79...Rg5+; 80.Kf8 Rh5; 81.Ra1. A little trick, which is another important rook endgame technique. If Black captures the pawn at h6, the rook is lost after a check at a6. 81...Rf5+! 82.Ke8 (82.Kg7 Rg5+; 83.Kh7 and the king cannot escape, so the pawn cannot advance.) 82...Rb5 threatens mate at b8. 83.Ra6+ Kf5; 84.h7 Rb7! The horizontal check threat prevents White from promoting. 85.Rh6 re-establishes the threat, but the Black rook now occupies h8 via a check. 85...Rb8+; 86.Kd7 Rh8; 87.Ke7 Kg5; 88.Rh1 Kg6; 89.Rg1+ Kf5; 90.Rg7 Ra8! The horizontal check at a7 prevents White from winning with Rg8. This position is a draw.

Imagine having to work all that out at the board, and save energy for the last, and best move. 68.Re5! is the right play. Facing an infiltration at g6, Black must exchange at g5. 68...hxg5; 69.Kxg5 leaves Black with a choice.

The aggressive 69...Kd6 is met by 70.Kf5! This analytical refinement was contributed by Nogovichin. 70...Re7; 71.Re1 Re8; 72.Kg6 Re7; 73.Re2 Kd5; 74.h6 gxh6; 75.Kf6 is a simple win. 70...Ra8; 71.e7 Re8; 72.h6! gxh6; 73.Kf6 h5; 74.Kf7 is also straightforward.

A better defense lies in 69...Ra1; 70.Kg6 Rf1, protecting from the rear, even at the cost of the pawn. 71.Kxg7 Rg1+; 72.Kh6.

Black cannot prevent White from building a bridge to get the king out of the way of the h-pawn. This is another important tactic in rook endgames. The rook will provide shelter to the White king, in this case by moving to g5. 72...Rg2 73.Rg5 Rf2; 74.Kg7 Kxe6; 75.h6 Rf7+; 76.Kg8 Ra7; 77.h7.

The position is now a win. If Black checks on the home rank, the White king goes to g7, and can then hide on h6. Even if Black manages to play ...Rh8, White can simply answer with Rg8.

The rook is a mighty warrior, but can be humbled by mere pawns if they advance far enough up the board. In the endgame two connected passed pawns on the sixth rank will usually defeat a rook. Many beginners and intermediate players fail to take this into account, often to their ruin. When the pawns are not sufficiently advanced up the board, however, it is easy for a rook to sneak behind and capture them, but if they are connected and passed, they are formidable opponents. Dr. Tarrasch showed the power of the pawns in his game against Janowski from the Ostende tournament of 1907.

Black has just played 78...Ra4 and threatens to place the rook on the b-file and get a queen. White must sacrifice the rook to stay in the game.

79.Rxb2. 79.f6 Ra1; 80.Rxb2 Kxb2; 81.g5 Rf1 reaches the same position as the game. **79...Kxb2; 80.f6!** White has a winning position. The rook alone cannot handle the pawns. Note that the pawn at g4 is taboo, because the f-pawn then advances and Black can do nothing to stop it. 80.g5 is inferior. 80...Rg4 81.g6 Kc3; 82.Kf3 Rg1; 83.Ke4 Kd2; 84.Ke5 Ke3; 85.f6 Rxg6; 86.f7 Rg5+; 87.Ke6 Rg6+; 88.Ke5 Rg5+; 89.Kf6 Rg1 draws.

80...Ra1. Black should have played this back at move 78, saving a crucial tempo. **81.g5 Rf1; 82.Kd4 Kb3; 83.Ke5.** It was later demonstrated that 2.Kd5 would have been more efficient.

83...Kc4.

84.g6! Now that the f-pawn is defended, the g-pawn can advance. **84...Re1+; 85.Kd6**

Rd1+. 85...Rg1; 86.g7 Kd4; 87.Kc6 Kc4; (87...Rg6 loses to 88.Kb5!) 88.Kd7 Kd5; 89.Ke8 Ke6; 90.f7 Ra1; 91.f8N+ Kf6; 92.g8Q would have been a prettier finish, according to Tarrasch.

86.Ke6 Re1+; 87.Kf7. Black resigned, because the g-pawn queens.

ENDGAME ROLE OF THE QUEEN

It is difficult to give general advice about the queen in the endgame. Give her good targets and a meaningful plan, and she will be happy.

In queen and pawn endgames, it is helpful to place the king in a fianchetto formation and station the queen on the long diagonal. This makes it very difficult for the opponent to achieve counterplay by attacking the king.

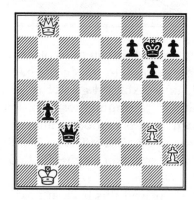

Max Euwe, playing Black against van Hoorn in Amsterdam, 1927, achieved this crushing position, and after **36.h4 b3,** White resigned. The pawn at b3 threatens the elementary mate at c2 and a2. In any case, Black's control of the long diagonal allowed him to advance the pawn easily.

ENDGAME ROLE OF THE KING

In the endgame, the king becomes a mighty fighting piece, a weapon of great strength. Watch how the White king manages to muscle its way to a draw in this seemingly hopeless position.

Study by Richard Reti

Every student of the game should know this position. It is the one I use to start my students thinking about the endgame. Trying to work it out by mere calculations is very difficult. Computers can do it with their inexhaustible computing resources. Humans, however, need only make the most of the abstract positional ideas available.

The king cannot catch the h-pawn, so the only possible defense must involve the c-pawn. Black threatens to gobble it up after ...Kb6, and the king is too far away to help. So all seems lost. The solution involves bringing the king to the d-file to protect the pawn, That takes four moves, which seems impossible.

1.Kg7 White's first move is obvious enough. 1.c7?? loses instantly to Kb7.

1...h4. 1...Kb6; 2.Kf6 transposes to the main line. **2.Kf6 Kb6.**

This position is easily predicted from the starting position. We now have to consider the rule of the square. If White can get to any of the squares on the first four ranks of the e-h files, this position is drawn. So White must now try to get to e4, f4, or g4 before the Black pawn advances to h3. At the same time, it must head for the d-file to protect the c-pawn. 2...h3; 3.Ke7 h2; (3...Kb6; 4.Kd7 h2; 5.c7 h1=Q; 6.c8=Q= is the same as the main line) 4.c7 Kb7; 5.Kd7 h1=Q; 6.c8=Q+ will draw.

3.Ke5!

3...h3. Otherwise the h-pawn falls. 3...Kxc6; 4.Kf4 h3; 5.Kg3 h2; 6.Kxh2.

4.Kd6! Now both pawns will promote, and the game will be drawn. **4...h2; 5.c7 h1=Q; 6.c8=Q.** The position is now a draw.

THE OPPOSITION

King and pawn endgames often come down to one simple concept — the **opposition**. This refers to the geometric relationship between the two kings. The kings act like sumo wrestlers, trying to get the enemy to move aside. The key position is the following:

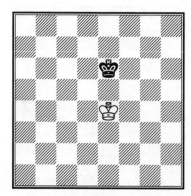

White's goal is to make progress up the board. The mighty king will try to assist a pawn to the 8th rank. The first step is to cross the meridian to the fifth rank. This can be accomplished here because it is Black's turn to move. White has the opposition, since any move by Black must give ground and allow the White king forward. If it were White to move, Black would have the opposition.

When the kings are close to each other, as in the previous diagram, this is fairly obvious. The same rule holds when the kings are far apart, but only when there are an odd number of squares between them.

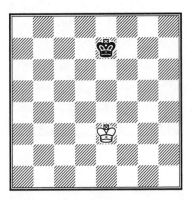

With White to move, Black has the opposition. If White plays 1.Kd4, Black plays 1....Kd6. On 1.Ke4 there is 1...Ke5. !...Kf4 allows 1...Kf6. In each case we get the simple opposition position, with White to move. White can move along the third rank, but the Black king will still make progress, for example 1.Kf3 Kd6 (but not 1...Kf6?? 2.Kf4 when White has the opposition!) 2.Ke4 Ke6!

Moving White's king back another rank, the opposition magically returns to White! There are now an even number of squares, four, between the two kings.

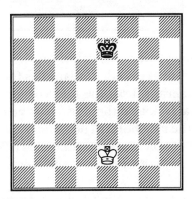

If it is White's turn, then 1.Kd3 seizes the opposition. If Black plays 1...Kd6, then 2.Kd4 reaches a simple opposition position. The same result follows 1...Ke6; 2.Ke4.

Unfortunately, most endgame battles do not take place on a single file. Long distance and short distance belly bumping can take place anywhere. There are many complex mathematical explanations, but here is a practical approach I adapt from Jeremy Silman, author of many fine instructional chess books.

Wherever the two kings are, draw an imaginary rectangle using the kings as the corners.

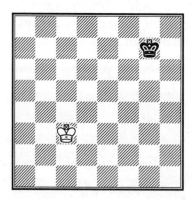

Imagine a line drawn from c3 to c7 to g7 to g3. That would form a square.

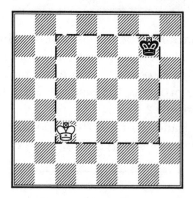

When the shape is a square, whoever is not on the move has the opposition. If White is to move in the diagram above, then Black has the opposition, and vice versa.

There is even a more general rule: if the four corners of the rectangle are of the same color, then the side that is not on the move has the opposition. Since c3, c7, g7, and g3 are all dark squares, the rule holds. The same would be true for a position with kings at c2, c6, e2, and e6. Try to picture that without a chess board. Are all the squares of the same color? If so, then wherever you put the kings, if it is White to move, Black has the opposition.

This rule is very important, especially when we get to king and pawn endgames. Let's look at one final example:

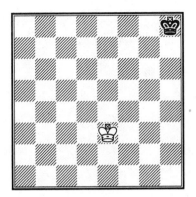

White grabs the opposition with 1.Kf4! If you are not convinced, set up the position on a chessboard and try it out. You can't give it to your chess computer, because technically the position is a draw according to the rules, and most chessplaying programs won't touch it!

This may make you wonder why the concept is considered so crucial. We'll get to that in just a bit, in the first of our four positions you need to remember. First, however, we need to discuss the rule by which the positions we just examined, fascinating though they were, are declared drawn.

MATING MATERIAL

You must always keep enough material on the board to be able to deliver checkmate. Our poor kings in the previous example would be doomed to wander aimlessly, perhaps playing endgames on the Flying Dutchman, were there not a sensible rule prohibiting such torture. The same rule terminates a game if neither side can set up a checkmate position. Essentially, you need one rook, queen, or pawn, or two bishops, or a bishop and a knight. Two knights will not do the job, unless your opponent commits chess suicide. Keeping a pawn around is always helpful, since it allows you to later obtain a new queen by advancing it to the promotion square.

ZUGZWANG

The German term **zugzwang**, is generally taken to refer to a position where a player loses because of the obligation to move. If a "pass" were possible, the game would not be lost. Here it is in its simplest form.

If it is Black to move, the only legal move is 1...Kc7, but then White plays 2.Ke7 and wins by promoting the pawn. On the other hand, with White to move, only 1.Kd6 saves the pawn, but that position is stalemate. Each player gets a worse result if on the move. Black loses instead of drawing. White draws instead of winning.

The squeeze is a related concept, often confused with zugzwang. A player who is in a squeeze has to move, and suffers the consequences, but even a "pass" would not help, because the opponent has waiting moves available. The following position shows the squeeze in action.

1.Ke5! White must not fall for 1.c6+ Kc8!; 2.Kd6 Kb8; 3.c7+ Kc8 is a draw. **1...Kc6.** 1...Ke7; 2.c6! bxc6; 3.b7 gains a new queen. **2.Kd4 Kd7; 3.Kd5.** We have the starting position of the diagram, and it is Black to move. Black has been squeezed into zugzwang.

3...Kc8; 4.Ke6 Kd8. Necessary, as the corner is not safe. 4...Kb8; 5.Kd7 transposes. **5.Kd6 Kc8; 6.Ke7 Kb8; 7.Kd7 Ka8; 8.c6 bxc6; 9.Kc7! c5; 10.b7+ Ka7; 11.b8Q+ Ka6; 12.Qb6#**

EXCHANGE TO WIN!

When you have extra material, you can often force a winning position in a simple endgame. This requires that you know which endgames are winning and which are merely drawn. That's why a lot of players let opportunities slip. They lack the confidence in their ability to convert a small advantage into a win. The more you know about the endgame, the easier it becomes to use the technique of exchanging to win.

As a trainer, I have often seen young players stubbornly refuse to trade queens when the result would be a straightforward winning king and pawn endgame. Such endgames require a great deal of calculation, unless you are familiar with the more general aspects such as those discussed in this book and more specialized treatises. Usually the students say afterwards that the calculation of the king and pawn endgame was just too long, and they didn't have faith in their ability to win from the position. They feared embarrassment if they went into the simple endgame and only achieved a draw. So the queens stayed on the board, and in many cases the queen and pawn endgames ended in draw by perpetual check.

In the hands of a great master, the technique of exchanging to win seems so easy. In the 1960/61 United States Championship, Bobby Fischer achieved the following position after 30 moves against William Lombardy, one of America's best players at the time.

White has just played the rook to e1, allowing a simplification maneuver with **30...Rxc3+!; 31.bxc3 Rxe5+; 32.Kd2 Rxe1; 33.Kxe1.**

The result of the position is an easy win for Black, thanks to the outside pawn on the a-file.

33...Kd5; 34.Kd2 Kc4; 35.h5 b6; 36.Kc2 g5; 37.h6 f4; 38.g4 a5; 39.bxa5 bxa5; 40.Kb2 a4; 41.Ka3 Kxc3; 42.Kxa4 Kd4; 43.Kb4 Ke3. White resigned.

FOUR CRITICAL POSITIONS

It is hard to say just how many positions you need to memorize to play the endgame well. There are surely at least a few hundred, but I have selected four. Criteria for inclusion here is that you should hang your head in shame if you fail to play them to the proper result!

OPPOSITION POSITION

This is the king position we discussed in the section on the opposition. We've now got a pawn at e5. To win the game, you need to promote your pawn to a queen. To do that, you have to drive the enemy king back, and off the e-file so that you can escort the pawn to e8. Ignoring the pawn, with White to move we have the opposition position, and know that progress cannot be made. The presence of the pawn adds a surprising twist. From this position we can drive the enemy back, but we still can't win the game!

LUCENA POSITION

The **Lucena** position is one of the most critical in all of endgame theory. It isn't by Lucena at all. It was in a book called *Il Puttino*, by Dr. Alessandro Salvio, published in 1634. Before you show off your knowledge of this arcane fact, better learn the position! If Black keeps the opposition (see p.204), then in the end White will be forced to abandon the pawn or allow stalemate. For example: 1...Ke7 2.Kd5 Kd7 3.e6+ Ke7 4.Ke5 Ke8! 5.Kf6 Kf8 6.e7+ Ke8 and now if 7.Ke6, the position is stalemate. Any other move drops the pawn.

White wins as follows. First, you bring the rook to c4, so that it can get to d4 and drive away the enemy king. Then you slip the king out, and use the rook to defend it from enemy checks. This is called **building a bridge**.

1.Rc4 Ra1. 1...Rd2, to stop the check, White takes the a-file with 2.Ra2, and the king comes to a7, after which the pawn can advance.

2.Rd4+ Ke7; 3.Kc7 Rc1+; 4.Kb6 Rb1+; 5.Rb6. White wins.

PHILIDOR'S POSITION

This endgame is seen frequently and is the basis for much of the theory of rook and pawn endgames. In **Philidor's position,** White has cut off the enemy king on the back rank, but Black can hold with accurate defense.

Black must defend the 6th rank, so that the White king cannot approach without the pawn occupying e6, which might otherwise be used as a haven for the king if Black gives check at f1.

Thus **1...Ra6** must be played. White will oblige by advancing the e-pawn, but first repositions the rook more effectively on the long side of the king. The rook generally is more successful from the side of the board which is furthest from the enemy king.

2.Rb7 Rc6; 3.Ra7 Rb6; 4.e6 Rb1!

Black will be able to check along the first rank, and the White king has no place to hide.

QUEEN AND BISHOP PAWN DRAW

Most queen and pawn endgames are quite difficult. The subtleties of the ending have been studied for centuries, but new discoveries are constantly being found. The one position you must remember is the case of queen against bishop pawn. This can be drawn if the stronger side's king is not too close. Even a king just a few squares away cannot achieve victory.

Black can easily bring the queen close to the enemy pieces.
1...Qg1+; 2.Kh8 Qh2+; 3.Kg7 Qg3+; 4.Kh8 Qh4+; 5.Kg7 Qg5+; 6.Kh8 Qh6+; 7.Kg8 Qg6+; 8.Kh8!

If Black captures the pawn it is stalemate, but otherwise no progress can be made. The position is a draw.

SUMMARY OF THE THREE STAGES

We've now examined the three main stages of the game: the opening, the middlegame, and the endgame. Each places unique demands on the chessplayer. You should try to develop your skills in each phase of the game, because if you only concentrate on one or two stages your hard work can be easily undone in the arena you neglected.

In the opening a master should play like a book, in the middlegame he should play like a magician, in the endgame he should play like a machine.

— Spielmann

The opening phase of the game is usually mostly a matter of playing out moves on the board that have been well prepared at home. Barring some sort of surprise on a part of the opponent you should be able to complete your development while still being in familiar territory. Once the middlegame and has commenced you have to think for yourself. Tactical and strategic planning requires not only knowledge of familiar patterns but also a fair degree of creativity. If you can come up with an idea that is both subtle and complex, your opponent is unlikely to spot it in time and you'll been rewarded with success.

In the endgame however technique usually triumphs over creativity. Technical prowess in the endgame will not only insure that you win those positions which are objectively winning also help you squeeze out points in positions that should by all rights end in a draw, and even draw or win games that are beyond salvation.

STRATEGY

Whosoever sees no other aim in the game than that of giving checkmate to one's opponent, will never become a good chessplayer. —**Euwe**

Except among rank beginners, games are not decided by checkmate in the first few moves. A long term strategy is needed to create the circumstances in which a mating attack is likely to be successful. Strategic skill is not easy to acquire. Where tactics are mostly a matter of pattern recognition, strategic planning requires intelligence.

Planning requires several things. You must have a good objective grasp of the situation. This is actually the hard part. Once you have worked out the relative merits of each side's position, you can determine whether attack or defense is appropriate. Then you can choose the appropriate form of action.

Although serious errors may change the direction of a game radically, Steinitz's concept that a chess game is won through the accumulation of small advantages still remains the foundation of modern chess. Attack or defend as the position requires, not as your mood dictates. Objectivity is crucial, and each configuration of pieces must be evaluated dispassionately.

The evaluation of a position takes into account both permanent and temporary factors. Of course no advantage is really permanent, a bad move can easily throw it away. Better to think of it as an advantage which you can hold on to.

KOTOV'S LIST OF ADVANTAGES

PERMANENT ADVANTAGES
- Material advantage
- More pawns in center
- Passed pawns
- Weak enemy squares (whether or not occupied by enemy piece)
- Healthier pawn structure
- More appropriate minor pieces

TEMPORARY ADVANTAGES
- Vulnerable enemy piece
- Superior coordination
- Control of the center
- Control of a line
- Advantage in Space

In this chapter we will consider coordination, control of the center, space, and pawn structures.

There is no magic formula to calculate the size of an advantage. Computer programs apply crude algorithms to come up with numbers, but rarely does any human have the capability to explain them. There are so many ways to calculate a numerical evaluation of the position. We learned early on that simply counting up material points does not suffice. Many factors are subtle, and while clear and simple logic is most often associated with chess, sometimes fuzzy logic is more appropriate.

One aspect of the game that Alexander Kotov should have included in his list of temporary advantages is the initiative. This is one of the most important factors in the middlegame, and also plays a role in the opening and endgame. The initiative is discussed in the middlegame chapter.

Strategic planning is best handled by non-linear thinking, absent of calculation. Look at the position. Imagine a similar, but more attractive position (from your point of view). Then try to come up with a plan to transform the present board to the desired one.

We will now look at six aspects of the game which can be especially useful in strategic planning. We start with piece coordination, the degree to which each side's pieces work together. Control of key squares is the next topic. We move on to the effect of control of greater space, which often confers the right to attack. Many books have been devoted to the subject of pawn structure, and we'll just get a brief overview here. We finish up with a discussion of purposeful moves and the importance of the "tempo," which is a unit used to measure time as it relates not to the chess clock, but to the abstract drama of the chessboard.

COORDINATION

Coordination refers to the ability of your pieces to work together. If they can bear down on a particular square, or defend each other agaisnt attack, their combined force is greater than pieces working alone. The better coordinated your pieces are, the more likely you are to win. Whether in attack or defense, pieces working together can easily defeat an army that is scattered. The most tightly coordinated pieces are those that form a **battery**, teaming up to attack enemy territory. Any two pieces can form a battery, though the plodding king and lowly pawn are not generally considered participants because of their limited range.

QUEEN AND ROOK

A queen and rook make up the most powerful battery. Against an exposed king, they usually deliver the fatal blow quickly. The following amusing position shows the underlying idea.

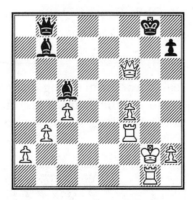

Tarrasch won this game against Pribulsky at Berlin 1880 despite the fact that both rooks are attacked, one is pinned and threatened with a capture and check. Tarrasch simply moved his king to h3 with discovered check. Black resigned, because taking the rook at g1 allows the other rook, no longer pinned, to slide to g3 and deliver checkmate.

The checkmating power of the queen and rook battery can be seen in artistic combinations even in scholastic chess. The game between Scott Thibaudeau and Wogae Sung from the Junior Varsity section of the 1998 National High School Championship featured a surprising turnaround.

At first, things look bad for White, because the queenside pawns are weak and there is pressure in the center. White has control of the h-file, but Black can defend against queen and rook by retreating the queen to the kingside via f7 and g8. White found the brilliant **33.Bh5!!** Black should not have taken the bait.

33...gxh5? This opens the floodgates and the White forces rush in. 33...Qf7; 34.Qg4 Rxa3 allows 35.Bxg6!! Qxg6; 36.Qd7+ Kg8; 37.Rh4! but 34...Rb7! would have left White grasping for a decent move.

34.Qxh5 Qf7; 35.Qh7+?! 35.Qh8+ Kg6; 36.Qh6# would have been more efficient. **35...Kf8; 36.Qh8+ Qg8; 37.Qxf6+ Qf7; 38.Rh8#.**

QUEEN AND BISHOP

Queen and bishop can wreak havoc from a long distance, and are a great team as long as there aren't too many pawns on the board. The White battery has to maneuver in surprising fashion in our example, which shows two useful queen and bishop formations.

26.Qc3. The battery aims at g7, the mating square. **26...Rd4; 27.Kg2 Red8; 28.Qc7 R4d6?** This lets White reconfigure the position for a different mating approach. The rook should retreat to d7, so that the f-pawn can be advanced and the g7-square will be protected. 28...R4d7; 29.Qe5 f5; 30.Qh8+ Kf7; 31.Qxh7+ Kf8; 32.Qxg6 will win eventually thanks to the extra pawns, but mate is not in the immediate forecast.

29.Bf6! The bishop cannot be captured, because the rook at d8 would hang. The rook cannot advance to d7, because then a check on the back rank would be deadly. **29...R6d7; 30.Qf4!** Checkmate blows in from another direction. **30...Re8?** This makes it simple. 30...Rd6; 31.Bxd8 Rxd8; 32.Qc7 loses both queenside pawns. **31.Qh6.** Black resigned, as mate at g7 is next.

QUEEN AND KNIGHT

The queen working in close proximity to a knight is a tremendous fighting force. Although the queen can cover all files, ranks and diagonals, only the knight can cover a square which is not on a straight line. The ideal coordination of queen and knight is found in the Smothered Mate, which is presented in the chapter on checkmating patterns.

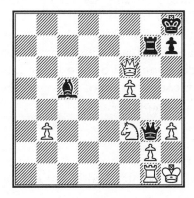

The game Jain vs. Musketh, Hastings 1995, saw mutual checkmating threats as the game approached time control.

After **39.Ne5 Qf2,** Black may have felt that White had nothing better than to repeat the position by retreating the knight, faced with mate at g1. White has other plans!

40.Nf7+! Kg8; 41.Nh6+ Black resigned. 41...Kh8; 42.Qd8+ Rg8; 43.Qxg8# is all that is left.

ROOK AND BISHOP

Rook and bishop are ideally coordinated when they converge on a single square. There are a number of checkmating patterns that use these two pieces, as you will see in the section on checkmate. Let's take a variation on one checkmating theme, the Opera Mate. The example is Spielmann vs. Hoenlinger from Vienna, 1929.

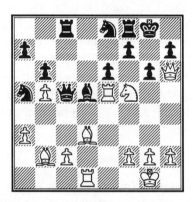

The queen, knight, and distant bishop stare menacingly at g7, but that square is defended by the knight. It is the rook, not the queen, who will deliver checkmate. Not at g7, but h8! First Spielmann gets the knight out of the way of the rook.

25.Ne7+!! Qxe7. The next shot is **26.Qxh7+!!** The queen sacrifices herself so that the rook can team up with each bishop in turn to create a beautiful checkmating combination. **26...Kxh7; 27.Rh5+.** This takes advantage of the power of the bishop at d3, which pins the pawn at g6. The Black king is driven back to the home rank.

27...Kg8; 28.Rh8. The dark squared bishop is the partner as the final curtain is lowered. For the most potent combination of rook and bishop power, see the section on the Windmill in the tactics chapter.

ROOK AND KNIGHT

The rook and knight do not get along all that well. Even working together, they are rarely effective. They can often be attacked by an enemy king, wedged in between them but not under attack.

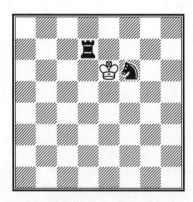

In an endgame with rook and bishop against rook and knight, the limited range of the knight makes life difficult in many cases. Sometimes, however, a knight can be a valuable assistant to the rook. When it occupies an outpost in enemy territory, the knight can safeguard a rook on the seventh rank, as in the following position.

This position was reached in Solt vs. Krizsan, from a game played in Hungary in 1974. The White rook is anchored by the knight at d5. The knight later plays an active role in the destruction of the enemy position.

26...Rd8. Black defends the bishop and thus protects the c-pawn, which cannot be captured by the knight, which must remain at d5 to protect the rook. If the bishop retreated, the c-pawn could be captured by the rook. **27.Bxg7!** This exchange strengthens the power of the rook at e7 by creating a more stable pin on the 7th rank. It also frees f6 for use by the knight.

27...Qxg7; 28.Nf6+! Kh8. If 28...Kf8; White can take the bishop with check, since the rook cannot be captured while the king must stay at f8 to protect the queen. **29.Bd5 Be8; 30.Rxc7 b6; 31.g5.** Black has no useful move.

The bishop has joined the attack, and now all of White's forces are coordinated, except for the queen at c3, which will quickly move to the e-file.

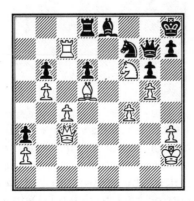

31...Rb8; 32.Qe3. Black resigned here. After 32...Qf8 33.Re7 the bishop is lost.

TWO ROOKS

> *All things being equal, the player*
> *will prevail who first*
> *succeeds in uniting the efforts of*
> *both rooks in an important direction*
>
> — Znosko Borovsky

When a pair are of coordinated rooks take part in attack, the defense usually has a difficult time. They are best used on adjacent files, because when doubled in a battery they control fewer relevant squares. A battery of rooks cannot smash through a well defended pawn barrier easily. Instead, they are usually used to make progress on open files.

A frontal assault can sometimes be effective but the most deadly infiltration is the occupation of the seventh rank. Doubled rooks on the seventh often threaten perpetual checks and can sweep enemy pieces off the board. An ideal rook battery consists of rooks on the seventh rank of the central files.

The ideal rook battery is seen in Luckis vs. Letelier from the 1946 Mar del Plata tournament. It is Black's turn to move but a defense to the threat of Nd6 and Rd8# is hard to find. Notice that the rooks control not only the seventh rank in its entire length, but also both central files. The control of e1 prevents checks, and the control of d8 stops the queen from getting back to defend. Defeat is inevitable.

The game concluded. **34...Kf8?!; 35.Nd6 g5; 36.Re8#.** That was just one of many possible mates!

CONTROL THE CENTER

All schools of thought agree that players should try to control key squares, especially in the center of the board. The center need not be occupied with pawns, but if a player can control the middle ground then winning chances are greatly enhanced.

> *Control of the center brings the possibility of influencing activity on both flanks simultaneously*
>
> — Nimzowitsch

Perhaps the most important aspect of controling the center is that it gives you the freedom to operate on either side of the board, or both! Your pieces can safely transfer from one side of the board to another, with the central zone being safe territory. The defensive side, however, having less room to maneuver, must somehow managed to guard both flanks if a counter attack in the center is not available. Chess masters frequently exploit this by developing threats on both flanks.

As with most of the topics in this book, entire treatises have been written on the importance of the center. Indeed, major philosophical debates have taken place, and the understanding of the center has been greatly refined since the days when occupation of the center by pawns was considered a goal in itself. Domination of the center is now understood to be achieved by a mixture of pawns and pieces. The pieces need not be stationed in the center, but must have scope over the central squares. To have scope over a square, a piece needs to be able to reach it in a single move.

Our example involves the game Timman vs. Portisch, from Tilburg 1979. The position is a hedgehog formation, which is discussed in the chapter on pawn structure. White has greater space, but Black's position is very solid. The defense was very much in vogue at the end of the 1970s. White has just played 17.f4, completing the domination of the middle of the board.

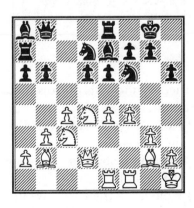

White completely dominates the center. The d5 square is within reach of five pieces, while Black has only three aiming at that spot. The pawn at e4 is supported by three pieces and attacked only by two. The knight at d4 cannot be disturbed except by an advance of the pawn to e5, which would critically weakened d5 and allow the knight to take up a strong post at f5. The e5-square is not yet under White's control, but since the pawn cannot advance from e6, it cannot be put to good use by Black.

17...Rc8; 18.Re2 Nc5; 19.Rfe1 Bf8. White has doubled rooks not to prepare the advance of the e-pawn, but to overprotect it. **20.Qd1!?** The overprotection strategy continues, as White prepares to triple on the e-file without conceding the g4-square to the Black knight.

20...Rac7; 21.Re3 Rd8; 22.Qe2 Rcc8?! 22...e5 might have been tried now, since the knight is easily driven off of its new home at f5. 23.Nf5 g6; 24.Nh4 seems only a little bit better for White. **23.f5!** Despite the buildup on the e-file, this is the intended advance. The e-pawn must stay at e4 or Black will exchange bishops and White will have problems on the light squares. **23...a5.** This allows White to create a serious weakness at e6.

24.fxe6 fxe6; 25.Rf1 Re8; 26.a3 Re7; 27.Ncb5. White is just maneuvering pieces to improve the landscape before the serious work begins.

27...Ncd7; 28.Rd1 Ree8; 29.Nc3 Ne5; 30.Bh3! White's overprotection of e4 allows the bishop to take up an active post, targetng the weakling at e6. **30...Kf7.** There is no other way to defend the pawn, which guards the critical central outpost square at d5. **31.Rf1 Rcd8.**

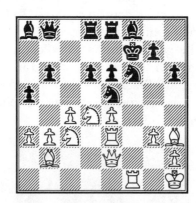

The stage is set for a sacrifice. White still controls three of the four central squares. The knight at f6 is an important defender, which is eliminated with a strong sacrifice.

32.Rxf6+! Kxf6; 33.Qf1+ Ke7; 34.Nxe6 Rc8; 35.Nd5+! Bxd5. Black has no choice. **36.exd5.** The remaining knight is now the critical defender. White can blast it from the board at any time. **36...a4; 37.Nf4 Kd8.** A prettier finish is 37...Rc7; 38.Bxe5 dxe5; 39.d6+ Kxd6; 40.Qd3+ Ke7; 41.Rxe5+ Kf7; 42.Qd5+ Kf6; 43.Rf5+ Ke7; 44.Ng6#.

38.Bxc8 Kxc8; 39.Ne6. By blocking the e-file, White cuts off a supply line to the knight at e5, which becomes vulnerable. **39...Kb7.** 39...Ng4; 40.Qf7! Nxe3; 41.Qxe8+ Kb7; 42.Qd7+ Ka8; 43.Nd8 is another win, with Qc6+ looming.

40.Bxe5 dxe5; 41.Qf7+. Black resigned. The end comes quickly as the remaining pieces fall. 41...Be7; 42.Nxg7 Rc8; 43.Qxe7+ Rc7; 44.Qxe5 Qh8; 45.d6! Rxg7; 46.Qxg7+ Qxg7; 47.Re7+ with a simple win.

If the center can be blocked, however, its loses some of its importance. Then the speedier flank operation will win. We see an excellent example from the game Rosenthal vs. Zagoryansky at the 1936 Moscow tournament.

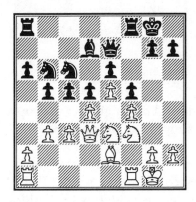

Black has just played 16...f5! White has a difficult choice. There is only one opportunity to capture en passant, but blasting open the kingside is also tempting. As it turns out, neither of these plans is correct. The best way to keep control of the center is, paradoxically, to remove the pawn at d4 by capturing at c5.

17.g4?

With the center closed, White tries to get the kingside attack going. Black's counterplay on the queenside seems insignificant, but it is not. Capturing at f6 would also be an error, but White could have retained the advantage by capturing the pawn at c5. This illustrates the difficulties that proper evaluation of the center can present. 17.exf6?! gxf6; 18.Rfe1 cxd4!; 19.cxd4. Capturing with the knight would have allowed Black to advance the e-pawn to e5 and annihilate the center. The superior 17.dxc5 Qxc5; 18.Rfc1 would have maintained the balance on the queenside. White would have a nice post for the knight at d4, as an exchange of knights would solidify White's advantage in space. **17...b4!** The base of the pawn chain is attacked. 18.gxf5 This also attacks the base of the pawn chain!

18...exf5; 19.Kh1 a5. Black continues to play on the queenside. **20.Rac1 cxd4; 21.cxd4 Nd8!**

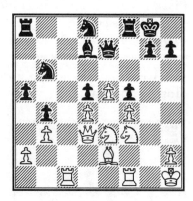

This is a multipurpose move. The knight will take up a new post at e6. At the same time, the bishop at d7 can support an advance of the a-pawn, and the c-file can be contested by a rook at c8.

22.Ne1? This is a very poor move contributes nothing to the kingside attack. White will soon regret his folly. The correct move was 22.Rg1.

22...Bc8; 23.Qd2. The knight is evidently headed for d3. In any case, White did not want to allow Black to move the bishop to a6. **23...Ne6!** White cannot complete the maneuver, because the pawn at d4 would not be defended if the knight gets in the way of the queen.

24.Rc6? White has no support at all for a queenside invasion. The impudent rook is chased away. **24...Qb7!; 25.Rc2 Bd7; 26.N1g2 Rac8!; 27.Rxc8 Nxc8.** The rook was unavailable for recapturing duty because it needed to remain in a position to guard the f-pawn.

28.Nc2 Ne7; 29.Bd3 Bb5!; Black exchanges bishops. The tide has turned and the blockaded White center is weak. **30.Rf3 Rc8; 31.Bxb5 Qxb5; 32.Kg1.**

White counts on using f2 as a safe square. The hole at c3 is the reward for Black's bold queenside strategy starting at move 17. In his concern for the king, White overlooked a simple tactic. 32.Nge3 was the best defense. At least the Black knight at e6 is tied to the defense of the pawns. 32...Rc3; 33.Rf1 Qd3; 34.Qg2 Qe4 would also be unpleasant. Black threatens to capture at d4, but the exchange of queens does not help. 35.Qxe4 dxe4; 36.Rf2 Nxd4!; 37.Nxd4 Rxe3; 38.Rc2 Rc3 followed by ...Nd5 would still be difficult to defend.

32...Rxc2!; 33.Qxc2 Nxd4; 34.Qc7 A desperate try to stay in the game, but after **34...Nxf3+; 35.Kf2 Nd4,** White resigned. 36.Qxe7 is mated by 36...Qe2+; 37.Kg3 Qf3+; 38.Kh4 Qg4#.

SPACE

When you control greater space, you can more freely maneuver your pieces and shift them quickly from one side of the board to another. The space you control is generally an area behind your pawn barrier, if it is intact, or within the scope of your pieces. Remember that a square is within the scope of your piece if it can reach that square in one move, and it doesn't matter whether or not your piece would be under attack on the target square.

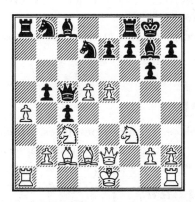

This position arose in a 1989 game between Glek and Yanvarov, played in the Soviet Union. White controls much more space in the center and on the kingside. Although there are no immediate threats, Black is in trouble. White starts by repositioning the bishop on the important central square d4.

16.Be3 Qb4; 17.Bd4 bxa4. Black is making progress on the queenside, but it is irrelevant. **18.0-0!** White mobilizes more force by bringing the rook to the f-file. From there it can maneuver, thanks to the free space, to the g-file or h-file as needed.

18...Nc5; 19.e6! Bxd4+? The best defense is 19...fxe6; 20.Bxg7 Kxg7; 21.dxe6 Qxb2; 22.Qe5+ Rf6; 23.Qxc5! Qxc3; 24.Ne5!! A fantastic move, blocking the defense of f6, so that now Qxe7 really is a threat. White controls the space all over the board. 24...Nc6 buys a little time, but 25.Qxc6 Qd4+; 26.Kh1 Ra7; 27.Qxc8 Qxe5; 28.Qxc4 Qxe6; 29.Qxe6 Rxe6; 30.Rxa4 is a simple enough win.

20.Nxd4 f6? 20...f5 is better. Still, White has 21.Nxf5 gxf5; 22.Bxf5 with a winning position, for example 22...Nb3; 23.Qh5 Rxf5; 24.Rxf5 and mate follows. **21.Bxg6!**

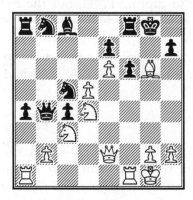

The remainder of the game is not available, but Black is lost in any case. After 21...hxg6; 22.Qg4 Kh7; 23.Rf3 f5; 24.Qh4+ forces mate in 6. 22...g5 is not much better. 23.Rf3. The rook lift is used to get to the h-file. 23...Qxb2; 24.Rb1 Qa3; 25.Qh5 forces mate in 7! 25...Nxe6; 26.dxe6 Bxe6; 27.Qg6+ Kh8; 28.Nxe6 Qc5+; 29.Nxc5 g4; 30.Rf5 Rf7; 31.Rh5+ Rh7; 32.Rxh7#.

Space is generally limited by pawns, either your own or enemy, and therefore will figure prominently in our discussion below.

PAWN STRUCTURE

Attacks on your major pieces require open lines, which means that the defending pawns have been cleared out of the way. If you are defending, you want to keep the pawn barrier intact so that it can continue to protect your territory. When you create weaknesses in your pawn structure, these attract the attention of your opponent, who will figure out a way to exploit them.

> *Take care of the Pawns and the Queens take care of themselves.*
>
> — Loyd

We'll look at ten different types of pawn structures and see how they can be exploited.

1. BACKWARD PAWNS

A backward pawn is one which has no neighboring pawn on a rank behind it to offer support. Pawns like to be supported by other pawns, and may be difficult to maintain if they have to rely on pieces instead. Here is a position where White must use all of his resources to defend the weakling.

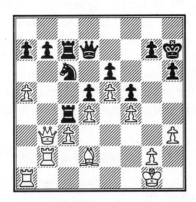

We join the game Szabo vs. Tal from the 1958 tournament at Portoroz. White has a backward pawn at c3, and Black has blockaded it by placing a rook at c4. Ideally, Black can attack c3 with all four pieces, forcing White to use all of his pieces to defend the pawn. How will Black make progress in this case? The plan involves maneuvering the knight to b5, supported by a pawn at a6.

24...a6; 25.Qb6. This stops ...Na7. **25...Ne7.** Black will try to get to a7 via c8. **26.Qd6 Qe8; 27.Rb6.** 27.Qxe6?? is a blunder. 27...R4c6 traps the queen.

27...R4c6; 28.Rxc6 Qxc6; 29.Rb1 Rd7. Tal puts the question to the enemy queen. If the queens are exchanged, the endgame with good knight vs. bad bishop is a straight-forward win. **30.Qb4.** 30.Qxc6 Nxc6; 31.Ra1 Na7; 32.Ra3 Rc7; 33.Kf2 Rc4 reaches a winning endgame. The plan is simply ...Nb5, and if the rook goes to b3, to maintain the pawn at c3, then ...Ra4 sneaks behind the a-pawn. 34.Ke3 Nb5; 35.Rb3 Ra4; 36.Kf2 Rxa5. This looks risky, because of the potential advance of White's c-pawn with a direct attack on the knight and a discovered attack against the rook. There is no danger, however, since 37.c4 is countered by 37...Ra3!

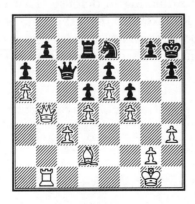

30...Nc8; 31.g4. White sees that Black will now be able to carry out the plan of ...Rc7 and ...Na7-b5. Opening lines on the kingside is intended to provide some counterplay on the kingside. Black keeps the position closed. **31...g6!; 32.Qf8.** A lone queen presents no danger. **32...Rg7; 33.Kf2 Qc4; 34.Rb2 Na7; 35.Rb6 Nc6!** The a-pawn is now the target. Eventually the Black queen strikes deeper into the enemy position and the knight can make use of c4.

36.Ke1 Qd3; 37.g5 hxg5! There can be no danger on the h-file because White still has a pawn on the file and the rook cannot get there anyway. **38.fxg5 Nxa5; 39.Rxe6 Nc4.** The e-pawn was of no real significance. The coordination of queen and knight leaves White defenseless.

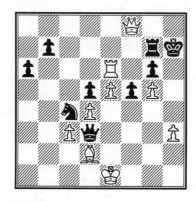

40.Bc1 Qxc3+; 41.Kd1 Qxd4+; 42.Ke2 Qe4+; 43.Kd1 Qf3+; 44.Kc2 Qe2+; 45.Kc3 d4+! 46.Kb4. 46.Kxd4 Qd1+; 47.Kxc4 Rc7+; 48.Kb4 Qe1+! 49.Kb3 Qc3+; 50.Ka2 Qc4+! 51.Ka3 Qxc1+; 52.Ka4 Qc4+; 53.Ka3 Qc3+; 54.Ka2 Qd2+; 55.Ka3 Rc3+; 56.Kb4 Qb2+ and mate next move. **46...a5+**

47.Kc5 Rc7+; 48.Kb5 Nxe5+; 49.Kb6 Rc6+. White resigned, because capturing the rook loses the queen to ...Nd7+.

An alternative to simply winning the backward pawn is to use it as a barrier to keep enemy forces from coordinating in defense. That can be seen in this excerpt from the game Smyslov vs. Rudakovsky, from the 1945 Soviet Championship. White has just played 17.Nd5, a powerful move which occupies an outpost in front of the backward pawn. Black is unable to secure an effective defense against the kingside attack which follows.

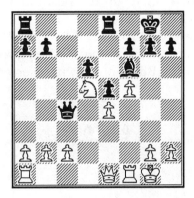

17...Bd8; 18.c3 b5. Black's queenside counterplay is non-existent. White enjoys a considerable advantage in space. 19.b3 Qc5+; 20.Kh1 Rc8. Black has no targets. White can now freely pursue the enemy king. 21.Rf3 Kh8; 22.f6! The barriers start to fall.

22...gxf6; 23.Qh4 Rg8; 24.Nxf6 Rg7; 25.Rg3 Bxf6; 26.Qxf6 Black resigned. White will bring the rook at a1, which has not yet moved, into the game with devastating effect. 26...Rcg8; 27.Rxg7 Rxg7; 28.Rd1 Qxc3; 29.h4 Qc7; 30.Rxd6. White wins.

If the backward pawn is such a liability, why then is it seen in many important variations of the Sicilian Defense? The answer is that a backward pawn can be remedied by advancing it. The pawn also serves as an anchor for a pawn at e5 or c5, which gives Black control of d4. In the Sicilian, Black has a semi-open c-file which can be used by a variety of Black pieces to indirectly support the pawn. The famous "Sicilian Break" is a case where the backward d-pawn advances to d5.

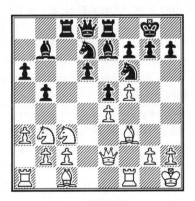

This position was reached in the game Van der Wiel vs. Browne, from the 1980 Wijk aan Zee tournament. White seems to have everything under control, as far as the d5-square is concerned. After all, the knight, pawn, and bishop at f3 all guard it, and a rook can come to d1 next turn. With the center under control, White looks forward to a kingside pawnstorm. Black has a strong move, however.

14...d5! The Sicilian Break opens up the position and leads to an initiative for Black. The initiative is supported by a pawn sacrifice.

15.exd5 e4! White realized that 16.Bxe4 Bd6; 17.Nd2 is countered by 17...Rxc3!; 18.bxc3 Bxd5 where White is in deep trouble. So he played **16.Nxe4 Bxd5; 17.Ned2.** Perhaps Black's best move is 17...Bd6, but Browne selected **17...Qc7; 18.Bxd5 Nxd5.**

The exchanges have not hurt Black, despite the pawn deficit. White's pieces are underdeveloped and uncoordinated. Black has plenty of time to get pieces to the kingside to attack the White king, which has only pawns as protectors. Black has eliminated the backward pawn and has an active game, which he eventually won after a long struggle.

2. DOUBLED PAWNS

A pair of pawns are doubled when they reside on the same file. **Doubled pawns** have been traditionally considered a weakness, but in recent decades quite a number of exceptions are found in respectable openings. One can no longer recommend following traditional advice to inflict doubled pawns whenever possible. Nowadays the specific circumstances of each doubled pawn structure must be considered. Let's start with an example of bad doubled pawns.

Doubled pawns are especially weak when they are isolated. Without the support of neighboring pawns they are difficult to defend. When the doubled pawns are part of what should be a healthy pawn barrier protecting the king, the consequences can be fatal. We can see this even in the opening, for example in the Max Lange Attack.

The following game is attributed to Muller vs. Bayer, played in 1908. It is stunningly beautiful, but perhaps is an example of a composed game. The opening starts out in exciting fashion.

MULLER - BAYER
1908
1.e4 e5; 2.Nf3 Nc6; 3.Bc4 Nf6; 4.d4 exd4; 5.0-0 Bc5; 6.e5 d5; 7.exf6 dxc4; 8.Re1+.

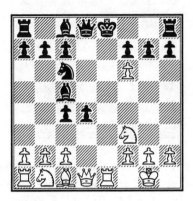

8...Kf8? Black should play **8...Be6.; 9.Bg5!** White threatens gxf7 attacking queen and rook so Black must capture.

9...gxf6; 10.Bh6+! Kg8; 11.Nc3! White continues to develop. The pin on the d-file is deadly, even though the Black queen is defended.

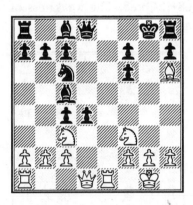

11...Bf8. 11...dxc3; The trap is sprung on 12.Qxd8+ Nxd8; 13.Re8+ Bf8; 14.Rxf8#. **12.Nxd4!** White offers yet another piece. **12...Nxd4?!** Hard to resist, unless you see what is coming. 12...Bxh6; 13.Nxc6 Qxd1; 14.Ne7+ Kg7; 15.Raxd1 would have left the game level, though the weak pawns and White's spatial advantage are meaningful. Black's extra pawn is not worth much, since it is also doubled, though defensible.

13.Qxd4!! Bf5; 13...Qxd4 loses to 14.Re8 which threatens mate at f8. 14...Qd6; 15.Nd5!! Black is mated in four moves.

Black continues to suffer from the isolated doubled pawns.

14.Qf4. 14.Nd5 is a simpler win. 14...Bg7 allows 15.Re8+!! Qxe8; 16.Nxf6+ Bxf6; 17.Qxf6 Qf8; 18.Bxf8 and wins. Or 14...Bxh6; 15.Re8+!! Qxe8; 16.Nxf6+ Kf8, when 17.Nxe8 Kxe8; 18.Qxh8+ Bf8; 19.Qe5+ Be6; 20.Qb5+ will be easy for White to win. **14...Bxc2?;** 14...Bxh6! is much stronger, though White has a clear advantage by taking either bishop. Of course such an end would have deprived us of the artistic finish.

15.Rad1!! Bd6. 15...Bxd1; 16.Qg3+ mates. **16.Nd5!!** White sacrifices the queen to force mate. **16...Bxf4; 17.Re8+!! Qxe8.** The weakness of the isolated doubled pawns finally leads to checkmate.

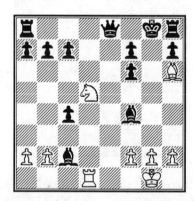

18.Nxf6#. So many brilliant moves by an obscure player and a suspicious oversight by Black combine to lend credibility to the notion that this was an invented game. I have not researched the matter, but would hardly be surprised to find that it had been composed.

When the doubled pawns are not isolated, they can be part of a strong defensive barrier. Nevertheless, in the endgame the pawn structure can be fatally unbalanced, if one side has a pawn majority that has no doubled pawns, and the other side has doubled pawns. This endgame can arise from many openings where a central pawn captures on the bishop file. The most recognizable example is the Exchange Variation of the Spanish Game, which begins **1.e4 e5; 2.Nf3 Nc6; 3.Bb5 a6; 4.Bxc6 dxc6.**

White will obtain a permanent kingside pawn majority with an early d4, for example **5.0-0 f6; 6.d4** which can lead to an early endgame after **6...Bg4 7.dxe5 Qxd1; 8.Rxd1 fxe5; 9.Rd3 Bd6; 10.Nbd2 Nf6; 11.Nc4 0-0; 12.Ncxe5 Bxf3; 13.Nxf3 Rae8; 14.e5 Bxe5; 15.Nxe5 Rxe5.**

We are following Grefe vs. Koelle, Australian Open 1975. White has two advantages. The bishop is better than the knight and the doubled pawns on the queenside hurt Black's chances of making anything with the pawn majority.

16.Bf4 Re2; 17.Rd2 Rfe8; 18.Kf1. White chases out the invader. **18...R2e7; 19.Rad1 Nd5; 20.Bg3 b5.** Black does not want the knight to be chased from d5, where it guards the pawn at c7 and blocks the d-file.

21.h3 Re4; 22.Kg1 Kf7; 23.f3 R4e6 24.Bf2 Ne3? A strategic error. Black needed to keep the minor pieces on. The closer the game gets to a pure pawn endgame, the worse Black's chances.

25.Bxe3 Rxe3; 26.Rd7+ R8e7; 27.Rxe7+ Kxe7.

Black had perhaps counted on a rook and pawn endgame which would be very difficult to win even with imperfect defense. This particular position does not allow for that possibility, as White can force the exchange of rooks.

28.Kf2 Re4; 29.Re1 Rxe1; 30.Kxe1 Kd6; 31.Kd2 Kd5; 32.Ke3. We arrive at a pawn endgame with no chance of survival by Black if White can manage to advance the kingside pawn majority.

32...c5; 33.f4 c4; 34.c3. White will not allow the Black pawns to get too close to the promotion rank. **34...a5; 35.g4 h6; 36.h4 g6; 37.h5!**

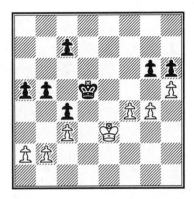

The pawn chain is weakened, but a passed pawn is created.

37...gxh5; 38.gxh5 c6; 39.Kf3! The battle for the tempo begins. Sooner or later Black must give way, and White's king will get to e4.

39...b4; 40.Ke3 c5; 41.Kf3 Ke6; 42.Ke4.

White has the opposition, and wins.

42...Kf6; 43.f5 Kf7; 44.Ke5 Ke7; 45.f6+ Kf7; 46.Kf5 a4; 47.a3 b3; 48.Ke5 Kf8; 49.f7. Any king move wins by force, but no doubt White had seen the game to the end, where the win comes on the wings of a single tempo.

49...Kxf7; 50.Kf5 Ke7; 51.Kg6 Ke6; 52.Kxh6 Kf6; 53.Kh7 Kf7; 54.h6. Black resigned.

There are some positions where the doubled pawns are not a liability. They can be an asset, keeping enemy pieces off critical squares. The file where the doubled pawn once stood is now open for use by a rook. Many times the doubled pawns are the result of an exchange of bishop for knight, so there is additional positional compensation. Our example shows how deadly the compensating factors can be. In Korody vs. Benko, Budapest 1921, White has just advanced 16.b5, since it was attacked at b4.

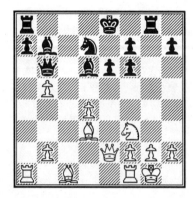

White has not been able to make any progress against Black's well-defended center. The d5 and e5 squares are overprotected, and both f-pawns play an important role in the central barrier protecting the king. The g-file is ready for action, and the bishop at b7 joins the rook in converging at g2. The knight is in the way, of course, but can be lured away. The surprise came in the form of **16...Qxd4!!** White is left without any good moves. 17.Nxd4?? is out of the question on this turn, because of 17...Rxg2+; 18.Kh1 Rxh2+; 19.Kg1 Rh1#. 17.g3? allows an elegant mate with 17...Bxg3!! 18.hxg3 (18.Nxd4?? Bf4+; 19.Bg6 Rxg6+; 20.Qg4 Rxg4#. 18...Rxg3+! 19.Kh2 Bxf3 and to prevent mate at h4; White must capture the rook. 20.fxg3 (20.Kxg3 Qg4+; 21.Kh2 Qg2#) 20...Bxe2; 21.Bxe2 Rc8 and Black is seriously behind in material.

So White chose **17.h3**, to which Black replied **17...Ne5!;** Trade a non-attacker for a defender! **18.Nxd4**. The alternatives were not much better. 18.Be4 still allows 18...Rxg2+!! 19.Kxg2 Bxe4; 20.Rd1 Bxf3+; 21.Qxf3 Nxf3; 22.Rxd4 Nxd4 winds up with Black a knight and pawn ahead, with the doubled pawns as healthy as ever! **18...Rxg2+.** The rest is simple.

19.Kh1 Rh2+; 20.Kxh2 Ng4+; 21.Kg1 Bh2#. The doubled pawn remains intact here, too. Doubled pawns are weak in many cases, but strong in some, so you should evaluate each case on its own merits. It is safest to accept doubling of your pawns when you can comfortably capture toward the center, as this does not bring with it the likelihood of a losing king and pawn endgame.

3. FIANCHETTO STRUCTURES

A **fianchetto** places a bishop at b2 or g2 (as White) or b7 or g7 (as Black) with some surrounding pawns, and it's formation is strong as long as there is a bishop at home. If the fianchettoed bishop is exchanged, very bad things can happen. The fianchetto is the base of operations for many opening strategies, including the King's Indian Defense and Dragon Sicilian. In the latter, the bishop is needed both for defense and to attack the enemy queenside. The fianchetto (both the Italian pronunciation *fee-ann-ket-to* and American *fee-ann-chet-to* are used) is one of the most dynamic formations and is considered positionally sound.

In the game Nunn vs. Mestel, from the 1982 Zonal at Marbella, two great Dragoneers met. Black was tempted by the pawn at e4, reckoning that it was insufficiently defended because of the pin on the long diagonal. After **15...Nxe4?!; 16.Bxe4 Bxe4; 17.Nxe4 Bxa1,** White established a strong position with **18.c3!**

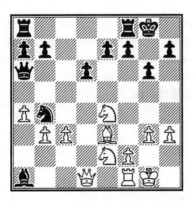

The Black bishop is trapped in the corner, and the dark squares on the kingside are vulnerable.

18...Na2; 18...Nc6 would have provided better defense. **19.Bh6 f5; 20.Qd5+ Kh8; 21.Rxa1.**

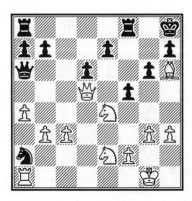

Now the knight at a2 is trapped, so Black has to capture at e2.

21...Qxe2; 22.Qd4+ e5; 23.Qxd6 fxe4. 23...Rf7; 24.Qxe5+ Kg8; 25.Nf6+ Rxf6; 26.Qxf6 and mate in 3. **24.Qxe5+. White won.**

4. HANGING PAWNS

Hanging pawns are adjacent pawns with no visible means of support. They can appear on various flanks and files, but are most often seen on the queenside. Hanging pawns on the c-file and d-file are very common in the Queen's Gambit Declined and Nimzo-Indian Defenses, where many main lines revolve around the weakness of the pawns and the need to protect them.

Because the hanging pawns cannot be protected by other pawns, they must be supported by pieces. If the defending pieces are eliminated, or sufficient force is brought to bear, then the pawns can be captured. The weakness of the hanging pawns is illustrated nicely in the following position from Karpov vs. Georgiev, Tilburg 1994.

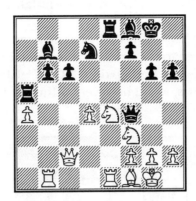

The hanging pawns at b6 and c6 are weak, and each has only a single defender. The remaining Black forces are in no position to assist with the defense of the pawns, so sooner or later one of them will have to step forward. This is not simple, because White has two pawn restraints at a4 and d4, as well as queen, rook, knight, and bishop all overprotecting the key squares.

22.Bc4. A cunning move, tempting Black to advance the c-pawn and open up an attack at e4 as well as d4. Black first swings the bishop into a better position at g7.

22...Bg7; 23.Re2 c5. Black must try to get into the game, and at least at e4 there is a target. 23...b5 would solve the problem if not for White's tactical refutation. 24.Qd2! Qxd2; 25.Bxf7+! and Black cannot take the bishop because of Nd6+ and the rook falls with check, after which White can recapture at d2. 25...Kf8; 26.Nfxd2 Re7; 27.axb5 Rxf7; 28.Nd6! Mate is threatened at e8, but the bishop at b7 is also under attack. Black must settle for 28...Bxd4; 29.Nb3! Ra4; 30.Nxb7 cxb5; 31.Nxd4 Rxd4; 32.Nd8! White wins the exchange.

24.d5! Raa8; 25.Rbe1. White is setting up more tactical threats. Black now tries to reorganize to go after the pawn at d5. The hanging pawns are still weak even in their new formation.

25...Rad8; 26.Qb3 Ba8; 27.g3 Qb8; 28.d6!

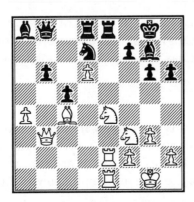

The bishop at a8 is released, but the pawn at f7 falls, and then the White pieces quickly move in for the kill.

28...Rf8; 29.Bxf7+ Rxf7; 30.Neg5!! White has no need to conserve material. Black's queenside forces cannot come to the defense of the king in time to make a difference.

30...hxg5; 31.Nxg5 Rdf8; 32.Re8 Qxd6; 33.Qxf7+ Kh8; 34.Ne6. Black resigned. Hanging pawns are not always, weak, however, as Karpov has demonstrated from the other side of the board.

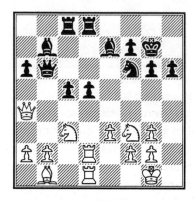

In the first game of the 1981 World Championship match Karpov obtained a favorable hanging pawn structure as Black against Korchnoi. Each pawn enjoys the support of three pieces.

24.a3? 24.Ne5 d4! (24...Bd6; 25.Nxg6 fxg6; 26.Qc2 gives White some serious attacking chances.) 25.exd4 cxd4; 26.Ne2 Rc5 and Black has an active game with pressure at b2 indirectly protecting the d-pawn. **24...d4! 25.Ne2.** 25.exd4 Bc6!; 26.Qc2 Bxf3; 27.gxf3 cxd4 is very strong for Black.

25...dxe3; 26.fxe3 c4. The pawn structure has changed radically. White has the weak pawns, and Black's pawns are fairly healthy. The bishop pair and mobile piece give Black a clear advantage.

27.Ned4 Qc7; 28.Nh4 Qe5; 29.Kh1 Kg8; 30.Ndf3 Qxg3; 31.Rxd8+ Bxd8; 32.Qb4 Be4 and White lost after another ten moves.

Handling hanging pawns takes a great deal of care, and is a task best left to professionals. You should avoid hanging pawns because they tie down your pieces in defense. When your opponent has hanging pawns, look for ways to attack in other areas of the board.

5. HEDGEHOGS

The **hedgehog** formation is a relatively modern innovation, at least as a serious defensive setup. Black places most of the pawns along the third rank, and usually fianchettoes both bishops. Many of the pawns are a bit weak and require the support of the other pieces, just as in the case of hanging pawns. The hedgehog formation can be reached from the Sicilian Defense, English Opening, Queen's Indian, and other popular openings.

> *T*he hedgehog is a peaceful creature.
> But those who try to hurt it soon
> experience the sharpness of its quills
>
> — Adorjan.

The hedgehog is not only a defensive formation. If White does not carefully over-protect the center, the entire White formation can come crashing down. We see a classic example from Garry Kasparov.

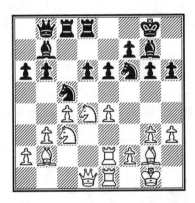

This is an excerpt from the game Hübner vs. Kasparov from the 1981 Tilburg tournament. Both sides have completed development and have slowly maneuvered through the first 22 moves. White seems to have a firm grip on the center but the weak pawn at d6 has no way to get to d5 and smash open the center. Or does it?

23...b5!; 24.cxb5 d5! This is a very instructive game because it shows how quickly the center can be undermined by well timed pawn advances combined with pieces that are situated to take advantage of the new environment.

25.exd5 Nxd5; 26.Nxd5 Bxd5; 27.b4 Bxg2; 28.Kxg2 e5! Black maintains the initiative. The remainder of the game, while not relevant to the question of the hedgehog formation, is worth viewing. **29.bxc5 exd4; 30.Rd2 Rxc5; 31.bxa6 Qa8+; 32.Qf3 Qxa6.** Material is now equal, and Black has a powerful passed d-pawn. **33.Red1 Rf5; 34.Qe4 Qa4!**

The pawn is indirectly defended because 35.Bxb4? loses to 35...Rfd5, exploiting the pin on the d-file. **35.a3 Re8; 36.Qb7 Rd8; 37.Rd3 h5; 38.R1d2 Qe8!**

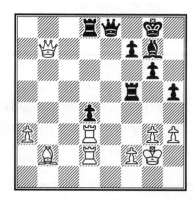

Black must find a way to remove the blockade of the d-pawn, and finds the means in an exchange sacrifice that will come at the last move of the time control (move 40).

39.Kf1 Rb8; 40.Qc7 Rxb2!; 41.Rxb2 Qe4. A clever move, which threatens both the rook and ...Qh1+. **42.Qc4 Qh1+; 43.Ke2 Qg1; 44.Rb8+ Kh7; 45.f4 h4! 46.Rb5 Rxb5; 47.Qxb5 hxg3; 48.Qg5 Qf2+; 49.Kd1 Qf1+.** White resigned. A very efficient win by Kasparov.

The hedgehog is hardly a perfect creature, however. The counter-punching can only take place if the defensive formation can withstand all of White's attacks. Our next example shows White exploiting the weakness of the queenside pawns. It is taken from the game Smyslov vs. Dzindzichashvili, played at Moscow, 1972.

Black's position seems solid enough, with all of the pawns defended. Smyslov exposes the hidden weaknesses of the hedgehog position with a fine sacrifice. The e5-square, which Black seems to have well under control, plays a major role.

17.Nxe6!! fxe6; 18.Qg4 Nf6; 19.Qxe6+ Kh8; 20.Nxb6. White has three pawns for the piece, and the central pawns, supported by rooks, crash through.

20...Rf8; 21.c5! Ra7. 21...dxc5?; 22.e5! wins a piece. **22.cxd6 Bd8; 23.Na4 Re8; 24.Qf7 Ba8; 25.d7 Rg8; 26.Qe6 Qb5** and in this pathetic position Black resigned, since the advance of the e-pawn will wrap things up quickly.

Weak pawns are targets, but so are empty squares which cannot be protected by pawns. We'll meet those next.

6. HOLES

A **hole** is a square near enemy pawn formations which cannot be defended by an enemy pawn. Holes are significant at every stage of the game. When a hole is occupied by a piece, we call it an outpost, because it represents a safe haven deep inside enemy territory. A couple of holes can easily lead to checkmate.

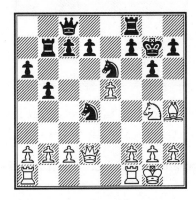

In Unzicker vs. Aarlund, from the 1974 Olympiad in Nice, Black suffers from serious holes at f6 and h6. White threatens 22.Bf6+ Kg8; 23.Nh6#. This often happens when the bishop is removed from the fianchetto formation. The king at g7 is less good as a defender. White owns both f6 and h6. The game cannot last long, and didn't. Black retreated the knight from d4 to f5, to cover h6 and g7.

21...Nf5; 22.Bf6+ Kg8; 23.Nh6+ Nxh6; 24.Qxh6 d5. Black has no way to save the game. After **25.Rad1,** Black resigned, because there is no defense to the rook lift to h3 and checkmate.

> *Weak points or holes in the enemy position must be occupied by pieces, not pawns*
>
> — Tarrasch

It is often tempting to place a pawn on a weak square in the enemy position. Such holes are better occupied by pieces. When a pawn sits on square it has control only over the two squares diagonally in front of it.

The pawn at f6 is useful of course, but the effect is limited by the short range. Black is deprived of two squares, and the pawn cannot reposition itself to inflict any serious damage.

A knight has a much greater effect because it attacks four points in the enemy position.

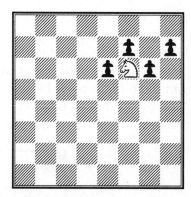

The knight would fork any two pieces on d7, e8, g8, and h7, possibly also enemy pieces to the rear at e5, h5, d5, and e4. It can move to any of those eight squares and reposition itself for another attack, should the immediate occupation at f6 not bring the desired result.

Bishops can be very powerful when operating from a hole in the enemy position. There are many checkmating patterns that involve a bishop on this square, as you will see in the inventory of mating positions in the Tactics chapter.

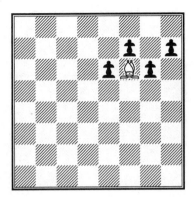

You can see that the bishop controls key squares at e7, g7, h8, and d8. The bishop does not have the ability to attack squares of both colors, so is somewhat more limited than the knight in this regard.

Because holes are, by definition, close to the enemy home rank, the queen is less effective. Often she can be chased away easily enough. In any case, the queen only adds an additional two squares to the coverage of the bishop, f7 and g6. Of course if the f-file is open for use by a rook, the pressure on f7 can be intense. And if the queen is backed up by a bishop on the long diagonal, the combinational possibilities are usually excellent, as we see in a game between Delmar and an unknown amateur, played in New York in 1890. We join it in the early middlegame.

The queen is now in position, and Black naturally had to worry about a subsequent knight move, for example ...Ng4 with three different checkmate threats, at h6, g7, and h8! So Black tried to chase the queen out of the hole with **17...Be7** but encountered the brilliant **18.Qh8+!! Kxh8; 19.Nxf7+ Kg8; 20.Nh6#**.

A rook strangely enough, is almost useless when it is occupying a hole. It is surrounded by well-defended pawns. In general, it is not better than a rook safely stationed further back on the file.

Therefore, it is usually best to occupy holes with minor pieces.

7. THE ISOLATED D-PAWN

Entire books have been devoted to discussion of the strengths and weaknesses of the isolated d-pawn. Many important variations of the Queen's Gambit, French Defense, Caro-Kann Defense, Nimzo-indian Defense and other major openings crucially revolve around this pawn, often called an isolani.

Siegbert Tarrasch was convinced that the traditional evaluation of an isolated pawn, that it is a major weakness, was wrong and that the isolated pawn was in fact a strong weapon. Let's first look at the pawn structure by itself.

If the game came down to a king and pawn endgame, Black would be lost. The pawn at d5 is weak, and can easily be blockaded by an enemy king at d4. In fact, the blockade is the best-known strategy for operating against an isolated d-pawn. The best blockaders are pieces of limited mobility and value, which means that a knight is ideal.

When there is a White piece at d4, the Black cannot advance the pawn from d5 and White can aim other pieces at it. Extreme views have been expressed on the subject of the "isolani." The great Hypermodern strategist Aron Nimzowitsch considered the blockade a potent weapon against the isolani, rendering it very weak. For the Classist Siegbert Tarrasch, on the other hand, the isolani is a source of dynamic strength, because it cramps the enemy position. Modern thinking holds that the isolani is neither good nor bad in isolation, but must be judged depending on the surrounding circumstances.

An isolated d-pawn on the fourth rank does indeed feel a powerful urge to get to the fifth rank. The pawn does not feel comfortable on the fourth rank, where it can be blocked by one enemy piece and then attacked from all sides. Advancing the pawn can be effective even when it merely seems to simplify the position. The following example is very instructive. We join the game Dolmatov vs. Larsen, from Amsterdam 1980, at the end of the opening, before White's 12th move.

> *The strength of an isolani lies in its lust to expand...*
>
> — Nimzowitsch

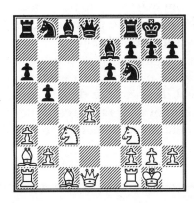

12.d5! exd5; 13.Nxd5 Bb7?! 13...Nxd5; 14.Qxd5 Ra7 would have been a better defense. **14.Nxe7+ Qxe7; 15.Bg5.** The bishop pair is a powerful force in this game, thanks to all the open space. **15...Nbd7; 16.Re1 Qc5?** Like it or not, Larsen had to retreat the queen to d8 here.

17.Be3 Qf5; 18.Nh4 Qe4; 19.Bg5 Qc6. Black tries to set up an attack, but White just drives the queen away with tempo. **20.Rc1 Qb6; 21.Be3 Qd8; 22.Nf5 Be4; 23.Nd6 Bg6.** Black has arranged the defense of the kingside, but White's advantage in space and control of the center bring the game to a rapid conclusion.

24.Qd4 Qb8; 25.f4. Black cannot preserve the bishop at g6 without critically weakening the kingside. **25...Rd8.** 25...h6; 26.f5 Bh7; 27.Rc6! White dominates the board. **27...b4 28.Bxf7+!** White wins at least a pawn, because the bishop cannot be captured. 28...Rxf7?; 29.Nxf7 Kxf7; 30.Qc4+ Kf8; 31.Rxf6+! gxf6; 32.Bxh6# is just one example of an embarrassing finish.

26.f5 Bh5; 27.h3 Nb6; 28.Qxb6 Qxb6; 29.Bxb6 Rxd6; 30.Be3 and Black resigned, since the bishop is lost.

The lesson here is that the advance of the isolated pawn is not just a way of getting rid of the nuisance. Since the holder of an isolated d-pawn often enjoys an advantage in space, the elimination of the pawn can increase that factor and result in a substantial advantage.

If you have an isolani, you must consider whether the advance of the pawn and offer of exchange will improve your position. If you release the tension too soon, you will be left with mere equality. If you wait too long, you'll be stuck with a sick pawn in the endgame.

When playing against the isolated pawn, try to blockade it with a piece and control the neighboring files, then you can try to win it. Do not rush the attack on the isolani. As the game progresses it becomes weaker and more vulnerable.

8. PASSED PAWNS

A **passed pawn** is a pawn which has no enemy counterpart directly in front of it or on either adjacent file. Each time a piece leaves the board there is one less resource to be used in stopping a pawn from marching up the board. That's why you should try to exchange pieces when you have a passed pawn. Reduce the number of potential defenders and you will have a significant advantage.

Our example shows this idea with a twist. It uses the important technique of letting your opponent capture one passed pawn while you create another one. Some players let themselves get tied down to the defense of a pawn and overlook simple winning combinations. A group of players representing the city of Nijmegen did not fail to spot the possibility to eliminate defenders in a correspondence game against The Hague.

A passed pawn increases it's strength as the number of pieces on the board diminishes.

— Capablanca

White has a passed pawn at d6, but there is no way to get it passed d7. The Black knight must stand guard over d7, at least until the bishop can get to a better position.

48.d7+! 48.g6? fxg6; 49.Nxg6 Bxg6; 50.Kxg6 Nc4 turns the tide, and it is White who must worry about the weakness of the pawns. 51.Kf5 Kd7; 52.Ke4 Nxa3; 53.Kd5 Nc2; 54.Kc5 Ke6 will end in a draw. **48...Nxd7+; 49.Nxd7 Kxd7; 50.Kxf7.** White has lost the d-pawn, but gained a passed g-pawn. The g-pawn, though only on the 6th rank, is even better, especially with the knights gone from the board. It is further from the queenside. Black's only hope is to get the king to a3, give up the bishop for the g-pawn, move the king to a4 and try to exchange the remaining White pawn. This plan is doomed, however.

50...Bd3; 51.Bc5 Kc6; 52.g6 Kd5; 53.g7 Bh7; 54.g8Q Bxg8+; 55.Kxg8 Kc4; 56.Bb6. Black resigned, because the bishop will come to a5, and the White king will eat the Black pawns as follows. 56...Kb3; 57.Kf7 Kxa3; 58.Ba5 Kb3; 59.Ke6 Kc3; 60.Kd5 Kd3; 61.Kc5 Ke4; 62.Kb6 Kd5; 63.Kxa6 Kc6; 64.Ka7 followed by 65.Kb6.

Keep in mind that when you have only one pawn your opponent can sacrifice a piece to remove it and will often achieve a draw as a result. This defensive plan is the key to many endgames.

> *The passed pawn is a criminal, who should be kept under lock and key. Mild measures, such as police surveillance, are not sufficient.*
>
> — Nimzowitsch

Things look bad for White, but there is an escape. Black captures the pawn at b2. If the king captures the bishop, then the White king grabs the e-pawn an the game is drawn because Black has insufficient mating material. If Black ignores the bishop at b2 and protects the pawn by moving the knight to g3, then White moves the bishop to e5, attacking the knight. The game is also drawn.

Your opponents passed pawn can be your worst nightmare. In the endgame, preventing a passed pawn from reaching to the promotions square is one of your most crucial tasks. The best defense is to keep it routed to its square, unable to advance. That is what it means being under lock and key. The surveillance Nimzowitsch refers to use pieces to control squares which live between the pawns current location and the promotion square. The problem with this form of defense is that such pieces can often be deflected or destroyed, sometimes through sacrifices, and then the pawn gets through.

9. PAWN CHAINS

Pawn chains are groups of pawns that are connected to pawns on adjacent files. They can be static, as in the case of stonewall formations, or dynamic, advancing to attack the enemy position. A pawn chain can look like this.

We rarely encounter such a long chain, but pawn chains are characteristic of certain openings, including the Saemisch Variation of the King's Indian Defense, the French Defense, Colle System, Torre Attack, and the older Benoni formations. Chains consist of at least three pawns and can have different shapes.

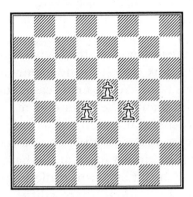

A three-pawn chain facing forward is called a **wedge**. It is seen in the French Defense, Caro-Kann Defense, and in other Semi-Open Games.

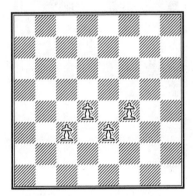

This is a **stonewall**. It is characteristic of the Colle Attack, some lines of the Torre Attack, and of course the Stonewall Attack. Black often adopts the formation in the Stonewall Dutch.

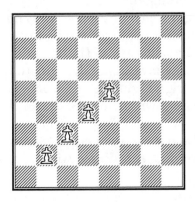

The basic pawn chain along a diagonal is a **straight chain**. It is seen in the French Defense and some other openings. We will use this simple chain for the remainder of our discussion.

We are often taught that the best way to attack a pawn chain is at its base. The base is the pawn which lies on the rank closest to the enemy home rank. In the diagram above, the base of the chain is at b2. Yet in many cases the target is the head, rather than the base. The head of the chain is the other end, at this case, e5. Sometimes, the intermediate pawns are the focus of attention.

In reality, there is no way to make a simple generalization about attacking pawn chains. It is true that most of the time a pawn at the base can be attacked by pieces, while the other pawns can only be hit by pawns (unless a pin or other tactic enables a piece capture). Let's look at four situations where a different pawn is the target in each case.

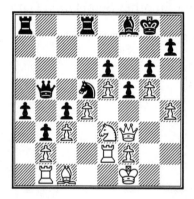

This position is from Ermenkov - Tukmakov, Vrnjacka Banja 1979. Black combines threats on both flanks to win, but the primary objective is the advance of the b-pawn. With **37...a3!** Black attacks the base of the pawn chain. This is especially effective because the pawn at c3 is supported only by the b-pawn, so that if White captures at a3, Black can capture at c3, forking the rooks.

38.Nxd5 Qxd5. The knight which threatened c3 is now gone. White has no good queen moves, so the queens must come off the board, too. **39.Qxd5 Rxd5; 40.Ke1.** 40.bxa3 Rda5 will result in the same sort of finish.

40...axb2; 41.Bxb2 Ra2. The invasion of the seventh rank leads to a winning position. **42.Kd1 Rda5.** White resigned during adjournment. Is the position really that bad? Yes, and all because of the pawn chains. 43.Rd2 h6! 44.Bc1 hxg5; 45.hxg5 Rxd2+; 46.Kxd2 Ra2+; 47.Ke3 Rc2; The base of the pawn chain, now at c3, is doomed. 48.Bb2. (Or 48.Bd2 f4+! 49.Ke2 Be7 and the g-pawn falls.) 48...Be7; 49.f4 Bd8; 50.Kf3 (50.Ra1 Rxb2; 51.Ra8 Rc2; 52.Rxd8+ Kf7 is a simple win.) 50...Ba5; 51.Ra1 Bxc3; 52.Bxc3 Rxc3+ etc.

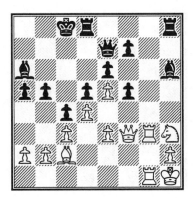

In Norwood vs. Tiviakov, from Calcutta 1993, Black opts to go after the pawn at c3.

23...b4!; 24.Bb1 bxc3; 25.bxc3 Kc7! Black will now use the open file for infiltration. **26.Nf4 Qa3; 27.Qf2 Rb8.** White is in a desperate situation. He tried a sacrifice at f5 but after **28.Bxf5!? Bxf4; 29.Qxf4 exf5; 30.Rg7 Rb2!; 31.Rxf7+ Kb6; 32.h4 Qxc3** the base of the chain falls, and the other pawns are vulnerable. Black won without difficulty.

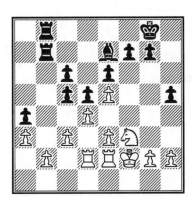

This is an excellent example of attacking the **neck** of the pawn chain, which is the pawn just below the head. Black not only uses the c5xd4 capture (twice!) but finished up with an attack on the head of the pawn chain, giving us two lessons in one! Our teacher is Bent Larsen, playing Black against O'Donnell in a 1970 game played in the USA.

24...cxd4; 25.exd4. Both pawns chains are undoubled. Larsen continues vigorously in pursuit of his target. **25...c5! 26.Rc2 Rc7; 27.Ke3 g5; 28.Ne1.** The knight heads for a more useful post at d3, where it can protect b2, at least temporarily.

28...cxd4+! 29.cxd4 Rb3+; 30.Kd2 Bd8!; 31.Rxc7 Bxc7; 32.Nd3. White defends b2, but the pawn at d4, our old target, is undefended. **32...Bb6!; 33.Ke3.**

Now there are pins at d3 and d4, which means that e5, despite all appearances, is actually undefended! Larsen relentlessly continues the assault, not minding a little sacrifice along the way.

33...f6!; 34.exf6 e5!; 35.Kd2. The pawn cannot be captured because of the pins, so the king retreats. **35...e4!** The knight is chased, and the b-pawn falls.

36.Nc5 Rxb2+; 37.Ke3. Black now enters a winning king and pawn endgame. **37...Rxe2+; 38.Kxe2 Kf7; 39.Ke3 Bxc5; 40.dxc5 Kxf6; 41.Kd4 Ke6; 42.Ke3 Ke5; 43.g3 d4+.** White resigned.

Summing up, the art of chess strategy lies in understanding broad and general concepts, such as those we have examined in this chapter. Now we turn to more specific matters, the tactical operations which take advantage of successful strategic planning or mistakes by your opponents.

TACTICS, SACRIFICES, AND COMBINATIONS

Strategy requires thought, tactics require observation. —**Euwe**

Tactics, sacrifices, and combinations are three closely related chess concepts. There are no universally accepted boundaries between them, and although each is "definitively" defined in various books and publications, the definitions vary widely. We'll begin this chapter with a look at what each of the terms means, or at least how they are generally used. The tactics will then be presented for pieces and pawns. Checkmating and stalemating tactics are cataloged, and you should spend some time making sure you know all of them, as otherwise you could find yourself on the receiving end of a nasty surprise in a game.

TACTICS DEFINED

A tactic is a means of achieving a goal. In that broad sense, almost anything can qualify as a tactic, but in chess the meaning is somewhat narrower. A chess **tactic** is a single move which accomplishes a significant goal. After all, every move does change the position, which could be considered a goal, and we mustn't trivialize the concept to the point where it becomes meaningless.

Chess tactics have names, such as fork, pin, skewer, etc. We will examine a collection of tactical devices below. Tactics are often contrasted with strategy, which involves longer term goals, as discussed in the previous section.

SACRIFICES DEFINED

A **sacrifice** is a simple concept. One side intentionally gives up material. If it is a small amount of material, say a pawn, and the sacrifice takes place in the opening of the game, then we refer to it as a gambit. Of course we don't really know if a player intended to part with the material, and often simple oversights are sometimes represented as sacrifices, especially if they turn out well. Who among us hasn't made an accidental sacrifice in a game, only to claim afterward that it was all intentional and planned!

Although strong players have always rebelled against this notion, it remains a fact. It is much harder to impress someone with a game that lacks a sacrifice, even though there may be beautiful strategic themes, or a fantastic endgame. Sacrifices are accessible, and even a weak player can appreciate them.

Do keep in mind, however, that tournament points and prizes are awarded according to points scored, not beauty. Unfortunately.

A sacrifices is a mean to an end, not a goal in itself. Some sacrifices are calculated precisely while others are of a more speculative nature. Often a speculative sacrifice will lead to a win when the opponent plays precise defensive moves. A worthwhile sacrifice may not stand up to the scrutiny of post game analysis but if it succeeds in bringing home the point in your game, then it was worth playing.

> *The beauty of a game of chess is usually assessed according to the sacrifices it contains.*
>
> — Spielmann

> *If I win, it was a sacrifice. If I lose, then it was a mistake.*
>
> — Koltanowski

COMBINATIONS DEFINED

There is no consensus of what a combination is. Many writers have worked hard to try to formulate the concept, but no definition is universally accepted. They can often get rather technical, and if you want to impress, or bore, your friends, you might quote the following definition:

In ordinary usage, the term **combination** is a simple notion. The basic idea is a series of moves, almost always involving a sacrifice, which leads by force to some tangible advantage. You can certainly call any sacrifice which leads by force to checkmate or the win of material a "combination." In modern chess, with refined defensive technique, often the sacrifices which are part of combinations are declined, the defender seeing less damage in conceding some positional point than in accepting the sacrifice with its dire consequences.

> *A combination is a rearrangement of the connection of pieces of both sides, which forces a coordinated connection of contacts, which is advantageous to one side.*
>
> — Averbakh

> *A combination must be sound. An unsound combination is no combination at all. It is merely an attempt, an error, a failure, a nonentity.*
>
> — Lasker

So in many games, the sacrificial portion of a combination is found in the notes, not the actual moves played. Many prized combinations, praised in the literature for decades, have been found to have flaws, detected by later analysts or computers. Imperfection in a combination is no longer considered a destroyer of artistic value.

Lasker's disdain for unsound combinations is shared by most top players. A combination is worth nothing at all if it can be refuted by correct defensive play. Combinations are easier to refute than sacrifices because the combination consists of a short series of specific tactical operations while a sacrifice may keep the opponent under pressure for a long time.

When a player is under pressure mistakes are more common. A mistaken combination can be refuted quickly with just a few moves.

Some attempts have been made to classify combinations, but since each combination may involve a variety of tactical devices the results are often confusing. It is perhaps best simply to list each of the tactics employed, as Leonid Shamkovich does in his *Tactical Chess Training*.

There are many combinations in this book, and we will examine some of the most common, as we turn to the topics of piece and pawn tactics. Because of the large amount of material which needs to be covered here, we will have to content ourselves with just a single example of each tactic. There are many books devoted to tactics and combinations, including *World Champion Tactics* and *World Champion Combinations* from Cardoza Publishing. See the bibliography for more suggestions.

PIECE TACTICS

We divide our attention between tactics involving pieces and tactics involving pawns, because pawns, with their extremely limited motion and special capturing rules, do things a bit differently. We'll start with the piece tactics.

1. BLOCKING

The **block** is a device which places a piece on a square so that an enemy pawn stationed in front of it cannot advance. In a trivial sense, a block can be as simple as the following position.

Black can play 1...Nb7, blocking the pawn. The term block is also used to describe a specific blocking maneuver, **Alekhine's Block**, which places a piece in front of an enemy pawn.

Blocking in Action

The most famous example comes from the game Fischer vs. Benko from the 1963/64 United States Championship. Here is the position after move 18, where Black has just captured at d4.

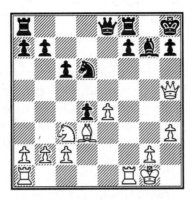

White wants to play e5, so that a mate threat at h7 is activated. 19.e5 fails to 19...f5! The White queen is now attacked, but if queens are exchanged at e8, Black recaptures with the knight and brings it to safely. Fischer found the elegant **19.Rf6!!** Black cannot capture the rook because then the advance of the e-pawn forces checkmate at h7. The f-pawn can no longer be advanced to f5 because the bishop is in the way, a result of having captured the rook at f6. Black tried **19...Kg8** but resigned after **20.e5 h6; 21.Ne2.** The knight cannot move and must fall to the pawn, since if it leaves, the White queen comes to f5.

2. CHOKE AND BRINKMATE

Jon Tisdall, in his brilliant book *Improve Your Chess Now*, added this category to the collection. **Choking** is a form of blocking an exit for an enemy piece of king. It is indeed remarkable that this valuable tactic has been overlooked in so much of the literature. Tisdall is concerned with combinations, but I prefer to examine the tactic in a simpler form first.

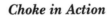

Choke in Action

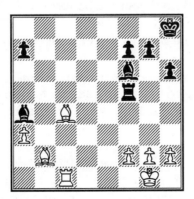

This is a position from a game I played in high school. I played 1.Bd3, threatening the crude back rank mate if the rook moves, because the flight square at h7 would be covered by the bishop. After 1...Bxb2 2.Rc8+ Kh7; 3.Bxf5+ g6; 4.Bc2 Bxc2; 5.Rxc2 Bxa3; 6.Rc7 I went on to win the endgame.

The idea behind the choke is that a piece will take away a flight square from the enemy king. When it is used in a combination, it can be called a **brinkmate**, John Fairbain's term derived from a Shogi concept. Out of deference to my friend Tisdall, I'll retain the term for the specific combination. In the **brinkmate combination**, a piece is sacrificed to achieve this effect. Tisdall presents the following example from the *Encyclopedia of Chess Middlegames*.

Brinckmate in Action

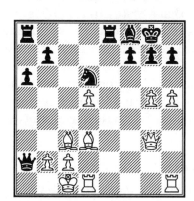

We know it was the game Luik vs. Vooremaa played in the Soviet Union in 1978, but the complete game score is not available so we do not know the move number of the position. White has a menacing kingside attack, and Black seems to be attacking only with the queen. If the d2-square were not available to the White king, checkmate at a1 is possible.

After **1...Re2!!** White had no defense. 2.b3 loses to 2...Ne4! when the bishop at f8 threatens to get to a3. White tried

2.Bxh7+ Kxh7; 3.Qd3+ but **3...Ne4** forced resignation.

3. CLEARANCE

A **clearance sacrifice** is used to free up a square for use by one of your pieces when that square is protected by an enemy piece. This can be accomplished by a simple move or a combination.

Clearance in Action

In the following position, from the game Tal vs. Timman at the 1972 Skopje Olympiad, White wants to play the knight to g5, setting up an exchange of bishops followed by capturing the pawn at h7 with the queen.

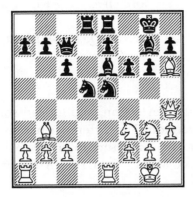

Tal played **18.Rxe5!!** and after **18...fxe5** the knight reached its goal with **19.Ng5.** Timman tried **19...Bf6** but after **20.Nxe6** realized that he was lost and resigned.

4. DEFLECTION

A **deflection** is exactly what the term implies. A piece is forced to leave its post, and the defensive formation falls apart. The goal may be to remove a defender, or a blockader, as in the next position.

Deflection in Action

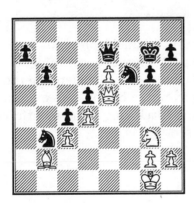

This position is from a meeting between Botvinnik, then a rising star, and Capablanca toward the end of his career. White obviously wants to get the Black queen to leave the e7-square, so that the pawn can be advanced.

Botvinnik played **30.Ba3!! Qxa3.** Or 30...Qe8; 31.Qc7+ Kg8; 32.Be7 Ng4; 33.Qd7.

31.Nh5+ gxh5. 31...Kh6 also loses. 32.Nxf6 Qc1+; 33.Kf2 Qd2+; 34.Kg3 Qxc3+; 35.Kh4 Qxd4+; 36.Ng4+; 31...Kh8 walks into 32.Qxf6+ Kg8; 33.Qg7#.

32.Qg5+ Kf8; 33.Qxf6+ Kg8; 34.e7! There is nothing to fear from checks! **34...Qc1+; 35.Kf2 Qc2+.** Black fares no better on **35...Qd2+; 36.Kg3 Qe1+.** 36...Qxc3+; 37.Kh4

Qe1+; 38.Kxh5 and there are no more checks. 37.Kh3 Qxc3+ is met by the winning move 38.g3!

    36.Kg3 Qd3+; 37.Kh4 Qe4+; 38.Kxh5 Qe2+; 39.Kh4 Qe4+; 40.g4 Qe1+; 41.Kh5. Black resigned.

5. DECOY

    The **decoy** is similar to the deflection, and indeed sometimes they are bundled together under the name **diversion**. The difference here is that the intention is not to drive a piece away from a square, but rather to lure it to a more vulnerable position. The classic game Mackenzie vs. Mason, from the 1878 tournament in Paris shows the decoy in spectacular fashion.

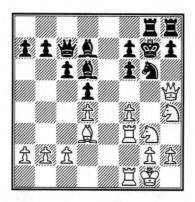

    17.Qh6+!! Kxh6; 18.Nhf5+. A knight prevents the king from retreating to g7. **18...Bxf5; 19.Nxf5+ Kh5; 20.g4+!** Another decoy brings the king to g4, where it can be checked by the king while the bishop is still defending the knight at f5.

    20...Kxg4; 21.Rg3+ Kh5. Now the bishop is free to move and deliver checkmate. **22.Be2#.** White now lures the Black king to h6 by offering up the queen, an offer which cannot legally be refused.

6. DESPERADO

A **desperado** is a move by a piece which is going to be captured anyway. Instead of standing in place awaiting the fatal blow, the piece makes an exit with a flourish and inflicts serious damage on the opponent.

Desperado in Action

We see an excellent example in the 1995 rapid game played by Kramnik against Yusupov in Moscow.

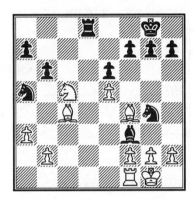

The material is even, but pieces are under attack at c5, c4, and f3. You might be tempted to capture the Black bishop, attacking the knight, but then Black would capture at c4, and both the knight at c5 and the pawn at e5 remain under attack. Kramnik uses a desperado knight to win quickly.

18.Nxe6! Re8. 18...fxe6; 19.Bxe6+ Kf8; 20.gxf3 gives White a decisive advantage. **19.Nc7.** The knight continues its rampage, again kicking at the rook on e8. **19...Rc8; 20.e6!** A fine move which defends the knight at c7 by opening a line for the bishop at f4. The pawn cannot be captured because of a huge fork on e6.

20...Nxc4; 21.e7. Black has an extra piece, but it is under attack and the White pawn threatens to queen. **21...Bc6; 22.Rd1!** The new threat is Rd8+. **22...Re8.** There is nothing better. **23.Nxe8 Bxe8; 24.Rd8 Nf6; 25.Bg5.** Black resigned because the defender of the pinned bishop at e8 is about to fall.

7. DESTROYING THE BARRIER

Destroying the Barrier, the destruction of an enemy pawn barrier, is a strategic goal which is often accomplished by a special tactic designed for the demolition of the pawn structure.

Destroying the Barrier in Action

We'll look at the thrilling conclusion to Andersen vs. Wagner from Swinemunde 1930.

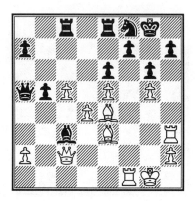

The White forces are in position to eradicate the Black king, but there is a strong pawn barrier in the way. There is a weak link at f7, and White exploits it to destroy the barrier. The combination starts with a deflection, taking the king away from the defense of f7.

25.Rxh7!? Kxh7. 25...Nxh7; 26.Bxg6 Nxg5; 27.Bxf7+! The final pawn is removed. 27...Nxf7; 28.Qg6+ Kh8; 29.Rxf7 and mate next move.

26.Rxf7+ Kg8. 26...Kh8 is an alternative defense, but it fails to 27.Bxg6. **27.Bxg6**.

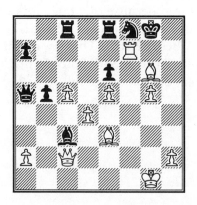

Again the destruction of the pawn barrier is complete. 27...Qd8; 27...Red8 gains some counterplay at d4 but it is insufficient. 28.Bh5 Rxd4!; 29.g6 Rh4; 30.g7! Nh7; 31.Qg6 forces mate! For example 31...Ng5; 32.Rf8+ Rxf8; 33.gxf8Q+ Kxf8; 34.Qf6+ Kg8; 35.Qxg5+ Kh8; 36.Qf6+ Kh7; 37.Bg6+ Kg8; 38.Qf7+ Kh8; 39.Qf8#.

28.Bh5? White should pay dearly for this choice. We'll look at the rest of the game, because it is very exciting and displays lots of tactics, but I should point out that the position is more likely to be won by other means.

28.Rxf8+ Rxf8; 29.Qxc3 was best at this point. White has three pawns for the double exchange, but Black has only one open file to work on, and that means that White has excellent chances to advance at least one of the pawns. For example 29...Qd5; 30.Qd3! Qxa2; 31.Bh5 Qa1+; 32.Kg2 Qa2+; 33.Kg3 Rc7; 34.Bg4 Rh7; 35.h4 b4; 36.h5 Qd5; 37.g6 Rd7; 38.h6 b3; 39.Qa6! Re7; 40.Bg5 and White wins.

28...Bxd4!; Black has pinned the bishop at e3 and threatens to get the queen into the game by threatening 29...Qxg5+! **29.Rxf8+.** White removes the defender of the infiltration square at g6. 29.Qf2 Bxe3; 30.Qxe3 Re7; 31.g6 Qc7!; 32.Qh6 doesn't work because of 32...Qxc5+; 33.Kg2 Qxe5; 34.Rxe7 Rc2+ and Black is the one who delivers mate.

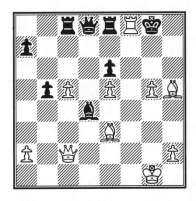

29...Kxf8?; The game might have been saved if Black chose the proper recapture: 29...Rxf8!; 30.Qg6+ Kh8; 31.Qh6+ Kg8; 32.Qxe6+ Kh8 is going to end in a draw by repetition. 33.Bf7 falls for the trick 33...Qxg5+ and Black wins.

30.Qh7 Qxg5+?? A move later, the trick backfires. 30...Bxe3+; 31.Kf1 Qc7 was a trivial win. **31.Kh1.** Black resigned, but why? 31...Re7!; 32.Qh8+ Qg8; 33.Qf6+ Rf7; 34.Bh6+ Ke8; 35.Bg5! (35.Qxe6+? Kd8 and White faces mate at g1.) 35...Kf8!; 36.Bh6+ repeats the position and draws. 31...Qxh5; 32.Qxh5 Bxe3; 33.Qf3+ Ke7; 34.Qxe3 Red8 followed by ...Rd5 should also draw. This is not the only case of resigning a position that was not lost. We'll see other examples in the section on resignation, later in the book.

8. DISCOVERED ATTACK

A **discovered attack** takes place when one piece is moved so that another piece attacks an enemy piece as a result. The piece being moved may capture, move into position to capture, or take part in a mating attack.

Discovered Attack in Action

I've selected an example that not only starts with a discovered attack, but runs the entire gamut of tactics before coming to the conclusion. It also demonstrates David Bronstein's artistic touch in all its glory. The game was played against Patzl at the Krems tournament of 1937.

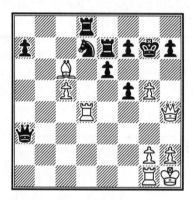

Bronstein played **32.g6!** The rook at e7 is attacked, but so are pawns at f7 and h7. **32...Qxc5;** This defends the rook and forks White's rook and unprotected bishop.

33.Qxh7+!? The direct attack wins in the end, but there was a cleaner kill. 33.gxh7 f6; 34.Bxd7 and neither rook can capture the bishop because the pawn will then promote at h8. 34...Qc7; 35.Rgd1 Rh8; 36.Bxe6 Rxh7; 37.Rg4+! fxg4; 38.Qxg4+ Kh6; 39.Bf5 forces mate, and would have been only slightly less artistic. Bronstein no doubt anticipated the pure aesthetic pleasure of his 35th move in the game.

33...Kf6; 34.g7 Qxd4. Black is now ahead by a rook and two pawns, but White has a surprise in store.

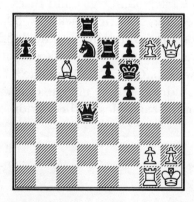

35.Qh8!! This is a form of brinkmate, because Black will not have e5 available when the pawn is promoted with discovered check! **35...Rg8.** A blocking sacrifice to stop the pawn from promoting. Black has an extra rook, so this is not a devastating loss.

36.Qxg8 Qg4; 37.Qd8! The pin wins! White threatens to promote, and reinforces the attack on the enemy knight. **37...Qxg7; 38.Bxd7.** White's extra bishop is enough to win. **38...Qg4; 39.Bc6 Qc4; 40.Qh8+! Kg6; 41.Bf3 Rc7; 42.h4!** The choke is applied. White finally threatens Bh5#.

42...f4. Black clears the escape square. **43.g4.** White adds another choke. **43...Qc3; 44.Be4+ f5; 45.gxf5+.** A double check is added to the tactical inventory. **45...Kf7; 46.Qh7+** Black had seen enough and gave up. After 46...Kf6; 47.Qh8 Ke7; 48.Rg7+! Kd6; 49.Qd8+ the final fork picks up the rook and forces queens from the board.

9. DISCOVERED CHECK

A discovered attack can involve a check, but that doesn't make it a discovered check. A **discovered check** only takes place if the piece which is not moved gives check as a result of another piece getting out of the way.

> *Discovered check is the dive bomber of the chessboard.*
>
> — Fine

Discovered Check in Action

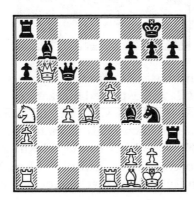

In Gerasimov vs. Smyslov, Moscow 1935, the future World Champion demonstrated the power of the discovered check with 21...Bh2+! 22.Kh1 Be5+ and White resigned, because after 23.Kg1 the bishop returns to h2 with check, retreats to c7 with another discovered check and grabs the enemy queen. This repeated use of discovered checks is the theme behind the windmill combination we'll cover later on.

10. DOUBLE ATTACK

A **double attack** is a simultaneous attack on two enemy pieces. We have divided this type of attack into two categories—the discovered attack we saw above and the fork which we will discuss a little later on. There are some double attacks which fall into neither category. These involve situations where one enemy piece is already attacked, and a player makes a move to threaten another. This type of attack is not generally considered in the literature. It usually involves an intermezzo, which will be explained in a later section of this chapter.

11. DOUBLE CHECK

A **double check** involves two pieces simultaneously attacking the enemy king. This type of check can never be headed by a queen or rook, as in that case the enemy king would already be in check. Nor can it involve a pawn, unless the pawn is involved in a capture. So the most common double checks are delivered by minor pieces.

Double Check in Action

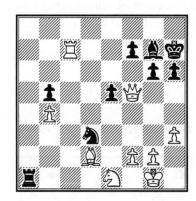

In Barcza vs. Bronstein, from the Budapest vs. Moscow match of 1949, White has just captured Black's queen at f5, and expected Black to recapture. Bronstein unleashed

32...Nxe1!! White had to try **33.Kf1** since he can't capture at f7 because of the threat of Nf3++, a double check which leads to mate because it also chokes the h2-square. 33.Qxf7 is mated by Nf3#. 33.Bxe1 Rxe1+; 34.Kh2 gxf5 is a hopeless endgame.

33...Nc2+. A simple discovered check. **34.Bc1.** 34.Ke2 Nd4+ is another way to go. **34...Rxc1+; 35.Ke2 Nd4+; 36.Kd2 Nb3+!** Black defends the rook and has time to capture the queen with the pawn.

12. FORK

A **fork** is a move which attacks two pieces at once. Since the opponent can move only one piece at each turn, one of the two attacked pieces must be left to its fate. Sometimes you read that forks are a property just of knights and pawns, and another term is used when the attacker is a bishop, rook, queen, or king. That is a rather artificial and useless distinction. Even if you want to distinguish short range and long range operations, the king would have to be included with the pawn and knight.

The Knight Fork

The **knight fork** is especially frequent at c7, where it gives check to the king and attacks a rook at a8. When a queen and king are both involved, then we have an example of a family fork. The following position, from Wexler vs. Germalm, Philadelphia, 1967, is a triple fork.

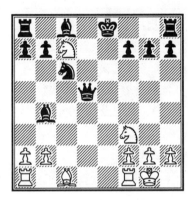

The Bishop Fork

The ability of the bishop to operate at long range makes it possible to fork two pieces on distant areas of the board with a **bishop fork**. The next game is barely out of the opening when Black delivers a terminal fork from f3. The next move would have been White's 13th, but the position was sufficiently unlucky to cause immediate resignation. White has an extra bishop, but will soon have one less rook and is missing a pawn as well.

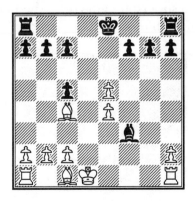

The king is in check, and the rook at h1 is lost. The doubled e-pawns are difficult to defend and the pawn at e4 can be removed. From Perlis vs. Wolff, Vienna (Gambit Tournament), 1904.

The Rook Fork

The rook can create a double attack in two ways. It can attack two pieces on the same straight line, or can attack one piece on a rank and another on a file. When it is really lucky, it can attack three or even in very rare cases four pieces at once!

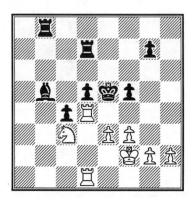

This seemingly quiet position came about in the 1892/93 between Lasker and Showalter. Lasker used a super rook fork, with the help of a later knight fork, to bring his opponent down. **37.Rxd5+!** This attacks king, rook, and bishop, none of which are adequately protected. **37...Ke6.** 37...Rxd5; 38.Rxd5+ Ke6; 39.Rxb5 was out of the question. **38.Nxb5! Rxd5; 39.Nc7+.** Knight fork! **39...Kd6; 40.Nxd5.** Black resigned.

The Queen Fork

With the ability to work on ranks, files and diagonals the queen has many opportunities to create forks. In the tricky queen vs. rook endgame, the win often comes by way of a fork. This is seen in a superstar game from the Barcelona World Cup tournament of 1989. Salov is playing White against Short.

The key to victory, White will win by forking the king and rook, so the rook must be forced to move away from the king.

90.Qe8! The threat of mate prevents the king from moving. **90...Ra7;** 90...Kh6; 91.Qf8! checkmates quickly. **91.Qh5+ Kg8; 92.Qg4+.** The queen maneuvers into position.

92...Kh7; 93.Qh3+ Kg8; 94.Qg3+ Kh7; 95.Qh2+ Kg8; 96.Qb8+. The fork is delivered. **96...Kh7; 97.Qxa7+ Kh8; 98.Qg7#.**

The King Fork

The king operates only at close range. He sort of waddles around and hits things with his elbows. Enemy pieces can only be knocked down when there is a real crowd around the attacking king. The king forks are usually seen in the endgame, when it safe for the monarch to take an active role in the game. The king cannot attack a queen, for it would have to walk into check to do so. It can, however, attack all the other pieces, though it must approach from a safe angle.

The king fork is most common against pawns. The following example is typical.

White wins one of the Black pawns.

13. FORCED MOVES

The concept of **forced moves** is not exactly a tactic, but it is an essential part of most tactical operations. A forced move is a move which must be made in order to avoid immediate disaster. The international symbol for such a move is a small square, and many players use the term "box" to describe a forced move.

A forced move is not usually considered a "good" move, and it is considered incorrect to award it a single exclamation mark (!), no matter how hard it is to find. This seems a bit unfair, but the usual view is that forced moves are inevitable. Some forced moves are considered brilliant enough to deserve the highest accolade (a double exclamation mark) in the chess literature.

The presence of a forced move makes calculation of variations easier to carry out, because alternative strategies for the opponent can be easily dismissed. On the other hand, many moves that seem forced, especially recaptures, need not be played immediately. See the intermezzo topic below for discussion and examples of this important set of exceptions.

For examples of forced moves, review the tactics presented earlier in the chapter.

14. INTERFERENCE

The **interference** tactic places a piece on a line (rank, file, or diagonal) so that it interrupts the communication of enemy pieces. Interference can be a simple tactic, as in the following position.

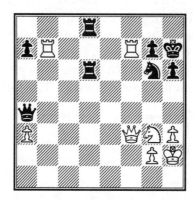

White threatens Rxg7+ and Rxa7, but Black can interfere with that plan by playing one of the rooks to d7. The interference tactic is seen in games, but is even more common in composed studies.

Interference in Action

The following 1934 study by Troitzky shows a spectacular example of an interference known as Novotny's Theme. This is a double interference where the solution involves a move that interrupts the function of two different pieces.

Black is a rook ahead but White threatens to make a new queen at a8, and also has a powerful passed h-pawn. White wins with **1.Ne4!!** The knight cannot be captured by either piece. If the rook takes the knight, then the pawn gets to a8 and makes a queen with check. After **1...Bxe4** the pawn advances to h7 and one of the pawns must queen.

15. INTERMEZZO

The concept of an in-between move, or **intermezzo**, has been one of the joys of chess since the early days. There is something especially pleasing about being able to ignore an opponent's threat to create one of your own. The chess literature has many terms for this concept, including the German **zwischenzug** (tsvi-shen-tsuug) and English **in between move**, both of which are somewhat awkward. I prefer the Italian term, which is elegant and easy to pronounce. Sometimes the tactic is described as an intermediate move, which engenders confusion between the tactic and the evaluation of a move as recommended for beginners or more advanced players. Xenophobes might use "tweener," though that hardly seems to convey the beauty of the concept.

Perhaps more professional games have been lost by overlooking an intermezzo than by most other tactics.

Intermezzo in Action
The Russian star Ilyin Zhenevsky used a triple intermezzo to defeat Sorokin at the 1931 Soviet Championship.

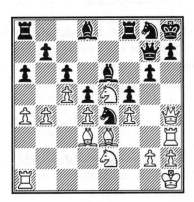

27.Qxh7+!! Qxh7. If White simply captures at h7, the exchanges will have cost him a rook. An intermezzo leads to the win of material.

28.Nxg6+! Kg7. The pin on the queen is broken. Now if White captures the queen, then Black takes the knight and has won a piece for the two pawns. **29.Nxf8!!** This is Ilyin Zhenevsky's brilliant conception. The knight chokes the queen by taking away the g6-square. The queen is now under a double attack, and can be captured next move. Black logically uses the desperado tactic to get a rook for the queen.

29...Qxh3; 30.Nxe6+! Since this is a check, as an intermezzo often is, Black cannot retreat the queen.

30...Kf6; 31.gxh3 Kxe6; 32.Rg1. White eventually converted the extra material into a win.

16. OVERLOADING

Overloading a piece means that the piece is given more defensive work than it can possibly handle. When a piece is overloaded, a simple decoy or deflection can remove it from the defense of a key square. You should always examine your opponent's pieces to see if any of them are overworked.

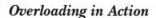

Overloading in Action

In a game from the 1996 match between Yugoslavia and Hungary, Minic flattened Honfi with a powerful exploitation of the overworked queen. The burden of defending the rook at d8 weighs heavily on the shoulders of both the queen and the rook. With **1.Qa7!!** White forced Black's resignation. A back rank mate at d8 is in the near future.

17. PIN

A pin is one of the most powerful weapons in all of chess. The simple pin is at the heart of many of the most complicated combinations. A piece is pinned when it cannot move off of the line on which it is attacked, if the result of moving would lead to loss of a more important piece, or check to the king. The first is a relative pin and the second is an absolute pin.

> *The pin is mightier than the sword*
>
> — Reinfeld

Absolute Pin

An **absolute pin** is a pin against the king. These pins cannot be broken by moving the attacked piece. The absolute pin is a consequence of the rules. A player may not move in such a way as to leave the king in check at the conclusion of the move.

The Black bishop is pinned to the king by a rook. The exploitation of the pin involves attacking it with more pieces than your enemy can mobilize to defend it. The bishop can be defended by retreating the rook to a5 or advancing the f-pawn to f6, but in either case White replies f4, and can add further pressure with Bb2, leading to the win of material.

Relative Pin

The **relative pin** involves a pinned piece that is of greater value than the piece it shields.

Terminal Pin

There is one pin which doesn't clearly fit either the class of absolute pin or the class of relative pin. The **terminal pin** is a pin not against a king, but against a mating square. It might be called a terminal pin, because moving the pinned piece will terminate the game.

The knight is pinned to the e8 square. If the knight moves, Black delivers checkmate at d8. The terminal pin is a close relative of the absolute pin, as they both involve the enemy king.

The most intense form of a pin is the **cross**. This special tactical device uses pins and counter-pins and is also known as a double pin. Victor Charusin has made a thorough study of this device, and his *Combination Cross* includes the following types of crosses.

Perfect Cross

In a **perfect cross**, one side pins an enemy piece absolutely, in other words a piece is pinned to the king. The pinned player reacts by creating another pin, also an absolute pin.

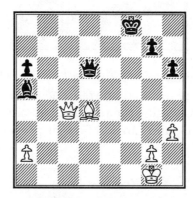

In Brunstrup vs Budrich, played in Berlin in 1954, White seized the opportunity to pin the queen to the king, and played **1.Bc5!** Black responded with **1...Bb6** which "saves" the queen because the White bishop is now in an absolute pin. Yet the Black queen remains pinned to the king, so White wins with **2.Qf4+!!**

Black resigned, because on the next move White will capture the Black queen at d6 with the queen.

St. Andrew's Cross

The **St. Andrew's cross** involves two pins, one against the enemy king and another against a second piece. It has been seen in a number of games, and is hard to anticipate. Alekhine employed one to defeat Capablanca in the 11th game of their 1927 World Championship game.

Capablanca, as White, resigned, because if he blocked the check with 67.Qg2, then 67...Qh1 is checkmate.

The king pin is on the f1-h3 diagonal, while the pin against the queen at a8 is on the h1-a8 diagonal.

Oblique Cross

The **oblique cross** also involves a diagonal pin, but has a rank or file pin as its partner. My favorite example of this one comes from the game Shumov vs. Winawer, played in St. Petersburg 1875. Black has just responded to White's check at a4 by interposing with the queen. White in turn ignored the threat to his own queen at a4 and moved the rook from e1 to c1.

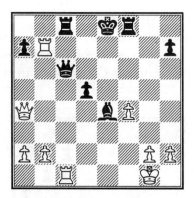

All three White pieces are attacked, but none can be captured! If Black captures at a4, White takes the rook at c8 with checkmate. Black cannot touch either of the rooks because the queen is pinned by the enemy queen at a4. Black tried to defend by sacrificing the queen, but after **28...Rf6; 19.Rxc6 Rfxc6; 20.Rxa7.** White won without difficulty.

Maltese Cross

A **Maltese cross** exploits pins on a rank and a file. It is quite rare, and usually comes as quite a surprise. I have selected the finish of Zek vs. Travin, from a game played in the Soviet Union sometime before World War II. Black has checked at b2, and White defended by moving the rook from d1 to d2.

The killer move **1...Qd1!!** forced Black's resignation. You can understand why White could not have foreseen Black's resource. The d1 square had been occupied by a White rook. That rook, and, presumably that square were under the control of the Black queen. When the rook advanced to d2, the queen no longer controlled d1. The rook at d2 also does not control d1, because the rook is pinned. Such a situation does not usually come into consideration when calculating variations. You should learn this tactic so that you do not fall victim to it.

18. PURSUIT

Pursuit is a tactic used to save a lost game. It involves attacking an enemy piece relentlessly. While the piece cannot be captured, the enemy must move it at each turn, and therefore can do nothing to try to win the game. This is known as harassment. If a piece can escape the pursuit, the tactic fails. The most common form of pursuit is **perpetual check**.

Perpetual Check in Action

The diagram shows the final position of Geller vs. Gurgenidze, from the 25th Soviet Championship in 1958. The players agreed to a draw, even though Black has an extra rook for just two pawns.

White has just sacrificed a piece at f6, and a draw was agreed after **29.Qd7+,** since the king cannot escape the checks. The g-file is covered by the rook at g2, and the f-pawn prevents the king from using that square. The Black king must shuffle between f8 and f7 while the White queen goes to d8 and d7. If the players had not agreed to a draw, the three-fold repetition rule would have kicked in after a few more moves.

Harassment in Action

When the target is a piece other than the king, we can use the term **harassment**. In this case a piece of greater value than the attacker is threatened move after move.

The Black queen must helplessly slide back and forth between g8 and h7. After **1...Qh7; 2.Bf5** the g-pawn cannot intervene because it is pinned by the bishop at e5.

19. REMOVING THE DEFENDER

The tactic of **removing the defender** is a simple and logical concept. If a piece is defended, the elimination of the guardian can lead to the win of material. This tactic is very common in all stages of the game, and is often part of the battle for the initiative in the opening. The Spanish Game begins **1.d4 d5; 2.Nf3 Nc6; 3.Bb5.**

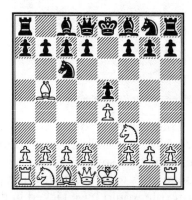

With the second move, White threatened to capture the pawn at e5 with the knight. Black responded by defending the pawn. White's third move threatens to capture the knight at c6 and deprive the pawn of its defender. This is not a serious threat at the moment, because Black can capture the bishop with the d-pawn, and meet Nxe5 with ...Qd4, forking the knight at e5 and pawn at e4.

Removing the Defender in Action

Later on, however, the tactic can be more meaningful. For example, John vs Caro, from the 14th German Chess Congress in 1904, continued **3...Nf6; 4.0-0** and here Black blundered with **Be7?! 5.Nc3 0-0?**

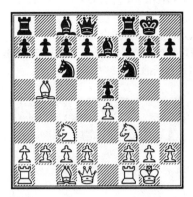

This allowed **6.Bxc6 dxc6; 7.Nxe5** with a healthy extra pawn. Black tried **7...Nxe4; 8.Nxe4 Qd4** but the desperado **9.Nxc6!** secured the advantage.

20. SKEWER

The **skewer** is an inverted pin. One side attacks a distant target by forcing an intermediate piece to flee. It is often seen in the form of a check, as in this elementary rook endgame.

White wins by playing **1.h7!** The only way Black can stop the pawn from promoting is by playing **1...Rxh7** but **2.Rb7+** skewers the king and rook. The king must get out of the way, and the rook at h7 is captured.

The skewer is also known as an **x-ray attack**, because one piece attacks through an obstacle. In a sense, the skewer is also a discovered attack.

21. TRAPPED PIECES

When a piece has no escape route, it is **trapped**. If a king is trapped and in check, the result is checkmate. When the trapped piece is something other than the king, the piece may be captured. It may also be left to rot, having no significant role in the game.

Trapped Knight in Action

The knight can be trapped in enemy territory even in the opening, as in the Frankenstein-Dracula Variation of the Vienna Game.

1.e4 e5; 2.Nc3 Nf6; 3.Bc4 Nxe4; 4.Qh5 Nd6; 5.Bb3 Nc6; 6.Nb5 g6; 7.Qf3 f5; 8.Qd5 Qe7; 9.Nxc7+ Kd8; 10.Nxa8 b6.

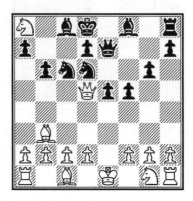

The knight at a8 cannot escape. White has an extra rook, but when the knight is eventually captured, the difference will just be the exchange. Black has enough compensation to justify the small sacrifice.

The knight is easy to trap at the edge of the board because it has very few moves. In the corner, there are only two possible escape squares, and they are easily covered. The king can trap a knight all by himself.

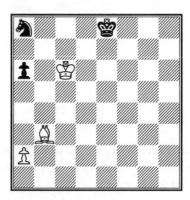

After 1.Kb7 the knight is lost.

Trapped Bishop

The bishop has a greater range than the knight, but can still be trapped in squares near the corner. To trap a bishop, you must take away all but one of the available diagonals. On the edge of the board, there are never more than two available diagonals, so you just need to close one of them. In the corner of the board, the bishop has only a single diagonal.

Trapped Bishop in Action

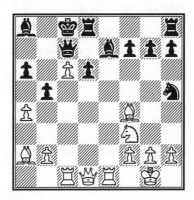

In the 1962 British Junior Championship, Boyers took advantage of the trapped bishop to defeat Feavyour. The material is equal, but Black is effectively a piece down because the bishop at a8 is trapped.

17.axb5! White ignores the threat against the knight, and destroys the pawn barrier. **17...Nxf4; 18.Qa4!** The threats on the queenside allows this powerful intermezzo.

18...a5. Black closes the line. 18...axb5?? is a blunder. 19.Qa6+ Kb8; 20.Qxb5+ Kc8; 21.Qa6+ Kb8; 22.Re3 wins. **19.Rxe7 Nh3+?** The desperado is just a waste of time. The disruption of White's pawn structure has no effect on the game, but the tempo is important. 19...Qxe7; 20.Qxf4 is still almost hopeless for Black.

20.gxh3 Qxe7; 21.Qxa5. The result of the clearance sacrifice is a position where Black can no longer move the king to b8, because the c-pawn, no longer blockaded by the queen, can advance.

Trapped Rook

The rook is a little harder to trap than the bishop. It is possible, however, to use a minor piece to close the lines, since then a sacrifice of the exchange can be forced.

Trapped Rook in Action

The game Anderssen vs. Neumann, from Berlin 1866, is a clear example.

All White has to do is bring the king to g7 to win.

46.Kg6 Kf8; 47.c4. The king cannot abandon g7, and pawn moves only delay the inevitable. Black is headed for a squeeze, so didn't waste time and conceded the exchange with **47...Rxg8+; 48.hxg8Q+ Kxg8; 49.Kf6.** Black resigned, because the king and pawn endgame is a trivial win.

Trapped Queen

Since the queen can move in all directions, trapping the queen would seem to be difficult. In the opening, however, it has no room to maneuver. It is particularly vulnerable to an attack by a knight at e6 if there is a Black knight at d7. Several opening traps involve this idea.

Trapped Queen in Action

Here is one of them, from a game between Dadiani and Doubrava played in Kiev, 1896.

1.e4 d6; 2.Bc4 Nd7; 3.Nf3 g6; 4.Ng5 Nh6; 5.Bxf7+ Nxf7; 6.Ne6.

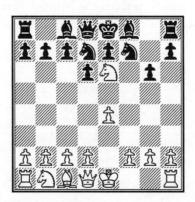

Trapped King

When a king is trapped, then all that is needed is a check to finish it off. That's checkmate! Even a pawn can do the job.

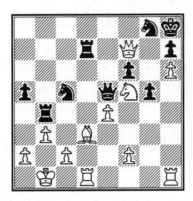

In Stangl vs. Buchal, from the 1994/95 season of the German League, White won brilliantly with **32.Qg7+!! Rxg7; 33.hxg7#.**

22. WINDMILL

The **windmill** involves repeated use of a discovered check to win material. The piece that is moved, giving discovered check, captures a piece. It then returns to the scene of the crime, also with check, before engaging in a feeding frenzy. The windmill is at the heart of many famous combinations.

Windmill in Action

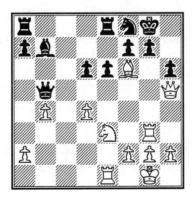

A shocking combination brought Carlos Torre world recognition when he defeated Lasker in Moscow at 1925. The last move, 25.Bf6!!, offered up the queen. After **25...Qxh5; 26.Rxg7+** the windmill goes into motion.

26...Kh8; 27.Rxf7+ Kg8; 28.Rg7+ Kh8; 29.Rxb7+ Kg8; 30.Rg7+ Kh8.

The rook could also grab the a-pawn, but that would only open a line for the Black rook on the a-file. Instead, it is time to switch directions and pick off the queen.

31.Rg5+ Kh7; 32.Rxh5 Kg6; 33.Rh3 Kxf6; 34.Rxh6+ Kg5; 35.Rh3.

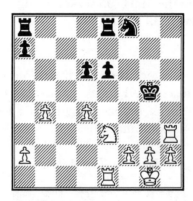

The carnage is complete and White had an easy win in the endgame, thanks to the extra pawns.

Now let's move onto pawn tactics.

PAWN TACTICS

Pawns do not have the full range of tactics available to the other pieces. They can operate only at short range, and have no power to pin or skewer enemy pieces.

1. EN PASSANT

En passant is a tactic available only to pawns. It arose because of the rule change that allowed pawns to advance two squares on their first move. It was only reasonable that this attempt to speed up the opening should not deprive a player of the right to capture the pawn as it zooms past. Most experienced players do not fail to spot an en passant capture, but beginners sometimes do.

En Passant in Action

The following position arose in Timman vs. Campora, Biel 1995. Black has a dangerous protected passed pawn, but the pawn at f7 is weak and under attack.

This is the position after White's 53rd move. Black cannot capture the knight at h6, because the new h-pawn would queen. The pawn at f7 cannot be defended, so it must advance.

54...f5 allowed the en passant capture **55.exf6**. Not 55.gxf6?? Bxh6.

55...e5 56.Ng4 e4; 57.Nf2 e3; 58.Nd3. Black resigned. White will break through with 59.h5 gxh5; 60.g6. The breakthrough is our next topic.

2. BREAKTHROUGH

Pawns are drawn like lemmings to the eighth rank where they are promoted to higher rank. They can smash through a pawn barrier using a technique called a **breakthrough**. It is seen in the opening, the middlegame, and the endgame. The breakthrough can be used to attack an enemy king or to promote a pawn.

Breakthrough in Action

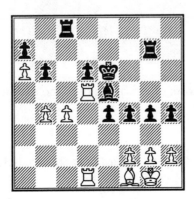

In the 1998 Polish Championship, Palus was on the receiving end of a breakthrough by Cyborowski after **39...g3!** White tried **40.f3** 40.hxg3 fxg3; 41.fxg3 h3!? finishes the demolition of the pawn barrier by using another breakthrough move. 41...Rxg3 is also strong. **40...h3.**

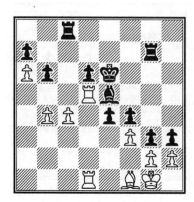

White resigned as the pawns come crashing through, for example 41.gxh3 [41.hxg3 hxg2; 42.Bxg2 Rxg3; 43.Kf2 e3+; 44.Kf1 Rxc4; 45.Re1 Rc2 when the bishop is lost.] 41...exf3; 42.R1d2 f2+; 43.Kh1 g2+! 44.Bxg2 f3! White is forced to part with the bishop, as the Black rook must not be allowed access to g1. 45.Rxf2 fxg2+; 46.Rxg2 Rxg2; 47.Kxg2 Rxc4 is obviously hopeless.

In the endgame, the classic example is

White wins with **1.b6! axb6;** (1...cxb6 2.a6! is the only alternative.) **2.c6! bxc6; 3.a6** and the pawn promotes.

3. FORKS

The fork is the pawn's favorite tactic. It is the basis for a great deal of opening theory. For example, after 1.e4 e5; 2.Nc3 Nf6; 3.Bc4 Nxe4; 4.Nxe4 d5 the fork regains the piece.

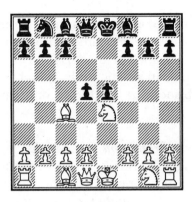

4. PROMOTION

Promoting a pawn to a queen is a central concept in the endgame. Usually the key to victory is getting the pawn to the last rank before the opponent manages to get a new queen. This concept is simple enough to need no illustration, but there are some twists, for example promoting to a piece other than the queen, which we will deal with a little later on.

First, a practical point must be made. Chess sets come with only one queen, which can be very inconvenient. Players have to be resourceful. Upside-down rooks, salt shakers, even candy bars have been drafted to serve as temporary members of the army, but what do you do when the number of queens reaches seven?

That's what you need to play over the famous game "Sumpter vs. King, Australia 1965." Seven queens appear on the board.

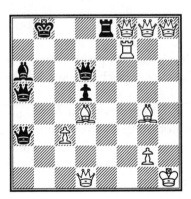

The game is a fake, as pointed out by Krabbé, whose collection of chess curiosities is a chess desert island book. Only five simultaneous queens have been recorded in serious play. There are plenty of fakes, however. But it would be nice if chess sets came with at least one extra queen!

5. UNDERPROMOTION

Never neglect the possibility of **underpromotion**, promoting a pawn to something other than a queen, as a tactic in the endgame. It is easy to overlook, especially if the promotion is buried deep in a branch of analysis. The underpromotion theme can be trivial, or can be buried deep in an artistic study. Underpromotion can involve replacing the pawn with a rook, bishop, or knight but only underpromotion to a knight, giving check, is common.

Promotion to a Knight

The promotion to a knight is usually made with check, which is a simple and obvious move, though sometimes it needs to be anticipated well in advance. In rare occasions, such as the following, the knight is chosen not to give check, but to threaten checkmate.

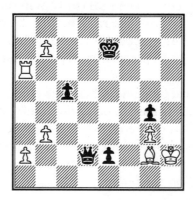

In the 1995 Yugoslav Championship, Vujosevic counted on Jovic, promoting the pawn to a queen. Then White would have time to make a queen, since Black has no safe checks, the h6-square being under the protection of the rook at a6. Instead, 53...e1N won the game, because of the threat of checkmate at g2.

Promotion to a Rook

Many cases involving promotion to a rook are merely the use of a rook because the result of the move would be no different, e.g. a back rank mate or when the piece can be captured. The presence of an extra rook near the board, when no second queen is at hand, is responsible for those trivial cases.

In this excerpt from a study by Platov, White must promote to a rook, because if 1.h8=Q? then 1...b1=Q! 2.Qb8+ Kc4 and if Black captures the queen, then stalemate results. With the rook, however, Black still has an escape at d3, so there is no stalemate.

Promotion to a Bishop

The bishop promotion is extremely rare, because the queen serves the same diagonal function while adding power along the rank and file. The only reason to promote to a bishop is to avoid stalemate, as in the previous section on rook promotion.

In another Platov study, we find the stalemate theme again. This one is a bit tricky, even though we are close to the final position of the study. White must promote to a bishop, because after 1.c8=Q b1=Q 2.Qf5+ Ke2!; 3.Qxb1 Black is stalemated. So White promotes to a bishop instead, and after 1.c8=B b1=Q; 2.Bf5+ and after the king moves, White captures the Black queen and then can checkmate with the bishop pair, picking off the g-pawn at will.

CHECKMATING PATTERNS

Lots of books contain catalogs of checkmating positions, and recognizing mating patterns is one of the essential skills required to make progress in chess. I have taken the traditional mates and present them as they actually occurred in tournament play. Most books only show mates when the enemy king is at the edge of the board, so I have had to expand the collection considerably to show additional checkmating patterns which are important. The wisdom here speaks directly from the chessboard, so I have confined myself to the briefest of introductions.

For each mating pattern, I present a diagram showing it in pure form, with only the key pieces represented. Then there is a game with a small combination leading to the final position. Keep in mind that most mating patterns can be found on either flank, and of course can apply to White or Black. Many can also be rotated 90 degrees, though not those which involve pawns, of course.

Many authorities use the names of the checkmates to refer to a pattern of attack to reach the final position. I have always found this approach a bit confusing, since it is not clear, when a mating position can be reached by several means, what the name of the checkmate actually refers to. I have therefore used just the final checkmate position for purposes of classification.

1. ANASTASIA'S MATE

This checkmate got its name in a novel by W. Heinse called *Anastasia and Chess* (1803). The **Anastasia mate** involves a knight and rook working against the enemy king.

Anastasia's Mate in Action

In Bayer-Falkbeer, Vienna 1852, White just captured a rook at a8. White forces Anastasia's Mate in three moves with **1...Ne2+; 2.Kh1 Qxh2+!!; 3.Kxh2 Rh4#.**

2. ANDERSSEN'S MATE

In this checkmate, the corner is used by a White rook or queen to trap the enemy king, with support from a pawn or a bishop on the long diagonal. The **Anderssen's mate** version with a pawn is more interesting.

There is a certain elegance in this checkmate, which has been used in some magnificent games. Unlike many checkmates, which come as a surprise, Anderssen's mate is often visible in advance when there is nevertheless nothing that can be done about it.

Anderssen's Mate in Action

In the old swashbuckling days, we often saw brawls from the opening notes to the final curtain. Gunsberg vs. Schallop, from the London tournament of 1886, is a typical example. After White's 23rd move, the position was ready for Anderssen's inspiration to take root.

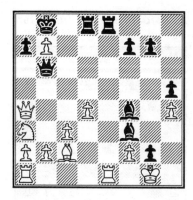

Schallop simply played **23...Qf6!** White resigned. There is no defense against the threat of ...Bh2+, ...Qh4+ and ...Qh1#.

3. ARABIAN MATE

The **Arabian mate** pattern exploits the unique properties of the knight, which works well against kings trapped in the corner. The knight will always be two diagonal squares from the enemy king, but the rook can operate either on the rank or on the file.

Arabian Mate in Action

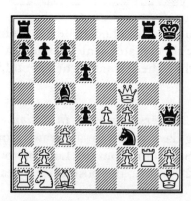

Rainer-Steinitz, Vienna 1860 saw the future World Champion unleash an Arabian Mate with **1...Qxh2+!! 2.Rxh2 Rg1#**.

4. BACK RANK MATE

Who among us has never fallen for the old **back rank mate**? This is one of the most common checkmating patterns in chess. It is also known as the **corridor** mate.

Back Rank Mate in Action

The sacrifice of the queen at a8 brought about the back rank mate in Anderssen vs. Wywill, London 1851. **1.Qxa8!! Rxa8; 2.Rd8+ Rxd8; 3.Rxd8#.**

5. BLACKBURNE'S MATE

Blackburne's mate combines the forces of three minor pieces, converging on the enemy castled king. One of the bishops can operate at a great distance, but the other two pieces must be close to the target.

The rook (which could be a bishop or queen) plays an important role in eliminating a flight square at f7. This mating pattern is comparatively rare, but threatening Blackburne's mate can force Black to weaken the position.

Blackburne's Mate in Action

Black obtained a strong attacking position after just 17 moves in Korody vs. Benko, Budapest 1951. The rook and the g-file and the bishop at b7 are aimed at the enemy king. Black has just brought the knight to e5, ignoring the attack on his queen.

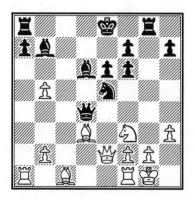

White accepted the offer of the queen, but was quickly checkmated. There wasn't any way of holding the position in any case.

18.Nxd4 Rxg2+; 19.Kh1 Rh2+!! 20.Kxh2 Ng4+; 21.Kg1 Bh2#.

6. BODEN'S MATE

Boden's mate uses two bishops against a king whose escape is blocked by his own pieces.

Boden's Mate in Action

This checkmate is named after a famous game by Boden. White has been credited as MacDonnell (London 1869) and Schulder (London 1853, 1860, or 1865)! In any case, there was a predecessor, Horwitz vs. Popert, Hamburg 1844. Poor Popert never got the credit! The oft-cited game starts out:

1.e4 e5; 2.Nf3 d6; 3.c3 f5; 4.Bc4 Nf6; 5.d4 fxe4; 6.dxe5 exf3; 7.exf6 Qxf6; 8.gxf3 Nc6; 9.f4 Bd7; 10.Be3 0-0-0; 11.Nd2 Re8; 12.Qf3 Bf5; 13.0-0-0 d5; 14.Bxd5.

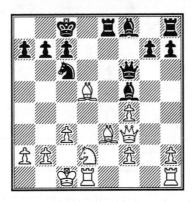

Boden played the brilliant **14...Qxc3+!!; 15.bxc3 Ba3#.**

7. CORNER MATE

The elements of the **corner mate** are simple. The king is stuck in the corner, with a rook or queen cutting off escape toward the center, and a knight delivering the fatal blow.

The corner mate is seen quite frequently.

Corner Mate in Action

The White queen finds herself pinned in Anka vs. Ireneusz, Geneva 1995. She sacrifices herself to bring about the corner mate.

White captured the rook, and then delivered mate: 1.Qxb7 Bxb7; 2.Nf7#.

8. COZIO'S MATE

Cozio's mate is an upside down version of the Dovetail mate, which we'll get to later. The 1766 study by Cozio gave it its name.

The Black king has nowhere to run after **1.Qh6+** except **1...Kg3**, but then **2.Qh2** is mate!

Cozio's Mate in Action

The Cozio mate is no stranger to battles at the chessboard. In the 1954 Soviet Championship, Simagin blundered into it against Batuyev: **1...e2?? 2.Qg1+ Kd2 3.Qc1#.**

9. DAMIANO'S MATE

Damiano's mate is one of the oldest observed checkmating patterns. The diagram shows the typical final position. The Black rook could be a bishop or queen, without making any difference.

The checkmate position is not the real secret of Damiano's mate. It is the method of arriving at this position, which often involves a sacrifice of a rook along the h-file, followed by moving the queen to the h-file with check and delivering mate at h7. Damiano's mate had appeared in composed studies for a long time when it appeared at the board. It was published as a study by Damiano in 1512!

Damiano placed no White king on the board, and this has prevented this classic from entering many databases which will not accept illegal positions! Of course it makes little difference where the king is, as long as it is out of the way. The composition is not supposed to illustrate a practical idea, but rather sheer beauty. The sacrifice of both rooks leads to checkmate:

1.Rh8+ Kxh8; 2.Rh1+ Kg8; 3.Rh8+ Kxh8; 4.Qh1+ Kg8; 5.Qh7#.

Damiano's Mate in Action

This theme was exploited in Moll vs. Falkbeer, Vienna 1864. That game began in a very odd fashion. **1.e3 e5; 2.c3 d5; 3.d4 Bd6; 4.Bd3 Nc6; 5.Ne2 Nf6; 6.0-0 e4; 7.Bc2 Ng4; 8.Ng3 h5; 9.f3.** White's inept play opens the door to a mighty sacrificial finish. **9...Nxh2; 10.Kxh2 h4; 11.fxe4 hxg3+; 12.Kg1.**

12...Rh1+; 13.Kxh1 Qh4+; 14.Kg1 Qh2#.

10. DAMIANO'S BISHOP MATE

The standard mate with queen and bishop is very important, because it is part of many classic combinations. The **Damiano's Bishop mate** is shown below.

It is usually not implemented directly. Instead, it is the end result of an attack against other vulnerable points in the enemy position.

Damiano's Bishop Mate in Action

The New York Times columnist Israel Horowitz was quite a good player, and at a tournament in New York in 1931 he delivered a magnificent Damiano Bishop mate.

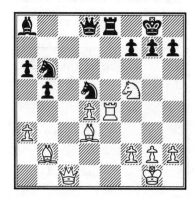

Actually, he didn't have to play the moves. He announced checkmate in seven moves, starting with **22.Qg5!** Indeed, checkmate is inevitable. 22...g6. 22...Qxg5?? 23.Rxe8# mate. 23.Qh6 gxf5; 24.Rg4+ fxg4; 25.Bxh7+ Kh8; 26.Bg6+ Kg8; 27.Qh7+ Kf8; 28.Qxf7#.

DAVID AND GOLIATH MATE

Yes, getting checkmated by a pawn is embarrassing, but it does happen! The **David and Goliath mate** can take many forms, but the essential ingredients are checkmate by a pawn, with both friendly and enemy pieces in the vicinity.

A shame hath he that at the Checkes pleyeth, when that a pown seyth to the kyng, checkmate!

— Lydgate

David and Goliath Mate in Action

In Martinez vs. Pollock, at the American Chess Congress of 1889, White finished the game with a rare pawn checkmate.

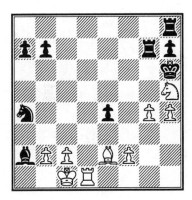

26.Rd6+ Rg6; 27.g5#. This is not the sort of thing you see everyday.

> **Deadly hate id play check mate with me, poor pawn.**
> *(Deadly hath it play checkmate with me, poor pawn – fatally mated by a lowly pawn!)* — Gascoigne (1573)

We turn now to the more common checkmating positions.

12. DOUBLE BISHOP MATE

The **Double Bishop mate** is a simpler form of checkmate than Boden's mate, as the two bishops are assisted only by a lowly Black pawn which has not moved from its original home. If the coward had ever entered the battle, Black might not be checkmated here!

Double Bishop Mate in Action

The double bishop checkmate motif was used in the famous game Corzo vs. Capablanca, Havana 1902, although it only led to a different type of checkmate.

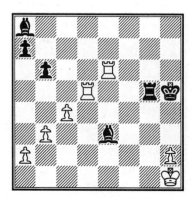

White seems to be hanging on, since Black's rook at g5 is pinned, even though White's rook at d5 (which arrived there on the last move, capturing a Black rook) is also pinned. Black can't play ...Rg1 on this move because of the pin, but after Black captures the rook at d5 with check, Black will deliver the fatal blow on the next move.

13. DOVETAIL MATE

Tisdall added this stange bird to the catalog. The **Dovetail mate** uses a rook at c1 instead of a pawn at d5 with 1...Bxd5, but it really doesn't matter how the queen is supported, as long as it cannot be captured. Similarly, the other Black pieces can be anything but a knight.

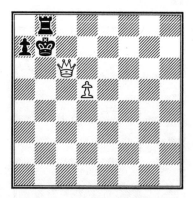

This checkmate is comparatively rare, because Black has to more or less blunder into it. Sometimes a dovetail mate is found at the end of long attacking combinations.

Dovetail Mate in Action

As with so many basic mates, we can find an example in Giacchino Greco's 17th century text.

1.e4 e5; 2.Nf3 Nc6; 3.Bc4 Bc5; 4.c3 Qe7; 5.0-0 d6; 6.d4 Bb6; 7.Bg5 f6; 8.Bh4 g5; 9.Nxg5 fxg5; 10.Qh5+ Kf8; 11.Bxg5 Qe8; 12.Qf3+ Kg7; 13.Bxg8 Rxg8; 14.Qf6#.

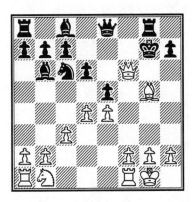

In Platz vs. Rothman, New York 1945, White exploited this theme beautifully.

34.Nxf7+. The knight will eventually fall, but the mating net has been cast. **34...Kf8; 35.Qxd6+ Kxf7; 36.Rf2+ Kg7; 37.Qf6#.**

14. EPAULETTE MATE

This mate resembles a pair of epaulettes, those little strap-like things that often adorn military uniforms, riding on the shoulder. The **Epaulette mate** can take place anywhere on the back rank. It is sometimes seen in the center, when one side forgets the importance of castling early in the game. The epaulettes just get in the way when the king is being stared down by an enemy queen.

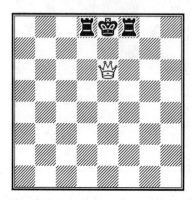

The queen can deliver checkmate by herself, because the king has no flight squares.

Epaulette Mate in Action

The epaulette mate often comes as a nasty and unexpected blow. In this position from Fedorov vs. Lastin, Perm 1997, Black did not appreciate how important the knight at d5 was to the defense.

35...Nf4?? The position is terrible in any case, but this move is unforgivable. **36.Bxf4 Qxf4??** Black just fails to see the haymaker coming. Capturing with the rook was essential. **37.Qxe6#.**

15. GRECO'S MATE

Greco was one of the early catalogers of checkmates, so he certainly deserves to have one named for him. History has chosen several, but many have been reassigned and now this pattern bears the name. Here is the **Greco mate:**

The queen gives check along the edge of the board, with a bishop supplying the necessary containment, helped by Black's g-pawn.

Greco's Mate in Action

Our position is taken from the classic game Rotlevi vs. Rubinstein, Lodz 1907.

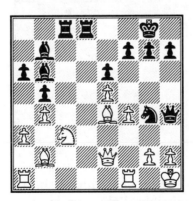

White played 22.g3 in the game, and fell to a brilliant combination starting with 22...Rxc3. Suppose, however, White had chosen **22.h3?** Surprisingly, the same reply wins, though in a rather different fashion.

The game would have continued **22...Rxc3!!** Of interest to us here is **23.Bxc3.** On 23.gxh4 Rxh3+!! White would have no choice but to capture with 24.Qxh3, and then 24...Qxh3+ 25.gxh3 Bxe4+ would lead to a successful king hunt.

23...Bxe4+; 24.Qxe4 Qg3!

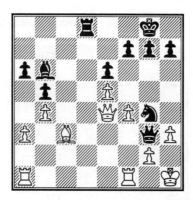

Black threatens ...Qh2#, so White must play **25.hxg4** and now we get Greco's mate with **25...Qh4#.**

16. HOOK MATE

The **hook mate** necessarily involves a rook, a knight and a pawn, in optimal configuration. This leaves one enemy flight square uncovered, but it may be occupied by a Black piece or may be controlled by another White piece. Here is the pure form:

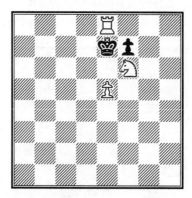

The rook is protected by the knight, which is in turn protected by a pawn. The pawn also covers one of the possible flight squares.

Hook Mate in Action

Adolph Anderssen, one of the greatest players and at one time an unofficial World Champion, showed his combinative prowess in the following position, taken from a game against Mayet at Berlin in 1855.

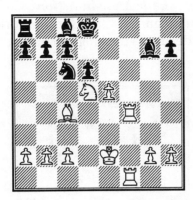

White won by force with **22.Rf8+ Bxf8; 23.Rxf8+ Kd7; 24.Nf6+ Ke7; 25.Re8#.**

17. H-FILE MATE

The **h-file mate**, using a bishop and rook, usually arises from a position where the target has castled kingside with a fianchetto formation. The king is trapped on the edge with a pawn or piece (other than a knight) blocking the escape path at f7.

Often the attacker will use a series of sacrifices on the h-file to open up the line toward the enemy king.

h-file Mate in Action

In Euwe vs. Loman, Rotterdam 1923, the future World Champion has only the threat of Qh7+, which is not deadly, as the king can hide at f8. White has just captured a pawn at d4.

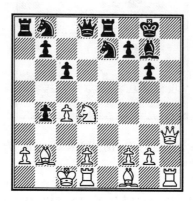

Black carelessly captured the knight, but after **16...Bxd4; 17.Qh8+!! Bxh8; 18.Rxh8#** could only hang his head in embarrassment.

18. LEGALL'S MATE

The famous **Legall's mate** is not of much practical value. It can happen only in a very few openings, and then only after a terrible blunder by Black. Indeed, in most cases Black has only moved one piece in the key position. In the classic study *The Art of Checkmate*, Georges Renaud and Victor Kahn argue that Legall's mate is nevertheless very important, and should be learned by heart, with special attention to the opening moves used to reach it. The mate itself looks like this:

Legall's Mate in Action

The purest form of Legall's mate is seen in Legall de Kemeur vs. St Brie, Paris, 1750. Black's game is destroyed before it can begin to ripen.

1.e4 e5; 2.Nf3 d6; 3.Bc4 Nc6; 4.Nc3 Bg4?; 5.Nxe5!!

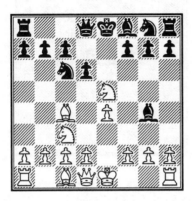

The queen is sacrificed for a quick checkmate. **5...Bxd1; 6.Bxf7+ Ke7; 7.Nd5#.**

19. LOLLI'S MATE

The infiltration of an enemy fianchetto position is one of the most common mating patterns, and is called **Lolli's mate**. It uses a queen and a pawn to slam dunk the enemy king.

Reaching this position often involves a sacrifice along the h-file, so that the queen can come to h6 with gain of tempo.

Lolli's Mate in Action

In Blackburne vs. Steinkuhler, Manchester 1871, White smashed through the defensive pawn barrier..

White played **29.Rxh7+** and **Black resigned**, because after 29...Qxh7; 30.Rxh7+ Kg8; 31.Rh8+! Kxh8; 32.Qh6+ Kg8; 33.Qg7# we have the desired position. No better is 30...Kxh7; 31.Qh6+ Kg8; 32.Qg7#.

MAX LANGE'S MATE

The maneuver known as **Max Lange's mate** is usually the result of some tactical operation. The queen and bishop are used together to checkmate an enemy king trapped by two of its own pawns or pieces.

The queen arrives via the back rank, and often after a discovered check when the bishop has forced the king to the corner, as in the following example.

Max Lange's Mate in Action

Although Anderssen was a great player, he did occasionally get ambushed. Here Max Lange teaches him a lesson and earned a place in history with a brilliant combination. The game was played in Bratislava, in 1859. The opening is Spanish Game.

1.e4 e5; 2.Nf3 Nc6; 3.Bb5 Nd4; 4.Nxd4 exd4; 5.Bc4 Nf6; 6.e5 d5; 7.Bb3 Bg4; 8.f3 Ne4!; 9.0-0. 9.fxg4? falls into the trap. Black wins with 9...Qh4+; 10.Ke2 Qf2+; 11.Kd3 Nc5#.

9...d3! 10.fxg4.

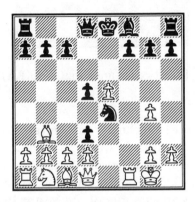

9...Bc5+; 11.Kh1. Black may have expected Black to check at f2 here, regaining some material. That is not the case.

11...Ng3+!; 12.hxg3 Qg5. Black is ready to unleash Greco's mate with ...Qh6#! **13.Rf5.**

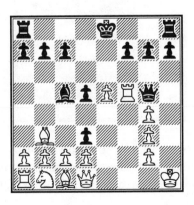

15...h5! If White takes the queen, then another Greco mate follows on 14...hxg4#. **14.gxh5 Qxf5.** Now the idea is a classic deflection with 15...Qf1+; 16.Qxf1 Rxh5#.

15.g4 Rxh5!; 16.gxh5 Qe4. Greco is lurking at h4. **17.Qf3 Qh4+; 18.Qh3 Qe1+; 19.Kh2 Bg1+.**

Now we are at last ready for Max Lange's mate! **20.Kh1 Bf2+; 21.Kh2 Qg1#.**

21. MINOR PIECE MATE

We often worry about how to checkmate with bishop and knight against lone king, since that must be executed carefully in order to complete the operation within the fifty moves allowed by the rules. Paradoxically, situations arise when it is much easier to accomplish when the Black king has protection! The piece can deprive the king of critical flight squares. Here is an example of the **Minor Piece mate.**

The knight only covers two squares, and the bishop accomplishes the same, but since Black pieces occupy the other two squares, the king is checkmated with a **minor piece mate.** Black doesn't have to have a pawn and knight, thus any pieces that cannot stop the bishop will do.

Minor Piece Mate in Action

It is not easy to see how our mate will be achieved from this position. The bishop is at g2, and d5 is occupied by the knight which must get to g6. In Doeserich vs. Burschowsky, Goetzis 1995, things changed quickly.

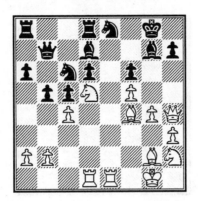

White attained the goal with **28.Ne7+ Kh8; 29.Ng6+ Kg8; 30.Bd5+ Be6; 31.Bxe6+.** Black resigned. It is not checkmate, but after 31...Qf7; 32.Bxf7+ Kxf7; 33.Qxh7 there is no point in playing on.

A young player found the minor piece mate in the 1995 Lingen Championship for players under 11 years.

37.Nxg6+ Kg8; 38.Rb8# did the trick. A discovered checkmate! Knowing the classic mating patterns certainly comes in handy!

22. MORPHY'S MATE

Paul Morphy delivered many great checkmates, including the opera house checkmate we will see. The checkmate that bears his name, **Morphy's mate**, is like the corner mate, except that the attacker uses bishop and rook instead of knight and rook.

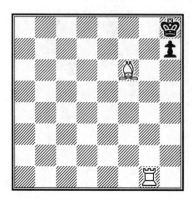

The cooperation of a Black pawn or bishop at h7 is necessary, as any other piece could interpose at g7 or capture the bishop at f6.

Morphy's Mate in Action

The idea of this checkmate was anticipated in a game between an unknown amateur and Sarratt played in 1810. The threat of Morphy's mate is used to set up a corner mate.

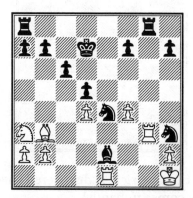

Black played **28...Bf3+!!** If White retreats the rook to g2, then the bishop captures the rook with checkmate. So the bishop must be captured. **29.Rxf3 Nef2+; 30.Rxf2 Nxf2#.**

23. RETI'S MATE

This checkmate requires the cooperation of four enemy pieces, which must occupy four flight squares. The bishop controls the diagonal squares, and a rook or queen covers the open files and protects the bishop. Let's see the **Reti's mate**.

Reti's Mate in Action

There is no better illustration of this theme than Reti vs. Tartakower, in a casual game played in Vienna 1910. That's how the checkmate got its name.

1.e4 c6; 2.d4 d5; 3.Nc3 dxe4; 4.Nxe4 Nf6; 5.Qd3 e5? This is now known to be a blunder. **6.dxe5 Qa5+; 7.Bd2 Qxe5; 8.0-0-0 Nxe4?**

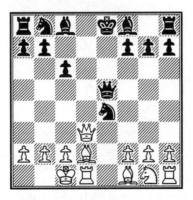

White has too great a lead in development for Black to be indulging in such foolishness.

9.Qd8+!! Kxd8; 10.Bg5+ Kc7; 11.Bd8#.

24. OPERA MATE

In the **Opera mate**, White uses a rook on the back rank, supported by a bishop which also cuts off the escape route of the enemy king. An enemy pawn or piece, other than a knight, occupies the other possible flight square.

Opera Mate in Action

The opera mate is named after a famous game played by Paul Morphy against royal opposition at the Paris Opera during 1858. This game is found in most introductory books and involves a model combination.

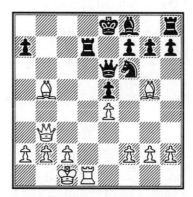

The winning plan was cleanly executed by Morphy.   **15.Bxd7+ Nxd7; 16.Qb8+!! Nxb8; 17.Rd8#.**

25. PILLSBURY'S MATE

The bishop and rook also combine forces in **Pillsbury's mate**. This time the rook works the open file, while the bishop removes the remaining flight square. The king can be either at g8 or h8.

> *There you lie then, and the game's ours—we give you checkmate by discovery, king, the noblest mate of all.*
>
> — Middleton, A Game at Chesse

· The mating position is usually achieved with a discovered check, with the bishop retreating to open up the file, but it is sometimes seen with a capture at f6.

Pillsbury Mate in Action

1.d4 d5; 2.c4 e6; 3.Nc3 Nf6; 4.Bg5 Be7; 5.e3 Nbd7; 6.Nf3 b6; 7.cxd5 exd5; 8.Bb5 Bb7; 9.Ne5 0-0; 10.Bc6 Rb8.

Another disaster would have followed 10...Bxc6; 11.Nxc6 Qe8; 12.Nxe7+ Qxe7; 13.Nxd5 Qe4; 14.Nxf6+ gxf6; 15.Bh6 Qxg2; 16.Qf3.

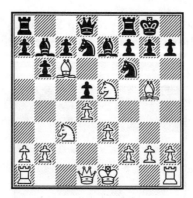

How do we get from this picture to the Pillsbury mating position? By forcing the play, and accepting a little help from the opponent.

11.Bxb7 Rxb7; 12.Nc6 Qe8; 13.Nxe7+ Qxe7; 14.Nxd5 Qe4; 15.Nxf6+ gxf6; 16.Bh6.

It is unlikely that a modern player would be foolish enough to capture at g2, opening up the dangerous g-file, even if the combination itself was not anticipated.

16...Qxg2?? 17.Qf3! White gives up the queen to get the g-file. **17...Qxf3; 18.Rg1+ Kh8; 19.Bg7+ Kg8; 20.Bxf6+ Qg4; 21.Rxg4#.**

26. QUEEN AND PAWN MATE

This basic checkmate is similar to the end of Damiano's Bishop mate, but here a pawn is used instead of a bishop. The **Queen and Pawn mate** is shown below.

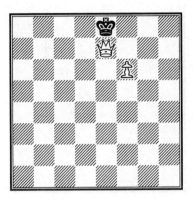

This pattern is not often seen on the chessboard, but the threat of it has won many a game.

Queen and Pawn Mate in Action

In Von Balla vs. Reti, Kosice 1918, the rising star found himself checkmated in the humiliating queen and pawn mate. In the diagram, Black seems to have both f7 and e7 defended, but a sacrifice quickly dispels that notion.

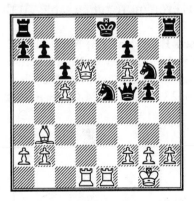

25.Rxe5+! brought a swift end to the game after **25...Nxe5; 26.Qe7#.** On 25...Qxe5, the conclusion would have been 26.Qd7+ Kf8; 27.Qf7#.

27. SMOTHERED MATE

The **smothered mate** is delivered by a knight. Black's king is trapped in the corner, entombed by his own pieces.

Smothered Mate in Action

For our illustration, we will turn to an ancient game, perhaps the very first time the smothered mate was employed in competition. William Lewis, the greatest British player of the early 19th century, played it against B. Keen in a match played in 1817, where Lewis gave odds of a rook or knight in each game, and nevertheless won 4.5-0.5.

This sparkling game contains a combination in the opening, a powerful middlegame attack, and finishes with a smothered mate! When you consider that Lewis spotted his opponent a rook, the game is even more remarkable. At the start of the game, there is no rook at a1.

1.e4 e5; 2.Nf3 Nc6; 3.Bc4 Bc5; 4.c3 d6; 5.0-0 Nf6; 6.d4 exd4; 7.cxd4 Bb6; 8.h3 Nxe4; 9.Re1 d5; 10.Bxd5 Qxd5; 11.Nc3 Qd8; 12.Rxe4+ Ne7; 13.Qe2 Be6; 14.Bg5 Qd6; 15.Bxe7 Kxe7; 16.d5 Rhd8; 17.Ng5 c6; 18.Nxe6 fxe6; 19.Rxe6+ Qxe6; 20.Qxe6+ Kf8; 21.d6 Re8; 22.Qf5+ Kg8; 23.Ne4 Rf8; 24.Qe6+ Kh8; 25.Ng5 Bxf2+; 26.Kh2 Rae8.

This is the classic form of the smothered mate, with the queen sacrifice at g8.
27.Nf7+ Kg8; 28.Nh6+ Kh8; 29.Qg8+ Rxg8; 30.Nf7#.

28. SUFFOCATION MATE

The **Suffocation mate** is similar to the Smothered Mate. The knight will attack the enemy king from a safe distance. The king cannot escape with his own pieces and an enemy bishop depriving him of air, even in the corner of the board.

Suffocation Mate in Action

In Gustke vs. Ballo, German Boys Under-11, 1996, Black had to give up the queen because that was the only way to get out of check. White went on to win easily.

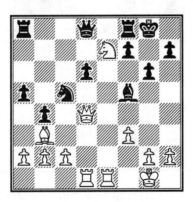

29. SWALLOW-TAIL MATE

The **Swallow-tail mate** is also known as the Gueridon Mate. Black pieces, which can be anything except knights, cut off the diagonal retreat.

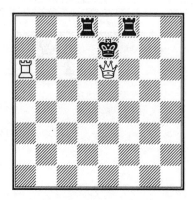

Swallow-tail Mate in Action

1.e4 e5; 2.Nf3 d6; 3.d4 Nd7; 4.Bc4 exd4; 5.Nxd4 Be7; 6.Bxf7+ Kxf7; 7.Ne6 Kxe6; 8.Qd5+ Kf6; 9.Qf5# mate.

This is the final position of a trap in the Philidor Defense. It was seen in Polo vs. Pasqualini from Ferrara, 1923.

Remember that this is just a selection of common checkmates. There are others scattered throughout the book, and you can find them using the thematic index at the end of the book.

STALEMATING PATTERNS

A **Stalemate** is a situation where the side to move has no legal moves, and thus the game ends in a draw. Stalemating patterns are not as well studied as checkmating patterns, and this is a pity, since they are of equal practical importance. Stalemate is often the last, best hope of a defender who is under attack. This is only logical, since the attacker will try to deprive the enemy king of as many flight squares as possible. If all the exits are closed, then Black need only sacrifice remaining material to achieve stalemate.

The stalemating patterns in this section are only those which are seen with some frequency in actual games. There are many more which are the

> *I* pray you, Sir, is it your will, to make a stale of me among these mates?
>
> — Shakespeare, The Taming of the Shrew

subject of endgame compositions, designed for artistic merit. I have included some examples of artistic stalemates from practical play, however.

1. CLASSIC PAWN STALEMATE

The most common stalemating pattern is found in king and pawn endgames. In fact, stalemate is the key drawing resource in many of these minimalist endgames.

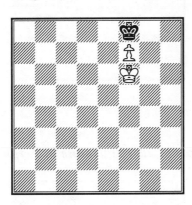

Classic Stalemate in Action

This was seen in Burn vs. Pillsbury, Vienna 1898, and of course in many other games. Here is a spectacular variation on the same theme.

Znosko Borovsky vs. Salwe, Ostende 1907. White is threatened with a back rank mate, but there is salvation in **46.Ra8!! Rxa8; 47.h8Q!! Rxh8** stalemate.

2. ROOK PAWN STALEMATE

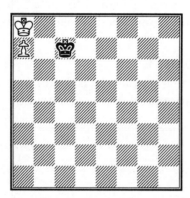

White to move is stalemated, Black to move plays **1...Kc8** and the result is the same.

Rook Pawn Stalemate in Action

In Maroczy vs. Treybal, from the great Carlsbad tournament of 1923, White captured a knight at a8. Black played **65...Kc7** and the position was stalemate.

3. MATTISON'S STALEMATE

This stalemating pattern involves a king trapped by a queen (or rook), a king and a knight. **Mattison's stalemate** is very uncommon, but can easily be overlooked.

Mattison's Stalemate in Action

If Black captures the rook with **1...Qxg5**, then White is stalemated. Otherwise, White wins the queen.

4. QUEEN CORNER STALEMATE

The **Queen Corner stalemate** is one of the simplest stalemates. The White king is trapped in the corner by an unassisted queen.

Queen Corner Stalemate in Action

In Albin vs. Csank from the 1890 Kolisch Memorial, White escaped with **89.Qg7+!!** because after **89...Kxg7** he is stalemated.

5. WOLF'S STALEMATE

Wolf's stalemate will often come as a surprise, because the king is not at the edge of the board. A rook cuts off the file, and a protected pawn eliminates another two flight squares. A friendly pawn and enemy king are involved, too.

Wolff's Stalemate in Action

Schlechter vs. Wolf, Nuremburg 1906. White has just played 55.b6??, a terrible blunder. After **55...Re1+!!** White had no choice but to play **56.Rxe1**, with stalemate.

6. TOWER STALEMATE

In the **Tower stalemate**, the king is prevented from fleeing from his cell in the corner, because a rook eliminates all flight squares.

Tower Stalemate in Action

Schelchter vs. Janowski, Ostende 1907. Black tried to win quickly with **76...Rg2??**, but after **77.Rh6+!! gxh6** the game ended in stalemate.

7. ENGLISCH STALEMATE

The **Englisch stalemate** is a very unusual stalemate, but it reflects a common theme of sacrificing all remaining material once the king is in a stalemate position. It is named after a German, explaining the odd spelling.

Englisch Stalemate in Action

This was the situation with White to move. This stalemate gets its name from the game Bird vs. Englisch, London 1883. White wins Black's remaining pawn and threatens to advance one of the g–pawns. The game may be headed for a draw under normal circumstances, but we are treated to a wonderful display of stalemate. White captured the pawn with **41.Nxf6**, and English offered up both rooks with **41...Rh1+; 42.Kxh1 Re1+; 42.Kh2 Rh1+!!**

After **23.Kxh1**, Black was in stalemate.

8. PAULSEN'S STALEMATE

Here is an example of **Paulsen's stalemate**.

Paulsen's Stalemate in Action

In Schallopp vs. Paulsen, Nassengrund 1888, the king and a bishop are all that are required to eliminate all legal moves by the White king.

The amazing **81.g6!** forced a draw. After 81...hxg6, the position was stalemate.

9. CONGDON'S STALEMATE

And now, **Congdon's stalemate**...

Congdon's Stalemate in Action

In Congdon vs. Delmar, New York 1880, White saved this position, down a full five pawns, with **1.Qg8+!! Kxg8** and stalemate.

10. KING'S HEAD STALEMATE

This is a rare example of the king being stalemated in the middle of the board. It was seen in a game I played as a member of the King's Head Pub, in a critical championship game. Here is the **King's Head stalemate**...

King's Head Stalemate in Action

This position was reached after White's 45th move in Macaulay vs. Schiller, London 1982. I played **45...Kd5!** Black's king will now be in a stalemate position if the e-pawn is removed. **46.Kf5** was played, because 46.f4 exf4; 47.gxf4 Rh4+!! 48.Kf5 Rxf4+! 49.Kxf4 is stalemate! After **46...Rh5+; 47.Kf6 Rh6+; 48.Kf5 Rh5+** the game was eventually drawn.

These are just a few of the many stalemating possibilities in chess. Others are scattered throughout this book, and many more are seen in tournament competition. You can see from these examples that when a king is in the corner, there are many stalemating possibilities. On the back rank, there are a lot, too. Even in the middle of the board, we saw some trapped kings. Whenever there is a trapped king, keep in mind that stalemate may be a defensive option.

ANALYSIS

Do not believe in anything simply because you have heard it.
Do not believe in anything simply because it is spoken and rumored by many.
Do not believe in anything simply because it is found written in your books.
Do not believe in anything merely on the authority of your teachers and elders.
Do not believe in traditions because they have been handed down for many generations. But after observation and analysis, when you find that anything agrees with reason and is conducive to the good and benefit of one and all, then accept it and live up to it. **—Buddha**

The proper evaluation of actual and predicted positions is crucial to success in chess. In this chapter we sill look at various ways of evaluating positions. This practical advice comes from many top players and trainers. We'll consider some of the great myths of chess, such as the absolute values of chess forces and the tree of analysis before turning to modern advice on calculation and how to analyze in time pressure.

VALUE OF THE PIECES

> *...some scientists have calculated the approximate mathematical value to be as follows: taking the Pawn as the unit, the Knight worth 3.05, the Bishop 3.50, the Rook 5.48 and the Queen, 9.94.*
>
> — Steinitz, Modern Chess Instructor

Steinitz is citing work published in *Staunton's Handbook*, but which was probably borrowed in turn from some source in the first half of the nineteenth century. Mathematicians have long been fascinated by chess. The idea that absolute values can be assigned to individual chess forces is appealing, but, as we shall see, fatally flawed.

> *On the scale of comparative values, three pawns compensate approximately a knight, four a bishop, five a rook, and nine a queen.*
>
> — David Bronstein,
> The Sorcerer's Apprentice

Many books for beginners assign values to each piece, and although they do warn us that these values are not absolute, there is nevertheless a tendency to keep believing that pieces have an intrinsic worth that is independent of the position. Unfortunately, there is a great deal of disagreement about the numbers! Assigning values to pieces is useful for teaching absolute beginners, but in order to progress in chess you must free yourself from the yoke of materialism and learn to value the potential of pieces, not a point count!

Usually pieces are assigned values in a hierarchy, from most valuable to least valuable, Queen, Rook Bishop, Knight, Pawn. The king is omitted because the king must be preserved at all costs. In reality, a piece must be evaluated in terms of its current usefulness and potential value. Bishops are generally considered better than knights because they can operate at long range, which is very important in attacking positions and certain endgames. In other cases, however, a knight is worth much more than a bishop. Revisit the examples of bad bishops in the book to see convincing evidence.

Even in endgames with a large imbalance in material, the potential activity of a piece may be so limited as to reduce its value to nil. Leaving aside the occasional bizarre positions, we find plenty of examples where even an advantage equivalent to a rook in point count systems is not enough. A queen is considered the equivalent of approximately two rooks, but sometimes one rook alone is sufficient to handle a queen, as in the following example.

We have the position after White's 68th move in Luberti vs. Schiller, from the 1997 Western States Open. There is no way to contain a rook on the e-file using just king and queen, even if there is a zugzwang against the White king. The rook at e3 has seven possible moves on the e-file. The king can cover at most three. The queen can cover another three. To cover seven squares, the open square must be one where a check along the a8-h1 diagonal will pick off the rook. Yet the Black king cannot cross the e-file, so it can never cover e3, e2, or e1.

I decided to play **68...Qxe3.** Instead, 68...Qc2 should have been tried. 69.Re7 Qc5; 70.Re3 Qd5+; 71.Kg1 Qd1+; 72.Kg2 Qd6; 73.Kf1! Qd1+; 74.Re1 Qd3+; 75.Kg2 is a draw.

69.fxe3 Ke4; 70.Kf2 Kd3; 71.e4! Kxe4. I had some small hope that White would overlook **72.Ke2!** But he didn't, and a draw was agreed.

In my earlier calculations, leading up to the win of the enemy queen for a rook and pawn, I did not properly evaluate the importance of the fortress position in reducing the value of my material advantage. This didn't make a practical difference, since winning the enemy queen was the best option at the time.

We are going to take a long journey through a fascinating complete game now. Let's just concentrate on the evaluation of the pieces, as might be done by a modern master, even though the game is an ancient one. Some powerful computer chess programs were used to analyze this game, and we will consider some of their evaluations, made under normal tournament time controls, with those of Petrov himself. Computers can be thought of as enhanced point count machines. They do apply positional factors in their evaluations, but they are still, by and large, mechanically calculating various factors and coming up with numbers, then playing the moves which are evaluated has having the most points.

Although the sacrifice in the following game is unsound, the machines were unable to understand the long term situation clearly enough to find the best moves at many points.

PETROV - SURNY
Paris, 1863

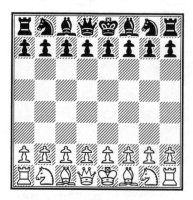

Right at the outset, only pawns and knights can move. The potential of the other pieces remains untapped.

1.e4. The value of the White queen and bishop has increased as a result of this move. **1...e5; 2.f4** White offers a gambit, in order to gain control of the important central square d4. **2...exf4.**

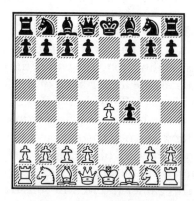

Black has a pawn, but what is the value of the pawn. It is so weak that it can only really be defended by advancing the g-pawn, but that creates further weaknesses in Black's position. The evaluation of the position remains about even.

3.Nf3 g5; 4.h4 g4. If Black captures at h4, there are two extra pawns, but they are hardly worth anything at all, and both will soon be captured, with additional weaknesses at f7 and h7 to work on.

5.Ne5. The knight shows its potential for forking, with g4 and f7 under attack. **5...Nf6; 6.Bc4 d5.** Already Black must return the pawn, or face destruction at f7. **7.exd5 Bd6.**

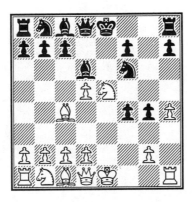

What value do you place on White's pawn at d5? It is doubled and weak and in the way of the White bishop. On the other hand, it controls e6 and c6. White's next move adds to the value of the bishop at c1. If White retreated the knight to d3 instead, then the value of the bishop would have to be reduced, as its short-term potential drops off the scale.

8.d4 Nh5; A knight on the rim has less mobility and therefore is usually reduced in value, but here the knight not only defends property at f4, it also can enter the White kingside at g3. I'd say the knight is more valuable now than it was before! **9.Bb5+.**

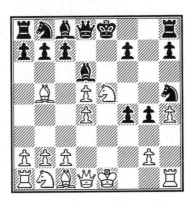

It is interesting that when I fed this position to computers, they all moved the king to f8, as in the game. True, the king is safer there, but what is the future of the rook at h8? It won't be able to play an active role until the endgame. Actually, in this game it never moves at all! So the king move lowers the value of the rook, which in the end, as we'll see, is absolute zero. Black should, in fact, embark on a sacrificial path.

9...Kf8?; The bold 9...c6! is correct, even though it loses a pawn. And that's just for starters. 10.dxc6 bxc6; 11.Nxc6 Nxc6; 12.Bxc6+ Kf8.

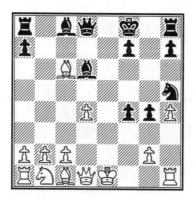

Yes, it's a whole rook sitting at a8. Looking at the position, however, we see that the bishop has more power than the rook, at the moment. It is the only developed White piece, and the king is in great danger on the e-file. 13.Bxa8 Ng3; 14.Rh2. White has defended against the immediate threats, but the rook at h2 has been greatly devalued. 14...Qe7+; 15.Kf2 Ne4+; 16.Kg1 (16.Bxe4 g3+; 17.Kg1 gxh2+; 18.Kh1 Qxe4; 19.Nc3 Qe7; . White has an extra pawn, but Black's bishops are powerful, while White's does nothing. The rook at h8 will enter the game at g8.) 16...f3; 17.g3 Bxg3; 18.Bxe4 Bxh2+; 19.Kxh2 Qxe4; 20.Bh6+ Ke7; 21.Qd2 g3+! 22.Kxg3 Rg8+.

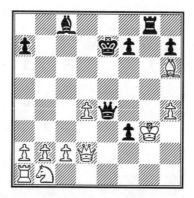

White has greater potential value, with an extra knight and pawn, but almost all of Black's pieces are operating at full potential, while White needs to activate the queenside forces. In fact, the king cannot retreat here without significant loss of material, so White must allow the bishop to be sacrificed to buy time for development. 23.Bg5+ (23.Qg5+ Rxg5+; 24.Bxg5+ f6 wins quickly for Black, though White has almost as many "points" as Black.) 23...f6; 24.Qb4+ Kf7; 25.Qc4+ Be6; 26.Qc7+ Kg6.

Though White has a whopping 4-point advantage, under most counting systems, eight of his points—the rook and the knight— are doing nothing on the queenside, and the bishop is unable to retreat for tactical reasons. 27.Nc3 (27.Bd2 Kf5+ leads to checkmate!) 27...Qg4+; 28.Kf2 fxg5; 29.Qd6 Qxh4+; 30.Kxf3 Qh3+; 31.Kf2 Re8. White's point count advantage has been reduced quite a bit, but White can now activate the rook and survive. Still, Black should have some sort of perpetual check to get the half point.

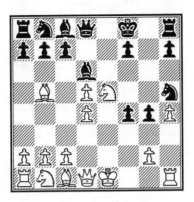

Now we return to the move played in the game and recommended by computers, the flight of the king to f8.

10.Nc3 Ng3; 11.Bxf4!? White decides to make the sacrifice. Activating the bishop and adding the threat of a check at h6 is, in Petrov's opinion, worth the investment of the rook.

11...Nxh1; 12.Qd2 Qxh4+; 13.g3 Nxg3; 14.Qf2.

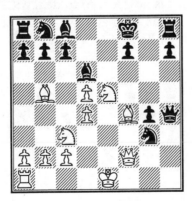

What on earth is going on here. White is giving away the store! Let's see, Black has an extra rook, worth five clams or whatever, and can eat another one at a1. Must be winning, right?

14...Nf5. The greedy 14...Qh1+; 15.Kd2 Qxa1 gets mated in three after Bh6+. Of course Black could try some other move, such as capturing at e5. **15.Qxh4.** Remember that rule about trying to trade queens when you are way ahead in material? Has Petrov forgotten? Or perhaps it wasn't discovered yet?

15...Nxh4; 16.Bh6+.

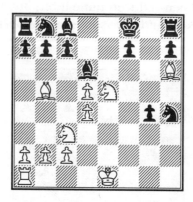

Here we have a classic example of materialism leading to defeat. Black doesn't want to give back the knight, so moves the king to g8 where it reduces the value of the rook, which would have much preferred to see the king to go e7, to nothing. By the way, one of the strongest chess computers, searching millions of positions to six moves by each side, came up with the same foolish plan, evaluating it as twice as good as the transfer of the king to the center.

16...Kg8?; Black should have played 16...Ke7!; 17.Bg5+ f6; 18.Bxh4 to bring the point count advantage down to three, but look how the value of the rook has increased, and the three connected passed pawns are a sure winner in the endgame.

17.Ne4! Be7; 18.Be8! Black is now forced to deal with the threat at f7. Recall that when we evaluated the pawn at d5 long ago, we were not so impressed. Yet here, by simply eliminating the defense ...Be6, it shows that it is worth its weight in gold!

18...Nf3+; 19.Kf2 Nxe5; 20.dxe5.

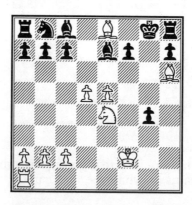

Time to evaluate the position again. Black still has more points, with an extra pawn and the exchange. White, however, has every piece in an active position. Since neither Black rook can move, we might want to deduct ten points from Black's total.

That would be overkill, however. The rook on h8 can move if the bishop vacates h6.

20...Bf5; 21.Nf6+ Bxf6; 22.exf6 Nd7? 22...Na6!; 23.Re1 Rd8 would have won. White can go after the rook at h8, but only at the cost of the bishop. For example 24.Bg7 Bxc2; 25.Bxh8 Kxh8; 26.Bxf7 Rf8; with an easy win for Black.

23.Bxd7! Again White confounds the pundits by exchanging pieces while a rook down. **23...Bxd7.**

There is an extraordinary tale to be told here on this 19th century chessboard. White is a whole rook down, and a pawn. The question is, can he win, or merely draw! Computers evaluate the position as about four pawns better for Black, but what do they know? An exhaustive analysis of this position is beyond the scope of this book, so I invite you to match wits with another Petrov, a chess composer from Volgograd. Almost a century he later published analysis showing that moving the rook to the h-file, to either get around the pawn at g4 or later destroy it, was the proper plan. The player of the White side in the game agreed, noting after the game that the next move was inaccurate.

24.Re1. 24.Rh1 Bf5; 25.Rh5 Bxc2; 26.Re5 was the 19th century analysis. The main line of the 1955 article by D. Petrov runs as follows. 26...Rd8; 27.Kg3 a5; 28.b3 a4; 29.Kxg4 axb3; 30.axb3 b5; 31.Kf4 b4; 32.Re2 and the pawn cannot be captured because the rook comes to the g-file with check. The analysis does not stop here, of course, but it is interesting to note that computers already count up their points a little less optimistically for Black, though they still evaluate Black as being almost three points ahead. 32...Bd3; 33.Re7 Rc8; 34.Ke5 Bb5; 35.Kd4. White threatens to gobble the b-pawn. Machine evaluations continue to drop. Now they think the position is a draw. 35...c5+; 36.dxc6 Bxc6; 37.Re3 Rd8+; 38.Kc4 Be4! Black offers to sacrifice both the bishop and the rook for the ultimate draw—stalemate!

The computers say draw, but humans persevere. 39.Kxb4! (39.Rxe4?? Rd4+; 40.Kxd4 is stalemate.) and White's winning plan is illustrated by the sequence 39...Rb8+; 40.Kc3 Rc8+; 41.Kb2 Bf5; 42.b4 Bg6; 43.b5 Rb8; 44.Kc3! The pawn is taboo because of the back-rank mate. White wins by advancing the b-pawn to b7. 44...Rc8+; 45.Kd2 Rc2+;

46.Kd1 Rc8; 47.b6 Rd8+; 48.Ke1 Rb8; 49.b7 Rd8; 50.Rc3 Bf5; 51.Rc5 with checkmate in seven.

24...Re8; 25.Rxe8+ Bxe8.

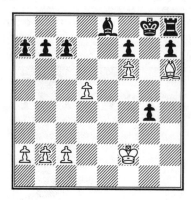

Yet again White has stubbornly stuck to the plan of exchanging pieces while behind in material. Black has an extra rook and an extra pawn. Six points in an endgame, with no tactical tricks or passed pawns for White. The machines are rejoicing. Humans start to grow puzzled looks.

26.Kg3 Bd7; 27.c4 a5; 28.a3 a4; 29.c5 Bc8; 30.d6 cxd6; 31.cxd6 Bd7; 32.Kf4 Be6; 33.Kg3.

The game was agreed drawn at this point. Black can do nothing with the extra rook. White just moves the king back and forth, g3-f4-g3-g4 etc. How long would it take a computer to realize that the game is drawn?

KOTOV'S TREE OF ANALYSIS

Alexander Kotov's classic, *Think Like a Grandmaster,* advises us to calculate each branch of a variation once, and not to retrace our steps. This idea is rarely achieved, but it remains an elusive goal which troubles the sleep of some chessplayers. You can relax.

Kotov would have us reduce the analysis procedure to the kind of number crunching a computer program uses. Humans are rarely capable of such disciplined thinking. We notice things. That gets in the way of pure calculation, but leads to inspired leaps of creative thinking.

No one applies the Kotov technique in all its glory. Exhaustively analyzing a few branches individually can lead to a stifling of creativity and interfere with the exploitation of little bits of ideas picked up while analyzing. Often you travel down one path, but spot some characteristic of a piece or pawn structure which is relevant to some other branch that you have already examined. With this new knowledge, you are tempted to leap back to the relevant branch.

This sort of thinking violates the Kotovian system, but is in fact more productive. From Kotov's brilliant work we must extract only the broad outlines. You definitely should select a number of candidate moves and them examine each in detail. Flitting back and forth is a waste of time. Yet rigidly following a single path is like walking with blinders. Perhaps it works for machines, but not for humans. Despite some overstatements, Kotov's book is still valuable reading for instruction on the art of calculation.

Tisdall, in his excellent book, *Improve Your Chess Now!,* advocates a different approach. He points out many flaws in Kotov's approach and suggests the following three step procedure:

1. To aim towards the choice of a single critical variation. Deal with branches only when unavoidable.

2. At all times, evaluate the position objectively.

3. Determine appropriate candidate moves

This is actually a very radical view, especially the first step. Instead of casting a wide net, Tisdall urges us to focus on what strikes us as the most important line. Under his system, you scan the available plausible lines and zero in on one that seems most critical. I think he has the right idea, because in practice, most players intuitively adopt one or at most two lines as critical when approaching a position. In addition, this thought process will bring to the forefront the relevant tactical and strategic considerations which will appear in many different lines.

ON CALCULATION

It is not enough just to calculate. The creative side of chess must be exploited to achieve maximum results at the board. All of the discipline of calculation can stifle the creative muse, and may overlook possibilities which involve bizarre moves or unlikely sacrifices. Man does not live by calculation alone, and there is other food for thought.

You must be able to imagine variations and positions that are beyond your ability to calculate. By doing so, you create a set of patterns in your mind which can be invoked later in calculating tactics.

Let your fantasy roam from time to time, especially when your opponent's clock is running. Imagine different possibilities that might arise if one of your opponent's pieces were to be moved elsewhere. This can lead you to discover decoy and deflection combinations. Start considering endgame possibilities early in the middlegame. For example, when your opponent has few pawns left, and one is a rook pawn, see if the opponent has the right color bishop to advance it. If so, perhaps you might want to eliminate that piece.

> *In chess, as played by a good player, logic and imagination must go hand in hand, compensating each other.*
>
> — Capablanca

Only after you have some goals in mind should the concrete analysis begin. Don't rush into consideration of a long variation before you have a good grasp of the overall terrain, and possible directions the game might take.

Above all, do not think one move at a time! Never start out by calculating what your opponent will do in response to a planned move. Set out your goals, find ways to achieve them, and then find variations which lead toward that goal.

ANALYZING IN TIME PRESSURE

Analyzing when short of time is a special art. When you don't have the luxury of evaluating the overall position, just ask yourself one question—what does my opponent threaten? If the answer is nothing, then ask—why did my opponent make that move? Be careful, however, because often when the opponent is in time trouble a player will make a move which is hard to figure out because it really doesn't have a direct purpose. This is known as a "confusionary riff."

Concentrate on concrete threats.

Time permitting, try to think of how each exchange of pieces might affect the game. Try to make favorable exchanges, and avoid unfavorable ones. Watch out for drawing tricks, whether you have the advantage or disadvantage. If at all possible, postpone important decisions until after the time control.

THE CHECKLIST

When I teach beginners and intermediate students, I advise them to ask the following questions after each opponent move:

1. What did your opponent play?

2. What is the point of the move?

3. Can I capture any enemy pieces now?

4. Can I give any checks?

5. Can I threaten any enemy pieces?

6. Can I improve the position of any of my pieces?

These questions should be taken literally, including all legal possibilities. It may seem stupid to look at capturing a pawn with your queen when your opponent can simply recapture. However, it is just possible that a clever combination may lie just beyond your horizon. More important is the possibility that while useless now, the move may become an option later, if the opponent makes some changes in the position.

That's why you consider these options even when your reply is "obvious". When your opponent captures one of your pieces, and you have a defender, you will normally capture the piece that inflicted the damage. But there may be a better move! The checklist will open up your options.

After you have completed the checklist, you now have a set of moves that you can consider as candidate moves. Discard the ones that are clearly bad, but make sure you take a look at each. You will try to analyze each of the remaining candidates as best as you can. Then discard the moves that are obviously bad, and select a move that will give you the best result, at least as far as your skill will carry you.

TRAINING

A man who is well prepared has already fought half the battle. —*Cervantes (Don Quixote)*

Chess training can be accomplished alone, in groups, or in formal instruction. Most readers of this book will be relying on their own efforts, perhaps with the inclusion of occasional lessons. This chapter contains tips for effective training.

> ***W**hat the chess public needs is a method of winning easily without first mastering the difficult and unnecessary technique of making good moves.*
>
> — MacMurray (1933)

Alas, all too many chess players agree with this statement, and are unwilling to put in the work required to master the fundamentals of the game. Actually, chess is a lot like reading. The more you do, the better you become. The better you are, the easier it is to do! Time spent learning basic opening and endgame strategies will serve you well throughout your chess career.

To assist you with your preparation, the following sections will provide advice on studying many different aspects of the game, including physical training. You'll get some surprising advice at the end of the chapter!

STUDY THE CLASSICS!

There is plenty to learn about all aspects of the game from studying the classics. We have classical games, played in the Classical Era between roughly 1886 and the outbreak of the First World War. There are classic games which have been reprinted in many anthologies. Some great books have achieved the status of classics, and most masters have read them at one time or another.

> *I will pray you at the same time to send me Philidor on chess, which you will find in the book room, 2d. press on the left from the door of the entrance: to be wrapped in strong paper also.*
>
> — Letter by Thomas Jefferson

We must be careful not to believe everything we read, however. We'll consider the question of attitude toward chess authorities in the psychology chapter, but here let's remind ourselves that even the greatest of chess authorities can be very, very wrong.

The great international tournament in New York, 1924, is filled with remarkable games. The notes in the tournament book are by Alekhine himself. These notes are studied at some time in almost every successful chess master's career. They are not without serious errors, as Edward Lasker has demonstrated.

Here is a position from the tournament where Edward Lasker had White against Efim Bogoljubow. This is the picture after move 40 by White.

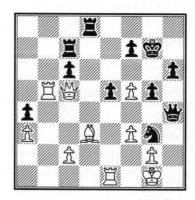

Black played **40...f6,** an obvious move but one which fails to anticipate the coming sacrifice. **41.Rxe5!! fxe5?;** Bogoljubow should have tried exchanging queens with 42...Qd4+!; 43.Qxd4 Rxd4; 44.Rc5 Nh4 with the threat of ...Nf4+. **42.Qxe5+ Kg8; 43.Rb4!** This is the move Black overlooked. The attack on the queen leads to a decisive advantage.

43...Qh1+; 44.Kf2 Rf7.

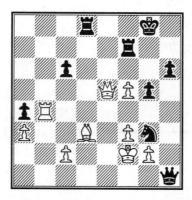

45.Rb8? The time control for this game was at move 45, and Lasker had only a few seconds left for this critical move. The exchange of rooks leads to a draw. He explains that he forgot that the rook at b4 covers h4, so he could have just captured the knight.

45...Rxb8; 46.Qxb8+ Kg7; 47.Qe5+ Kf8; 48.Qb8+ Kg7; 49.Qe5+. Here the game was agreed drawn. Alekhine wrote that the position would have been easily won for Black after 40...Rd5; 41.Qb6 cxb5.

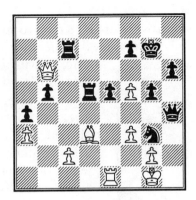

He considered only 42.Qxc7?! There is an immediate win with 42.f6+! Kg8; 43.Qb8+. The picture he paints of the entire game is one where Black was winning, but threw away the game with a blunder. In fact, Lasker's play was impressive, and it was he who threw away the win with a blunder.

Both Alekhine and Lasker agree that after the superior 45.Kxg3 the Black king would be doomed. Is this evaluation correct?

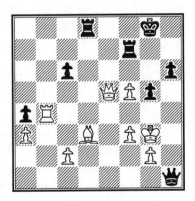

Black can play 45...Qh5, which allows the queen to come to f7 after the rook evacuates. It is hard to see how White can win by direct means. The rook is still rooted to the fourth rank because of the threat at h4. White may be able to win slowly by picking off the weak Black pawns, but Lasker is surely too optimistic when he writes, "To realize the threat Bc4, I had only to play the king back to f2." In fact, 46.Kf2 Rfd7 forces the bishop to remain at its defensive post, since the check at c4 accomplishes nothing when the king runs to h7. White can grab either pawn on the queenside, but chances for counterplay would remain.

STUDYING GAMES

There is no better way to improve your chess than to study games by great players, especially games with insightful explanatory commentaries. You can study your games alone, or with friends. Either way, a good procedure is to first play through the games without pause, following just the actual moves and not being distracted by any variations, sidelines or commentary. Just observe the flow of the game, and try to notice when the position changes radically and one side obtains a decisive advantage.

> *H*istory repeats itself –
> the first time as tragedy,
> the second time as farce.
>
> – Karl Marx

Return to the game, and play it through again. This time pay attention to the commentaries, but don't examine each piece of analysis in detail. Instead, try to concentrate on the general point that the author is trying to make. The commentaries should use words, not abstract symbols. Pages cluttered with hieroglyphics can be deciphered by masters, but are generally unhelpful to amateurs. The symbol "+=" means that White has an advantage. A small, slight, meaningful, or significant advantage? Such statements don't tell you anything other than that the author would, all things considered, prefer to be sitting on the White side of the board. Words inform, symbols usually just confuse. In your second pass of the game, you are just trying to get a feel for how the game was viewed by the commentator.

Your third examination of the game is where the work really begins. Read every bit of analysis and commentary, and challenge anything you don't immediately agree with. When a piece of analysis ends with an evaluation, extend it a few more moves to make sure that you agree. Be especially critical of any analysis that includes the words "clearly" or "obviously." This is often where errors lie. I first noticed this trend in the linguistic work of Noam Chomsky, but it applies just as well to chess.

You should, of course, also study your own games. Learn from your defeats! Recognize the errors in your games and you won't have to suffer through endless repetitions of the same old blunders.

STUDYING OPENINGS

> *T*o study opening variations without reference to the
> strategy that applies to the middlegame is, in effect,
> to separate the head from the body.
>
> – Petrosian

You cannot achieve much in chess by merely memorizing opening moves. It is absolutely essential that you understand the underlying concepts and strategies which are part and parcel of a major opening. A chess encyclopedia with grids of moves evaluated by the standard chess informant symbols can be very useful as reference material, particularly if you're a strong player, but even the best players need strategic explanations when learning a new opening.

The quote below is especially amusing since Picasso said it first in reference to painters — but Stravinsky stole it as his own! In any case, one must study the classics in order to gain inspiration and find models for correct play. You should never decline to play an opening idea just become someone has done it before! Try to find original ideas that are improvements over mistakes in games that have been the foundation for evaluating openings.

> *Great composers do not borrow - they steal.*
>
> — Stravinsky

If you insist on trying to play strange moves in the opening purely for originality, remember that many bad openings have multiple refutations. Perhaps you find a new move which rehabilitates the Frobisher Gambit and refutes one of the main lines. There is likely to be an alternative line for the opponent which is also good for a healthy advantage, if not as great an advantage as was credited to the one you have just repaired.

The best way to learn a new opening is to play over complete games by top players which use the opening. Observe the typical middlegame and endgame strategies for both sides. Don't try to memorize any moves. Memorization should be the final stage of opening study, not the start. Then get a good book on the opening, one which explains the ideas in words rather than symbols. You can supplement this basic understanding with technical knowledge later.

Try out your new opening strategy in informal games, for example, on the Internet. Every time you win, identify the crucial mistake that cost your opponent the game. When you lose, don't settle for such a superficial examination. Find every single inferior move you made in the game. A computer chess program can help you by analyzing the positions and suggesting improvements.

STUDYING MIDDLEGAMES

The middlegame is best studied by examining games played by the best players, preferably with their own notes. In this way, you can get a picture of how each player approached the positions, and how they weighed the various factors involved. It is all too easy for an analysts to point out that one player successfully employed a particular strategy, but that is only one part of the thought process.

Most of the best players have published extensive collections of games with notes.

From Steinitz to Kasparov, the World Champions have all contributed greatly to the literature. When champions meet, often they each write detailed commentaries to the games. These analyses can be quite different. At times, reading Botvinnik's and Bronstein's notes to their encounters, they hardly seem like the same games!

Each of the World Champions has a unique style, and their games teach different lessons. All are, of course, well versed in the art of strategy and tactics, but each had some outstanding characteristics.

STRENGTHS OF THE CHAMPIONS

Morphy	Attack against uncastled king
Steinitz	Defense and active use of king
Lasker	Taking advantage of mistakes
Capablanca	Endgames
Alekhine	Combinations
Euwe	Attack from Stonewall positions
Botvinnik	Balance of attack and defense
Smyslov	Positional maneuvering
Tal	Attack against castled king
Petrosian	Counterattack from cramped positions
Spassky	Balance of attack and defense
Fischer	Transition to favorable endgame
Karpov	Exploiting positional advantages
Kasparov	Positional Sacrifices
Kramnik	Avoiding weaknesses

It must be admitted, however, that even these exalted players sometimes present incorrect information. They occasionally make mistakes in tactical analysis. Modern scholars, aided by powerful computers, have reversed some of their judgments. Their opinions on opening strategies must always be taken in the context of the prevailing views at the time, and sometimes seem rather quaint today. Nevertheless, you can't go wrong by studying games by the very best players.

STUDYING TACTICS

Chess tactics consist of individual patterns which often interact to form spectacular combinations. You need to burn these patterns into your memory. Many newspapers have a chess column with puzzles for you to solve, and there are many collections of self-tests available. Tactics should be practiced daily, if possible.

STUDYING ENDGAMES

The endgame is the hardest aspect of chess to study by yourself. Mastering the complexities of the seemingly simple positions that dominate practical endgame play requires knowledge of all of the concepts mentioned in the endgame chapter, a keen ability to calculate, and a lot of experience.

Some teachers like to concentrate on "practical" endgames from tournament situations, and others use exclusively composed studies. The majority of teachers use both, with good reason. Practical games contain many instructive errors, while studies draw your concentration primarily to the correct solution.

The themes encountered in compositions are frequently used to bring victory in practical play. In many cases, they represent a pure, more abstract form of the critical ideas. A beautiful composition will stamp the theme indelibly in your mind, ready for use when opportunity arises.

In this 1905 composition by Behting, White has an extra pawn, but a win is not easy to find. The solution is beautiful, and teaches a trick about knight pawns. White cannot play 1.Ke2? Kg2; 2.g4 fxg4; 3.f5 g3; 4.f6 because 4...gxf6 5.h6 f5; 6.h7 f4; 7.h8Q f3+; 8.Kd3 f2; 9.Qb2 Kg1; 10.Qd4 Kg2 is just a draw. Even worse is 1.g4?? fxg4; 2.h6 gxh6; 3.f5 g3 and Black wins!

1.Ke1! is the only path to victory. **1...Kg2;** 1...Kh2 also loses. 2.Kf2 Kh3; 3.Kf3 Kh2; 4.g4 fxg4+; 5.Kxg4 is a simple win.

2.g4! fxg4; 3.f5 g3; 4.f6! Black is doomed. **4...gxf6.** 4...Kh1; 5.fxg7 g2; 6.g8Q g1Q+; 7.Qxg1+ Kxg1; 8.h6 is no problem. **5.h6 f5.** 5...Kh1; 6.h7 g2; 7.h8Q+ Kg1; 8.Qh3 f5; 9.Ke2 f4; 10.Kf3 and mate.

6.h7 f4; 7.h8Q f3; 8.Qf6 f2+; 9.Ke2 Kg1; 10.Qa1+ Kg2; 11.Qf1+ Kh2; 12.Kf3 leads to checkmate. Note that the White king was in correct position to win the queen vs. two pawn endgame. Such subtleties are among the lessons that endgame studies have to offer.

To study the endgame properly requires a partner, preferably an experienced coach. Books are helpful, but once you turn the page and look at the solution, the lesson is less valuable. Trying to find the solution is an integral part of the learning process. Your coach should gently guide you to the correct move, providing small hints and disclosing short term and long term goals.

Studying one endgame per day will improve the results of almost any player. Most students spend far too much time on opening study and neglect this difficult but essential phase of the game. When I teach, half of each lesson is devoted to endgame theory. I have watched my students outplay players rated much higher when the pieces start to come off the board. Invest in endgame training and you will reap many rewards!

PHYSICAL TRAINING

The physically fit chessplayer has a large advantage over the couch potato. Chess is a game that requires stamina in large amounts. Both players and trainers have a wide variety of regimens, covering everything from physical exercise to diet. On the latter, little has changed in four hundred years. Here is the wisdom of a Sicilian priest, from 1617:

> *Whoever is to play an important game must avoid filling his belly with superfluous food, because fullness is contrary to speculation and obfuscates the sight, so that it is necessary he should observe strict sobriety.*
>
> — Pietro Carrerea, Il Giogo degli Scacchi.

It is impossible to recommend a single plan for all players. I can, however, offer a piece of advice that dates back at least to Botvinnik. When you are playing serious games, make sure that after the third or fourth hour you boost your energy with something to eat. Preferably something that isn't full of chemicals and sugar, but I must admit that a candy bar works well for young people. I tend toward low fat, low sugar granola bars myself these days. Fruit juice often works well. When my students play, I try to check that they have suitable energy sources available as they head to the game.

During tournaments, I find that I play better if I can swim for an hour or so each day. My performance rating is generally about 100 points higher, in fact! Cardiovascular exercise seems to be beneficial, and many top players find it in one form or another.

THE LAZY WAY

Some people just don't want to work on chess, preferring to learn by osmosis and experience. Most will never amount to anything, but one must always remember Emanuel Lasker's words:

> *Of my 57 years I've applied at least 30 to forgetting most of what I learned or read, and since I succeeded in this I have acquired a certain ease and cheer which I should never again like to be without. If need be, I can increase my skill in chess, if need be I can do that of which I have no idea present.*
>
> *I have stored little in my memory, but I can apply that little, and it is of good use in many and varied emergencies. I keep it in order, but resist every attempt to increase its dead weight.*
>
> — Lasker

It must be noted that no professional chessplayer would agree with this sentiment today, when even amateur players arrive at the board well-prepared and familiar with recent theoretical developments.

Some Grandmasters claim that they don't really work at the game, but few people believe them.

PSYCHOLOGY

I don't believe in psychology.
I believe in good moves. —**Bobby Fischer**

The game of chess is played in the mind, though the moves are played out on a physical board much of the time. The mind is a complex thing, and there are many psychological considerations which affect the game of chess in a tournament situation. In this chapter you'll discover aspects of practical chess psychology.

QUESTION AUTHORITY!

If there is one theme that runs throughout this book, it is that you should not take advice on chess matters without question. Even the most accepted principles and analysis is subject to revision, especially in these days of powerful computer programs. Timothy Leary coined the slogan "Question Authority!" It is useful to keep those two wise words in mind during your chess studies. Consider, for example, that old chestnut, the "Immortal Game." You'd think that a century would be sufficient to get at the true evaluation of the famous sacrifice, but it has been re-evaluated many times.

As a trainer, I often have to "unlearn" concepts which have been taught by my student's former teachers. With young players, there is a reluctance to believe that the information they received is wrong. Usually it isn't a matter of the advice being wrong, but rather that advancement in chess has rendered some old methods obsolete, and some of them, especially in opening strategy, can be harmful.

A beginner may be encouraged to play gambits in order to learn how to attack. This works well against opponents who do not know how to defend, but against more advanced players such crude methods will no longer work and an adjustment is needed.

IF YOU NEED A DRAW, PLAY FOR A WIN

It is common knowledge among chessplayers that it is very difficult to play a game where you need a draw to achieve your goal, whether it is winning the tournament or achieving an international norm. Professional players and trainers say that to survive this pressure, you must play for a win, not a draw. The advice is good, but hard to follow. Although I repeat it to every player I coach, I often fail to follow it myself.

There are many good reasons to play ambitiously when you only need a half point. Much of it is physiological. The aggressive attitude keeps you sharp and on the look-out for tactical tricks. If you concede the initiative to your opponent, you place yourself on the defensive. From a strategic view, playing sharply for a win also provides many chances to grab the half-point. The opponent, under pressure, may wish to exchange pieces to ward off threats, leading toward endgames which can be held.

In the final game of the 1985 World Championship, Kasparov just had to draw to claim the throne for the first time. Instead of playing a quiet opening, he dared to do battle in the Sicilian Defense. He bravely sacrificed material, and pressed all out for the win. Kasparov became World Champion as a result.

KASPAROV - KARPOV
World Championship, 1985

1.e4. Switching to the king pawn under the pressure of needing a win was not a good idea. Karpov was forced to switch to a more aggressive style, leading to game of the sort that Kasparov loves to play. Even with a nominal opening advantage, the weight of recent experience lay with his opponent.

1...c5; 2.Nf3 d6; 3.d4 cxd4; 4.Nxd4 Nf6; 5.Nc3 a6; 6.Be2 e6; 7.0-0 Be7; 8.f4 0-0 9.Kh1 Qc7; 10.a4 Nc6; 11.Be3 Re8; 12.Bf3 Rb8; 13.Qd2 Bd7; 14.Nb3 b6; 15.g4.

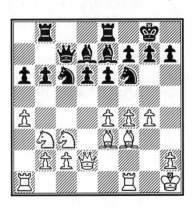

Karpov's prepared novelty, but a direct attack against an enemy king is atypical of his style.

15...Bc8; 16.g5 Nd7; 17.Qf2 Bf8; 18.Bg2 Bb7; 19.Rad1 g6; 20.Bc1 Rbc8; 21.Rd3 Nb4; 22.Rh3. The rook lift is one way to carry out an attack, but now a pawnstorm is not possible. Black finds an excellent defensive plan in reply.

22...Bg7; 23.Be3 Re7!; 24.Kg1 Rce8; 25.Rd1 f5! Kasparov is playing both aggressively and defensively. Using the concept of prophylaxis he has overprotected many key squares in the center and on both flanks. Only h7 is weak, and even that can be defended along the seventh rank.

26.gxf6 Nxf6; 27.Rg3 Rf7; 28.Bxb6 Qb8. The pawn sacrifice was designed to ruin the coordination of White's forces, and it has succeeded. **29.Be3 Nh5; 30.Rg4 Nf6; 31.Rh4 g5!!**

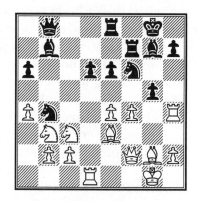

A phenomenal move. Kasparov offers this pawn to open the f-file, which would not be so dangerous were it not for the weakness of the a7-g1 diagonal. Weakness? Yes indeed, despite the powerful queen and bishop battery, the diagonal will soon be vulnerable.

32.fxg5 Ng4!; 33.Qd2 Nxe3; 34.Qxe3 Nxc2; 35.Qb6. White must play this move or else Black can play the queen to the critical diagonal. **35...Ba8; 36.Rxd6?** Karpov was in great time trouble and under psychological pressure, too, so a mistake is not all that surprising. Karpov should have exchanged queens, hoping to hold an inferior endgame.

36...Rb7!; 37.Qxa6 Rxb3; 38.Rxe6 Rxb2; 39.Qc4 Kh8; 40.e5? Another error, right at time control. The Black queen gets to a7 and the diagonal is used to finish the game. **40...Qa7+; 41.Kh1 Bxg2+; 42.Kxg2 Nd4+.** White resigned, and Kasparov became the 13th World Champion.

IF YOU NEED A WIN, BE PATIENT!

Steel nerves are needed when a win is necessary at all costs. The temptation to play sharply in the opening should be resisted, because sharp openings often dissolve into sterile positions. A better approach is to play to secure a small advantage with White, or a level but unbalanced position as Black.

When Garry Kasparov had his back against the wall in the 24th and final game of the 1987 World Championship match against Karpov, he kept his nerve and scored the point. Needing a win to keep his title, he played quietly in the opening and waited for his chances. The opening is Reti Opening.

KASPAROV - KARPOV
World Championship, Seville, 1987
1.c4 e6; 2.Nf3 Nf6; 3.g3 d5; 4.b3 Be7; 5.Bg2 0–0 6.0–0 b6; 7.Bb2 Bb7; 8.e3 Nbd7; 9.Nc3 Ne4; 10.Ne2!? a5; 11.d3 Bf6; 12.Qc2 Bxb2; 13.Qxb2 Nd6.

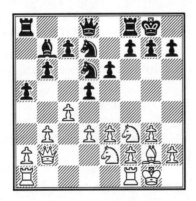

Karpov has succeeded in removing a pair of pieces from the board, but now White will be able to play d2-d4 without locking in his bishop. Of the remaining bishops, White's is clearly the more powerful, and the White queen is also more active.

14.cxd5 Bxd5. At first it seems as though White has only assisted Black by unlocking the light-squared bishop, but in fact it only becomes more exposed.

15.d4! c5; 16.Rfd1 Rc8; 17.Nf4. It is clear now that White is trying to work the queenside, while Black is merely defending. If the bishop retreats, then White will dominate the center, so Black captured at f3. **17...Bxf3.** 17...Bb7; 18.d5! exd5; 19.Nxd5.

18.Bxf3 Qe7; 19.Rac1 Rfd8; 20.dxc5 Nxc5; 21.b4! axb4; 22.Qxb4.

White concludes that the subsequent weakness of his a2-pawn will be less significant than the weakness of the b6-pawn. One supporting point is the strategic possibility of advancing the a-pawn and taking control of both the a-file and the b-file. Then the advantage of bishop versus knight will be felt.

22...Qa7; 23.a3 Nf5; 24.Rb1 Rxd1+; 25.Rxd1. Considering that all Karpov needed was a draw to become World Champion, Kasparov is remarkably cooperative when it comes to exchanging pieces. But he has concrete strategic goals, which can, and will be met.

25...Qc7; 26.Nd3. White has a small advantage, with bishop against knight. Karpov advances the wrong pawn now. **26...h6.** 26...g6 would have been wiser, since the dark squares are safer than the light squares, because White has only a light-squared bishop.

27.Rc1 Ne7; 28.Qb5 Nf5; 29.a4!

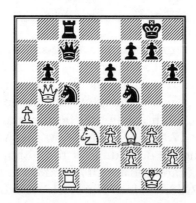

29...Nd6!; White was threatening to play 30.a5, undermining the position of the c5-knight. **30.Qb1 Qa7; 31.Ne5!** White renews the threat. Now 32.a5 brings with it the threat of Ne5-c6.

31...Nxa4; 31...Qxa4; 32.Qxb6 Qa3; 33.Rd1 gives White a significant advantage: 33...Nde4; (33...Ne8; 34.Rd8 Rxd8; 35.Qxd8 Qa1+; 36.Kg2 Qxe5; 37.Qxe8+ Kh7;

38.Qxf7±) 34.Bxe4 Nxe4; 35.Qb7 and White wins.

32.Rxc8+ Nxc8; 33.Qd1? An error in time pressure. Kasparov later pointed out that 33.Qb5! was the correct move. **33...Ne7?!** Karpov returns the favor. 33...Nc5 would have held the game. Kasparov provides the following line 34.Qd8+ Kh7; 35.Kg2 f6! 36.Nc6 Qd7; 37.Qxd7 Nxd7; 38.Nd8 Nc5; 39.Nxe6! Nxe6; 40.Bg4 with a likely draw.

34.Qd8+ Kh7; 35.Nxf7 Ng6; 36.Qe8! The threat is 37.Be4 and 38.Qh8 mate! **36...Qe7.** 36...Nc5; 37.Bh5! and 38.Ng5+!

37.Qxa4 Qxf7. The stage is set for the remainder of the game. The weak b6-pawn will fall, and then it will be a question of whether White can improve his position sufficiently so that Black will run out of moves.

38.Be4! Kg8; 39.Qb5 Nf8; 40.Qxb6 Qf6; 41.Qb5 Qe7; 42.Kg2.

The sealed move. Kasparov was able to analyze overnight, and found the correct plan with the help of his team.

42...g6. This seems like an early concession, but Black obtains additional breathing room for his queen, which has an additional square from which to protect the f8-knight.

43.Qa5 Qg7; 44.Qc5 Qf7; 45.h4! h5. Black should just have played ...Kg7. This creates permanent weaknesses.

46.Qc6 Qe7; 47.Bd3 Qf7; 48.Qd6 Kg7.

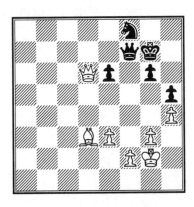

49.e4! An important move which launches the winning plan. The pawn will be established at e5, and the e4 square can later be used by the bishop.

49...Kg8; 50.Bc4 Kg7; 51.Qe5+ Kg8; 52.Qd6 Kg7; 53.Bb5 Kg8; 54.Bc6 Qa7; 55.Qb4! Qc7; 56.Qb7 Qd8; 57.e5! Qa5; 58.Be8 Qc5; 59.Qf7+! Kh8; 60.Ba4 Qd5+; 61.Kh2 Qc5; 62.Bb3 Qc8; 63.Bd1 Qc5; 64.Kg2! Karpov resigned because there was no defense to the simple plan of bringing the bishop to e4, followed by the capture of the g6-pawn, after which the queen ending is not worth disputing.

PLAY THE POSITION OR THE OPPONENT?

There is vigorous disagreement on whether you should take into account your opponent's likes and discounts to the extent that you abandon your most familiar territory. Preparing a new opening for a particular opponent is a risky business. It can easily backfire, because you will be new to the middlegame positions and can often get caught by surprise in the opening.

One often hears the advice "play the position, not the opponent." That is a maxim that is more true at the end of the game than at the beginning. In the endgame, objectivity rules. In the middlegame, small sacrifices, especially positional sacrifices, can be uncomfortable for a defender, particularly in time trouble. In the opening, a variation may be chosen to lead the game into positions which are known to be uncomfortable for the opponent, or to avoid positions which have been played many times by the opponent.

When opponents are mismatched in ranking, special considerations apply. The weaker player should try to play mainline theory, according to US Champion Joel Benjamin. The stronger player is then up against the collective wisdom of professional players. Sometimes the stronger player is put in a position of having to reveal an opening secret that would be better put to use against a top competitor. The player may decide to play a second best move instead, rather than tip off future opponents.

Stronger players should avoiding overplaying their hand early in the game. Patience is a wiser course. There is no need to play sharply. Inferior opponents will sooner or later make a positional error. If all else fails, head for a complicated endgame where superior technique will increase winning chances even in positions that should theoretically be drawn.

UNBALANCE THE POSITION AND UNBALANCE YOUR OPPONENT!

In a critical game each player enters with a certain psychological state. Players who are in a position where they must not lose tend to play cautiously and avoid taking risks. The presents a useful opportunity to the opponent. By offering material in a situation where acceptance is risky, but to decline leads to positional disadvantage, should one accept the offer?

> *A disturbance of material equality often mentally upsets the 'fortunate' possessor of the extra material*
>
> — Alekhine

Passive defense usually does not work well in tense situations, because the opponent is able to try many different strategies, not facing any significant threat. Psychologically, passive defense is uncomfortable, and this leads to many errors.

Accepting an offer of material, when no disastrous consequences are on the horizon, is usually a correct plan. As Alekhine pointed out, however, there is also a psychological danger when you have extra material. The game takes on a sharper character, and draws become less and less likely.

In the last round of the 1942 international tournament in Prague, Alekhine trailed a young star by the name of Klaus Junge. Junge was not yet twenty years old but had already won the German championship. Alekhine had to win, and he did so by exploiting this psychological weapon. The game even earned the brilliancy prize!

ALEKHINE - JUNGE
International Tournament, Prague, 1942
1.d4 d5; 2.c4 e6; 3.Nf3 Nf6; 4.g3 dxc4; 5.Qa4+ Nbd7; 6.Bg2 a6; 7.Qxc4 b5; 8.Qc6 Rb8; 9.0-0 Bb7; 10.Qc2 c5; 11.a4. This is the Catalan opening. Alekhine started our slowly, but suddenly offers a pawn at d4 to the tournament leader.

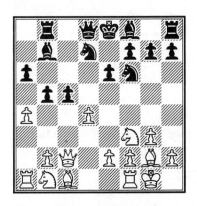

Accept or decline? A few months later, Foltys made the correct choice when he played 11...Qb6! 12.axb5 axb5 with a solid position. Junge confidently accepted the sacrifice, perhaps the lingering impatience of youth over-rode his sense of danger.

11..Bxf3; 12.Bxf3 cxd4; 13.axb5 axb5; 14.Rd1 Qb6. Not 14...Bc5, which would be met by 15.Bf4! **15.Nd2 e5; 16.Nb3 Nc5; 17.Nxc5 Bxc5.**

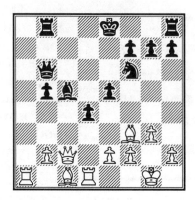

Basking in the light of his extra pawn, Junge hardly dreamed that the pawn was a mere token sacrifice with bigger things to come. Alekhine gives up an exchange to make sure that Black cannot castle.

18.Ra6! Qxa6; 19.Qxc5 Qe6!; Black defends well. Nevertheless, the king is dragged out of his cave. **20.Bc6+ Nd7; 21.Bxd7+ Kxd7; 22.Qa7+.**

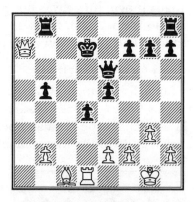

22...Kc6. Black's move has been criticized by Alekhine, who recommended that the king go to d6. Strangely, Alekhine wrote that he would then have had nothing better than the drawing line 22...Kd6; 23.Bf4 exf4; 24.Rxd4+ Kc6; 25.Rd1 Rhc8; 26.Rc1+ Kd5; 27.Rd1+ with a perpetual check.

Pachman found a better plan: 22...Kd6; 23.f4. Then 23...Kc6 doesn't work. 24.Be3! Rhc8; (24...dxe3; 25.Rc1+ Kd5; 26.Qc5+ Ke4; 27.Qc2+ Kd5; 28.Qd3#) 25.fxe5 dxe3; 26.Rd6+ picks up the queen. The best reaction is 23...Qd7!; 24.fxe5+ Ke6; 25.Qa6+.

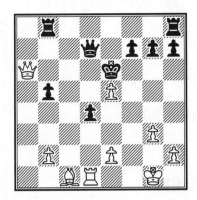

25...Ke7; 26.Bg5+ Ke8 was Pachman's prediction on how the game would go. I doubt that. There is a stronger alternative in 25...Kf5! This is how I think Black should have played. 26.Bh6 sets a little trap, but it can be avoided. 26...Ra8!; (26...gxh6; 27.Qf6+ and mate in six!) 27.Rf1+ Ke4; 28.Rf4+ Kd5!; 29.Qb6 threatens to capture at d4, but Black can take the initiative. 29...Ra1+; 30.Kg2 Rd1; 31.Bxg7 Rc8; Alekhine would have perhaps bravely considered playing for a win with the pretty line 32.Rxd4+ Rxd4; 33.e6 Qxe6; 34.Qxd4+ Kc6; 35.e4. The position is not worse for White, despite the material deficit. Crucially, the bishop on the long diagonal defends the pawn at b2. In any case, that is not how the game went.

23.Bd2 Rhc8; 24.e4 Qb3; 25.Ra1 b4.

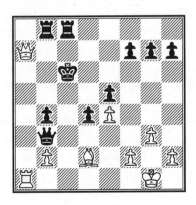

Alekhine is reported to have announced mate in seven here.

26.Ra6+ Kb5; 27.Ra5+ Kc6; 28.Qc5+ Kd7; 29.Ra7+ according to *Alekhine's Best Games of Chess*. **Black resigned** here, since it is mate in three.

KINDNESS AND COMPASSION

Mercy has no place at the chessboard. Though often a stronger player will agree to a last-round draw if it leads to a guaranteed prize, or may occasionally grant a draw to someone who needs a final half point to achieve a norm, brutality is the norm in a chess battle. You must always strive to create as many difficulties as possible for your opponent!

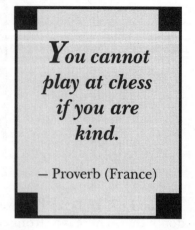

You cannot play at chess if you are kind.

— Proverb (France)

CLOCK MANAGEMENT

In most tournaments you are given an average three minutes for each move, at least in the first time control. No players move at such a steady pace, however. Some moves are played instantly, some after a deep contemplation of 20 minutes or more. Sometimes a player will go into meditations of over an hour! It is possible to become World Champion even addicted to time pressure, as Petrosian demonstrated.

For practical success, you must try to maximize your time. This doesn't mean always staying at the board. You may need to take a stroll to keep your circulation going and catch a breath of fresh air. A cup of coffee may stimulate your thought process. The point is that when you are at the board, you must try to concentrate and use your time effectively.

Usually, a player combines strategic planning with a calm evaluation of the position. Many players find it useful to split these tasks, doing evaluation while the opponent is thinking and keeping the focus on planning when their own clock is running.

It is not a good idea to waste time in the opening staring at the board, trying to give your opponent the impression that you did not come fully prepared for the position on the board. This childish attempt at deviousness just rebounds when the critical minutes are missing later in the game. At the same time, don't rush your early moves, as sometimes the quick pace leads to a blunder when the early middlegame is conducted too quickly. It is embarrassing to be obviously caught unprepared in the opening, but chess truth can always be found at the chessboard.

Assuming that you have to make forty moves in two hours, you should try to use no more than twenty minutes for the first fifteen moves. These moves should, for the most part, be familiar to you as you become an experienced player. The early middlegame is one of the most dangerous periods, and you must allow yourself time for thinking. Getting to move 20 in the first hour should be possible if you get the first moves played quickly. For the last part of the time control, moves 36-40, try to leave yourself at least three minutes.

STYLE

The concept of chess style is very misleading. Most professional players manage to handle a wide variety of positions well. For non-masters, the term "style" should usually be interpreted as meaning that the player prefers to play positions which are suited to the abilities of the player. In other words, style is a cover word for a group of weaknesses that someone is trying to hide or avoid! Instead of seeking openings which lead to positions you feel comfortable in, you will be better served, in the long run, by addressing the defects in your play. If you prefer sharp positions, learn how to handle quiet ones well and create a double threat every time you sit down at the board!

Established masters have usually reached a point where their talents are known and it is perhaps necessary to play for positions which seem comfortable. Over time, the number of positions which are known to the player expands, and more types of positions become easier to play. This is especially true in the endgame. Many young players try to avoid endgames on the grounds they may misplay them. You must play a lot of endgames before a true understanding of that phase of the game develops. Might as well start early!

PSYCHOLOGICAL WARFARE IN THE OPENING

The opening phase of the game offers opportunities to disrupt your opponent's peace of mind. Not only can you steer the game into variations which do not fit the opponent's style, you can even bluff your opponent into avoiding critical variations. Transpositions can be carefully chosen, leading the game toward desired positions.

Suppose you want to play the White side of the Sicilian Defense (1.e4 c5), but are afraid of the Najdorf Variation (1.e4 c5; 2.Nf3 d6; 3.d4 cxd4; 4.Nxd4 Nf6; 5.Nc3 a6)? You might try **1.e4 c5; 2.Nc3.**

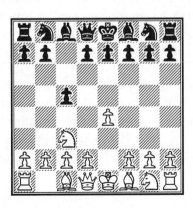

Most defenders choose **2...Nc6** here. After **3.Nge2!? Nf6; 4.d4 cxd4; 5.Nxd4** we have a Sicilian in which the Najdorf is no longer possible, since in the Najdorf the knight usually goes to d7, not c6.

The broader your opening, the more psychological tricks are available. You can work out favorable paths to your favorite positions, or those which are known to be unfavorable to your opponent.

A gambit can often be offered as a bluff. If the opponent is unfamiliar with the territory, the offer may be declined. No player wants to be in uncharted waters in the opening. This leads some players, mostly amateurs, to explore offbeat, unorthodox openings. To maintain psychological balance in these circumstances, you should simply try to figure out what your opponent is up to. Consider this situation, when White opens **1.d4** and Black responds **1.d6**.

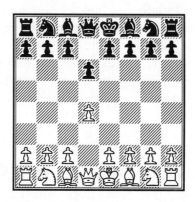

What does Black have in mind. Clearly an invitation is being extended to enter the paths of the Rat, but when White plays 2.e4, 2...Nf6 can force White to abandon the idea of an early c4, as 3.Nc3 is indicated. In this case White has left the normal Queen Pawn Game and must operate in the sphere of the King's Pawn Game. Establishing the ideal pawn center is desirable, but not if it means abandoning home preparation.

If White plays the normal 2.c4, Black can respond with 2...e5, the Purdy Defense, which has risen from obscurity to become a popular and respected opening. Capturing the pawn at e5 and trading queens is not considered advantageous for White because the pawn at c4 gets in the way of any attack, and the Black king eventually goes to c7, where it is safe.

When you are unprepared for this situation, it shows that your opening repertoire is not complete. During the game, you can't do anything about that, so forget about it. You can play **2.Nf3** and preserve most of your options in the opening. You do give up the Saemisch Variation and the Four Pawn Attack against the King's Indian, because both of those openings involve advancing the f-pawn before developing the knight.

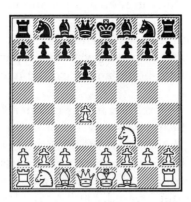

Whatever Black does next, White can play 3.c4, returning to normal Queen Pawn Games. The only serious non-transpositional move is **2...Bg4.** Black threatens to capture at f3, but that is not a significant worry because the disruption of the pawn center isn't worth giving up the bishop. White gets a small advantage against that plan. After **3.c4 Bxf3; 4.gxf3** White can build a strong center with e4, and can use the g-file for an attack. Castling queenside will soon be possible. The advantage is far from decisive, but it is a nice position to get in the opening as White. In the long run the bishop pair can be effective.

Don't let unfamiliar positions throw you off your game. If it is your intention to play aggressively as Black, and White offers a gambit, you may not want to enter the complications of the main line. Usually there is a way of declining that does not lead to a bad game; you can just push the advanced pawn one more rank.

For example: The Smith-Morra Gambit starts **1.e4 c5; 2.d4 cxd4; 3.c3.** You can play 3...d3.

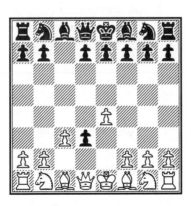

This is not the best move, but it is not bad. White can set up a Maroczy Bind with an early c4. White may have a slight opening advantage, but that is the case in most normal openings. All you have done, psychologically, is grant White the usual opening advantage. You get something in return. Your opponent does not get the kind of position that a gambit approach is supposed to lead to. If you have prepared this variation and are familiar with the most useful strategies, you have a large psychological advantage. If confronted by the opening when unprepared, you can use this method of declining the gambit, then go home and learn the main lines and strive for more next time.

Many other gambits can be declined in this manner. In the French Defense, 1.e4 e6; 2.d4 d5; 3.Nc3 dxe4; 4.f3 can be met by 4...e3. In the Caro-Kann, the same logic applies with 1.e4 c6; 2.d4 d5; 3.Nc3 dxe4; 4.f3 e3. Even in the Göring Gambit, 1.e4 e5; 2.Nf3 Nc6; 3.d4 exd4; 4.c3, 4...d3 is possible. In no case is this strategy the best available for Black, and I don't recommend using it for a long time, but it is a safe reaction the first time you are caught unprepared. Let it be the last time!

INTUITION

There are many times during the chess battle that you have to trust your gut. Actually, you need to rely on your experienced as recorded, consciously or subconsciously, in your mind. Your mind stores far more patterns than you can recall. When we play chess, sometimes access is granted to these patterns, even if we don't realize it.

It has often been observed that many times errors are made when an initial move selection is retracted. An inferior move is often played in its place. Psychologists have studied chess mistakes, though they don't seem to have come up with a method for avoiding errors.

As a practical matter, whenever you reject your initial plan, you should return to it one last time before making your move. Make sure your instincts are proven false by objective calculation.

A sense of danger is helpful. If you feel uncomfortable about your position, but are not sure why, check for vulnerable points and try to overprotect them. If you have no weaknesses, you can only lose through a major mistake.

ETIQUETTE

Politeness: The most acceptable hypocrisy.
—Ambrose Bierce

Part of becoming a tournament player is learning the etiquette of the game. If you don't behave well, you will soon find yourself without friends in the chess world. Competitive pressures can force even nice, gentle people to act badly. You should try to follow the etiquette presented below, yet forgive lapses by others. We'll look at the timing of draw offers and resignations, analyzing after the game, kibitzing, and even offer a brief note on playing chess for money.

TIMING OF DRAW OFFER

According to the rules, you must make an offer of a draw on your own time, after you have completed your move but before you press your clock. Even Garry Kasparov screws this one up frequently. If someone offers you a move while your clock is running, it is improper, but if done when there is no time pressure and immediately after making the move, it is a minor infraction. When your opponent offers you a draw before making a move, you have the right to wait until the move is made before responding. It is best to get into the habit of making the offer properly to avoid trouble. Make your move, and say one of the following before pressing the clock.

OFFERING A DRAW

• I offer you a draw?
• Would you like a draw?
• Remis? (pronounced *ray-me*. It's French, but is internationally recognized.)
• Nichya? (pronounced *nee-chyaa*)
Use mostly against Russian speaking opponents

If your opponent does not seem to understand you, you may use a hand signal which is widely understood, crossing your index fingers to form a letter 'x'. Most of the time your opponent will understand your intent, because during the game you are only permitted to speak to your opponent to resign, to offer or accept a draw or to adjust the pieces. Announcing "check" is in improper in tournament chess but is often helpful in casual chess, especially among beginners.

That's the timing of the draw offer, but when should you offer a draw? That is a question that is far from simple. As a matter of etiquette, you do not offer a draw to a stronger player just because the position is level. A draw offer is always appropriate if the position is theoretically drawn. If you offer a draw, and your opponent declines, do not offer again. Let the opponent do so if the position eventually merits it.

Draw offers can be used as part of chess strategy. In a given tournament situation, you may be content with half a point, for example, to win the tournament or achieve an international norm. Relatively early in the game, you may offer a draw, just to find out if your opponent is in the mood for a fight. Of course you are not allowed to agree to a draw before the game begins. Happens all the time, to be sure, but it is not legal.

There used to be a series of splendid tournaments in Ramsgate, England. They were held at a convivial hotel (the owner was a player in the event!) with a friendly disco and a bar that had its own definition of opening hours. The night before the last round, two players with no possibility of prizes or other awards agreed that they would draw their game. One of the two turned up at the board ready for action, but the opponent stopped off at the bar and started the post-tournament celebrations early. They played a few moves, and the beer had its effect, the player got a bad position. Before things went too far, he offered a draw, expecting the pre-arranged deal to hold up. The opponent, with a winning position, declined the draw, confusing the "relaxed" opponent.

Since I am an international arbiter, though was just a player at this event, many players would confer with me before filing official protests. So Mr. Beer (as we shall call him) came to me and said "Eric, I am going to make a protest. My opponent agreed to a draw before the game but refuses to honor it!" I had to explain that you can't enforce an illegal contract, but a better solution was found. Another player went up to the sober opponent, took him aside, and gently explained the sorts of things that happen to people who back out of deals. The game was quickly drawn. That's real life.

There is a prevailing attitude in the chess world that agreeing to a draw before a game is a "wink wink, nudge nudge" kind of offense, but agreeing to lose a game is nastly, ugly crime. There are some players who engage in both, sad to say. FIDE does recognize that in some cases it is in the best interest of one or both players not to play for a win at all costs, but arranged games are forbidden. If you are approached before the game by your opponent, who asks, "are you playing for a win?", and you say "not necessarily," and then you sit down and draw the game, that does not seem to contravene the rules. If the opponent says, before the game, "Would you like a draw?" and you say yes, then it does. A fine line. My best advice is don't do anything you know to be dishonest. Your gut should tell you right from wrong.

The manipulative draw offer is legal. That's when you make a move and offer a draw in a position where the opponent can choose either a sharp or quiet plan. In many cases, the opponent will be reluctant to play the quiet move, and if the draw is unacceptable, may be provoked into choosing the riskier path. Sometimes you don't even have to make an explicit offer, as there are many openings that lead to drawn positions, and you can offer one of them. Here is a somewhat silly example, known as the Bird Invitation in the French Defense.

After **1.e4 e6**, White can try the bizarre **2.Bb5.**

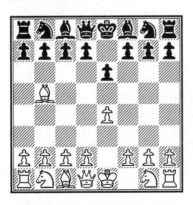

This is usually an invitation to a draw. Black can respond **2...Qg5,** attacking the bishop and the g-pawn. So **3.Bf1** is logical. Then **3...Qd8** repeats the position. The game is drawn whenever the same position is repeated three times on the board, with the same player to move, so the opponents can just repeat the maneuver to claim a draw.

How soon can you offer a draw? This is not at all clear. There is nothing in the rules prohibiting a draw offer on the very first move. In the 1972 Student Olympiad in

Graz, Austria, I was the co-captain of the American team. Fresh out of high school, I was placed in an interesting situation when the game between our Ken Rogoff and German rising star Robert Hübner, started out like this. Rogoff was Black. **1.c4.**

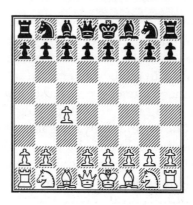

Ken came up to me (consulting with captains regarding draw offers is legal and appropriate) and advised me that Hübner had offered a draw! I responded with the normal "Can't you play a few more moves, for appearances sake?" but Ken said that Hübner had insisted it was now or never, for he had played a long adjournment session that morning. He felt in no condition to play, and was annoyed that his captain had ordered him to play, though fresh reserves were available. At the time, even a tired Hübner (rated 2590) was a clear favorite over Rogoff (2430), especially with White, so my decision was to accept the draw.

The arbiter didn't see it that way. He rejected the game and ordered them to play again. The two players were most annoyed. Before recounting the rest of the tale I'll point out that a decade later, at a FIDE meeting, the arbiter admitted he was quite wrong. The matter took an embarrassing turn.

This was a long game, rather a game of many moves, which lasted just a couple of minutes. The replay went like this (very quickly):

1.c4 Nf6; 2.Nf3 g6; 3.Ng1 Bg7; 4.Qa4 0-0; 5.Qxd7 Qxd7; 6.g4 Qxd2+; 7.Kxd2 Nxg4; 8.b4 a5; 9.a4 Bxa1; 10.Bb2 Nc6; 11.Bh8 Bg7; 12.h4 axb4 and a draw was agreed. I won't give you a diagram, you need to play this one through to appreciate the absurdity.

This also failed to pass muster. The tournament book quoted Becker, commenting on the rules as adopted at the FIDE congress in 1964. Here is my translation: "It is expressly determined that the abolishment of the 30-move-rule in no way means that the intention, which led introduction of this rule is removed. It is expected also further by the tournament directors that this sin against the spirit of the game should be punished by forfeit." I can't agree with this interpretation.

The organizers could not have been disturbed merely that the game was a short draw, for there were several of those, though they were not published in the tournament book, which contained only selected games. It was the extreme shortness of the game. They would have been content had the two players reeled off a dozen or so moves and then shaken hands. That is what most players do. Hübner has strong principles, however, and did not want to play "pretend" moves. A final game was ordered, after a long meeting in which other team captains (rivals) tried to get both players forfeited.

Hübner had seen enough. He refused to come out for round 4 of the farce. Rogoff wanted to do the same, but Hübner insisted that since Ken did nothing wrong, he should not be penalized for his actions. In the end, the Americans were awarded the game, though we would have been satisfied with the original draw offer!

The acceptance of a draw brings the game to an end. There are many famous cases where a player agrees to a draw only to find that the position was a win. Even worse, sometimes a game is adjudicated, with an outside official intervening. They can make mistakes, as ex-World Champion Max Euwe did when called on to decide the result of this position from Epen vs. Roislag, at Amesfort 1946. It is Black to move.

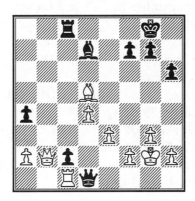

Euwe determined that the game should be drawn, and the result was so entered. 1...Qh5! wins on the spot. The threat is simply ...Bh3+, followed by the return of the queen to d1, after which the king can no longer escape to g2. 2.Bxf7+ is therefore pretty much forced. 2...Kxf7; 3.Rxc2 still fails to save the game, because of 3...Bc6+! with devastation on the light squares.

Sometimes time pressure accounts for a premature acceptance. Often a player will settle for a perpetual check when no clear continuation of the attack can be seen and no time remains to examine the complications. Against Nestler at Venice 1950, the great attacker Rossolimo invests a double exchange and a piece in a brilliant attack, but this must have consumed too much time. He does manage to resist the perpetual check himself, but gave his opponent a chance to repeat the position three times. In effect, Rossolimo offered a draw. Here is the position after twenty moves. Black has just castled.

21.Rxf6!? Bxf6; 22.Rxf6 gxf6; 23.Nd5 Bxd5; 24.Qg4+ Kh8; 25.Qf5. White has at least a draw here. **25...Rg8.** 25...Qc8; 26.Qxf6+ Kg8; 27.exd5 Qg4; 28.Bf5 Qg7; 29.Qh4 is given by Kotov, but Black continues 29...e4 and no win is in sight! Therefore White would have had to take the draw with 27.Qg5+ and a perpetual check.

26.Qxf6+ Rg7; 27.Bh6 Rag8; 28.exd5 Qc3. Black tries to get into position to attack the White king. **29.Kf1!?** 29.Bxg7+ Rxg7; 30.Qd8+ Rg8; 31.Qf6+ is available if White is willing to settle for a draw.

29...Qd4. 29...Qa1+; 30.Ke2 Qxa3; 31.d6 Qxb4; 32.h3 Qd4; 33.g4 Qd5; 34.Bf5 Qg2+; 35.Ke1 Qg1+ with a draw. **30.d6 Qd5; 31.Bf5.** White ignores the threat at g2.

31...Qxg2+; 32.Ke1 Qg1+; 33.Kd2 Qf2+; 34.Kc1 Qg1+; 35.Kb2 Qd4+; 36.Kb1? White must play the pawn to c3, as in the analysis below the next diagram. Instead, Rossolimo allows the position to be repeated. **Qd1+; 37.Kb2 Qd4+; 38.Ka2? Qd5+; 39.Ka1 Qd1+; 40.Ka2? Qd5+; 41.Kb1 Qd1+.**

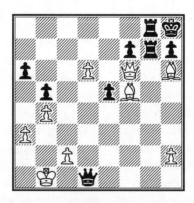

Black claimed a draw here, according to Rolf Schwarz. He then presents Kotov's analysis, which has somehow been confused with the actual game. 42.Kb2 Qd4+; Some sources suggest that Black resigned without further play, but this is not the actual game, and there is more to the analysis. 43.c3 Qf2+; 44.Kb3 Kotov says that White wins with d7. Not so! 44...Qb6!; This pins the d-pawn. 45.Bxh7!! (More efficient than 45.Bxg7+ Rxg7; 46.Qxe5 Qd8; 47.Qe7 Rg8; 48.Qxf7 Rg7; 49.Qd5 is very good for White, but the game is far from over.) 45...Kxh7; 46.Qh4 Kg6; 47.Qg5+ Kh7; 48.Qh5 Rh8; 49.Be3+ Kg8; 50.Bxb6 Rxh5; 51.d7 and White gets a new queen.

TIMING OF RESIGNATION

It is bad manners to play on in a position which is utterly without prospect of salvation. This has different meaning at different levels of competition. Most masters will not play out endgames with king and pawn versus lone king that are known to be relatively uncomplicated. Beginners require "proof of technique," no certificates accepted!

> *You should not continue playing in a position in which, by your own personal evaluation of the situation, there are no hopes of saving the game.*
>
> — Bronstein, Sorcerer's Apprentice

It is never easy to resign, even when the position is hopeless. Some teachers advise their students always to play on to the bitter end in the hopes the opponent will blunder terribly. Players who follow that advice often gain reputations as annoying and unpleasant cretins.

So when should you resign? It is often said that you should resign only when even a mere beginner in the audience would understand why. That is good practical advice. The last thing you want to do after a game is to explain to someone why you gave up!

Be nice. Congratulate your victorious opponents, even if they don't deserve it. Even if they are smug, self-centered little slugs who really annoy you. Don't pull a "Von Bardeleben!" The 19th century player had a habit of simply walking away from the board. Eventually, he'd exceed the time limit and his opponent would finally get the point.

On the other hand, and there is another hand, premature resignation is not merely embarrassing, it is humiliating! And yet, it happens to the best of players.

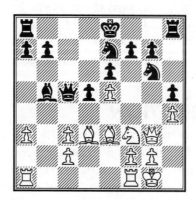

This position arose in a game between Liberzon and Petrosian, played in Moscow in 1964. The World Champion, playing Black, gave up in the face of White's 15th move, moving the bishop to attack the queen. He could have just played 15...d4! Then his position would have been a bit worse, but surely nothing to give up on.

This is nothing compared to the startling finish to the second game of the famous Man vs. Machine contest in 1997, pitting the World Champion against a supercomputer.

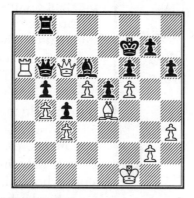

Kasparov resigned, but could have saved the game with 45...Qe3!; 46.Qxd6 [46.Qd7+ Kg8; 47.Qxd6 Rf8; 48.Qe6+ Kh7; 49.Qe7 (49.Ra1 Qxe4; 50.d6 Qd3+; 51.Kg1 Qxc3 wins for Black.) 49...Rg8!; 50.Bf3 Qc1+; 51.Kf2 Qd2+; 52.Kg1 Qc1+; 53.Kf2 Qd2+; 54.Kg1 Qc1+; 55.Kh2 Qf4+; 56.Kg1 Qc1+; 57.Kf2 Qd2+ and White cannot escape the checks.] 46...Re8.

Now there are several important branches. We will look at four of them, to give you an idea of just how much Kasparov needed to see to save the game.

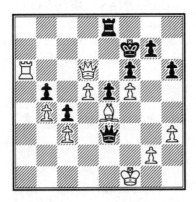

A) 47.Qd7+ Re7; 48.Qxb5 Qxe4 is not a problem for Black.

B) 47.Qc7+ Re7; 48.d6 Rxc7; 49.Bd5+ (49.dxc7 Qf4+; 50.Kg1 Qc1+; 51.Kh2 Qf4+; 52.g3 Qxe4; 53.c8Q Qe2+ draws.) 49...Ke8; 50.dxc7 Kd7; 51.Rc6 Qc1+; 52.Kf2 Qd2+; 53.Kg1 Qc1+; 54.Kh2 Qf4+; 55.g3 Qd2+; 56.Bg2 Kc8 and Black has the better chances. 47.Qe6+ Rxe6; 48.fxe6+ Ke7; 49.Bg6 Qc1+; 50.Ke2 e4; 51.Bxe4 Qb2+ will be drawn.

C) 47.Bf3 Qc1+; 48.Kf2 Qd2+; 49.Be2 (49.Kg1 Qc1+; 50.Kh2 Qf4+; 51.g3 Qxf3; 52.Ra2 Qxf5; 53.Qc5 Qb1; 54.Ra7+ Kg8; 55.Qxb5 Qc2+; 56.Kg1 Qd1+ with perpetual check.) 49...Qf4+; 50.Ke1 Qc1+; 51.Bd1 Qxc3+! 52.Kf1 Qc1; 53.Ke2 Qb2+; 54.Ke1 (54.Kf3 loses to 54...Qc3+; 55.Kg4 Qe3!; 56.Qd7+ Re7; 57.Qxe7+ Kxe7 and White cannot hold on to the remaining pieces.) 54...Qc3+; 55.Kf1 Qc1 with a draw.

D) 47.h4!? is the critical line. Black must now play 47...h5! After 48.Bf3 Qc1+; 49.Kf2 Qd2+; 50.Be2 Qf4+ the king cannot find shelter.

One would expect correspondence players to be less quick to give up. Perhaps White wanted to save some stamps, but had he properly evaluated the position, resignation would have been out of the question. Our next game takes a disastrous turn early.

MEIRONAS - BEDINOV
Correspondence, 1989
1.e4 e5; 2.Nf3 Nc6; 3.Bc4 Nf6; 4.Ng5 Bc5; 5.Nxf7 Bxf2+; 6.Kf1 Qe7; 7.Nxh8 d5; 8.exd5 Nd4; 9.d6 cxd6. The opening is Two Knights Defense.

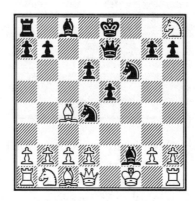

10.Kxf2?! Pure unadulterated greed. With 10.c3 the powerful enemy invader would have been eliminated, either through retreat or capture. Then Black would have been justified in resigning! The bishop at f2 was not attacking the White king, it was defending him!

10...d5; 11.Be2?! Again, the advance of the c-pawn cried out to be played. **Ne4+; 12.Kf1 Qh4.** The White king begins to sweat. **13.Qe1 Qf6+; 14.Kg1 Nxc2.** White resigned.

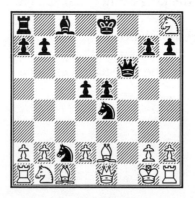

White must have been disgusted at this point.. It isn't just a matter of losing the rook at a1. The queen falls because of the threat of 15...Qf2. 15.Qf1 loses to 15...Qb6+. 15.Bb5+ Bd7; 16.Bxd7+ Kxd7 only postpones the inevitable. Notice that White's waste of time is written all over the board. Despite being a rook and knight ahead, the only two developed pieces are the bishop at e2 and the knight off in the corner. Black is two moves away from completing development in the diagrammed position, and will recover the rook at a1 at will. To achieve some sort of normal position, White would in any case require six or seven developing moves.

Nevertheless, is the position completely hopeless? What happens after **15.Bh5+ g6**? There is no need to seriously consider alternatives for Black, because this obvious move attacks both the bishop at h5 and the knight at h8. White now plays **16.Qe2.**

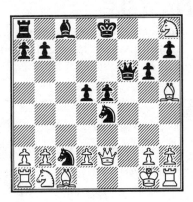

Remember, White is still up a rook and a knight, even though the one in the corner is doomed. If the queen captures the knight, then the pressure is off f2 and White can try to attack with bare queen via a check at b5. Black's scattered forces will start to drop. There is no rush to capture the rook at a1, and if Black does, then White retreats the bishop to f3. When the queen captures at h8, White exchanges at e4 and eventually collects the knight at a1.

So Black probably has to try **16...gxh5.**

17.Qxh5+. Not 17.d3 Bg4; 18.Qxc2 Bd1!; Or 17.Nc3 Qb6+! **17...Kf8; 18.Qf3.** Now a plausible continuation is **18...Nxa1; 19.Na3 Qxf3; 20.gxf3 Ng5; 21.Kg2 Ne6; 22.d3 Kg7; 23.Bd2** when both knights in the corner are devoured. Surely no reason to resign!

Whether a correspondence game or not, White should not have resigned without at least trying a few more moves. Even if a preliminary evaluation of the position after 15...g6 was not positive, the position is still too messy for resignation.

POST-MORTEM ANALYSIS

When the game is over, usually both players spend some time analyzing it. This is called a post-mortem. It is an autopsy of the game. Why did one king die? What factors contributed to the death? For the loser it can be a morbid affair. Nevertheless, you can learn more from a post-mortem than from any book, especially if your opponent is a strong player.

So no matter how badly you feel, you must always try to summon the courage to analyze the game objectively. If you have

> *...after having lost a game at Chess, it is my custom to ponder on the past moves until I find out the false step that led to my defeat ...*
>
> — Letters of a Hindoo Rajah, 1796

won the game, and would prefer to celebrate, remember that it is your obligation to at least offer to go over the game with your opponent.

Some players do not like to discuss the opening in a post-mortem. They don't want to give away any secrets. Others spend most of the time on the opening moves, giving away information but gaining other knowledge in return. Once out of the opening, the post-mortem is usually objective, with nothing held back. Even in World Championship matches players have remained on stage to look at the game, at least briefly.

It is consider polite for the winner of the game to offer a beverage (appropriate to age and mood) to the loser. Relax, but remember that the post-mortem is a great opportunity to learn new things. You can find out how many tactics you overlooked, and whether or not your positional evaluations were well grounded.

KIBITZING

Kibitzing is offering unsolicited advice during a game or post-mortem. During a game it is against the rules. If you receive advice, you can be forfeited. When someone approaches you during the game and offers a comment on the game, cut them off quickly to avoid getting into trouble.

During a post-mortem kibitzing may or may not be welcomed by the players. If you saw some important tactic in the game and want to offer advice, it is best to wait until invited to join in. In practice, most people can't resist jumping in, and if you are conducting a post-mortem and don't want kibitzers, do it in private or politely ask onlookers to leave. The latter rarely

> *It is better to remain silent and be thought a fool, than to open your mouth and remove all doubt.*
>
> — Groucho Marx

happens. A post-mortem is an attempt to find the truth, and sometimes dispassionate onlookers can contribute to the discussion.

When a strong player offers suggestions, you should certainly welcome them. At the Reykjavik international in 1986, Mikhail Tal was in a great mood, and was often helping others with analysis. He even looked at all of my games with me, not just because we were friends (Tal was a friend of almost anyone he ran into frequently), but because the positions were interesting, even if the games were far from perfectly played. Once during the event, American star Yasser Seirawan was conducting a post-mortem with his opponent, also a Grandmaster. When Tal stood by and offered a few comments, Yasser gave up his seat to the former World Champion and remained standing during the analysis!

Although you may think that you and your opponent have worked out all the details, a third party can often spot what you have missed. In one of my games from the Reykjavik tournament, I had a long endgame against a Swedish International Master. During the post-mortem he, and many other strong players, criticized my strategy of playing on opposite wings in an even endgame.

By playing with less risk I could have easily drawn the game. True enough, but I have always tried to win against higher rated players. It was one of my best tournaments ever, and I was playing with great confidence. I was sure my strategy was correct. Tal came by and rattled off a fascinating variation, pointing out that I had the right strategy, just not the means to execute it!

Many times outside analysts can shed more light on the game than the players themselves. You don't always appreciate this as you listen in, because the players will often respond to a long tactical variation by implying that they had, of course, considered that plan. Often, this is just a little white lie. No one wants to admit overlooking a tactic!

Of course there are many times when you have no idea who is offering the advice, not recognizing the person. It doesn't hurt to ask. A few times I have had players insist to me that the advice I was offering was incorrect, because "Schiller's book says...". Then I must admit that I was wrong in my earlier analysis, but have a better view now.

Take advantage of the opportunities offered by a good public discussion. Put up with a few irrelevant or even stupid comments, because others may be hold great value. Don't hold back too much of your opening analysis. The discussion can find flaws in your logic, and even if a few people know about it, there will be plenty of other opponents to surprise later.

As a kibitzer, try not to annoy the players. Don't point out the obvious, and above all, think before you ask a question or suggest a line! When looking at the opening, it is best to keep quiet. Sometimes you may know of an important recent game in the variation under discussion. Then it is acceptable to mention it. Otherwise, wait until the position has entered the middlegame or endgame. Do not speak to players during the game, and offer no audible comments where you can be heard. Even if the players seem to be just playing blitz for fun, there may be stakes involved and kibitzing during blitz games is never welcome.

PLAYING FOR MONEY

Playing for stakes is illegal in most places, but friendly games for small stakes have been going on for a thousand years or more. There was a term coined in the 1980s for players who were particularly good at playing for quarters — **metalheads**. With even a little money at stake, the atmosphere can become a little more tense, with minor infractions of any rule taken most seriously. In parks and public thoroughfares one sometimes comes across a **chess hustler**, who offers to play for small, but ever increasing stakes. For some it is an honest living, but others have many tricks. Old fashioned chess clocks could be fiddled so that one side ran more quickly, or during the game a hand may surreptitiously reach behind the clock and turn the knob. The ne'er-do-well might lie about his name or rating.

One sign that there may be more to your opponent than meets the eye is when you are not asked your rating. Once upon a time, in New York's Washington Square Park, a well known chess hustler was plying his trade against anyone he didn't recognize (the prestigious Marshall Chess Club is but a few blocks away). A young man with a Philadelphia accent approached, and eventually they started playing. The hustler knew all the top American players, and was an excellent blitz player who could easily handle most ordinary masters. On this occasion, he got thumped. He was clearly being out-hustled by an unknown master of the art. Grandmaster, actually, for his opponent was a top European player with American roots. In chess, at least, "don't ask, don't tell" is not always a good policy!

But the temptation to take back a move is very great with a beginner and it has been found desirable for this purpose to play for a small stake, as this causes it to be considered a point of honor to play strictly according to the rules. This practice has become usual in the principal Chess clubs of Europe, as well as in larger cities of the United States and in Havana. Other advantages of playing for a small stake are that it tends to promote greater care in the play and to check comments or suggestions from the bystanders.

The game of Chess is so utterly unsuited for gambling that no danger is incurred by the practice, and the players usually know each other's strength, and either the score is about even or the weaker player fully expects to lose, but is willing to pay a fee for the amusement and instruction which he receives from his adversary.

— Steinitz, Modern Chess Instructor

RULES

*Rules are for people who don't know
how to get around them.*
—*Tori Harrison*

Most of the laws of chess are known to even the most casual players. In this section we look at some of the rules which apply in serious competition, especially in sanctioned tournaments. We'll consider some of the variations among professional organizations in the section on Local vs. Standard Rules. Other topics include how to properly adjust a misplaced piece, the infamous touch move rule, castling, time controls, chess notation, the scoresheet, and ratings. I am sure you will find things here that you didn't previously know. Very few players, for example, can give a precise definition of the castling rule. So read this chapter well, because these factors can influence the outcome of a game to the same extent as a brilliant move or a blunder!

Eileen Tranmer relates how she played a pair of games with an elderly opponent in a local chess club. In the first game she captured *en passant* not entirely certain whether he understood the rule. The game continued, and later she learned that he was just being polite, figuring that she didn't know the rules of how pawns capture! The second game was even more amusing. At one point her opponent blundered terribly, so she suggested a better move. Her opponent offered to continue the game, having played both the original more, and the suggestion. Tranmer learned that knowing the rules is an important part of the game.

Usually, the rules are enforced by the referees, called *arbiters* in most of the world, *tournament directors* in the United States. There is only one thing you really need to know about the powers of the *arbiter*. They are virtually unlimited! The rules allow the arbiter to take action to solve problems, using discretion, precedent, and, one hopes, a little common sense. You can almost never win an argument with an arbiter, and most of the time it isn't worth the effort.

ADJUSTING THE PIECES AND THE CLOCK

Sometimes, especially in the heat of battle, a piece will not be placed in the center of a square. You can adjust the piece so that it is in proper position, provided that your clock is running and you alert your opponent, usually by saying the French term "J'adoube." This is usually pronounced something like ZHA-DUUB. Since the majority of chessplayers do not speak French, just about anything that comes close is acceptable. You can use the English expression "I adjust" if you wish.

Some pieces are nicely symmetrical, for example pawns, rooks, and queens. It doesn't make any difference if they are rotated. Knights, however, have always presented a problem. Some players, for example World Championship challenger Viswanathan Anand, like the nose pointed straight ahead, some sideways (Garry Kasparov points them to the left), and some at an angle. There is no rule concerning adjustment of knight positions. If the nose of your knight points to your back rank, that would be decidedly odd and one could hardly object to the opponent repositioning it. If the nose is pointed forward, in any direction, that is considered normal. It is considered poor etiquette to constantly adjust enemy knights to your own preferred angle. As an International Arbiter, I've never been called upon to make a ruling in such matters. If it happened, I'd probably rely on the guidelines in this paragraph.

Many players wonder when they are permitted to adjust the chess clock. The simple answer, under standard rules, is that you may not. During the game, only the arbiter can start or stop the clock. Usually you only stop the clock when the game is over, either accepting a draw or resigning. Stopping the clock when there is no offer of a draw is usually interpreted as resigning. Unintentional stopping of the clock will result in a warning from the arbiter, and more serious consequences if the action is repeated.

DON'T TALK TO YOUR OPPONENT

In tournament chess, you may speak to your opponent only under the following circumstances:

1. To resign
2. To offer a draw
3. To accept a draw
4. To adjust the pieces

All other conversations should take place through the arbiter or tournament director. Of course, this musn't be taken to extremes. In addition to wishing your opponent good luck at the start of a game, it is perfectly acceptable to point out when your opponent's clothes are on fire! In fact, in European tournaments I have had my opponent offer me a cup of coffee in the middle of a game, a technical violation, but not an unwelcome one.

TOUCH MOVE

If you touch a piece, you must move it provided that you can make a legal move with the piece that you touched. If you touch a piece, but the arbiter rules that it was an unintentional act, you may be excused from this rule. If your opponent accidentally knocks over his king while moving a piece further down the board, it is not a resignation. In most cases, good sportsmanship would in any case prevent a player from claiming a touch move violation that was clearly an accident.

> *A very important point is always to observe strictly the law of 'touch and move'.*
>
> – Steinitz, Modern Chess Instructor

The move cannot be changed when your hand releases the piece. In some events, videotape has been used for an "instant reply" to assist the arbiter in making a final ruling, but that is a very rare case. This is very clearly stated in the 1997 edition of the *Laws of Chess* of the World Chess Federation (FIDE). The touch move rule is enforceable by the arbiter. A player may also claim an infraction of this rule, but only before that player touches a piece.

In recent revisions to the rules, castling is considered a move of the king, and must be made by touching the king first. The penalty for touching the rook first is a warning from the arbiter. You may not castle on that side and the touch move then applies to the rook. If both pieces are touched simultaneously, but castling is illegal to that side, then you must either castle in the other direction, if legal, or make a different move with the king.

CASTLING

Castling is simple in theory. You slide the king toward a rook on its home square, and the rook leaps over the king to the adjacent square. Yet there are many complicated rules which apply, and many players, even some professionals, get confused.

The official definition of castling is "This is a move of the king and either rook of the same colour on the same rank, counting as a single move of the king and executed as follows: the king is transferred from its original square two squares towards the rook, then that rook is transferred over the king to the square the king has just crossed."

Castling is illegal if the king has already been moved, or with a rook that has already been moved. Sometimes a player forgets.

In the Chess-in-the-Schools International Grandmaster tournament of 1996, Viktor Korchnoi, one of the greatest players of all time, asked me, as the arbiter, whether he could borrow his opponent's scoresheet. I had to decline, for reasons which will be explained in the section on the scoresheet below. The reason for his request, which I only discovered later, was that he had forgotten whether he had moved his rook from a8, and his own scoresheet was, as usual, illegible! Korchnoi has had a problem or two with the castling rule in his career, and he didn't try to castle (which would have been illegal, since the rook had moved), thus avoiding another embarrassing incident.

Castling is prevented under the following circumstances. First, when the square on which the king stands, or the square which it must cross, or the square which it is to occupy, is attacked by an enemy opponent's pieces. It is also illegal if there is any piece between the king and the rook with which will be participating in the castling operation. Here is a summary in pictures.

White can castle in either direction. If we place an enemy queen at e6, Black cannot capture because the king is in check.

Sliding the queen one file to the left or right prohibits castling in either direction.

A queen at b6 would prohibit queenside castling, because it covers d8.

What about a queen sitting at b2? This situation is one which will befuddle many players.

The queen covers b8, which is vacant, and also attacks the rook at h8. Neither of these factors matter! It is the safety of the king that is of paramount concern. Did you realize that castling is legal here? If not, you are in good company. You can guess who almost fell victim to the castling rule —our friend Korchnoi! It almost cost him a game in a World Championship qualifier. It was the 1974 Candidates Final against Anatoly Karpov. The winner would go on to be the challenger to Bobby Fischer, who retired and did not defend the match.

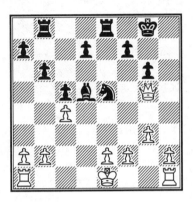

The rook at h1 is under attack Korchnoi wasn't sure of the rules, so he asked the arbiter. When he was assured that castling was legal, he returned to the board and castled. The game only lasted two more moves, as after **18.0-0! Bxc4; 19.f4,** Black resigned.

Had Korchnoi not inquired, the result of the game might have been different.

Against rival Jan Timman at the Dutch Championship of 1977, the position on the following page was reached.

> *In the two and a half thousand games that I had played before, there had never been an instance where it had been necessary for me to castle when my rook was attacked, and I was not sure that I understood correctly the rules of the game.*
>
> — Korchnoi

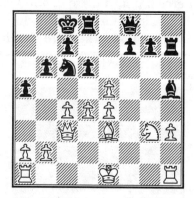

Timman played **21...Bf3?** He didn't realize that White could actually castle. Korchnoi, who would never forget the experience in the Karpov game, castled, and won without great difficulty.

The other situation, with b8 covered by an attacking piece, led to controversy in Averbakh vs. Purdy, Australian Open Championship 1961.

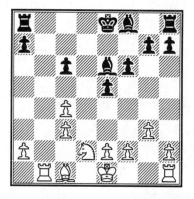

Averbakh, who was on his way to becoming a senior chess official, believed that queenside castling was illegal and protested when Purdy played it. The rule had to be explained to Averbakh, who never forgot the lesson!

50 MOVE RULE

If fifty moves by each player pass without a piece being captured or a pawn being moved, then the game is a draw. In the modern age with very fast time controls, the arbiter must sometimes keep track of the number of moves made, though it is not clear if intervention is appropriate even when the 50 moves are up! In most cases, however, a claim of a draw is based on a complete scoresheet demonstrating that the limit has been reached.

This may sound like a modern refinement of the rules, but it is not. The old Bishop Ruy Lopez included it in his set of rules back in the 16th century. Modifications to this rule were made in the twentieth century, but they have been repealed, so the rule is once again a simple one. If a player tells you about "exceptions" to the rule, have them check the 1997 FIDE rules, available on the Internet.

The idea of the rule may have been, as Roycroft speculates, to limit the length of games, which were often played for considerable stakes. Being a chess master was a dangerous occupation back then. Some top players were even assassinated!

TIME CONTROLS

Chess is usually played with a timing device that controls the amount of time each player is allotted. This insures that the game will end within some definite period of time. Chess clocks have been in use for over a century. There are many different time controls, and we'll get to those in a moment. There is one "inherent" time control, which is not appreciated by many players.

The rules require that each player arrive at the board within 60 minutes or the published starting time of the game. This is not the same as an hour after the game has started, which is what many people believe the rule says. If the game starts late, after a series of typically annoying announcements and speeches by a loquacious tournament director, the deadline may be long past when the flag indicates an hour elapsed on the clock. If the posted starting time is, say, five o'clock in the afternoon, then if the opponent doesn't arrive by six o'clock, the game is forfeited and the latecomer is awarded a big fat pumpkin (0) on the wall chart, while the player who was present records a win. It doesn't matter that the chess clock shows less than an hour remaining.

In recent changes to the rules, it is now required that you press the button on the clock with the same hand used to make your move. This has long been a requirement in rapid time controls, but is now part of the standard laws.

STANDARD TIME CONTROL

The modern standard time control is forty moves in two hours by each player, followed by either all remaining moves in an additional hour each, or another 20 moves in the next hour, followed by all remaining moves in thirty minutes.

Things are changing, however, and incremental time controls are increasingly popular. These involve reserving a fixed period of time for each move. In serious chess, this time period is often thirty seconds per move. So the first time control might be forty moves in 100 minutes, with an additional 30 seconds per move. That works out to the same control as forty moves in two hours, except that under all circumstances a player must have at least thirty seconds for each of the moves, where without the increment one can run out of time altogether. The second time control is twenty moves in fifty minutes, again with thirty seconds per move. The final time control can be all moves in twenty minutes, with thirty seconds per move.

AMATEUR TIME CONTROL

Amateur tournaments tend to be designed to get as many games as possible into a fixed period of time. Often these events are held at schools and other facilities which have a strict limit on when events must end. It is not uncommon to see three or even four games played in one day. In general, however, amateur tournaments have two games per day. Time controls vary greatly, but some of the more popular ones are all moves in two hours, thirty moves in ninety minutes, followed by all moves in an hour, and 45 or 50 moves in two hours.

David Bronstein recommends 15 minutes per player per game for casual chess, and thirty minutes for more "creative" games. In the incremental control, this could be 10 minutes per game with a 5-second increment in the friendly games, and 20 minutes with a ten second increment for more serious encounters.

BLITZ CHESS

Blitz chess, also known as "rapids," is usually played at a rate of five minutes per player per game. Sometimes the game is even faster, with three-minute chess and "bullet" chess, which allows only one or two seconds per move, especially popular on the internet.

Blitz players sometimes use special rules, which are not consistent. The World Blitz Chess Association has not yet had its rules adopted in many localities. In many cases, the official FIDE rules are used for blitz chess as well.

WHATEVER HAPPENED TO ADJOURNMENTS?

Until rather recently, most professional tournaments and matches allowed for adjourning the game, which means stopping the game at some point, usually after the first or second time control, and resuming later. Often games were not finished until a second, third, or even fourth day! At first, players were not allowed to consult with other players, analysts or computers but eventually the rules were relaxed. In most of the World Championships, especially after World War II, the combatants employed teams of seconds to assist with the analysis of adjourned games.

Modern tournaments do not allow for adjournments, but have had to accelerate the time controls in order to complete the games in a single playing session, usually six or seven hours. This is not too much of a burden, but when there are two games per day, as in the overwhelming majority of American tournaments, playing over 12 hours a day is not at all uncommon. The other casualty of the death of the adjournment process is the lack of an opportunity to bring all powers of concentration to the analysis of a complex endgame position. Adjournment sessions were a major training ground for endgame proficiency for young professionals for decades. There was also a certain thrill that came from analyzing an adjourned game from a World Championship contest, matching wits with the players themselves, and their human and silicon seconds!

Still, it is hard to find professionals who miss the adjournments, which took the game out of their hands and put it in the hands of teams of analysts.

LOCAL VS. STANDARD RULES

Chess is played all over the world by players of all ages. It is hardly surprising to find different rules in different places, at least among amateur players. Most of the official chess federations follow the rules of the World Chess Federation (FIDE). Indeed, all internationally rated games are supposed to be played under these universal rules. Nevertheless, in some places, especially in America, provincial rules are used which are often confusing to competitors.

For example, the rules specify that at the start of the game, White's clock should be started. White then makes a move, and starts Black's clock. In America, however, White is not obliged to make a move until the opponent is physically present at the board. The idea, presumably, is that this prevents the player of the Black side from entering the room, seeing White's first move, and scrambling to some computer or book for assistance. This rather ridiculous notion can lead to some silly situation. White comes to the game, starts Black's clock without making a move, then goes for a stroll to watch other games. Black enters, and starts White's clock and goes away. White returns to the board, sees no physical sign of the opponent, and starts Black's clock again!

Another USCF rule requires that in order to claim a win on time forfeit by the opponent, a player must have a complete and sufficiently accurate scoresheet before the opponent's flag falls. This is the case even though you are not required to keep score in the final five minutes! There have been many arguments about the legibility and accuracy issues. Foreign players often don't get to win games on time forfeit because they are not aware of this provincial rule.

In general, the USCF rules have been modified so that the arbiter plays less of a role in enforcing the rules. Players are left to be their own referees during the game. These changes have been made so that tournament organizers can save money by hiring fewer arbiters. Even in the United States Open, players must make claims against rule infractions. Imagine the United States Open tennis championship having the players call the balls in or out!

Then again, in America it is common to be required to bring your chess pieces and clock, even in professional events. Usually Black gets to choose the equipment, but only if it sufficiently "standard," and the tournament director makes that call. With clocks it is more complex, but the usual case is that a digital clock, especially one that has the features of the clock the USCF commercially endorses, rules. In better tournaments, sets and clocks are provided, and everyone uses the same equipment.

The standard rules are developed and revised by the World Chess Federation (FIDE) but retain core elements which do not change. I have written a book on the subject with scholastic organizer Richard Peterson. *The Official Rules of Chess* contains the standard rules online, and each organization with its own set has them available on a website. All of the material below is based on the standard rules.

THE SCORESHEET

The scoresheet is an important part of tournament play. The large chess databases of tournament games grows because the recording of games is obligatory at chess tournaments. When the organizers provide scoresheets, these are considered property of the tournament. This affects the rules of the game.

You are generally obliged to keep a legible record of the game in a standard form of algebraic chess notation until you have less than five minutes remaining on your clock in any time control. After each time control is reached, you must fill in any missing moves in your game record. This must be done as soon as time control has been reached. If your opponent has a complete scoresheet, you may ask him (while it is your turn to move) to let you borrow the scoresheet to assist you. The opponent does not have the right to refuse.

When the game ends, it is customary for the players to sign both copies of the scoresheet. It is considered extremely rude, and sometimes against tournament regulations, to fail to sign the scoresheets. When scoresheets include more than one copy, the top copy should be submitted to the tournament arbiters following the procedure of the particular tournament. Failure to turn in a scoresheet may constitute a serious breach of tournament regulations. In American tournaments, the players are also responsible for marking the result of the game on the pairing sheet.

Some players deliberately hide their scoresheets, or make them illegible, in hopes that their game, and therefore their opening strategy, will not be published. This doesn't work. As a bulletin editor, I'd track the games down. Even if the whole game couldn't be deciphered, I'd make sure the opening got published. In big open tournaments where the official bulletin only included selected games, I'd try to include every single opening by the players who refused to cooperate. If they really annoyed me, I'd annotate games by researching their repertoires and discussing them in the tournament bulletin. It is my belief that all professional games should be recorded and made available. The game belongs to everyone. In any case, failure to cooperate with the bulletin editor can be a big mistake. The pen is mightier than the checkmate!

Sometimes, of course, legibility isn't a matter of intent. Some people just have awful handwriting. As mentioned earlier in the book, Korchnoi can't read his own scoresheets. American GM John Fedorowicz usually produces a mess. Both of these players are willing to cooperate with bulletin editors. I've seen John sit down and play out the game for the editor. Nice guys like that make the difficult job of publishing the games much easier.

RATINGS

There are several rating systems in use, applying various mathematical formulas to tracking chess performance. Here we will concern ourselves only with the significance of the ratings, not their mathematical properties. Dr. Arpad Elo's book is listed in the bibliography, for those who want the gory details. All of the major ranking lists use some form of the rating system devised by Elo. The scale is roughly zero to 3000, though no one has achieved either of those numbers.

The numbers can be translated to meaningful terms as follows:

RATING SCALE

Rating		Title
2800	•	World Champion
2700	•	World Championship contender
2600	•	World Class Grandmasters
2500	•	International Grandmaster
2400	•	International Master
2300	•	FIDE Master
2200	•	National Master
2000	•	Candidate Master
1800	•	Advanced Tournament Player
1600	•	Tournament Player
1400	•	Club Player
1200	•	Casual Player
> 1200	•	Beginner

These designations should not be confused with official titles. The requirements for international titles are more complicated. To become an International Master or Grandmaster, you must have three certified qualifying results, called "norms." Put simply, you need to perform at over 2650 for Grandmaster (2450 for International Master) in three events of at least nine rounds, against competition of suitable caliber.

A performance rating differs from a published rating in that is tied to a single event. You can approximate a performance rating by averaging the rating of your opponents and adjusting it for your result. An old formula is that the adjustment is your net wins (i.e., wins minus losses) times 400, with that result being divided by the number of games. So if you play in a ten round event and score seven points, your net wins is +4 (7-3). 400 times that is 1600, and we divide that by the number of games (10) to get +160. Add this to the average of your opponents rating. For example, if your opponents average 1600, your performance would be 1760. That is not the precise formula, but it is an easy way to approximate it.

Modern tournament software does all the rating and norm calculation for you. This is a good thing, because chessplayers are not always good at arithmetic!

Ratings play an important role in tournament competition, as the rating not only determines the pairings (matches between two players), but are also used for prize qualification. This is especially true in America, where tournaments are often run to create a profit for the organizers, and huge prizes are awarded to players who barely know how to move the pieces. Prizes reserved for players under 1200, for example, can involve thousands of dollars! These prizes can be so large that some people deliberately lose games to keep their rating low, just to qualify for the prize. This makes it hard for the honest player to win them. Many sane people wonder why such large prizes are awarded, but the math is simple. Offer up one big prize, get lots of people to ante up entry fees of hundreds of dollars, pocket the profit. That's the way some organizers look at it. In Europe, these "class prizes" are modest sums, intended to cover the cost of attendance, no more.

A tip to chess coaches: if your students play for class prizes, demand a cut! One good idea in the opening may win them a lot of money, and if you provided it, you deserve something. My policy is to allow students to keep all unrestricted prize money, but get 15% of any money won in a class ranked 2000 or lower. Since I always encourage my students to play in higher sections than their current rating, I don't get much, but it is the principle of the thing, after all.

Ratings are not just used by organizations, they also track your progress Until you reach master (2200), you should be able to put on at least 100 points per year if you work at the game. Younger people can move even faster. The youngest master in American history was once Bobby Fischer, a comparatively old man of 13. His record was smashed in the 1990s, by Jordy Mont-Reynaud (11), Vinay Bhat (a few months younger), and in 1998 by 10 year-old Hikaru Nakamura. This does not reflect rating inflation. Instead, it is a testimony to the resources available for teaching and coaching. These kids are good, and you can meet them in the Cardoza book, *Whiz Kids Teach Chess*.

FIDE RATINGS

The most widely accepted ratings are those of the World Chess Federation (FIDE). These are published twice a year and are available on the internet. This list only includes players rated 2000 and above, and is expected to include 25,000 players by the year 2000. The top players are updated monthly. Starting in 1999 FIDE will offer ratings to all players for games one hour in duration or less.

FIDE TOP 10 LIST—DECEMBER 2002

Rank	Name	Country	Rating	Birthday
1	Garry Kasparov	RUS	2836	1963-04-13
2	Vladimir Kramnik	RUS	2809	1975-06-25
3	Viswanathan Anand	IND	2755	1969-12-11
4	Michael Adams	ENG	2745	1971-11-17
5	Veselin Topalov	BUL	2743	1975-03-15
6	Peter Leko	HUN	2743	1979-09-08
7	Ruslan Ponomariov	UKR	2743	1983-10-11
8	Evgeny Bareev	RUS	2737	1966-11-21
9	Vassily Ivanchuk	UKR	2709	1969-03-18
10	Alexander Morozevich	RUS	2707	1977-07-18

USCF RATINGS

The United States Chess Federation maintains a list of ratings for over 40,000 players, from absolute beginners through Grandmasters. At the upper end, their ratings are considerably higher than FIDE's which leads to some confusion. There is a smaller differential in the 2000 to 2400 range. The current average rating on the USCF list has dropped into the 1200s, as more and more beginners are being enlisted for rated tournament play. They have even subcategorized players with ratings under 1000. If you ask an amateur player what their rating is, and you are talking to an American, you are likely to get the USCF rating in response. The USCF also awards a separate rating for quick time controls, but no one pays much attention to it.

OTHER NATIONAL RATINGS

Most national federations use a form of the Elo system. The British have traditionally used their own, quite different system, but then they do drive on the wrong side of the road. Their traditions also produce great beer, magnificent cheeses, and many of the best chess tournaments of all time. When someone offers you their local rating, the best thing to do is ask how that translates to the Elo system. Most players know where they stand.

ICC RATINGS

The Internet Chess Club maintains a ranking list for thousands of members. There are four different ratings. The most quoted one is that for rapid chess, but they also have a ranking for lists played at slower time controls, super fast chess, and chess variants. These ratings are not used by other organizations, and can be influenced by use of books, computers or human assistance. Nevertheless, many players who do not pay large membership fees to national chess organizations have no other rating, and this can be used as an approximate guide to their strength.

WBCA RATINGS

The World Blitz Chess Association, based in Berkeley, California, has their own ranking list, and it is a generally accepted list for games played at 5 minutes per player. American Grandmaster Walter Browne founded and nurtured this organization, which has affiliates all over the world. Nevertheless, the ranking list is not used for much outside of WBCA events.

PCA/WCC RATINGS

The Professional Chess Association, founded by Garry Kasparov in 1993, is now defunct, replaced by an even smaller organization known as the World Chess Council. They publish lists of rankings, but these ratings are used only in their own events. The rating list for April, 1998, is not much different from the FIDE list, except that Karpov is lower.

PROFESSIONAL TOP 10 LIST—DECEMBER 2002

Rank	Name	Country	Rating	Birthday
1	Garry Kasparov	RUS	2805	1963-04-13
2	Vladimir Kramnik	RUS	2789	1975-06-25
3	Veselin Topalov	BUL	2712	1975-03-15
4	Ruslan Ponomariov	UKR	2697	1983-10-11
5	Viswanathan Anand	IND	2694	1969-12-11
6	Peter Leko	HUN	2688	1979-09-08
7	Evgeny Bareev	RUS	2685	1966-11-21
8	Alexei Shirov	ESP	2682	1977-07-18
9	Alexander Grischuk	RUS	2677	1988-10-31
10	Michael Adams	ENG	2667	1971-11-17

LAST WORDS

Avoidance of mistakes is the beginning,
as it is the end, of mastery in chess.
—Znosko-Borovsky

Old Znosko-Borovsky was right. Chess games are not won, they are lost. It is not the clever move that truly determines the fate of the game, it is the inaccurate move which made the brilliancy possible. Without errors, chess would be a dull game indeed. Perhaps what you have read here will reduce the number of errors you make at the chessboard. That would make me very happy indeed.

To enjoy chess fully you need to aspire to a certain level of mastery of the game. I believe that anyone of average intelligence or above can become at least a Candidate Master. Following the advice given in this book should make your path easier, though it won't be without its mountains and valleys. Even Grandmasters make simple mistakes. Don't take a loss as a setback. Look at it as a learning experience. Resolve never to make the same mistake twice, and you'll do just fine.

I hope you've enjoyed our excursions through the wide world of chess. Practical tips you have learned should help you advance through the ranks of the chess world and, I hope, reach the coveted master title. You should revisit relevant sections of this book as frequently as you need to, to refresh your understanding of the important chess concepts at each stage of the game. As you compete, or study games, try to match patterns you see with those you have found here. Successful chess is largely pattern recognition, so the more frequently you encounter useful ideas, the better your results will be.

If you understand concepts presented in this book, you won't need to remember them explicitly. Instead, they will become part of your overall chess knowledge to be drawn upon as necessary in the course of competitive games. Your success of the chessboard will improve steadily as you apply your new wisdom. You're enhanced chess knowledge will also make your games more enjoyable and allow you to come closer to the elusive goal of artistic perfection.

So keep playing, studying, and enjoying the wonderful game of chess!

RECOMMENDED READING

These are books which I found useful in the preparation of this book. There are of tens of thousands of books on chess, and you can usually learn something from any one of them. The books listed below all feature good prose explanations of important chess concepts. They can be useful to players of all levels.

I have not included any books where advanced chess knowledge is a prerequisite. This is a highly subjective selection, of course, and hundreds of additional titles could have been added. In any case, it is a good place to start on your further chess education.

GENERAL

Modern Chess Strategy by Edward Lasker. David McKay 1953.
The Sorcerer's Apprentice by David Bronstein & Tom Fürstenberg. Cadogan, 1995.

THE OPENING

B.C.M. Guide to the Openings in 178 games. Selected and arranged by "Hobart." Trubner & Co., ca. 1896.
Standard Chess Openings by Eric Schiller. Cardoza Publishing, 2002.
Unorthodox Chess Openings by Eric Schiller. Cardoza Publishing, 2003.
World Champion Openings by Eric Schiller. Cardoza Publishing, 2002.
Gambit Chess Openings by Eric Schiller. Cardoza Publishing, 2002.
Survive and Beat Annoying Chess Openings by Eric Schiller and John Watson. Cardoza Publishing, 2003.

THE MIDDLEGAME

Plan Like a Grandmaster by Alexei Suetin. Batsford, 1988
Play like a Grandmaster by Alexander Kotov. Batsford, 1978.
Saving Lost Positions by Leonid Shamkovich & Eric Schiller. Batsford, 1985.
The Art of Defense in Chess by Lyev Polugayevsky & Iakov Damsky. Cadogan, 1996.
The Middlegame by Max Euwe & H. Kramer. Hays Publishing, 1994.

THE ENDGAME

Essential Chess Endings Explained Move by Move by Jeremy Silman. Chess Digest, 1988.

Improve your Endgame Now! by Eric Schiller. Chess Enterprises, 1997.

Questions and Answers on Practical Endgame Play by Edmar Mednis. Chess Enterprises, 1987.

639 Essential Endgame Positions by Eric Schiller. Cardoza Publishing, 2000.

STRATEGY

Pawn Chains by Colin Crouch. Schachverlag Olbrich, 1994.

Strategy for Advanced Players by Eric Schiller. Chess Digest, 1991.

Development of a Chess Master by Eric Schiller. Cardoza Publishing, 2002.

TACTICS, SACRIFICES AND COMBINATIONS

Alekhine's Block by Victor Charusin. Pickard & Sons, 1997.

Combination Cross by Victor Charusin. Pickard & Sons, 1997.

The Art of Checkmate by Georges Renaud & Victor Kahn. Simon & Schuster, 1953.

Tactics for Advanced Players by Yuri Averbakh. Sportverlag Berlin/ Chess Digest, 1992.

World Champion Combinations by Raymond Keene & Eric Schiller. Cardoza Publishing, 1998.

World Champion Tactics by Leonid Shamkovich & Eric Schiller. Cardoza Publishing, 1998.

ANALYSIS AND TRAINING

Improve Your Chess Now! by Jonathan Tisdall. Cadogan, 1997.

Reassess You Chess by Jeremy Silman. Siles Press, 1993.

Think like a Grandmaster by Alexander Kotov,. Batsford, 1995.

PSYCHOLOGY

Decisive Games in Chess History by Ludek Pachman. Dover, 1972.

The Chess Mind by Gerald Abrahams. Penguin, 1960.

RULES

Chess Curiosities by Tim Krabbe. George Allen & Unwin, 1985.

The Rating of Chessplayers Past and Present by Arpad Elo. Arco, 1978.

The Chess Organizers Handbook by Stewart Reuben. Cadogan, 1998.

The Official Rules of Chess by Eric Schiller. Cardoza Publishing, 2003.

For more resources, check out the following internet sites:

Newsgroup: rec.games.chess.misc

Chess City: http://www.chesscity.com

Chessworks Unlimited: http://www.chessworks.com

The Week in Chess: http://www.chesscenter.com/twic.

These resources make reference to most useful chess sites and are a great way to start surfing for chess information on the net.

CHESS NOTATION

Chessplayers like to record their games, and we have records of games from a thousand years ago! You never know when you will come up with a brilliant game that will be published all over the world, so it is best to keep a record of all of them, even the ones you lose, because those often contain valuable lessons. Almost all tournaments require you to write down the moves, so you may as well learn right away. If you are unfamiliar with the code used for reading and writing about chess, this section will explain it all and help you follow the discussions and games we present in this book.

Recording a game score isn't very hard at all, once you know how. The board is divided into a grid, with letters from a to h along the base and numbers from 1 to 8 along the side, so that files are lettered and ranks are numbered. Each square thus has a name, consisting of a letter and a number.

At the beginning of the game the pieces are in their original positions.

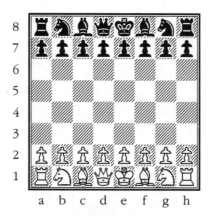

We refer to the horizontal rows as **ranks** and the vertical columns as **files**. The ranks are numbered 1-8, from White's point of view. The files are designated by letters, from a-h. After you get used to playing out chess games from the notation, you won't need any help in remembering them. For this introduction, however, we'll add the letters and numbers to help you follow the discussion.

In order to keep track of a game, you'll need a scoresheet. On it, there are spaces for White and Black moves, and they are all numbered. You start by filling out the names of the players and the date. A White move and a Black move make up one move. White moves are written on the left hand side and Black moves are written on the right hand side.

THE MOVES

Each move on the board can be described with six pieces of information:

    1. The name of the piece being moved.

    2. The square the piece is moving from.

    3. The square the piece is moving to.

    4. Whether or not the move captures an enemy piece.

    5. Whether or not the enemy king is placed in check.

    6. The place in the game where the move was played.

The most common form of notation is the *American style*. We start by indicating the number of the move. We use a number followed by a period. Then we add an abbreviation for the piece being moved.

The pieces have the following abbreviations: king is **K**; queen is **Q**; rook is **R**; bishop is **B**; knight is **N** (not K, because that is reserved for the king). The pawn has no abbreviation. Don't ask why it's not "P." It may be to make the notation more "efficient," though in reality it just makes it more complicated! The lowly pawn gets left out, but as long as there is no other capital letter indicated, then we understand that it must be a pawn move.

After the abbreviation for the piece, the square the piece lands on is usually indicated next. However, we can give some information about the square that the piece is moving from, but only if we have to. We will skip this for the moment, but return to it soon.

We'll make our first move, with the king pawn moving two squares forward. We write, **1.e4.** The position after the move is shown in the diagram:

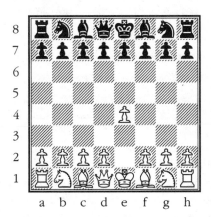

Now the pawn rests on the 4th square of the e-file. If you need to, count the letters from the left edge of the diagram (a, b, c, d, e) and count up from the bottom (1, 2, 3, 4). It will take a little time for you to master the chessboard in your mind, but you will find that it comes easily enough over time.

Now suppose we want to describe Black's reply, also moving the pawn on the kingside to a position two squares in front of the king.

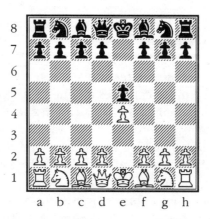

This move would be written **1...e5**. We use an ellipsis (...) to indicate that it is not White's move, but Black's. If we want to describe the entire game so far, we write simply **1.e4 e5**. In this instance, we didn't use the ellipsis, since the White and Black moves are represented together. As you can see, the White move is always shown first, then the Black move after.

Now let's say that White brings the bishop to b5.

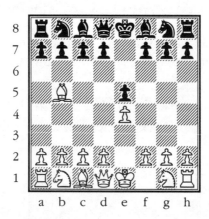

That move is written **2.Bb5**. The "2" indicates White's second move, the Bb5 shows that a bishop has moved to the b5 square. The game now reads **1.e4 e5; 2.Bb5.**

Black responds by bringing a knight to c6. We notate that as **2...Nc6**. We don't have to say which knight, because only one of the Black knights can move to c6. Let's try a few more moves. We'll let the game continue with White bringing a knight to f3, transposing, by the way, into the Spanish Game.

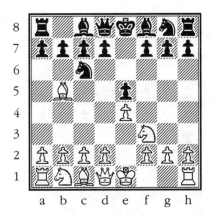

That's **3.Nf3**, giving us **1.e4 e5; 2.Bb5 Nc6; 3.Nf3**. Black responds by moving the a-pawn forward one square, attacking the White bishop. **3...a6.**

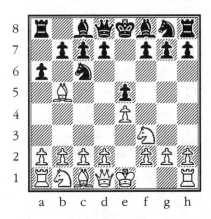

Now let us introduce a new element. We will capture the knight with our bishop. Because we are capturing an enemy piece, we add an "x" between the piece and a capture. We represent the move with **4.Bxc6**. Annotation of the game so far would be as follows: **1.e4 e5; 2.Bb5 Nc6; 3.Nf3 a6; 4.Bxc6**.

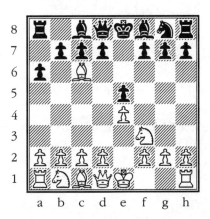

Earlier we said that we'll only mention the square the piece is leaving from if we have to. Now we have to. We can't just write 4...xc6 because that would not tell us which of the two possible pawn captures are possible.

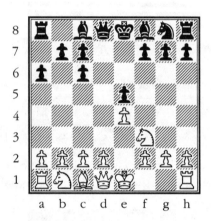

Because we need to clarify the situation, we add the file that the pawn is leaving from: **4...dxc6**. We see that it is the pawn on the *d-file* that is making the capture, not the pawn on the b-file.

Now it is White's turn, and let's suppose that the sensible move of castling takes place.

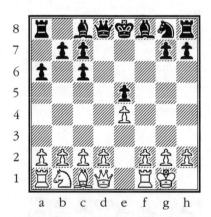

Our system has no easy way of combining the king and rook moves, so instead there is a simple convention. We use two zeros separated by a hyphen to indicate castling on the kingside (castling short): **5.0-0**. For queenside castling, we would add another hyphen and another zero "0-0-0".

Our game so far is **1.e4 e5; 2.Bb5 Nc6; 3.Nf3 a6; 4.Bxc6 dxc6; 5.0-0**. Let's try a few more moves, without commentary. **5...f6; 6.Nxe5 fxe5**.

These moves should be easy to spot. We have now reached the following position:

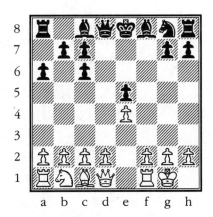

I have chosen these moves just to illustrate the last important part of the notation. If White now plays the queen to h5, the enemy king will be in check. We indicate this by appending a suffix in the form of a plus "+" sign. We are at move seven, so the notation is **7.Qh5+**. Our entire game can be described as **1.e4 e5; 2.Bb5 Nc6; 3.Nf3 a6; 4.Bxc6 dxc6; 5.0-0 f6; 6.Nxe5 fxe5;. 7.Qh5+.**

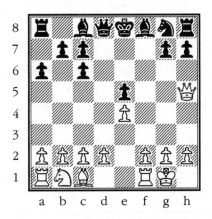

An actual checkmate will be indicated by "++" or "#".

One final point. If you are lucky enough to promote a pawn into a queen, it is written by marking the square that the pawn promotes onto, affixing an equal "=" sign, and then indicating the piece the pawn is promoted to. For example, e8=Q means that the pawn moves to the e8 square and is replaced by a queen.

THE SYMBOLS

There are many special symbols used in specialist chess literature, but in this book, words are generally used instead for easier comprehension. Still, we use a few symbols to point out moves of special, or doubtful, merit.

! = a good move
? = a bad move
!? = an interesting move
?!= a dubious move
!!= a brilliant move
??= a terrible move

These symbols are not to be used while playing the game. You add them later when studying, or, if you are playing against a human opponent, during the "post-mortem" which is what we call post-game analysis.

*'Are there not games played on boards?
To play them would surely be better
than doing nothing at all.'*

–Confucius

INDEXES

The two indexes here will help you locate topics of interest. The first is an index of important concepts. You might want to refer to it as you read the sections relating to the concepts, to find additional examples which will reinforce your understanding. The second index lists the openings that are mentioned in the book. You can look up references to the openings that you play.

INDEX OF CONCEPTS

INDEX OF OPENINGS

CARDOZA PUBLISHING CHESS BOOKS

- OPENINGS -

WINNING CHESS OPENINGS *by Bill Robertie* - Shows concepts and best opening moves of more than 25 essential openings from Black's and White's perspectives: King's Gambit, Center Game, Scotch Game, Giucco Piano, Vienna Game, Bishop's Opening, Ruy Lopez, French, Caro-Kann, Sicilian, Alekhine, Pirc, Modern, Queen's Gambit, Nimzo-Indian, Queen's Indian, Dutch, King's Indian, Benoni, English, Bird's, Reti's, and King's Indian Attack. Examples from 25 grandmasters and champions including Fischer and Kasparov. 176 pages, $9.95

WORLD CHAMPION OPENINGS *by Eric Schiller* - This serious reference work covers the essential opening theory and moves of every major chess opening and variation as played by *all* the world champions. Reading as much like an encyclopedia of the must-know openings crucial to every chess player's knowledge as a powerful tool showing the insights, concepts and secrets as used by the greatest players of all time, *World Champion Openings (WCO)* covers an astounding 100 crucial openings in full conceptual detail (with 100 actual games from the champions themselves)! *A must-have book for serious chess players.* 384 pages, $21.95

STANDARD CHESS OPENINGS *by Eric Schiller* - The new definitive standard on opening chess play in the 20th century, this comprehensive guide covers every important chess opening and variation ever played and currently in vogue. In all, more than 3,000 opening strategies are presented! Differing from previous opening books which rely almost exclusively on bare notation, *SCO* features substantial discussion and analysis on each opening so that you learn and understand the concepts behind them. Includes more than 250 completely annotated games (including a game representative of each major opening) and more than 1,000 diagrams! For modern players at any level, this is the standard reference book necessary for competitive play. *A must have for serious chess players!!!* 768 pages, $24.95

UNORTHODOX CHESS OPENINGS *by Eric Schiller* - The exciting guide to all the major unorthodox openings used by chess players, contains more than 1,500 weird, contentious, controversial, unconventional, arrogant, and outright strange opening strategies. From their tricky tactical surprises to their bizarre names, these openings fly in the face of tradition. You'll meet such openings as the Orangutan, Raptor Variation, Halloween Gambit, Double Duck, Frankenstein-Dracula Variation, and even the Drunken King! These openings are a sexy and exotic way to spice up a game and a great weapon to spring on unsuspecting and often unprepared opponents. More than 750 diagrams show essential positions. 576 pages, $24.95

GAMBIT OPENING REPERTOIRE FOR WHITE *by Eric Schiller* - Chessplayers who enjoy attacking from the very first move are rewarded here with a powerful repertoire of brilliant gambits. Starting off with 1.e4 or 1.d4 and then using such sharp weapons such as the Göring Gambit (Accepted and Declined), Halasz Gambit, Alapin Gambit, Ulysses Gambit, Short Attack and many more, to put great pressure on opponents, Schiller presents a complete attacking repertoire to use against the most popular defenses, including the Sicilian, French, Scandinavian, Caro-Kann, Pirc, Alekhine, and other Open Game positions. 192 pages, $14.95.

GAMBIT OPENING REPERTOIRE FOR BLACK *by Eric Schiller* - For players that like exciting no-holds-barred chess, this versatile gambit repertoire shows Black how to take charge with aggressive attacking defenses against any orthodox first White opening move; 1.e4, 1.d4 and 1.c4. Learn the Scandinavian Gambit against 1.e4, the Schara Gambit and Queen's Gambit Declined variations against 1.d4, and some flank and unorthodox gambits also. Black learns the secrets of seizing the initiative from White's hands, usually by investing a pawn or two, to begin powerful attacks that can send White to early defeat. 176 pages, $14.95.

COMPLETE DEFENSE TO QUEEN PAWN OPENINGS *by Eric Schiller* - This aggressive counterattacking repertoire covers Black opening systems against virtually every chess opening except for 1.e4 (including most flank games), based on the exciting and powerful Tarrasch Defense, an opening that helped bring Championship titles to Kasparov and Spassky. Black learns to effectively use the Classical Tarrasch, Symmetrical Tarrasch, Asymmetrical Tarrasch, Marshall and Tarrasch Gambits, and Tarrasch without Nc3, to achieve an early equality or even an outright advantage in the first few moves. 288 pages, $16.95.

COMPLETE DEFENSE TO KING PAWN OPENINGS *by Eric Schiller* - Learn a complete defensive system against 1.e4. This powerful repertoire not only limits White's ability to obtain any significant opening advantage but allows Black to adopt the flexible Caro-Kann formation, the favorite weapon of many of the greatest chess players. All White's options are explained in detail, and a plan is given for Black to combat them all. Analysis is up-to-date and backed by examples drawn from games of top stars. Detailed index lets you follow the opening from the point of a specific player, or through its history. 240 pages, $16.95.

SECRETS OF THE SICILIAN DRAGON by *GM Eduard Gufeld and Eric Schiller* - The mighty Dragon Variation of the Sicilian Defense is one of the most exciting openings in chess. Everything from opening piece formation to the endgame, including clear explanations of all the key strategic and tactical ideas, is covered in full conceptual detail. Instead of memorizing a jungle of variations, you learn the really important ideas behind the opening, and how to adapt them at the chessboard. Special sections on the heroes of the Dragon show how the greatest players handle the opening. The most instructive book on the Dragon written! 208 pages, $14.95.

HYPERMODERN OPENING REPERTOIRE FOR WHITE *by Eric Schiller* - Instead of placing pawns in the center of the board as traditional openings advise, this complete opening repertoire for White shows you how to stun opponents by "allowing" Black to occupy the center with its pawns, while building a crushing phalanx from the flanks, ready to smash the center apart with Black's slightest mistake. White's approach is simple to learn because White almost always develops pieces in the same manner, but can be used against all defenses no matter what Black plays! Diagrams and explanations illustrate every concept, with games from the greatest players showing the principles in action. The Réti and English openings form the basis of the Hypermodern and lead to games with brilliant sacrifices and subtle maneuvering. 304 pages, $16.95.

SECRETS OF THE KING'S INDIAN *by Eduard Gufeld and Eric Schiller* - The King's Indian is the single most popular opening and offers great opportunities for spectacular attacks and clever defenses. You'll learn the fundamental concepts, critical ideas, and hidden resources along with the opening traps and typical tactical and strategic mistakes. All major variations are covered, including the Classical, Petrosian, Saemisch, Averbakh, Four Pawns, Fianchetto and unconventional lines. You'll learn how these strategies and tactics were applied in the brilliant games of the best players, how to apply them to your own games. 240 pages, $14.95.

GAMBIT CHESS OPENINGS *by Eric Schiller* - Gambits, where one side sacrifices material for an advance in development, are the most exciting and popular openings in chess! Every important gambit opening and variation ever played and currently in vogue is here—more than 2,000 opening strategies in all! Each gambit is covered in detail with a diagram showing the standard position representative of the gambit, the move orders taken to reach that position, and an explanation in plain language of the thinking behind the moves. More than 100 complete games are included so that readers can see how the ideas behind the gambit are influential not only in the beginning of the game, but later on in its development. 240 pages, $14.95.

SURVIVE & BEAT ANNOYING CHESS OPENINGS *by Eric Schiller and John Watson* - This is the chess doctor's handbook to the very popular traps and pitfalls faced by beginning and intermediate chess players. Opening traps are the single most annoying stratagem, that is, for unprepared players. There is nothing worse than getting caught in a quick trap and going down to a quick defeat. This book puts the power back into the hands of prepared players and not only shows them how to handle these traps as both Black and White but to set them themselves! Schiller and Watson provide practical remedies for both White and Black to the annoying variations that their opponents will often choose instead of the well-known main lines. Finally, there is now a reliable single-volume resource to neutralize or defeat these strategies. For key openings, the authors provide two separate remedies to appeal to both the attacking and positional player. Unique charts and graphics make learning these remedies easy and fun!. 256 pages, $17.95.

- MIDDLEGAME/TACTICS/WINNING CONCEPTS -

ENCYCLOPEDIA OF CHESS WISDOM, The Essential Concepts and Strategies of Smart Chess Play *by Eric Schiller* - The most important concepts, strategies, tactics, wisdom, and thinking that every chessplayer must know, plus the gold nuggets of knowledge behind every attack and defense, is collected together in one highly focused volume. From opening, middle and endgame strategy, to psychological warfare and tournament tactics, the *Encyclopedia of Chess Wisdom* forms the blueprint of power play and advantage at the chess board. Step-by-step, the reader is taken through the thinking behind each essential concept, and through examples, discussions, and diagrams, shown the full impact on the game's direction. You even learn how to correctly study chess to become a chess master. 432 pages, $19.95.

10 MOST COMMON CHESS MISTAKES and How to Fix Them *by Larry Evans* - This fascinating collection of 218 errors, oversights, and outright blunders, will not only show you the price that great players pay for violating basic principles, but how you can avoid these mistakes in your own game. You'll be challenged to choose between two moves; the right one, or the one actually played in the game. From neglecting development, king safety, misjudging threats, and premature attacks, to impulsiveness, snatching pawns, and basic inattention, you will get a complete course in exactly where you can go wrong and how to fix it. 256 pages, $14.95.

WORLD CHAMPION TACTICS *by Leonid Shamkovich and Eric Schiller* - The authors show how the greatest players who ever lived used their entire arsenal of tactical weapons to bring opponents to their knees. Packed with fascinating strategems, 50 fully annotated games, and more than 200 diagrams, players learn not only the thinking and game plan behind the moves of the champions, but the insights that will allow them to use these brilliancies in their own games. Each tactical concept is fully explained with examples and game situations from the champions themselves. 304 pages, $18.95.

WORLD CHAMPION COMBINATIONS *by Keene and Schiller* - Learn the insights, concepts and moves of the greatest combinations ever by the greatest players who ever lived. From Morphy to Alekhine, to Fischer to Kasparov, the incredible combinations and brilliant sacrifices of the 13 World Champions are collected here in the most insightful combinations book written. Packed with fascinating strategems, 50 annotated games, and great practical advice for your own games, this is a great companion guide to *World Champion Openings*. 264 pages, $16.95

100 AWESOME CHESS MOVES *By Eric Schiller* - This collection of brilliant ideas from real tournaments are not just regular combinations or tactical swindles, but moves of stunning originality. Schiller has selected 100 *awesome* moves, and through positions, examples, and clearly explained concepts, shows you how to improve your grasp of deep positional understandings and swashbuckling tactics. You'll learn how to reinforce your gut instincts to not just reach for the best move, but the *inspired* move. 224 pgs, $18.95.

WINNING CHESS TACTICS *by Bill Robertie* - 14 chapters of winning tactical concepts show the complete explanations and thinking behind every tactical concept: pins, single and double forks, double attacks, skewers, discovered and double checks, multiple threats - and other crushing tactics to gain an immediate edge over opponents. Learn the power tools of tactical play to become a stronger player. Includes guide to chess notation. 128 pages, $9.95

303 TRICKY CHESS TACTICS *Fred Wilson and Bruce Alberston* - Both a fascinating challenge and great training tool, this is a fun and entertaining compendium of two and three move tactical surprises for the advanced beginner, intermediate, and expert player. The arrangement of tactics are in order of difficulty so that the player may gauge his progress as he advances from simple to the complex positions toward the end. The examples, drawn from actual games, illustrate a wide range of chess tactics from old classics right up to the 1990's. 192 pages, $12.95.

DEVELOPMENT OF A CHESS MASTER *Eric Schiller* - Players of all levels will learn how to improve their chess play by cutting down on tactical and strategic mistakes. Using examples from his own games, Schiller illustrates the types of errors typically found at each stage of chess development, from early scholastic games to professional encounters with Grandmasters. In each case, Schiller shows how such errors can be overcome while at the same time showing how professional players can fall prey to the same problems as amateurs. Learn from the author's mistakes and you won't suffer the terrible fate that awaits most blunders! 128 pages, $12.95.

- BEGINNING CHESS BOOKS -

THE BASICS OF WINNING CHESS *by Jacob Cantrell* - A great first book of chess, in one easy reading, beginner's learn the moves of the pieces, the basic rules and principles of play, the standard openings, and both Algebraic and English chess notation. The basic ideas of the winning concepts and strategies of middle and end game play are shown as well. Includes example games of great champions. 64 pages, $4.95.

BEGINNING CHESS PLAY *by Bill Robertie* - Step-by-step approach uses 113 diagrams to teach novices the basic principles of chess. Covers opening, middle and end game strategies, principles of development, pawn structure, checkmates, openings and defenses, how to write and read chess notation, join a chess club, play in tournaments, use a chess clock, and get rated. Two annotated games illustrate strategic thinking for easy learning. 144 pages, $9.95

WHIZ KIDS TEACH CHESS *Edited by Eric Schiller* - Today's greatest young stars, ranging from 10 to 17 years of age—some perhaps to be future world champions—present a fascinating look at the world of chess. Each prodigy tells of their successes, failures, world travels, and love of the game, show off their best moves, and even admit to their most embarrassing blunders. At the heart of this inspirational book targeted toward beginning, under-17 players, is a basic chess primer with large diagrams, clear explanations, and winning ideas. Features Jordy Mont-Reynaud (14), who smashed Bobby Fischer's record by over two years to become the youngest USCF Master, Vinay Bhat (14) the Pan American champion who eclipsed that record, Hikaru Nakamura (10) the America's youngest national master ever, Master Irina Krush (15) the Pan American girl's champion, and stars Gabe Kahane (16), Asuka Nakamura (11), Jennifer Frenklakh (17), Matthew Ho (10), Jennifer Shahade (16), more. 160 large format pages, $14.95.

COMPLETE BOOK OF BEGINNING CHESS *by Raymond Keene* - In just 10 easy lessons, beginning players learn everything they need to know to play and win at chess. From setting up a chess board and moving the pieces, to basic concepts and winning strategies, and even how to get rated and play on the internet. Chapters cover basic openings, strategy, tactics, computer chess, middlegame play, endgame play, history and more. 360 pages, $19.95.

- MATES & ENDGAMES -

639 ESSENTIAL ENDGAME POSITIONS *by Eric Schiller* - From basic checkmates to sophisticated double-rook endgames, every important endgame concept is explained. Topics include every key combination of king and pawn endgames, bishops, knights, rooks, and queens, plus tricky endgames with no pawns. The thinking behind every position is explained in words (unlike diagram-only books) so that players learn which positions are winning, which are drawn, and which cannot be saved. Frequent diagrams show starting and target positions, so readers can visualize end goals and steer the middlegame to a successful conclusion. 400 pages, $18.95.

303 TRICKY CHECKMATES *by Fred Wilson and Bruce Alberston* - Both a fascinating challenge and great training tool, this collection of two, three and bonus four move checkmates is great for advanced beginning, intermediate and expert players. Mates are in order of difficulty, from the simple to very complex positions. Learn the standard patterns and stratagems for cornering the king: corridor and support mates, attraction and deflection sacrifices, pins and annihilation, the quiet move, and the dreaded *zugzwang*. Examples, drawn from actual games, illustrate a wide range of chess tactics from old classics right up to now. 192 pgs, $12.95.

MASTER CHECKMATE STRATEGY *by Bill Robertie* - Learn the basic combinations, plus advanced, surprising and unconventional mates, the most effective pieces needed to win, and how to mate opponents with just a pawn advantage. Also, how to work two rooks into an unstoppable attack; how to wield a queen advantage with deadly intent; how to coordinate pieces of differing strengths into indefensible positions of their opponents; when it's best to have a knight, and when a bishop to win. 144 pages, $9.95

BASIC ENDGAME STRATEGY: Kings, Pawns and Minor Pieces *by Bill Robertie* - Learn the mating principles and combinations needed to finish off opponents. From the four basic checkmates using the King with the queen, rook, two bishops, and bishop/knight combinations, to the King/pawn, King/Knight and King/Bishop endgames, you'll learn the essentials of translating small edges into decisive checkmates. Learn the 50-move rule, and the combinations of pieces that can't force a mate against a lone King. 144 pages, $12.95.

BASIC ENDGAME STRATEGY: Rooks and Queens by Bill Robertie - The companion guide to *Basic Endgame Strategy: Kings, Pawns and Minor Pieces*, you'll learn the basic mating principles and combinations of the Queen and Rook with King, how to turn middlegame advantages into victories, by creating passed pawns, using the King as a weapon, clearing the way for rook mates, and other endgame combinations. 144 pages, $12.95.

CHESS ENDGAME QUIZ *by Larry Evans* - This challenging book features 200 challenges in the multiple choice format that has proved so popular for chess-playing readers. These instructive, elegant and entertaining positions not only will challenge and entertain readers but teach them how to improve their endgame while trying to find the best move of the three choices presented. The problems are divided into various sections such as king and pawn endings, so that players can concentrate on areas for either training and learning purposes, or just flat out fun. Take the plunge and find out! 224 pages, $14.95.

BECOME A BETTER CHESS PLAYER!

YES! I want to be a winner! Rush me the following items: (Write in choices below):

Quantity	Your Book Order	Price	

Subtotal	
Postage/Handling: First Item	$5 00
Additional Postage	
Total Amount Due	

MAKE CHECKS TO:
Cardoza Publishing
P.O. Box 1500, Cooper Station
New York, NY 10276

CHARGE BY PHONE:
Toll-Free: 1-800-577-WINS
E-Mail Orders: CardozaPub@aol.com

SHIPPING CHARGES: For US orders, include $5.00 postage/handling 1st book ordered; for each additional book, add $1.00. For Canada/Mexico, double above amounts, quadruple (4X) for all other countries. Orders outside U.S., money order payable in U.S. dollars on U.S. bank only.

NAME_____

ADDRESS_____

CITY_____ STATE _____ ZIP _____

30 day money back guarantee!

Wisdom '03

FREE - CHESS CITY MAGAZINE
www.chesscity.com

Go online now to visit our free online chess magazine with articles, columns, gossip and more. The web's most interesting and informative chess magazine is free to you from Cardoza Publishing!

Chess City is a sprawling metropolis of chess information, a magazine with the lastest news and analysis, where you can find gossip, trivia and many fun features. Travel around the world to visit the most fascinating chess competitions, preview books long before they hit the shelves and read informative columns on openings, meddlegames, endings, tactics, strategies, mates, and much more.

Chess City is the newest and most exciting chess web site on the World Wide Web. You'll be able to catch up on the latest news and find out where the tournaments are, get secret tips from top professionals and trainers, read about the exploits of the Whiz Kids, and delve into the history and personalities of the chess world. View games online with commentary by Cardoza authors, or download chess games annontated with words, not hieroglyphics.